THE
NOTE-BOOKS OF
SAMUEL BUTLER

Volume I
(1874-1883)

Edited by

Hans-Peter Breuer

LANHAM • NEW YORK • LONDON

Copyright © 1984 by

University Press of America,™ Inc.

4720 Boston Way
Lanham, MD 20706

3 Henrietta Street
London WC2E 8LU England

All University Press of America books are produced on acid-free
paper which exceeds the minimum standards set by the National
Historical Publications and Records Commission.

This is the first volume of the complete edition
of Samuel Butler's manuscript
Note-Books (1874 - 1902)
edited by Hans-Peter Breuer and Roger E. Parsell

TABLE OF CONTENTS

ACKNOWLEDGMENTS

Two stipends made possible the research for this edition: a summer grant from the National Endowment for the Humanities, and a faculty grant from the University of Delaware Research Program. To both institutions I wish to express my heartfelt gratitude, but to the Research Program I must signal my particular gratitude and indebtedness, for without its considerable generosity beyond the grant this work would not have been launched in any case.

Many people have readily come to my assistance, and for their courteous helpfulness I am most thankful: Mr. Norman C. Buck, the now retired sub-librarian of St. John's College Library (Cambridge), has often aided me as has my partner in this editorial project, Prof. Rogert E. Parsell; Mr. D.E. Allen of Winchester has contributed considerable information about a number of Worsleys, and Mr. Frank Pring of Awliscombe (in Devon) has freely shared his knowledge of his ancestors and the Taylors; information was also furnished by Mr. J.C. Wilson, Archivist and Deputy Director of the Canterbury Museum, Christchurch, New Zealand; by Mrs. Jean Spring of Dorking and Pam Nunn of Bracknell (Bucks.); by Prof. Guy Lee, Librarian of St. John's College, and by Mr. Wayne Hammond of the Chapin Library, Williams College (Williamstown, Mass.). My colleagues at the University of Delaware often helped illuminate obscurities and solve puzzles: Prof. Merton Christensen, Prof. Edward A. Nickerson, Prof. Nicolas P. Gross, and Prof. Gerald R. Culley. I am also beholden to Mr. John Johnson, a student assistant, for fulfilling so conscientiously the research tasks I assigned him. Many thanks are due to Mrs. Betty Sherman, who typed the first MS. of the edition and to Mrs. Shirley Anderson, who produced the final copy: I remain indebted to them for their patience, forbearance, and friendship. I must mention two men who cooperated with me on this project but who did not live to see its completion: Mr. H. Richard Archer, the late Custodian of Chapin Library who not only gave of his time, but who also most generously extended his hospitality to me; and Mr. Brian Hill of London, the late co-executor of Butler's remaining estate (now at St. John's College), who also invited me into his home and offered many helpful suggestions, and criticisms. I wish to thank *English Literature in Transition* for permission to use portions of my article ("Samuel

Butler's Note-Books: The Views of Victorian Black Sheep") for the Introduction to this edition.

Finally, all honor to my family—Angela my wife, Nicola and Alexander, our children—for living good-humoredly through the ups and downs of academic drudgery, and to Mrs. Theresia S. Callicott, my mother, and Frau Wilma Prollius, my aunt, who helped in other quite indispensable ways.

HPB

General Note on the Text

At his death Butler left a mass of miscellaneous literary "remains" that included his MS. Note-Books, written and typed in a uniform format, bound into five volumes, with enough loose notes to fill a sixth, intended quite obviously for posthumous publication despite repeated disclaimers to the contrary in the Prefaces to the volumes. The original set of six volumes (A) is now housed with the Butler Collection in the Chapin Library at Williams College, Williamstown, Massachusetts; of the two pressed copies of this set, one (B) is in the British Library, the other (C) is in the Butler Collection in the St. John's College Library, Cambridge, England. Butler himself bound five of the volumes, covering the years 1874 to 1900 (February); the notes kept from March of that year to shortly before his death in June, 1902 were bound into a matching sixth volume by Henry Festing Jones. All but this volume (which holds 132 folio pages) run to more than 240 folio pages and contain handwritten indeces.

The first three volumes, mostly in typescript after folio 74 of Volume 1, contain the notes kept up to January, 1890, which Butler systematically edited or revised a final time between March, 1891 and March, 1899; the other three volumes, almost entirely in his hand, contain the notes Butler began keeping from May, 1890 on, during the time he edited the older notes, and beyond, up to March 20, 1902 (the last entry). Volumes I, II, and IV--this last with notes kept between May, 1890 and June, 1893--were already bound when in 1899 he completed the editing of the remaining older notes, only to find he had not sufficient matter to swell Volume III to the size of its fellows; consequently, as he tells us in the Preface to it, he added some materials not, strictly speaking, notes but essay-length accounts and memoranda, some belonging not to the period of the re-edited notes, but to the years falling between 1890 and 1898. Jones followed Butler's plan when he made up Volume VI by adding some miscellanies from Butler's papers, including the sayings of Mrs. Boss (the laundress of Butler's cousin, Reginald Worsley) which had been kept separately from the Note-Books, and a collection of "Black-guardisms and Improprieties." Sometime in 1919 he also pasted a few additional pages to the end of Volume III containing three published letters pertaining to Butler's account of his friendship with Charles Paine Pauli that is included in the volume, and that was published (in part) for the first time in Jones's biography of Butler, *Samuel Butler, Author of "Erewhon" (1835-1902): A Memoir*, 2 vols. (London: Macmillan, 1919). This explains why sets B and C of the Note-Books are not exact copies of A: B does not contain all of the supplemental materials of this volume as well as of Volume VI. Furthermore, Butler's occasional hand-written afterthoughts or corrections in A are not found in either set.

The Chapin Library Catalogue of the Butler Collection lists two other volumes (of which no copies exist) as part of the Note-Books set.[1] These volumes, however, of unequal size, bound differently (by Jones or A. T. Bartholomew) from the Note-Books volumes, bear the title "Notes and Extracts, Italian etc." and do not even by format belong to the set; they contain chiefly jottings, mostly unedited, related to Butler's journeyings in Italy, some of them mere pencilled scribbles on slips of white paper pasted on the MS. pages. The more extensive and substantial matter in the first of these volumes had been composed as part of a projected book similar to *Alps and Sanctuaries*; hence A. T. Bartholomew and Jones included most of it in the expanded edition of *Alps and Sanctuaries* (1913), reprinted later as Volume VII of the *Shrewsbury Edition of the Collected Works of Samuel Butler* (London: Jonathan Cape, 1923-1926).[2] Another substantial segment of the volume consists of notes preparatory to the Homeric theory Butler developed in *The Authoress of the Odyssey* (1897). The second volume nevertheless does contain about 50 MS. pages of undated notes similar to those in the Note-Books, some highly condensed, others mere shorthand phrases, some of which refer to specific pages in the "commonplace book" Butler kept, as he explains in the Preface to the present Volume, from about 1874 on. None of these notes appear to belong to a period later than 1884, and since some of them reappear in fuller form in the Note-Books proper, this collection most probably is the outcome of the winnowing of older notes that Butler undertook in September, 1884, before finally destroying the commonplace book. A number of notes unique to these pages (and the first of these two volumes) were included in A. T. Bartholomew's selection, *Further Extracts from the Note-Books of Samuel Butler* (London: Jonathan Cape, 1934).

In the British Library there is yet a third unique volume of bound MS. materials entitled "Life and Habit, Vol. II," containing four essays intended for a sequel to *Life and Habit* as well as an undated collection of notes under a number of headings, many condensed and referring also to the commonplace book. The main part of this volume is estimated by Bartholomew to belong to 1885, and these notes must have been gathered during yet another winnowing, this time in relation to specific topics. Again, many of them reappear in the Note-Books and the more substantial matter in the volume has been printed in Vol. XVIII of the *Works* (see p. 103). Bartholomew, in his Preface to *Further Extracts*, lists this volume with the "Notes and Extracts" volumes as constituting part of the Note-Books set of 9 volumes. Consequently, there is a confusion between Bartholomew's listing of the Note-Books and that of the Chapin Library catalogue: it was created because in both cases the notes Butler entered systematically in a uniform format are not distinguished from the materials (all three supplementary volumes were bound in 1924) that are either miscellaneous or the outcome of editing preliminary to the final revision of notes undertaken in 1891.[3] For a complete inventory of these unconnected volumes, see Bartholomew's Preface.

Excerpts from the Note-Books were first published in several issues of *The New Quarterly*, edited by the Butler admirer Desmond McCarthy, between November, 1907 and May 1910, appearing in both the first and final issue of the journal. Henry Festing Jones selected and edited them freely according to an editorial scheme he was to use again when compiling the first book-length selection, *The Note-Books of Samuel Butler, Author of "Erewhon"* (London: A. C. Fifield, 1912):[4] he condensed notes on similar topics into one, often altering or shortening them to give the amalgam the necessary coherence, and eliminated all chronology. In the *New Quarterly* selections he identified his sources by volume and page references to the MS. Note-Books, but in the 1912 edition he omitted them (though all but a handful are identified in Jones's copy now in the British Library), arranged the amalgamated notes under 24 chapters each corresponding to a general topic, leaving the odd ones for a chapter headed "Higgledy-Piggledy," and included some of Butler's poems and early essays. An American edition, made from the English sheets appeared in the following year (New York: Mitchell Kennerly); another American edition, provided with a brief introduction by Francis Hackett, came out in 1918 (New York: Dutton). The 1912 volume is reprinted in the main as Volume XX of the *Works*, with some alterations, two additional sonnets, and the text of the "oratorios" *Narcissus* and *Ulysses*. Other notes from the Note-Books and from the "Notes and Extracts" volumes which Jones withheld in

1912 appeared as documentation in his 1919 Butler biography.

The next stage of the Note-Books public life was ably supervised by A. T. Bartholomew, who took custody of Butler's literary estate as Jones's executor after Jones's death in 1928. First he published a reduced version of the 1912 edition for the Traveller's Library series (London: Jonathan Cape, 1930). Then, with the assistance of G. W. Webb of the Cambridge University Library, he compiled, between 1930 and 1932, a complete inventory of the Note-Books and the other MS. volumes, and re-examined them to see "whether there is enough good stuff left unprinted to justify the publication of a further Selection."[5] As a result of these editorial labors he published some new notes (with Butler's complete account of his friendship with Pauli) in the October, 1931 issue of *Life and Letters*, and in several issues of *The English Review* for 1931/2 (vols. 54 and 55), and in a small new volume that appeared only in the U.S., *Samuel Butler's Note-Books: Some New Extracts* (New York: Random House, 1932). With an expanded version of this volume, made up entirely of new notes, Bartholomew finally provided the first textually reliable selection already referred to, *Further Extracts from the Note-Books of Samuel Butler*, published a year after his death, in 1934.

This edition is divided into sections corresponding to the dates of each MS. volume, and the notes from each volume, though without individual dates, are listed in chronological order, edited without substantial alterations into polished form that required only occasional omissions or slight changes. Into this chronological listing Bartholomew worked some quotations from Butler's published works for which he had "a peculiar affection,"[6] and, as mentioned already, some notes from the "Notes and Extracts" volumes, as well as from "Life and Habit, Volume II." His preface provides a thorough bibliographical description of the "nine" volumes of bound MSS.

The most recent volume of selections, published in 1951 by Jonathan Cape, was edited by Sir Geoffrey Keynes and Brian Hill: in addition to entirely new notes it reprints notes and materials from both of the earlier book-length editions, from *Butleriana* and Jones's biography, listing them in chronological order without however dividing them into the six divisions corresponding to the MS. volumes as Bartholomew had done. Though Jones's 1912 edition contains a few footnotes and some explanatory matter for each of his chapter headings, none of the three editions is fully annotated.

Bartholomew and Keynes and Hill approached the text in their respective editions with a relatively liberal but commonsense editorial policy, for they were intent on providing a volume of the best of Butler's witticisms and opinions to a general public. The present complete edition of the Note-Books has been conceived primarily (though not exclusively) as a reference work, and an addendum to the biographies of Butler and his collected *Works*. The edition follows as faithfully as is reasonable and practical the original MS. of set A, arranged in a format corresponding generally to the one Butler settled on by the time he was well into compiling Volume I. Rather than reproducing scrupulously in print the written or typed page, with Butler's shorthand devices, abbreviations, and inevitable slips, the editors have decided to provide a text that is readable and typographically consistent while reflecting, as a scholarly edition of the Note-Books ought, the somewhat roughhewn features of many entries, and the most prominent idiosyncracies of Butler's style. A minimum of editorial interference was consequently exercised: obvious errors were corrected (unless of interest) without making substantial alterations, and in this the editors were sometimes guided by the texts of the two previous editions. Square brackets, whenever marked by an asterisk, enclose whatever substantial changes had to be made; Butler's punctuation and other orthographic vagaries, wherever necessary or convenient, were brought in harmony with modern usage; his errors when quoting were allowed to stand if they were minor; the composition and editing dates made to appear as they do in the MSS.,[7] and later additions to the notes identified where possible. Furthermore, occasional overscored passages have been recovered in the footnotes, the notes have been numbered for convenience, and Butler's index, since not entirely useful for such an edition, has been replaced by that of the editors into which, however, many of Butler's references and subject entries have been absorbed.

HPB

NOTES

[1]*Catalogue of the Collection of Samuel Butler in the Chapin Library, Williams College, Williamstown, Mass.* (Portland, Me.: The Southworth-Anthoensen Press, 1945), p. 4.

[2]Henceforth referred to as *Works*.

[3]The Chapin Library Butler Collection lists yet another unique volume of "Extracts, Notes and Drafts" separately from the Notebooks. It contains Butler's notes and lengthy quotations from other works for his studies of Homer, the Shakespeare Sonnet sequence, and evolution; the MS. of "Essay Upon the Art of Feeling" (unpublished), and a rough draft of "The Genesis of Feeling" printed in Volume XVIII of the Works.

[4]Second impression, 1913; third (popular) edition, 1915. According to Harkness (*The Career of Samuel Butler (1835-1902)* [London: The Bodley Head, 1955], p. 55) Jonathan Cape brought out a "Library edition" of the 1912 edition. I have not been able to verify this. A French translation of the 1912 edition, by the French novelist Valèry Larbaud, appeared in 1936 (Paris: Librarie Gallimard).

[5]Bartholomew in a letter to Carroll Wilson, June 3, 1930; the letter is in Butler Collection of the Chapin Library.

[6]*Further Extracts*, p. 10.

[7]These dates present the only real textual difficulty to the exact editor. Butler entered both composition and editing dates in the left upper corner of each page. Occasionally a larger note runs over the next page headed by an editing date different from the previous one, suggesting either that Butler finished his work when he had filled a page or at the note's conclusion on the new page which would bear the date, however, of the next editing session. It is of course a niggling point, but the editors have placed such divided notes under either the first or second editing date unless quite long, when the note is listed under both editing dates.

INTRODUCTION

I

The 19th century, in England as elsewhere was, from a literary point of view, an increasingly self-conscious age, when writers more apparently than before became their own subject matter, and confessional literature--autobiographies, memoirs, "lives and letters," diaries, note-books-- came into its own. To some degree this literary self-consciousness was a symptom not simply of the universal desire to record observations of people, places and events, but also of the characteristically modern impulse to examine independently inherited beliefs, assumptions, and traditions--the impulse, in other words, to consider the past impersonally as a relic that rapid changes and the intersection of the ascending curve of positivist science and the falling one of Western Christian humanism had awakened, an intersection which occurred in the mind of every significant English thinker in the last century.

In Samuel Butler's life certainly this dramatic intersection played a decisive role, and his six volumes of Note-Books are consequently best regarded in this context. In the main they do indeed form a personal account of his life-long quarrel with the older tradition and with Charles Darwin, one of the chief contributors to the newer, as well as of his subsequent accommodations with the reigning positivist spirit of the time. As writer Butler consistently quarrelled with respectable opinions in religion, science and literature, and naturally had many strong opinions to set down. His urge to do so, however, was intensified when his published works, except for *Erewhon* (1872) and *Erewhon Revisited* (1901), his first and last book, went all but unnoticed during his lifetime. Quite understandably he wished to leave behind as much of himself as possible for a posterity that could (and would he doubted not) give him his due once the prejudices of contemporaries and the controversies in which he had become embroiled had been forgotten.

The Note-Books, in fact, are the third, perhaps most important, pillar on which his reputation now rests. When his friend and biographer Henry Festing Jones first published a book-length selection from them in 1912 (*The Note-Books of Samuel Butler*), it was almost universally

1

and generously praised: the full substance of Butler, so it seemed, was contained there in the most attractive and quotable form. Arthur Clutton-Brock, to cite a relevant example (*TLS*, December 5, 1912), comparing Butler with Germany's iconoclast, Friedrich Nietzsche, concluded that no one could fully know Butler without reading this anthology which was destined to become "the most read and valued of all his books." This was written when Butler's fame as the great solvent of Victorian stuffiness was at its height, when Butler, through the influence of G. B. Shaw, his self-proclaimed defender, and the scholarly assiduity of Jones and R. A. Streatfeild, had become a recognizable influence upon the literature of the time.

Despite the inappropriate comparison, Clutton-Brock's assessment remains justifiable. For in the strict sense, Butler was not a literary artist at all. He was at his best experimenting with ideas, recording anecdotes, witticisms, and paradoxes. In the two works most widely associated with his name at that time, the didactic elements dominate the mimetic and imaginative: *Erewhon* (1872) is a philosophical tale in the manner of Voltaire; the post-humously published novel, *The Way of All Flesh* (1903), is more a mixture of satiric episodes and philosophic reflections than a well-sustained anti-Victorian novel of education. By temperament and ability, Butler was in fact a philosophic wit and in the published notes readers met him in the form most congenial to him and could sense his affinity to La Rochefoucauld, Lord Chesterfield, Montaigne, and the Samuel Butler who wrote *Hudibras* (and also kept a notebook). They were his intellectual kinsmen, and he shared their pragmatism and worldly cynicism.

Of course, the *Selections* (and the two subsequent and more carefully edited anthologies) contained the very best the Note-Books had to offer, and consequently emphasized the unconventional and rebellious rather than the rough and at times even bigoted side of Butler's character and outlook that the notes in their entirety would have revealed. The editorial procedure was perfectly understandable. Jones, and the other editors, wished not only to publish a readable scrapbook of Butlerisms, but with it also to strengthen Butler's growing reputation as the great debunker of his age that had been established by the success of *The Way of All Flesh*. Butler would have approved heartily, for he always had fancied himself as a persecuted *enfant terrible*. But he would also have welcomed a complete edition of his notes; for so strong and immodest was his belief in himself that he was anxious to impose himself as fully as possible on posterity and was not afraid of having even his blemishes made public. As we shall see, he had his reason.

II

His writing career was essentially as much a sustained battle against the father and his symbolic representation in society, as it was a justification of his moral and intellectual position. Born in December, 1835, he had grown up as the dutiful son in the often joyless, severe atmosphere of his father's rectory at Langar, and of the public school at Shrewsbury. It seemed quite natural he should follow both his grandfather, Dr. Samuel Butler (former Headmaster of Shrewsbury School, later Bishop of Lichfield) and his father, Canon Thomas Butler, into the church. His studies at Shrewsbury and St. John's College, Cambridge, were directed to this end, but he appears to have given his future profession little thought. He accepted the Church's teachings on trust (so to speak), for he moved chiefly in clerical circles, and, diffident by nature, would have been easily frightened into submission, should rebellion have stirred within him, by overbearing masters or his stern, brow-beating father. Even at St. John's he showed little curiosity about the faith he was to serve. His first serious doubts arose only after he had taken his B.A. (in classics) in 1858 and was already working as lay assistant--in preparation for ordination--to the curate of St. James's, Piccadilly, among the poor of the parish.

It must have been a difficult experience for which he was entirely unprepared, the people among whom he worked usually indifferent if not hostile to his position and what it represented.[1]   Then at the eleventh hour he shrank back from ordination, sparking a violent, year-long struggle between himself and his father over a suitable alternative professions. It was to be Butler's first bitter battle with intransigent authority from a position of weakness; for having turned abruptly from what he had unreflectively prepared himself for, he became, given his inexperience, dependent on the financial assistance (hence good will) of his father to help him in whatever direction he now chose to strike out. His suddenly realized ambition to become a painter was morally repugnant to Canon Butler; only emigration to New Zealand's Canterbury Province, recently (1850) opened to settlement under Church of England auspices, proved in the end acceptable to both for a fresh start.

From 1860 to 1864 Butler worked as successful sheepherder (and occasional explorer) in the rugged back-country of the Province, in an atmosphere free from the restraints of clerical or academic milieus,

3

among vigorous, independent, practical men. Living in "exile," away from what was familiar, exercising successfully his latent abilities upon practical tasks, was bound to be bracing to his self-reliance. He began to nurture bitter resentment against family, church, and school. On the voyage out he had already prepared the way for breaking with his past: once on board ship he left off saying his prayers, and plunged into Edward Gibbon's *The Decline and Fall of the Roman Empire*. When settled on his sheep station, he scrutinized the Gospels with a stubborn skepticism nurtured obviously by the famous 18th century historian, and eventually found the discrepancies in the Resurrection accounts sufficient grounds for renouncing his faith entirely. By 1864 he felt free to make of Christ and the Bible what he wished.[2] At the same time, only a year after its publication, he read with great enthusiasm Charles Darwin's *Origin of Species* (1859), sensing immediately the subversive implications Darwin's theory had for a literal Christian understanding of man and his purpose. Undoubtedly this work, so instrumental in buttressing the increasing dominance of positivist thought, encouraged his development as freethinker and, despite what his later attacks on Darwin might suggest, became an authority with which to justify his intellectual revolt.[3] The suggestive concept of Darwinian evolution, with its implied morality of successful survival, applicable by analogy to so many spheres of inquiry, would certainly remain a permanent aspect of his slowly developing outlook.

More immediately, he began to understand his past under Darwin's sign as a bitter struggle between parent and offspring. He believed his education had been designed, without real regard for his personal welfare, to inculcate unrealistic, impractical goals about which his opinion had never been solicited; it had been a continuous stunting of his natural growth to self-sufficient manhood by intimidation and the application of strictures intended to weaken the protesting will; it had served to betray his self into a foolish trust in, and a sense of duty toward, his father or other spokesmen for established (or respected) authority, while instilling a corresponding lack of confidence in the urgings of his impulses and budding reflections. In short, he had been hoodwinked into an untenable position from which doubts and un-easiness had rescued him in the nick of time.

His analysis was to be fundamental and far-reaching. By the time he returned to England in the summer of 1864, he had severed his ties with the world of his father, even though he would not be entirely free of Canon Butler's influence until his death in 1886.[4] He established

4

himself in bachelor quarters in Clifford's Inn and devoted himself single-mindedly to the study of painting, his deferred vocation, "with the intention of making it my profession."[5]   For more than six years he would study and paint (getting hung at the Royal Academy occasionally) as if making up for time lost in pursuing goals set by others. But his rebellion did not end there.

For why (we might ask) was Butler so utterly a black sheep, an Ishmaelite (as he put it) in his day, fated to endure until shortly before his death almost total obloquy, when other freethinkers and rationalists who in plain hearing had also rejected or attacked the older tradition in one way or another--T. H. Huxley or John Morley for example--could rise to prominence?   His first books to appear after reluctantly surrendering as hopeless his painting ambitions, *Erewhon* and *The Fair Haven* (1873), were direct assaults on Christianity--the first for celebrating the unChristian "virtues" of good looks, good health, cash in hand, and light-hearted obedience to Mrs. Grundy; the second for offering (albeit as the misleading confession of a religious enthusiast), the positivist interpretation of the Resurrection he had developed in New Zealand somewhat along the lines of Friedrich Strauss' *Leben Jesu*. Much to his disappointment hardly anyone was shocked or took offence. When, however, he found grounds for sharply attacking, in four subsequent works, the *Origin of Species* and the theory of natural selection which by the 1870's were orthodoxies among freethinkers, he did offend and cut himself off from an audience with which he otherwise would have had much in common and to which his works were really addressed.[6]   Furthermore, lacking, unlike his later admirer George Bernard Shaw, the gift of aggressive self-advertisement, he damaged his position further by proposing, in the 1890's, that the *Odyssey* had been composed, not by Homer, but by a young Sicilian woman disguised as Princess Nausicaa in the poem; and that Shakespeare's sonnets incontrovertably revealed the revered Bard's homoerotic love for an obscure naval cook.   Both eccentric theories were calculated to offend literary authorities, who responded, predictably, by either ignoring or rejecting them entirely.

From these literary disappointments he derived however a crucial lesson: the vice of bullying, of self-righteous authoritarianism, was not, after all, restricted to Church and retory.   It was found among free-thinkers, scientists, literary big-wigs--anyone, in fact, who had risen to position and influence.   His failure to make a mark, he believed, was due entirely to the intellectual intransigence of those whose views

5

he had challenged. In this he was more flattering to himself than correct, for failing to get a fair hearing had much to do with the ironic whimsicality with which he stated his views, with his love of paradox, his undisguised scorn for opponents, and the complacent sense that he together with an imagined host of sincere, sensible people was really right. But he assessed his case so defensively because he had become keenly sensitive to the dogmatism of authorities, and to the hypocrisy and venality so often characteristic of them, precisely because he had lived well beyond the threshold of manhood in a state of naive trust in authority before realizing the consequences of this mistake. The struggles with his father, and with respected specialists in science and literature, disposed him increasingly to an automatic distrust of well-established reputations or verdicts. Having (as he thought) "seen through" the foundations of Christianity, only to discover his initial enthusiasm for Darwin's theory unwarranted, he decided to be hoodwinked no more and see for himself always, whatever the subject, before accepting the official view. Not surprisingly, he looked for his truth in out-of-the-way places. His interests were always roused by a desire to disparage whoever or whatever had made a big noise in the world, and it is this skeptical, doggedly self-assertive and yet defensive and easily wounded spirit which informs the entries in the six volumes of notes.

As early as 1874 he jotted down ideas and references to his reading in a "common-place book," primarily however for purposes of gathering the raw materials for his books. This was the seed from which the Note-Books proper were to grow, and they would never lose that original function entirely: many entries found their place in his published works, and others are segments deleted from his manuscripts during revising and re-writing. But as his desire to be heard remained frustrated by the neglect of his books, the notes came to mean a great deal more: by 1891, when he began to edit them a final time after several previous winnowings,[7] he saw in them a record of his intellectual life, a diary in which he could record his grievances and observations, have it out with his *bêtes noirs*, and comfort himself with repeated self-assurances, quite heedless of the decorum required of the published word.[8]

What appears to have crystallized this attitude toward his jottings was the experience of editing his grandfather's papers. In the fashion characteristic of him he had satirized Dr. Samuel Butler, who had died in 1839 when Butler was only four, as the egotistical domestic tyrant

6

George Pontifex in *The Way of All Flesh*. At the time of writing, in the full heat of his revolt (he would not touch the novel again after 1885) he could not imagine that a man who had been both headmaster and bishop could have been anything but a bully. But he was wrong. In December 1888, two years after his father's death, his sisters gave him Dr. Butler's papers so that he might use them for a brief biography. Though sifting through the mounds of materials proved laborious, for they were in total disarray, the task turned into a labor of love, issuing eventually in the bulky two-volume *Life and Letters of Dr. Samuel Butler* (1896). Already by March 1889 he was in love with his grandfather, who, instead of a patriarchal ogre, had in fact been a fair-mined, even-tempered, firm but kindly educator; further researches and interviews with Dr. Butler's former pupils only confirmed the impression. It was an unexpected revelation and must have brought home to him the importance of leaving behind personal memorabilia (preferably in a state of orderliness), especially if he was to have the posthumous hearing he devoutly yearned after. A year later he was putting his own literary "remains" in order --the notes, his correspondence (eventually to fill 16 volumes), and other unused bits of writing--a task that would occupy him intermittently for the remaining ten years of his life.[9]

As he left them at his death, the Note-Books are a remarkable rubble-heap of opinions and obsessions, many repeated again and again, more than 4,200 entries in all, dated and indexed, reflecting, despite the variety of his concerns, his consistent opposition to established intransigence and hero-worship. Regarded in the best light, they present Butler as the champion of the democracy of the mind, as the critic who developed a practical philosophy from an instinctive distrust of those who sought to impose on an unsuspecting public by an appeal either to hidden and recondite matter, or to the verdict of fashion and authority.

III

On first perusal, however, one is bound to be struck by the inordinate number of cranky, unqualified dislikes recorded in the Note-Books--most of them understandably excluded from the published selections--which serves to point up Butler's lack of sympathy for the cultural climate of the times. In literature, for example, he despised Wordsworth, Charles Lamb ("full of false sentiment and prolix"), Tennyson, Browning, Carlyle, Thackeray, George Eliot (*Middlemarch* particularly, which he studied as possible model for *The Way of All Flesh*), Mrs. Humphry Ward, and George Bernard Shaw (though attracted by his wit Butler was repelled by Shaw's propagandizing of Wagner and Ibsen at Handel's and Shakespeare's expense). The tragic Greek playwrights he disliked, Plato, Horace, Marcus Aurelius Antoninus, as well as Virgil, Dante, Spencer, and Francis Bacon (who, he thought, had belabored what the world "had known for many hundreds of years already"). His literary theories and translations of the *Iliad* and *Odyssey* into "Tottenham Court Road" English (that is, man-in-the-street English) set him at loggerheads with prominent Shakespearean and Homeric scholars (Sidney Lee and Andrew Lang, for example). He had little esteem for prominent intellectuals such as Crabb Robinson, Sydney Smith, Leslie Stephen, John Ruskin, Matthew Arnold, John Morley (a "master of style" but a "a jawing ass"), and Augustine Birrell (whom he dismissed as a "poseur" despite agreeing with some of his views). In art he found little to admire beyond the time of Giovanni Bellini, disliked Michaelangelo, Raphael, da Vinci particularly, and found the paintings of contemporaries such as Holman Hunt, D. G. Rossetti, Burne-Jones, and George Frederick Watts (full of "weak brag") odious. He was bored by the music of Bach and Beethoven, as much by Wagner's grand effects as by the delicate refinement of Mendelssohn (a mere "musical hairdresser")--by all music, in fact, written after Handel, with the exception of Sir Arthur Sullivan's comic operas. In politics (which hardly interested him) he was a Tory Conservative, contemptuous of Liberals and Radicals alike, despised Gladstone while unreservedly admiring his opponent Disraeli. His attack on Darwinism, as we have seen, earned him the disdain of prominent naturalists, and he reciprocated by abusing men such as T. H. Huxley, G. J. Romanes, Ray Lankaster, Grant Allen, and others.

An astonishing litany of hatreds, to be sure! One is inclined to dismiss Butler himself as a narrow-minded dogmatist, all the more because rarely (except in the case of the Darwinists) did he elaborate his reasons. G. B. Shaw, though an admirer, was quick to see how much "country parsonage" bigotry had stuck to him despite the often pointless jibes at Christ and Christianity he could not resist making to the end of his days. His attitude in fact was as authoritarian and narrow as his father's, only exercised on a different set of prejudices and preconceptions. To justify his sweeping rejection of those he could not like, he set up a small clique of his own--kindred spirits like H. F. Jones and his cousin Reginald Worsley--and made it represent the silent majority of common-sensical readers whose spokesman he fancied himself

8

to be, and who in their genial unpretentious sincerity could not but embrace his point of view.

Nonetheless, his unabashed subjectivism rested on a significant axiom: he firmly believed in the "personal heresy." He found work of any sort, unless completely botched, admirable only insofar as it revealed what he called a "nice" personality–an amiable, kindly, genuine individual. If a work "does not attract us to the workman," he wrote, "neither does it attract us to itself."[10] He regretted more than once the impersonality of his idols, Homer and Shakespeare; in a note (written significantly when he was editing his grandfather's papers) he asked:

> Why did not Shakespeare make a few odd notes now and again
> about anything he saw or heard and anything that came into
> his head? If we could have one such volume of rubbish shot
> anyhow from Shakespeare or Homer, we would give up three
> parts of the *Iliad* and at least two of the plays--say *Hamlet*
> and *Othello*.[11]

He could not separate the work from the workman, a predilection that grew to a ruling passion during the 1890's (nurtured no doubt by the editing of notes) when he confidently set out to unmask the "authoress" of the *Odyssey* by deciphering the epic, and to piece together the details of Shakespeare's secret love-affair from the counters of his 156 sonnets. Painting, music, philosophical, even scientific disquisitions were, in the final analysis, extensions of personality, and he was inclined therefore to judge tone and manner first. A great artist, he wrote, had to be a "man" first of all, and only then a craftsman or poet (II; April, 1885). He rejected the men we have listed because he did not find their personalities attractively human. In their work he sensed inevitably some aspect or residue of the sin of the father against which he had rebelled: "priggishness"--intolerant, self-righteous egotism, the very opposite of his moral standard of kindliness and niceness. The "essence of priggishness," he explained, "is setting up to be better than one's neighbour . . . more virtuous, more clever, more agreeable, or what not" (II; February, 1884).

This attitude explains even his unspecified dislike of Liberals. Temperamentally, in any case, he shrank from radical and sudden changes. But Liberals were reformers, political paternalist of the new order, intent (or so it appeared) on imposing their way of looking at things on an entire nation. Gladstone was of course such a reformer, and a

9

dour moralist to boot; that he was esteemed as the "G.O.M." and in public behaved accordingly would only damage him further in Butler's eyes. On the other hand, the Conservative Disraeli (not unlike Butler) was the outsider, both politically and (because of his background) socially--reasons enough for recommending him to Butler's sympathies. He was also doing battle against a successful, entrenched, and unrelenting "authority figure." And, finally, he was Gladstone's opposite in character--aristocratic, witty, urbane, prepared to laugh at his political convictions as the earnest, moralistic, Anglican Gladstone could not. Butler tells us that Disraeli, when asked for a rule of life, had replied, "Don't try to find out who is the Man in the Iron Mask."[12] That is just the sort of reply that Butler liked: it was a sure sign of a man who had escaped the vice of priggishness. Those, however, who in their self-importance made grand claims and raised themselves up as moral standard or prophet to mankind (Carlyle, T. H. Huxley, Ruskin, George Eliot, the Darwinist, for example), indulged in self-display (Wagner, Marcus Aurelius, or Michelangelo), or struck the self-important, review-puffed pose (Tennyson, or D. G. Rossetti) would almost certainly rouse his suspicions. Qualities such as these were not "nice," and boiled down to the intellectual egotism of the moral bully which he had encountered at home and in school.

For an illustration of Butler's instinctive response, we might turn to a simple reference in Volume I to a letter in the London *Times* (1883) from Professor Friedrich Max Müller, the well-known Oxford philologist, to which Butler added (though he had never met him), "What an odious person Müller is" (note 1132). The letter is a commemorative notice of a recently deceased Japanese student of Müller, a young Buddhist monk, written, Müller tells us, in the spirit of Dr. Johnson's advice about recording the lives of obscure good people who benefit mankind (the monk had left some incomplete but promising work). He recalls how once, as they watched a sunset on Malvern Hills, the monk, already ill, had pointed to it to say that it was the Eastern gate of " 'our Sukhavati, the Land of Bliss'," where he hoped to meet " 'all who had loved him, and whom he had loved' "; and how later, during their final parting, the monk had looked wistfully at Müller's house where "he had spent the happiest hours of his life." In Butler's eyes that must have been Mr. Pecksniff all over: the apparent eulogy of a promising scholarly career cut short was little more than a display of the laudable propriety of Müller's generous devotion to an unknown foreigner. The letter revealed not genuine interest in the unfortunate monk, but Müller's sanctimoniousness and barely disguised self-importance, however unconscious.

No doubt this was how Wordsworth's poetry must have struck him, characterised as it is by extended self-analysis and the celebration of the poet's sensitivity to nature; for Butler wrote that

> If a thing made such a noise (like a skylark, for example)
> that one could attend to nothing else, [then] Wordsworth
> could hear it, and immediately [think] he was the only per-
> son in the world who could (II; July, 1884).

Little wonder Tennyson's high-minded sentiments would seem insincere self-aggrandizement, and he felt confirmed in his appraisal when he learned (after Tennyson's death) that in private the poet laureate had been foul-mouthed and bad-tempered, and had a copy of Shakespeare's works buried with him.[13] Again, that da Vinci should not only save his caricatures, but also set great store by them proved that "there was a screw loose about him somewhere, and that he had no sense of humour . . ." (III; May, 1884). Finally, we can imagine the reasons for his dislike of Dickens; for his enormous popularity, the posthumous adulation heaped upon him, his fictional idealization of simple domesticity (the very opposite of Butler's sense of family in *The Way of All Flesh*), and his reformist zeal were sufficient to blot out whatever merit and humor he may have found in the novels.

These violent disapprovals have about them the ill will of one who, conscious of not having been accorded the credit he thinks his due, is determined not to concede merit in one who has. A deep-seated sense of inadequacy must have played its role in all this, for the success of his rivals only forced him into greater and greater resistance against them. The outlook he forged for himself with great labor had to be defended. So, for example he castigated Renan from a great distance, not only because he had become the prestigious secularizer of the Gospel, but also because he was able to look back fondly, and with regret, at his happy and orthodox youth (see note 969). Butler was painfully self-conscious about his inability to impress, and was consequently all the more sensitive to reproach or even silent reservation. From his close friends at any rate he exacted devotion, and could not easily forgive any real or imagined slight. To the end of his days he remained a "man with a grievance"[14] against the world, and this marred his judgments of contemporary culture. His own unpretentiousness, his colloquial common sensicalness, the source of much of the real charm in his writings, masked a powerful, proud but frustrated (and very Victorian) sense of self-importance: one does hate in others one's own vice.

11

This is not to say his assessments were entirely without merit. He had a point--as his earliest post-humous admirers quickly perceived--in insisting on the symptoms of smugness or bigotry in the lofty self-conscious poses and attitudes of the prominent intellectuals he attacked. The friendly and unsentimental simplicity of his outlook highlighted as much as any studied analysis could the false note and heavy-handed moralism that had entered the atmosphere of Victorian letters. That even his particular picques were not expressions of defensive jealousy only, but responses resting on not entirely inconsequential grounds is a subject to which we shall have to return.

IV

For Charles Darwin he reserved his fiercest and most articulated hatred. He was put off by the fulsome effusions (expressed while Darwin was still alive) about the nobility of his character, his "stately", "massive" brow, the magnificence of his achievement, his child-like simplicity and poor health, his not minding being compared to a gorilla, his spending many hours in the night when an old man observing earthworms in his slippers so as not to disturb them in their nocturnal doings. Such homage smacked of uncritical hero-worship. Darwin's well-known shyness and unostentatiousness, he decided, was only a shield hiding a high opinion of himself, an ostentatious unostentatiousness deliberately cultivated to impress the impressionable (like himself when in 1872, after his success with *Erewhon*, he was twice invited to Down). He found the *Origin of Species*, once he had located its weaknesses, filled with self-congratulation because of Darwin's habit of calling attention to the wealth of his facts and his countless "patient" researches. In his copy of the sixth edition--next to one such passage--he wrote, "bad prig *capable de tout,*" Butler's phrase for defining the heavy father. In short, Darwin personified everything objectionable in men who wielded authority or basked in the halo of established reputations: he was a sacred cow, and with impunity could afford to spurn the criticism of those in less secure and respected positions. Indeed when Butler published his criticism of the *Origin*, he was dismissed (though not by all reviewers) as an armchair amateur who, because neither a specialist nor laboratory scientist, could hardly be in a position to challenge the researches of a man of Darwin's eminence. But this easy superciliousness could only mean in Butler's mind that Darwin's defenders were unwilling to acknowledge that he had discovered a significant flaw in the Darwinist position.

In the 1859 edition of the *Origin*, Darwin had established natural selection as the supreme agent of true (as distinguished from ephemeral) evolutionary change: changed conditions (their "direct" and "indirect" influence on an organism) induced small, "fortuitous" variations which then were acted upon by natural selection (once again, the organism's external conditions). Specifically "biological laws" cooperated with this selective force–the principle of correlation; its corrolaries, the laws of balance and compensation; and the effects of use, disuse, and habit (that is, the inheritance of acquired characteristics). Under the action of natural selection, as less successful variant forms fell away, the difference between parent stock and a successful variant increased, and thus variations "accumulated" over innumerable generations, until, after the lapse of some hypothetical time, speciation occurred. The crux of the matter lay in Darwin's belief that *only* small, "fortuitous" variations were the prime material on which evolutionary change rested. Evolutionary change was gradual, almost imperceptible; the operation of the biological "laws" were distinctly secondary, and had, he insisted, no *direct* relation to the cause or causes that brought about eventual speciation. He rejected saltations (mutations) as causes since they were discontinuous and usually harmful to the organism. He assumed that variability in organisms was the rule, that small variations were heritable, and that, furthermore, organisms inherited the tendency to vary in the same direction, thus insuring (despite their fortuitousness) an element of cumulative progress in all changes: these phenomena sufficed to explain the origin of species under the operation of natural selection.

The validity of Darwin's explanation was questioned from the outset by reputable scientists without *a priori* objection to a theory of evolution.[15] The action of natural selection on Darwin's terms seemed insufficient to account either for speciation or phenomena such as reversions or the sterility of hybrids. It was suggested, for example, that though organisms do vary, they do so within the limits circumscribed by their morphology; and Darwin ought consequently to have distinguished concretely between ordinary variations and those leading to speciation. Furthermore, given the generally accepted hereditary law of blending by which offspring display a mixture of the characteristics of the parents, small, fortuitious variation–rare even by Darwin's account--would eventually be swamped by the dominant characteristics of the species; in fact, variations produced under domestication-- which Darwin relied on to illustrate what could happen analogously in nature–tended to disappear again in the wild state. Finally, his belief that organisms could vary in the same direction without limit was considered an unsupported assertion (Darwin would admit as much in the third edition). To meet these and other objections Darwin added numerous qualifications in the several editions of the *Origin* (to the last three especially), which not only modified but contradicted the terms of the original theory. The most significant of these changes was to assign an increasingly prominent role (to meet the difficulties posed by blending and swamping) to the inheritance of acquired characteristics, that is, to the effects of habit, use and disuse. He thus made the organism itself an operative force in its evolution, but maintained as absolutely as before that natural selection (an exclusively external force) acting on fortuitous variations, was the chief and sufficient agent of all development.

It is this contradiction which Butler detected after closely scrutinizing (sometime after 1873) all six editions of the *Origin*, and to which he would repeatedly point in his four works on evolution beginning with *Life and Habit*.[16] That Darwin had been forced to introduce the Lamarckian principle of the inheritance of acquired characteristics (Darwin had originally rejected Lamarck's works as insignificant) was for Butler sufficient demonstration that the theory of natural selection lacked logical rigor. In this he plainly echoed the criticism of William Henry Harvey (Dublin professor of botany) who declared that since Darwin had not accounted for the *origin* of variations, he had not told the story of the origin of species: a selective force cannot also be an originating force. Butler further emphasized that Darwin had provided no clear principle which would insure the *purposive* direction, observable in all organic development, to the merely haphazard accumulation of *fortuitous* variations. This last objection was for Butler the crux of the conflict between himself and the Darwinists.

He armed his criticism in *Life and Habit*, moderate, even conciliatory in tone, with his own theory which he innocently thought could resolve Darwin's difficulties. The theory, however, originated in purely philosophic considerations of some weight. If "cunning", that is habit, use and disuse, could contribute to an organism's development, however insignificant in comparison to the effect of outward events ruled by "luck" (fortuitousness), then organic development was essentially teleological, and would *always* reveal the principle of intelligence and purposiveness in action, no matter how unconscious; if, on the other hand, natural selection was the *only* efficient cause (as in the *Origin*), then development could not be purposive at *any* stage, and organisms

14

were perforce passive automata. Darwin had assumed that what man, the purposive breeder, could do with domesticated animals, natural selection could do as well; Butler's sharp eye noticed however that the consistency of the analogy depended upon Darwin's having transformed natural selection into a vague, omnipotent, even anthropomorphically realized power--always "intently watching" over accidental variations, carefully "selecting each alteration," capable of "adjusting each form to the most complex relation in life" (the phrases are Darwin's). A power of this sort could of course overcome all logical objections; but the language itself revealed unmistakably that Darwin had not succeeded in eliminating purposiveness from his argument.

Butler, on the other hand, held that intelligent action, or purposiveness in general, was an irreducible aspect of life itself. His proof he shrewdly drew from the evidence of machines.[17] Intelligently conceived instruments, cumulatively improved over many generations, essentially were extensions of man's limbs, incontrovertible evidence therefore of purposive attempts to solve problems of his existence. In fact, with machines man was changing and developing himself. But if man could act (and change) purposively, then so could all organisms, for what creature does not show some capacity to respond intelligently to its environment, or possess instincts sufficient for survival under normal circumstances? Darwin's fundamental mistake, Butler concluded, lay in explaining organic development without reference to this phenomenon.

Butler, however, went to the other extreme and assumed habit, use and disuse, as forming the *primary* causes of variation; natural selection could act only as a secondary force on existing or emerging variations. He tried in *Life and Habit* to give specific form to his hypothesis by identifying heredity with somatic memory; and in so doing, he believed he had provided the organic principle whereby acquired characteristics could be accumulated and passed on in a purposive direction. Since hereditary "memory" created a oneness of personality between offspring and parent, the habits of one became the habits of the other and tended to become over countless generations unconscious memories--that is to say, instincts. Such inherited memories guided somatic growth as much as specifically behavioristic activities; animals made even their limbs or improved their morphology in the same way they acquired their instincts--by responding intelligently to perceived needs. Consequently, organic development pointed *always* in the direction of purposive adaptation and did not occur somehow by

15

the action of a vaguely realized, anthropomorphized power. Furthermore, Butler claimed to have solved the riddle of reversions as a re-awakening, under the impact of relevant associations, of an older, more ingrained heredity; and of the infecundity of hybrids as the confusion caused by the merging of two divergent heredities.

Despite his claims, Butler's hypothesis can not stand as a satisfactory alternative to Darwin's. Butler had gone too far and driven the logic of his analogy too recklessly and rigorously without regard to biological facts. He equated memory and heredity so uncritically only because at the time almost nothing was known of hereditary laws, and because the distinction (first made by Weismann in 1885) between phenotypic and genotypic cells had not been established.[18] However, Butler's claim (when stripped of implausible assumptions), that life is characterized by goal-oriented (or, to use a modern term, "cybernetic") processes is by no means a quaint detail in a dead quarrel. Darwin had attempted to deal with organisms as if he could reduce purposiveness to a mere ephiphenomenon; and yet he had been unable to avoid language suggestive of what he denied. Scientists today use a not dissimilar metaphoric language when defining genetic processes as "memory" transfers, and the replication of DNA molecules as a "coding" and "programming" procedure.

They thereby admit (unawares perhaps) that these processes are *essentially* different from those of causally determined inorganic matter. Modern computer theory (the theory of *man-made self-regulatory* mechanism) is based on the analogy to life processes themselves, and consequently raises once again the philosophic issue of design in nature in very practical Butler-like terms. Finally, the possibility that strict causal determinism is suspended or restricted, or that acausality may operate in the microbiological realm, can no longer be considered unscientific speculations. The assumptions of 19th century mechanistic materialism have been superseded, and some modern scientists continue to express reservations about the demonstrable validity of a rigorous neo-Darwinist theory of natural selection.[19]

In his time, however, Butler's speculations were shouted down as regrettable relapse to Lamarck's primitive conceptions even though Darwin (as we have seen) himself had introduced them again into the revised edition of the *Origin*. That Darwin would not respond to his criticism and challenges,[20] or alert his readers to the import of the revisions and consequent contradictions in the theory, was for Butler

16

an unforgivable hypocrisy. The self-serving reverence with which the majority of fellow naturalists regarded Darwin made Butler's criticism of him seem not the exercise of an able, inquisitive mind, but a piece of outrageous obscurantism. It was father and son, master and pupil all over again, with the guilt, weakness, and impudence all on one side. Little wonder he felt Darwin and his *claqueurs* had less concern for the truth than for their reputations which were (after all) heavily invested in his revolutionary theory.

Butler's suspicions were not unfounded, though he saw deliberate conspiracy where none was. Grant Allen had on one occasion told him how useful he had found *Evolution Old and New*; however, in his review of it (*Academy*, May 17, 1879) he asserted that one could not derive a single idea from it (II; July 1885).[21] Then in an article written after Darwin's death (*Mind*, October 1883, pp. 487-505; see note 1209 in this volume), Allen rejected natural selection in favor of the inheritance of acquired characteristics as an explanation for the development of the nervous system. G. J. Romanes, another apparent Darwinian, in his work sailed very close to the concept of unconscious memory, yet attacked any sort of neo-Lamarckian criticism of the *Origin* (II; Aug. 1886). And Butler no doubt was disappointed when no support came from Herbert Spencer who quite clearly was a Lamarckian. Such behavior sufficed to persuade Butler, rightly or wrongly, that private misgivings were made to yield to the orthodox line in public debate. Such toadying had made it possible, as he saw it, to pull the wool over the public's eyes and transform Darwin's work into an all but unassailable authoritative original.

As in other quarrels, here too it was the manner more than the matter which roused Butler's rage. It must be emphasized that he questioned not Darwin's scientific findings, but his logic, to inspect which, it would seem, one need not be a specialist. In a letter to Edward Clodd (May 5, 1879) he mentioned he had heard T. H. Huxley (who disliked *Life and Habit*) maintain that Butler "had not the grasp of science" to enable him "to deal with such questions satisfactorily." "What nonsense!" he continued. "The matter is one which any barrister or business man can judge of just as well as Huxley himself." Butler complained that he could not "get chapter and verse for a single blunder from anyone" of his critics.[22] Yet he knew that Darwin had heeded not dissimilar criticism from St. George Mivart, a fellow scientist with a philosophic (and theological) bias against the *Origin*. What Butler could not have known was that by 1878 Darwin had withdrawn from the turbulent controversy surrounding his theory. He would die convinced of its rightness while fully aware of logical difficulties and his inability to demonstrate it empirically.[23] At the time, Darwin's silence, together with the reviewers' condescension could not but appear incriminating.

Butler was consequently determined to review the contributions of those forerunners whom Darwin in the introduction to the *Origin* had given short shrift. Perhaps he would find that in their case too there had been something other than honest appraisal. And so it turned out to have been: they had provided the basic principles, save that of a concept of natural selection, for a satisfactory theory of evolution. Darwin, in other words, had only puffed himself up by casting his teachers from the seat of honor. Refurbishing the reputations of Buffon, Lamarck, and Dr. Erasmus Darwin in *Evolution Old and New* was in effect an expression both of hurt pride (if not of revenge), and of heart-felt sympathy for the victims of a presumptuous new fashion. Before its publication when Darwin must have been on his mind, Butler had told Clodd (letter of June 2, 1878) that

> ... if I catch any one robbing the dead, especially the dead
> that have fallen honourably in battle, poor and neglected
> in their own day, after having borne its burden and heat,
> I will rob them of every stitch of clothing they have on
> their backs, so far as the law will allow me.[24]

That, in any case, is exactly what he did in the new volume and the two others in which he denied Darwin's originality and even impugned his honesty and reliability.

Butler's experience taught him that scientists, whom one associated with the very opposite of "country parsonage bigotry," were not exempt from self-righteousness or narrow dogmatism in the defense of their faith. He thought he detected the spirit of the Hebrew prophets in them--their intransigence, their absolutism, their demand for obedience to the established law. Scientists in fact were the priests of modern times, but far more dangerous than their traditional counterparts because unchallenged in their ascendancy:

> Science is being daily more and more anthropomorphized into
> a god. By and by they will say that science took our nature
> upon him, and sent down his only begotten son Charles
> Darwin or Huxley, into the world so that those who believe

18

in him etc.--and they will burn people [such as himself, no doubt] for saying that science, after all, is only an expression for our ignorance of our own ignorance (IV; Oct. 22, 1891).

Like theologians, scientists were enmeshed in violent (though bloodless) disputes, pretending, again like their counterparts, to final knowledge concerning the mystery-shrouded root of all things, and speaking furthermore from a position of revered authority heavily underwritten by money from foundations. So Butler had no alternative but to regard "the recognized exponents of both science and theology" with "equal distrust": in the matter of drawing conclusions from evidence, even in scientific disputes, no one ought be regarded another's superior simply on the ground of proper accreditation.[25] A phrase he copied from a letter by Lord Grimthorpe to the *Times* of August 13, 1883 summarized Butler's view: "Men of science have to find arguments for men of sense to weigh and judge of" (note 1071).

Appealing to the specialist or to authority, whether in justifying Aeschylus' greatness to schoolboys, or the "truth" of Darwin to laymen, was a form of intellectual intimidation that made it all the harder not only to get at the truth, but to know one's own thoughts and to have the confidence to express them. As such it was like looking everywhere but to oneself for one's most important convictions. That was the lesson Butler made his autobiographical hero Ernest learn in *The Way of All Flesh*. The duty he is taught to feel toward parents and schoolmaster makes him always feel guilty and vaguely (though intensely) unworthy if he has displeased them, and this experience of psychological inequity conditions him to persist in looking to men stronger and more assertive than himself. Consequently, as he grows up, he surrenders himself in good faith to a succession of self-appointed authorities until he is finally forced to fall back on his own resources when their advice leads to a dead end, lands him, in fact, in jail. Only then does he begin to break down the acquired habit of self-doubt and heed his smothered instinctual voice. Significantly, the two men who guide him to his own mind give no direct advice: the worldly dandy Towneley, and Mr. Shaw the tinker, who tells him to scrutinize the Gospels (as Butler had done in New Zealand) and judge for himself the validity of his religious faith. But a crisis is required before he learns, so deep is the habit of deference: he has inherited it from his father, who in his turn had been bullied by Ernest's grandfather, George Pontifex, the respectable bourgeois, who on the grand tour felt duty-bound to sit three hours before a painting in the Uffizzi, and record in his diary the ecstasy inspired by the sight of the Alps in the tritest clichés—not out of genuine enthusiasm but out of the urge, in the then fashionably romantic manner, to show to himself and others, the correctness and refinement of his sensibilities.

As an undergraduate Butler, like George and Ernest, did indeed try to be *comme il faut*, to conform, for example, to the rage for Beethoven among the smart set despite his instinctive preference for Handel. Then one day after his return from New Zealand—he was then thirty—he met a Bayswater curate at an at-home, and asked him who the greatest was--Bach, Beethoven, or Handel. "Handel" was the immediate answer and (Butler continues), "I knew he was right and have never wavered since. . ."26 Yet he had to be pushed before he could elevate his preference to a conviction. He was thrown into similar perplexity when at St. John's College he met George Trevelyan whom Butler's friends considered a genius: Butler readily believed them (though put off by Trevelyan), because he felt uncertain of his ground, "overawed by one I thought really did know things of which I well knew that I was myself mainly intent on trying to conceal my ignorance" (III; June 1887). As with Beethoven and Trevelyan, so eventually with Darwin and his theory: for some fourteen years he had accepted, more or less, despite strong reservations, the authoritative verdict that Darwin had done for the origin of life what Newton had for the heavenly motions, only to discover that the seemingly solid, irrefragable document was erected on a defensive self-righteousness as insufferable as that against which he had rebelled. There was thereafter no choice but to smell a rat in hero-worship. The reputations of the great discouraged independent thought, and their virtues were far "more dangerous to good work" than their vices. Let us not pretend, he wrote, that great men were other than they were, for "it paralyzes to be overshadowed too much" (IV; Oct. 29, 1890).27

V

If his suspicions of the fashionable and reputable crippled his sympathies for, and fuller understanding of, the dominant intellectual culture, he was correspondingly alive to what was unpretentious and sincere, to the poetry of the down-to-earth, to beauty, wit, and wisdom in common dress. He admired those who, if necessary, could suspend their firmest beliefs for kindness' sake; they truly were the "nice" people. In his preferences Butler reveals his attractive side,

20

the humanity hidden beneath the embattled, acrimonious, beetle-browed moralist, the kindliness (attested to by those who knew him) which moved him in old age, for example, to accompany young Desmond MacCarthy, whose parents he had recently met, to the table in a Swiss hotel restaurant to protect him from his father's wrath for being late for dinner.28 To this side we owe numerous charming anecdotes in the Note-Books:

> I saw [he wrote] a beautiful litter of nine sweet little pink
> pigs just a week old when I was on the Breidden ten days
> ago. I admired them and praised them to a cottager's wife
> who seemed to be more or less running them. "Yes," she
> said, "they are a very nice lot for a first belly" (II; July 1885).

Again:

> There was a man dying of painless, gradual decay, whose
> friends asked him if there was anthing he had a fancy for
> which they could get him. He said he had all his life
> thought he should like to have a cuckoo-clock, and the
> present would, he thought, be a proper occasion for ac-
> quiring one. A cuckoo clock was bought and placed
> where he could see it as well as hear it. He said the last
> few days of his life were much cheered by it (VI; Dec. 7, 1900).

How unsentimental, yet touching this last when we compare it to the conventional Victorian death-bed scene, little Nell's, say, or Stephen Blackpool's. Out of such stuff are made Shakespeare's Falstaff and Mistress Quickly, as well as Thomas Hardy's peasants:

> One sweltering hot day in June I saw a man in a railway
> carriage look wistfully up at the sky. "The snow," he
> said, "keeps off quite nicely, don't it?" (Note 321)

Folksy witticisms such as this brought Butler particular pleasure, for they were unselfconscious and bore no taint of undergraduate smartness or self-display: straight from the heart they came and had no designs upon him. Among those who spoke like this and in their world he felt most at ease; among people, that is, more apt to look up than down at him he felt free of intellectual bullying. And the art which reminded him of their down-to-earth spirit and which had not lost touch with their unconscious paganism he admired most.

All his life he inhabited drab, cluttered bachelor rooms in Clifford's Inn, just around the corner from the congestion and hurly-burly of Fleet Street with which Dickens was so familiar, close to the small, somewhat grimy shops in Fetter and Leather Lane where he did his shopping. He seems not to have shared the cultured outrage when the railway bridge was erected over Ludgate Hill, or when the historic Temple Bar (to be replaced by the Griffin monument) and the "Cock Tavern" (made famous by Tennyson and Thackeray) were pulled down to make way for the New Royal Law Courts. Their massive neo-Gothic facades, Barry and Pugin's Houses of Parliament, and other similar rising manifestations of Victorian architectural virility would not readily have commanded his attention. He loved the confusion of bustling life, the huddled comfort of the City where buildings had "grown" higgledy-piggledy and not in conformity to plan and symmetry. Among his favorite sights was the smoke-belching Cannon Street and Charing Cross Railway terminal. He enjoyed rambling in Cheapside, watching people or looking into shop windows. On his annual holidays in Italy he usually spent little time in the well-visited cities--Venice, Verona, Rome, Naples--but wandered from one north Italian or Ticenese sub-Alpine village to the next, relaxing expansively in the company of the simple folk he met there (some no doubt making much genuine fuss over their regular visitor). In later years, when gathering materials for his *The Authoress of the Odyssey* (1897), he made Sicily his destination where he formed friendships among the burghers of the then still remote Trapani. He was fond of extended walking tours through the southern counties,[29] visited pubs, or out-of-the-way cemeteries looking for quaint names and epitaphs. In the 1890's he often walked from Gravesend to Gad's Hill for a pint of beer at "The Falstaff" (even though the place was somewhat desecrated by the proximity of Dickens' house), managing to extort occasionally some freshly laid eggs from a local farmer on the pretense his wife was a poor invalid.[30]

In fact, he regarded himself as *vates sacer* to ordinary folk and his non-literary friends. He compiled a list of the sayings of Mrs. Boss,[31] his cousin Reggie Worsley's laundress, in whom he saw a veritable reincarnation of Mistress Quickly, a woman with an irregular marital past, a vulgar tongue, and several illegitimate children, with one of whom she lived, her son Tom (himself married bigamously). He questioned the propriety of preserving them, but "after consultation with men in high position at the British Museum, I have decided to retain them." Their charm is obvious: Once she told him that as a young woman she would snap her fingers "at any wh--re in Holborn, and if I was togged

22

out and had my teeth I would hold my own now with any fly-by-night of them all." "O Lor'," she complained to Worsley, "I never knew no bad words at all till I came to live with you. When you say 'bloody' it makes my backbone curdle and my heart jump out of its socket, and then I goes and tells it to Tom." Alfred Cathie, the Cockney man-servant he hired after his father's death also had his peculiar expressions, and showed his affection for Butler with stern reminders which were unconsciously comic and endearing. So Butler wrote these down as well; and he could not resist catching a few "improprieties" in flight, such as the one about the man who said he would not marry, since it was "cheaper to buy the milk than keep a cow"; or the pious lady who, anxious to convert a handsome young man, flung her arms about him to say she would do anything if he would love his Savior.

No doubt he preferred the society of the likes of Alfred because his easily wounded self-esteem and pugnacity made successful movement among his distinguished peers difficult if not impossible. It was quite natural he should gravitate to people whose thoughts and feelings were unburdened by an intellect trained to self-conscious artifice and sophistication. But he knew only too well he was not one of them. By virtue of his work and training he was more like members of that mandarin society which had rejected him. He had not shed their besetting vice, he was, he confessed, among the "damned," not among the saintly classes "who do not set up as instructors of other people" (II; Dec. 1884). He was given to sententious prosing, and not entirely unwittingly had turned friends such as H. F. Jones and Alfred Cathie into disciples. In his writings, at least, he tried to guard against tendentiousness, by reflecting the world of "nice" people, or rather what he fancied to be their common sense, tuning his language to theirs and introducing the rough-and-ready illustrations from life close at hand so characteristic of his style.

In the opening passages of *Life and Habit* he tells us, for example, that his arguments are directed to ordinary, matter-of-fact people, not scientific specialists; but, he continues, that ought not detract from the seriousness of his ideas, for "unless a matter be true enough to stand a good deal of misrepresentation, its truth is not of a very robust order . . ."[32] He never allows his most abstract speculations to fly too far from the ordinary world within which all matters must be judged:

The action, therefore, of an embryo making its way up in the world from a simple cell to a baby, developing itself eyes,

ears, hands, and feet while yet unborn, proves to be exactly
of one and the same kind as that of a man of fifty who goes
into the city and tells his broker to buy him so many Great
Northern A shares . . .

Or again:

No thief . . . is such an utter thief–so *good* a thief as the
kleptomaniac. Until he has become a kleptomaniac, and
can steal a horse as it were by a reflex action, he is till but
half a thief with many unthievish notions still clinging to
him.[33]

To be sure, he cites scientific treatises, and engages in logical argumentation, but the tone of a playfully ironic essay, with frequent digressions,
puns, and anecdotes, is allowed to predominate. The style was hardly
suited to a rebuttal of the *Origin of Species*, but Butler succeeded
(at his peril) in avoiding the authoritarian tone he disliked in many
of his contemporaries. "I wanted to please people," he explained to
Clodd in reference to the work, "and if there was anything in it they
had a fancy to, to keep it and set it straight for themselves." He was
breaking rules, but "such as I am I must be myself and travel by lanes
rather than highways, or I had better shut up at once."[34] He wanted
to tease his reader into seeing for himself rather than giving him the
sense that the matter could only be settled in the hermetic atmosphere
of the laboratory or of the academic colloquium.

If a grain of corn looks like a piece of chaff, I confess I
prefer it occasionally to something which looks like a
grain, but which turns out to be a piece of chaff only.[35]

The reader would less likely be taken in when the proposal was at
first glance unpresumptuous and even dowdily plain; it simply took
too much time (as he had learned) to ascertain the lion beneath the
skin.

That is why his critics could easily dismiss him. His ironic oblique-
ness made it difficult for them to know whether Butler was not after
all pulling their leg. They knew that with *Erewhon* and *The Fair Haven*
he had entered the public arena as satirist and paradoxalist. Some
readers (such as Canon Ainger, Charles Lamb's biographer) and reviewers in fact took the attack in *The Fair Haven* (published anony-

mously) on the foundations of Christian faith as a spirited defense against narrow and literalist theologians.36 The confusion delighted Butler so much that in the second edition, to which he appended his name, he cited the reviewers to point up their gullibility. But he thereby announced himself as a man whose real views were not always what they seemed. Since in tone and manner *Life and Habit* was so like its two predecessors, reviewers, Grant Allen among them, were understandably alert to the possibility of paradox. Clodd pinpointed the cause of Butler's vexation: readers prompted to ask, " 'Where was the joke?' " responded, when Butler assured them there was none, by saying that they were not as foolish as to believe that.37 Even much later, Butler's reputation made it seem possible to suspect that *The Authoress of the Odyssey* (1897) was nothing more than a literary hoax, a brilliant way of cocking his hat at the learned theories of classical scholars.

His Fleet Street realism also expressed his fundamental and literal minded anti-sentimentalism. He could not help but believe that fashionable representations of romantic or tragic emotions, or in general the imaginative, and figurative realism, were at bottom either hollow or insincere because out of touch with plain reality. His characteristic satiric weapon was deflation by means of a dry matter-of-factness. He tells us, for example, that Lohengrin in Wagner's opera was decidedly a prig, for in the bedchamber after the wedding he should have told Elsa that her question "rather put him up a tree, but that as she wanted to know who he was he would tell her and let the Holy Grail slide"; anyway, had she waited she would have "found his name on his shirt or his pocket handkerchief" (IV; June 30, 1890). Despite his love for Shakespeare, some plays did not sit right–*King Lear* and *Hamlet*, to mention two--and he was obviously delighted by a low-brow reaction to *Hamlet* from a critic in the American West who wrote that the author of this play indulges in too much "chinning," is behind the times, and seems to forget that "what we want nowadays is hair-raising situations, and detectives . . . Our advice to the author is, a little more action, a little more gurgling taffy, and a fair share of variety business in his next piece" (III; July 1887). Again he mused that one day he might meet three famous personages in Hades, only to find that Tantalus was getting "something not infrequently," that the vultures provided a rather gentle stimulus to Tityos' liver (thereby preventing congestion), and that Sisyphus found "no pleasure comparable to that of seeing his stone bound down hill. The effect is so fine that it is worth his trouble" (IV; June 6, 1891). On the subject of Tennyson's version of the famous legend he supposed that if "Lancelot had not flung Excalibur but had kept it to put in the [British] Museum, we cannot be sure that the consequence would have been so serious as we are given to understand" they would have been (IV; Oct. 25, 1892). Such commentary is not of course serious criticism: it is naughty boys throwing brickbats at revered portraits in the school hall. But that is the point: only an application of low-brow skepticism could break the spell of sanctity with which official culture so often invested great men, works, and ideas, and offset uncritical idealization.

Yet his serious though fragmentary art and music criticism in the Note-Books was also rooted in the bluff, no nonsense plain thinking and feeling expressed in these jokes. In Michelangelo he found too much striving after the transcendental, the exaggerated and idealized. To paint in this manner was a manifestation of *gnosis*--a pretense to arcane mysteries. On the one hand such art soared away from the solid world he knew (Michelangelo, he maintained, had refused to kiss the soil), on the other its grandeur seemed intended to impress and overawe the gazer rather than speak to him. The opposite approach was *agape*, the wish to lead one's fellow mortal by the hand and with one's talents, however humble, bring him enjoyment. This was what Giotto had done in painting, and Handel in his music, the straightforwardness of which suggested to Butler a man like himself--a bachelor, sensible, confident yet anxious to speak to his audiences in the most readily apprehensible way. Bach, by contrast, seemed to glory in abstract formality, forbidding fugal complexity, and tonal austerity; and, unlike Handel, he offered his works in the service of a deeply felt other worldly religiosity.

In fact, his ideas about painting were Pre-Raphaelitic and reflected the general fashion of his day. With Ruskinian precision he declared that the decline of Italian art had begun when the Carracce brothers opened the Art Academy at Bologna, late in the 16th century, initiating the academic system of training that eventually would predominate over the older apprentice systems. The trend encouraged painting by rules and thus--as Butler would have it--fostered the "formula" painting in imitation of admired models, a preoccupation with form at the expense of feeling, with technical polish of the sort he (and his contemporaries) deplored in the work of Raphael. His stylized sentiments, Butler insisted, showed neither genuine feeling nor a loving care for detail; he was after the grand and impressive effect.[38] Naturally, he could not enjoy the flamboyant moods of Salvatore Rosa (then still somewhat in vogue) either. *Agape* and genuiness he found in Raphael's

26

contemporary, Giovanni Bellini, whose inward intensity, expressed in quiet, faithfully rendered background landscapes and serene, unidealized, simple figures drawn from life, exuded kindliness and a delight in the everyday world. What he liked, he once wrote, was a *Santa Famiglia* with the wash flapping on the clothes-line in the background-- a proper balance, that is, between the ideal and real as he found it in the simple grandeur of Giotto and Dutch painters such as de Hooghe and Rembrandt, as well as in the mostly anonymous votive art in Ticinese and north Italian chapels, whose crudity in execution was offset by their endearing naivete and the absence of all show.[39] In all this he was expressing in his underdog sort of way (perhaps influenced by Ruskin, some of whom he must have read while an art student) the broad reaction that had set in by the 1850's against the idealization of High Renaissance art, against the "grand style" inspired by Raphael and established into dogma by Sir Joshua Reynolds. We may recall that John Everett Millais *Carpenter's Shop* offended because the Holy Family was portrayed naturalistically, and without a trace of Raphael--like sublimity, as a collection of plain and ordinary artisans,[40] and contained just the sort of flat factualness that would satisfy Butler's requirements. Still, he disliked most of the art of his day despite its tendency to go again to nature because much of it--especially D. G. Rossetti's work--did not escape self-conscious mannerisms and expressed the sort of romantic sentiments which, as we have noted, could only strike him as humbug.

In his literary tastes he was equally unsentimental. He preferred the plain style in form and matter. His two literary idols were Homer and Shakespeare, but he preferred Shakespeare's comic to his tragic creations. He cherished the sonnets, despite their ornate Petrachan quality, because he fancied to glimpse in them the otherwise inscrutable personality of the great Bard. He preferred the *Odyssey* to the *Iliad* because there too he thought he found the writer, not blind Homer, but a feminist princess with a dislike for masculine heroics and a loving concern for the details of her everyday world. He was in tune with the blunt realism of Defoe, Swift, Smollett, and *Hudibras* Butler; the unsophisticated, graspable allegorical figures (and simple Anglo-Saxon English) of Bunyan's *Pilgrim's Progress*; the hard common sense of Dr. Johnson and Jane Austen; the worldly-wise irony of Henry Fielding, and, as we have noted, the urbanity and wit of Disraeli. In short, his tastes show his affinity for the literature of the 18th century and its predominant philosophical attitudes:[41] there, it seems, he found reflected his own hard-won skepticism about the way of the

27

world, and an appreciation of the solidity of ordinary reality.

VI

Yet Butler did not merely mock, but tried to find a relativistic alternative to the Scylla and Charybdis of scientific and moral dogmatism. It is most clearly formulated in the *bon mots* and aphorisms found in the Note-Books selections published since 1912. Together with his posthumously published novel, *The Way of All Flesh*, they have exerted a traceable influence upon a disillusioned, skeptical generation of English (and American) writers working during and after World War I, and who, in revolt against the legacies of the previous age, were ready to hear the views of its black sheep. Bernard Shaw's life-long war on every sort of idealism and his "life-force" philosophy were nourished at its commencement by Butler's skepticism and anti-Darwinism. The general outlook of the members of the Bloomsbury Group who knew and were attracted to Butler (E. M. Forster most especially), in their distrust of ideologies, big causes, and "great" men, had considerable affinity with Butler's, although he probably would have felt uneasy about their preoccupation with beauty, art, and personal relationships.

The defining quality of his position derives from his neo-Lamarckian theory of evolution which served as an organizing metaphor (though he often as not took its terms literally) with which to express his convictions. The theory was in fact a substitute faith. It permitted him to redefine certain tenets of Christian dogma in entirely naturalistic terms.

The central concept of the theory is the continuous identity of parent and offspring up to the point of birth, united by the heritable fund of unconscious memories each generation has passed on to its successor since primordial beginnings. Inherited memory in fact defined a creature, was its store-house of instinctive knowledge tested by past generations in the struggle for survival, available as a resource from which each new individual could draw provided circumstances were favorable and not so foreign as to be perplexing. Life was a remembering, death, literally, a forgetting, though there could never be total forgetfulness since there was no absolute death. Vitality was the power of association, of "remembering" what to do in any given situation. Consciousness or mind, itself a corporation of countless consciousnesses, was a state of continual movement from static to dynamic aroused when confronted by something new enough to require

28

conscious cunning. For perfect understanding was a cessation of all awareness of differentiation, a state in which life would be lived absolutely unconsciously, purely instinctively. Like all creatures, man was a collection of tools made by, and in the service of, conscious cunning and unconscious memories, and God, by this account, was the original primordial personality that had proliferated into infinite species and individuals, the primordial will and intelligence, in other words, become and ever becoming flesh. God was the "baseless" (and unknowable) "basis of all that what we base most solidly, of all our thoughts and actions" (III; Jan. 1889).

His assumptions required a monistic conception of the universe; there were no definable limits to intelligence and memory, where they began, where they ceased: if intelligence was manifest in one cell, it had to be manifest in the atom. Intelligence was the unitary characteristic of all creation, the inorganic and organic, and there could only be one "real" substance and the multifarious forms of our universe but various aspects or manifestations of it. Consequently, though utterly beyond comprehension, "Eternal matter" permeated and sustained by eternal unfathomable mind, "matter and mind being functions of one another, is the least uncomfortable way of looking at the universe".[42] In such a universe it was impossible to draw fixed lines and establish clear definitions free of contradictions. It was impossible to define limits absolutely. As personal identity shaded imperceptibly into collective identity, mind into matter, the organic into inorganic, mental into mechanical, free will into necessity, life into death, so all categories most fundamental and necessary to our thinking, shaded into their logical opposite, and were indeed but makeshift formulations for grasping the ineluctable flux of things, rather than reliable symbols for fixed truth. The universe was one, yet at a touch always becoming discrete. Unavoidably at the heart of every rational inquiry we would come upon a contradiction, so that contradiction and paradox were the very foundation of our understanding of the universe, the foremost paradox of all being that mind and matter were simultaneous aspects of each other. The basis of consciousness itself, as we have seen, was paradoxical, for the more one knew the less one was aware, and *vice versa*. In God rested the most fundamental paradox of all, the extremes of all and nothing. Butler, in short, had argued himself into the position of the Greek philosopher Heraclitus.

But abstract formulations had practical implications. Materialists and positivists were committed to the assumptions of causal differential

29

determinism by which all phenomena could be explained in terms of the rigid laws of inert matter. He, on the other hand, had determined first of all that one could not explain purpose and intelligent action *in some other supposedly* more real category without contradiction, and secondly that absolutist positions of *any* kind were, in the final analysis, untenable. Butler simply refused to explain man's perceptions in terms from which the subjective aspect of experience had been eliminated for the sake of an objective and logically consistent description of it. Experience was anterior to the abstractions by which positivists "explained" it; and the experience of purpose, of goal-oriented actions, was one of those experienced realities behind which we could not go without undermining the very basis of all thinking, without "dehumanizing" man's sense of himself.[43]

That is why he declared as futile any striving after fixed truth and certitude. Truth as such was the most convenient formulation which for the time being best suited the known facts without an undue wrenching of common-sense ideas and instincts: "The firmest ground," Butler wrote, "is the most universally received and most unquestioned convention" (II; Jan. 1890), though, he cautioned, even common consent, if thought through too far, will prove--to the logical mind at least--a mere "chimera" (III; Nov. 1889). About the ultimate "why's" of experience, existence, and the universe man was and would remain profoundly ignorant. Hence, in a sense, illusions were as necessary as they were useful, for without them there would be no movement or progress of any sort. He admitted, for example, that Christian miracles were possible; but the question for him was, Are they "convenient? Do they fit comfortably with our other ideas?" (II; March 1885). Again, when in the 1890's he confronted the "Wolfian heresy" concerning the multiple authorship of the Homeric epics, he asked whether this view fitted with our sense of them, not whether it was true or logical. To hold firmly to dogmanic position was very much an escape from the monistic flux of life itself; instead, the only viable outlook had to be grounded on a continual (and shifting) compromise between extremes. Absolute virtue could easily produce the effect of its opposite; to be palatable and useful, it had to be mixed with a pinch of immorality. Just as there was always a little lying in truth-telling, and some truth in all lies, so respectability was all the more respectable and less presumptuous for being infected with a little naughtiness. Right and wrong, in short, were in an everlasting state of exchange; it was "wrong to be too right, and to be too good is as bad--or nearly so--as to be too wicked " (note 48). So when "the righteous man turneth away from

30

the righteousness that he hath committed, and doeth that which is neither quite lawful nor quite right, he will generally be found to have gained in amiability what he has lost in holiness" (IV; November 17, 1890). Butler's rule of thumb was that the one serious conviction a man should have is that nothing is to be taken seriously, a lesson Ernest, in *The Way of All Flesh*, learns in the end. Life was the practical art of "knowing" how to draw the right "lines"--and no one knew how to draw them "in respect to more than one or two things" (II; April 1884).

This sense of the uncertain meaning in our categories is implied in the celebrated satiric method Butler first employed in *Erewhon*, and which both Oscar Wilde and G. B. Shaw were to turn to such good account later. He simply turned an accepted idea, or more frequently, an analogy on its head, and ran it to see how much truth could be extracted. A favorite "misquotation" from Tennyson's *In Memoriam* furnished him with a perfect formula for reversals:

> There is more truth in honest lies
> Believe me than in half the truths (note 28)

There are other possibilities, as one can imagine. Again, we are treated to a new version of the famous parable:

> The lilies say, consider the Solomons in all
> their glory; they toil not neither do they spin,
> yet verily I say unto you that not a lily among
> you all is arrayed like one of these (II; Feb. 1887)

In this direction, needless to say, lies the path to nonsense, yet the fun of the game was that he could always find some kernel of unsuspected sense along the way. It was in fact a way of being serious, without seeming so. So when we are told that a bad digestion comes from our inability to convince the cells of our food to surrender their identity to our stomach cells, that the food quite literally "disagrees" with us, he half means it, as he does when he tells us that we choose our solicitors very much as we do our limbs, and that a man sometimes dies "through disease of his solicitor or failure of his bank's action" (III; Oct., 1889). With his theory he could connect everything to the purposive will; but above all, with his brand of serious playfulness he could snub his nose at all absolutist claims and pretensions and demonstrate both the limits of human reason and the consequent necessity

31

of a different court of appeal.

VII

If reason and logic were indeed inadequate guides, how did one find sound, that is, convenient conclusions in a world so completely in flux?

His answer was, With faith and common sense (the two terms often overlap each other). Since science no more than philosophy was allowed to answer ultimate questions, one had no choice but to rely on one's inner voice, one's own urgings: they had their own reasons (to adapt Pascal's phrase), and ruled according to laws transcending language and conscious thought. These reasons in fact were the irreducible and undefinable grounds of being itself. Man had shaped himself by ideas and desires for which in the last analysis he could provide no logical account, issuing forth, as they had from the urgings seated deeply within the structure of his being. This prelogical world was part of the unseen kingdom of God, its voice common sense, the voice of the Lord, and its standard the flexible balancing of considerations in pursuit of maximum convenience.[44] In comparison with this great and ancient pool of unconscious memories tested again and again in the practical business of survival, what was self-conscious reasoning but a tentative groping in the dark? So "there is nothing for it but a very humble hope that from the great unknown source our daily insight and daily strength may be given us with our daily bread. And what is this faith but Christianity, whether one believes that Jesus Christ rose from the dead or not?" (IV; Nov. 13, 1891). To supplant this faith with consistent positivist analysis, to dig around the foundations of being itself, in other words, was to risk utter intellectual and emotional paralysis. The awareness of this, coupled with his growing dislike of the "priests of science," moved him to make his peace eventually, in his manner, not with the letter but with the spirit of Christianity which, he discovered, was based upon an acceptance of the mysterious paradoxes of experience.[45] In fact, religion was (or ought be) a settling of first principles without over-defining them; and according to his reasoning, the Church was the visible representation of the ancient heritage which had given birth to them. So too Mrs. Grundy was to be respected rather than defied, for the truly sensible man would always do as his neighbour, unless this became absolutely intolerable. The knowledge of things, and the rules of conduct most especially, depended largely on what sensible and kindly people, those through whom the voice of the Lord spoke most clearly, could agree upon.

This conclusion, expressed in the Note-Books more than once, seems at odds with what we have already said of Butler the rebel and outsider. Readers of *Erewhon* will recall that the Ydgrunites, the successful and healthy people who pay due respect to Mrs. Grundy, are a kind of moral standard in that playfully ambiguous satire. If that was not a settled matter in Butler's mind in 1872, it certainly was not long thereafter, and he said so plainly and angrily, shortly before his death in a letter to the *Spectator*.[46] There is of course a contradiction: indeed Butler was not the Nietzsche-like rebel and individualist early commentators made him out to be, and he was decidedly not anti-bourgeois (in the modern sense), but only anti-rationalist. In championing common sense, or faith in unconscious memories,--essentially a conservative endeavor--he acknowledged the fact that common folk more often than not did have a consequential grasp of the essentials of their lives and that they, no less than the educated, must of necessity adjust their views to the exigencies of life, regardless of philosophic systems or logical consistency--which, in any case, always come limping after as mere gloss. The "common fellow," he insisted, "is the conscience and *verifying faculty* of the race" (note 105; italics mine). Butler assumed--and this renders his outlook so attractive--that the truth essential to daily life cannot depend on complicated, or abstract, arguments available only to the few. In fact, few have ever been guided to their most cherished conviction by logic, but have instead come to them by way of a more eluctable process--by faith, intuition, a sudden illumination. Experience as reflected in the totality of man's perceptions must be the foundation of metaphysical rationales, and not the other way round.

In this respect Butler echoed Petrarch's criticsm (in *De ma ignorance*) of Aristotle's notion of happiness: "the opinion upon this matter of any pious old woman, or devout fisherman, shepherd or farmer, would, if not so fine spun, be more to the point than his."[47] Increasingly in the 19th century this common faculty of knowing was ignored as a source of real knowledge, as the dismissive attitude toward the "primitive" and the "subjective" became, despite the Romantics efforts to rehabilitate the sensibility of simple folk, all but second nature among intellectuals. Truth became a matter of logical analysis detached from the experienced sense of reality. It is this habit of mind that Butler challenged in his general observations.

We can usually detect him trying to arbitrate between the claims of opposites with the intent of finding a comfortable compromise least ruffling to self-indulgence and kindly tolerance. "The Roman Catholic theory," he argued, "is the best--alternate fasts and feasts, and the same made movable so as to avoid too great regularity" (note 1103). It was not nice to be wedded to anything--not even a theory (II; Oct. 1883); it was best to be allowed to keep "a whole harem of ideas."[48] The one absolute he allowed was the freedom to follow where his prejudices led him, to sacrifice no possibilities in the name of abstract loyalty to cause or cogency. To insure this, he aimed at deliberate inconsistency, or rather, at deliberate intellectual elusiveness, and not (though he failed by clinging too tenaciously to his evolution metaphor) at another worked-out system. Life was rather like music--"it must be composed by ear, feeling, and instinct not by rule. But one had better know the rules, for they guide in doubtful cases--though not often"--(IV; Jan., 1891)--a lovely example, this last of Butler's shrinking back from what is about to become a dogmatic assertion. For everything is "one thing at one time in some respects, and another at another time in other respects"; what was needed was a means of expressing "the harmonies that lurk even in the most absolute difference and vice versa" (III; July 1888).

The cultivation of such a mixture of complacency and skepticism made Butler appear--when his fame began to spread--like a latter-day Epicurus, as someone, in other words, who had managed to free (his generation at least) from the terrors of the beyond and of constricting moral strictures.[49] He had elevated the principle of pleasure and the sense of need as respectable guides to sane life, and this essentially pagan principle is nowhere more strikingly manifested than in Butler's linking money to psychological health.[50] It is money, no less than hope, that helps us pierce the Alps, for will-force is nothing more than a form of money force. Butler knew from experience how debilitating lack of ready cash was. The fuel that nourished his rebellion was his financial success in New Zealand; after his losses in stock speculations he was hard pressed to enjoy his independence until after his father's death when he came to possess the tangible power of his inheritance. From this angle, keeping children financially dependent seemed the parents' way of delaying their self-reliance as long as possible. Ernest in *The Way of All Flesh*, for example, is not entirely free until he comes into the generous estate left him by his aunt Alethea. Butler compiled his own list of the seven deadly sins, and we find that the greatest next to bad health is the want of money (note 1295). Selfishness was for Butler not at all what traditional moralists claimed it to be; it was in fact a positive good. The world, if truth were stated baldly, had always been governed by self-interest and there was no use in trying to stop this. We should only try, he wrote, to make the self-interest of cads a little more coincident with that of decent people." (note 1088).

But we must not forget that this street-wise bluntness was one side of an outlook of which a deep sense of helplessness was the other-- a side earlier admirers too readily overlooked. In *Erewhon* he had made crime a disease, and disease a crime. The analogy impresses us as mere banter; yet it was the logical consequence of setting up the Ydgrunites as the satire's moral standard. Good luck and good health were, practically speaking, the only profitable virtues, that is to say, the only virtues that mattered. And it was a settled conviction: to possess such virtues, often as not the accidents of birth and breeding, as well as the requisite balance of cash in hand, was to be loved by the Lord (note 203). More: good breeding was nothing less than the *summan bonum* and the glory of God:

> It is a question of what is the Glory of God . . . We say
> it varies with the varying phases of God as made manifest
> in his works; but that as far as we are ourselves concerned
> the Glory of God is best advanced by advancing that of
> man. If asked what is the glory of man, we answer "good
> breeding"--using the words in their double sense, and mean-
> ing both the continuance of the race, and that grace of
> manner which the words are more commonly taken to
> signify (note 232).

For Butler, however, "grace" was fickle Fortune's gift, and not, as in the minds of many of his contemporaries, the Hellenistic inheritance which the gospel of Judea had deprived mankind of.

Though he has been celebrated as the great anti-mechanist, as the formidable opponent of a cosmogeny from which mind has been re- moved, Butler, by elevating unconscious above conscious cunning, could not escape the melancholy conclusion that what was most important to the good life was virtually beyond the grasp of deliberate willing. No brilliant attainment could outshine in his eyes the advantages of a comely body and sound instincts, the very qualities toward which nature had been travailing. To be blessed with them was to be in a state of grace, to possess the gifts necessary for navigating successfully through the multiplying perplexities of life to serenity and harmony. It was to have *savoir faire* without knowing it, and that was the very thing he, like St. Paul, lacked:

> Grace is best, for where grace is, love is not distant,
> Grace! the old Pagan ideal whose charm unlovely Paul
> could not withstand . . . [the voice of the Lord told
> him] let my grace be sufficient for thee--but in this he
> failed and so he stole the word and strove to crush its
> meaning to the measure of his limitations.

And we know now what the voice of Lord signified in Butler's thinking. His powerful sense of contingency that circumscribed this nostalgic ideal is expressed unequivocally in several places in the Note-Books. In life there was both luck and cunning, freedom and necessity even unto the very atoms; but luck was the stronger force.[51] Hence, to be aware of one's lack of fortune's favors was to know that one had fallen from the profoundest impulses of being. Performing dogs, he wrote in *Life and Habit*, "never carry their tails; such dogs have eaten of the tree of knowledge, and are convinced of sin accordingly--they know that they know things, in respect of which, therefore, they are no longer under grace, but under the law . . ."[52] The greatest poets never write, the greatest saints do not preach, painters and composers who theorize seldom produce lasting work.[53]

This is the conviction that lies behind his distrust of academic training. How easy it was for someone to block the way to one's own inner resources. The many notes on how to paint attest to his awareness of this possibility and are obviously the off-spring of bitter disappointments. Six years he devoted to following trustingly (as he tells us) the prescribed rules at the Heatherley Art School (and other painting schools). He learned to copy nature with Ruskinian attention to detail, but he was not encouraged to experiment and paint out of his own head. Early in the 1880's, when Festing Jones had urged him to write a little piano piece, he had sat down to find, to his great surprise, that he could indeed put one together. The experiment led to other short compositions in imitation of Handel, and to two secular "comic cantatas" (*Narcissus* and *Ulysses*). As an aid to composing the larger works, both he and Jones (who collaborated with him) took lessons in traditional counterpoint in 1890 from William Rockstro. In this instance, however, unlike in his art studies, he had allowed his first efforts, his *sense of need*, to precede academic training, and that was how he should have proceeded as a painting student. Let sincere effort rule, he counselled, not the mastery of rules, least of all a desire for public acclaim, and painting would come of its own: students should simply begin to paint, and like all organisms, solve problems as they arise, trusting in the sufficiency of their innate abilities to meet the challenge. They should have faith in their stock of unconscious and conscious intelligence, and learn only that without which they cannot get on. It was the only way both to discover one's capacities without falling victim to someone else's system and to do fresh, vigorous work instead of spiritless, stale imitations. Art academies, all academies in fact, went on the opposite principle as if intent on crushing all spontaneity out of their pupils. As in life, in art too there could be no fool-proof systems, no settled rules, no complete answers: there was no use trying to discover the man behind the Iron Mask. The best plan was to place oneself in the presence of effortless and sincere beauty, cultivate the "nice" people, and let their combined influence work upon oneself. The rest had to come from within.

VIII

Butler was exceedingly possessive about his ideas. The implications of hereditary memory, the crime-disease analogy, and the discovery of the authoress of the *Odyssey* he claimed as his own, and in the particular way he presented them they of course were.[54] But his general man-in-the-street outlook was very much part of a prevailing conservatism that runs like a connecting thread through many of the finest and most characteristic English writers of the 18th and 19th centuries. Perhaps we should look to John Locke as giving most systematic expression to that outlook.[55] Even when not articulated, it made itself felt, for it was rooted (as in Butler's case) in a concern with practical realities, a suspicion of metaphysics, and a disdain for the pretensions of crown and mitre. That brand of conservatism we find pre-eminently in Cobbett, in Johnson's *Rasselas*, where we learn that no way of life is free of sorrows, no system of difficulties and contradictions; it is the rugged force in Macaulay's essay on Bacon which sweeps centuries of philosophic inquiry into the rubbish bin to make room for the superior practical achievements of a mute and inglorious shoemaker. Even Ruskin's revolt against his younger aestheticism reveals its influence in the shape of his Puritan suspicions of sensuous beauty and his concern with social reform. John Henry Newman, despite his theological subtleties, reflected the tone of his age in the distrust of merely scholastic argumentation when he formulated the concept of the "illative

37

sense" in an attempt to account for knowledge gained directly from experience. It encompasses attitudes germane to Butler's understanding of faith and common sense. A Fleet Street grasp of realities we find embodied in Sam Weller (the necessary Sancho Panza to Mr. Pickwick's Don Quixote), in Dickens' wholesale distrust of legal institutions and political solutions, and his consuming concern with "fallen" girls and the ragged schools; in George Eliot's nostalgic recreation of rural types and Hardy's world of peasants, whose almost inarticulate communal wisdom derives from the land they cultivate and in Butler's old John Pontifex and Mr. Shaw the tinker.

So Butler's epicureanism is cut from the same cloth as is that of Thomas Love Peacock's self-indulgent Dr. Opinian (in *Gryll Grange*): Butler suggested that the Broad Church (of which he considered himself a member) ought to "sail as near, not philosophical stoicism, but good rollicking Paganism, as it dare . . . I think it would then draw" (note 1217). There was no point in dwelling on issues irrelevant to the enjoyment of the present, or in looking nostalgically back, or worriedly to the future. Discomfort, pain, indeed all untoward effort, was nature's way of telling us that we were going the wrong way. Our beliefs even, Butler argued, really ought follow the low road of least resistance" (IV; Oct. 29, 1890). All radical and sudden change was wrong; besides being uncomfortable, it brought one up against things so novel as to bewilder and render adjustment by one's wits all but impossible. On the other hand, since only perfect stagnation was perfectly moral, a comfortable degree of novelty was absolutely essential for keeping mind and body refreshed. So when Ernest has done what his sense of comfort demands and when his views have become settled and his life freed of the pressures once hindering his self-realization, he still must protect himself from complacency by going at least once a year to church, as a sop "to Nemesis."

What distinguishes Butler's conservatism is the whimsical ambiguity, the double-edged humor in which it is couched. It is true that a great deal of Victorian intellectual culture was not as marked by the Cockney earthiness he loved as was that of the 18th century; the discomforts of self-discipline were widely regarded, after all, as a good moral tonic. Yet, for all that, in fundamental matters he was not out of step with his time. If we compare Butler to Thomas Carlyle, the dogmatic prophet who raised hero-worship on its highest pedestal in England, and for whom seriousness was the fundamental virtue of life, we will find that despite obvious differences, both men began from a similar position.

38

Carlyle's thought represents a revolt against positivist materialism, and metaphysics in general, and for reasons identical to Butler's. When Carlyle lost his faith, he was forced by virtue of his promiscuous and encyclopedic reading to define his convictions in a chaos of contending outlooks. While searching for something to fill the spiritual vacuum he became convinced that the more he inquired the less he understood, that doubt grew as question led to question and dissolved to nebulousness the simplest assumptions and certitudes. In his torment he felt the blessedness of the unintrospective common man's estate. "Metaphysical Speculation," he wrote, "as it begins in No and Nothingness; circulates and must circulate in endless vortices; creating and swallowing itself . . . ;"[56] for he realized that the "attempt of the mind to rise above the mind" inevitably led to the complete skepticism and intellectual pyrrhonism of his fellow Scots David Hume. Scientific positivism at first seemed to be a solution to his dilemma; but it rested in what both he and Butler instinctively recoiled from--a mechanistic interpretation of man and the world. There were the possibilities opened up by German idealism, and though he relied heavily upon them, his pragmatic temperament prevented complete acceptance.

He fell back on the common sense knowledge one could gain from experience. "The healthy Understanding, we should say, is not the Logical, argumentative, but the Inituitive, for the end of Understanding is not to prove and find reasons, but to know and believe." With this axiom Carlyle robbed discursive thought of its regal perogative and deposed it to the role of servant. Doing came first, and to know what to do was, consequently, the "highest and sole blessedness." The impulse to action was the sign of health, while self-conscious cerebration infallibly was the symptom of disease: the artist, Carlyle asserted, whom we most esteem "knows not"--he is great, as Butler would have put it, in the unselfconsciousness of his achievement. Carlyle thus anticipated in the rough Butler's elaboration of unconscious memory.[57] Carlyle, however, despite attempts at humor, lacked the gift of wit, and inevitably fell into the typically Victorian habit of solemn,, if vituperative, tendentiousness, and his pronouncements came to wear a most unpleasant aspect in public; and Butler can not be linked directly to Carlyle's phillistine idealization of the great man, or the hard worker, engineer, and captain of industry. Yet Butler with his Ydgrunism was attempting, like Carlyle in his hero-worship, to find his way back to virtues and perceptions which had guided mankind long before the advent of positivism and the wholesale destruction of metaphysics by David Hume and Immanuel Kant. Positivists of course attacked meta-

39

physics (the second stage, in Comte's view, of man's intellectual evolution); Carlyle and Butler, however, in their attack sought to demonstrate the inevitability of returning to fundamental axioms which, as it turns out, are the very ones underpinning metaphysics and hence traditional philosophy.

That Butler did not appreciate this drift of his thinking was due to his impatience in distinguishing between logical and philosophical procedure. Logic is the tool of philosophy; by its rules alone we cannot arrive at universal principles. Logical consistency is no guarantee of truth, and Butler correctly sensed it led to the absurdities of nominalism and the annihilation of experienced reality. But in reversing analogies he provided no meaningful demonstration of the vanity of philosophy and metaphysics.[58] Butler was able to rescue himself from the fallacies of logicism by returning to the fundamental axiom he (and John Henry Newman) inherited from Bishop Joseph Butler's *Analogy* (1736) --that probability is our only reliable guide to ultimate Truth,[59] the very axiom that defines the intent of *Erewhon* where logicism is explored most fully: "There is no action save on a balance of considerations." By invoking a faculty transcending logic, he hearkened back (unawares) to the metaphysical conclusion that being, not thought (of which logic is an aspect), is the first principle and final reference of philosophic inquiry. For all content of the intellect originates in the senses, except intellect itself, the very process and mode of perception of which intuition is a fundamental aspect. That is the true significance Butler derived from his metaphor of unconscious memories, though he would not have put it this way. Inherited instincts aside, we do indeed construct from the body of intuitions and experiences our knowledge of reality, and consequently reason (in the broadest sense) does indeed transcend its own categories.[60] We cannot, in the end, escape metaphysics after all.

It cannot be surprising then that after elaborating the metaphysical concepts of purpose and design, he should discover the grounds for refurbishing beliefs essentially religious. The thrust of Carlyle's revolt was directed first of all against materialism, and not against his faith. He retained its general principles without recourse to dogmas to which he no longer could give real assent. In Butler's case, the return to such principles was stimulated, as we have seen, by his suspicion of science and scientists. The frequent jokes in the Note-Books, at times rather tawdry, made at the expense of Christ or Christianity are not, consequently, central to Butler's thought, even if they served him as a thera-

40

peutic ventings of his hostility to conventional morality.[61] Butler had indeed inherited the rationalism of the 18th century, but as his French propagandist, the novelist Valery Larbaud insisted (in the Introduction to his translation of the 1912 *Selections*), "sa pensée d'incroyant militant est toute impregnée de doctrine chrétienne."[62] It was one of his *bêtes noirs*, T. H. Huxley[63] who embodied more essentially the militant anti-Christian stance of his day. "On le voit bien lorsque, attaquant le mécanisme et le matérialisme de Charles Darwin et de ses disciples, il affirme et proclame contre eux le finalisme, l'efficacité de la Foi, et tous les elements surrationnels et surnaturels qu'il refuse d'admettre dès qu'il s'agit du Chrétianisme." When his struggles with the Darwinists were behind him, he asked, in the essay "A Medieval Girl School" (1889):

> And, after all, what is the essence of Christianity? . . .
> Surely common sense and cheerfulness, unflinching
> opposition to the charlatanism and Pharisaisms of a
> man's own times. The essence of Christianity lies
> neither in dogma, nor yet in abnormally holy life,
> but in faith in an unseen world, in doing one's duty,
> in speaking the truth, in finding the true life rather
> in others than in oneself, and in the certain hope that
> he who loses his life on these behalfs finds more than
> he has lost. What can Agnosticism do against such
> Christianity as this?[64]

Here he wrote without ironic edge, for he now possessed, in his evolutionary theory, a sufficiently non-theological justification of his position. In the end, then, he "naturalized" the spirit of Christianity much as Matthew Arnold had done before him in *Literature and Dogma* (1873), locating its truths in the psychological and ethical impulses of man's being. Still, with his kind of "natural supernaturalism" Butler as much as Carlyle had to posit one ultimate unseen, but felt, unifying reality behind, and immanent in, the world of appearances--the Unknown and Unknowable Intelligence (or God). That is panpsychism and pantheism--the very opposite of scientific materialism.

VIII

Yet he purchased the positive side of his outlook at great cost. He rejected too much too confidently. For all the freshness of his pragmatism and the general pertinence of his criticism, his sympathies

41

were extraordinarily narrow for a man of his considerable brilliance and range of interests. To this day it remains a difficult task to assess his real achievement with any sense of satisfaction: one remains troubled by the problem created by the deficiencies in thought and character these Note-Books so clearly reveal, deficiencies furthermore that cannot be separated entirely from the best of his published work.

In these notes we meet him face to face, without (usually) the deceptive veils of irony. Though one can insist that their publication in full had never been his expressed wish, it is clear he thought that all he noted down mattered. His modesty is a conventional apology. Why else so much care with them? The truth is he wanted to impose himself as fully upon posterity as possible, in part in the belief that if there was (as he doubted not) any soundness in him, the trivialities shot somehow from him would necessarily be invested with value, and discourage at any rate the sort of Victorian idealization he had a horror of. Even in his books--with the exception of *Erewhon*--he wished to sell himself as much as the ideas or theories: these were, as we have seen, *his* ideas, *his* theories. Whatever he ceded to everyone's common sense, in reality he desired the loyalty of discipleship. Jones tells the story of one day being caught by Butler looking into his Plato. Butler reproved him and emphatically expressed the hope that in the future he would know better than to read such nonsense again. Jones obeyed: Butler's opinion of Plato became Jones's, and after Butler's death he behaved unmistakably as the devoted disciple supervising Butler's posthumous literary career, interpreting and advertising his works, preserving reverently every detail of his life as if it had indeed belonged to a great prophet who had been stoned out of his own land.

His first admirers, in any case, perceived him as such: to a younger generation he appeared as the powerful, prophetic voice all the more unimpeachable because it had been so completely ignored. To the generation that suffered through the Great War he seemed to have lived, and given words to, their own anti-Victorian rebellion, and thus he, as much as what he had written, came to be transformed into a symbol of it. But admiration of this sort suggests that Butler is an author whom one either likes or rejects for reasons often irrelevant to the real measure of his achievements. Somewhat like D. H. Lawrence, he represents a point of view, and he does not, like his beloved Shakespeare, disappear behind a considerable body of writing with an independent life of its own. Butler's work inevitably leads to Butler the person; and hence the pattern emerging from Butler criticism is a continual alternation between warm (and forgiving) admiration and curt or qualified dismissal. To admirers, he is a remarkable, even towering, iconoclast; to detractors, to those who cannot take him whole, he is a weak, resentful, if clever, minor oddity. The appearance of the 1912 Note-Books *Selections*, and Jones's unselective biography (1919) made plain that Butler rather than a radical had been most stolidly bourgeois, and the revelation furnished material for the detractor's case which culminated in Malcolm Muggeridge's unsparing dissection of Butler's personality *The Earnest Atheist* (1936). The fury of the attack was as much directed at Butler as at the cultish devotion of earlier admirers--many of them, like Desmond MacCarthy, of note--who had helped elevate him to a modern classic. After this critique enthusiastic readers had to adjust their claims, but the alternation between admiration and dismissal has continued, the one party always resenting the conclusions of the other.

Consequently, to evaluate these very personal jottings quite frankly can seem an ungenerous response to someone whom many have accepted as a helpful friend. Yet two reservations should be aired, since it is on his ideas that his reputation must ultimately rest.

First of all, Butler shows us in the Note-Books that he too possessed the Victorian love for grand theorizing. During his involvement in the Darwinian controversy (1876-1888) we observe him again and again plumbing for the larger implications of his Lamarckian theory as if with it he had discovered the great key to the universe. He was intent, consequently, to bring his observations within the boundaries of its terms. But the efforts in this direction led him to conclusions devoid of all vitality. Entries under "God," "Life," and "Death" abound; perhaps he could not lay the ghost of concerns germane to his rejected profession. But they are abstract and puzzling. For example, we are told that there is either no death, or else there is no such thing as personal identity, since life is nothing but a gradual, gentle gradation toward the final change (II; Aug. 1884); or that the living never die really, but differentiate into the life of the world; and since all life is vibration or energy, it resolves itself into the feeling of vibrations" (II; Feb., April 1884).[65] These remarks lack the specificity of his best *bon mots* where the evolutionary terms play a less literal role and enrich rather than deprive: "Life is the income derived from the capital investment of our forefathers" (IV: Feb. 3, 1891). It is when he runs his theory that he is apt to be cryptic to one unfamiliar with it, and absurd to one who rejects it.

So too his love for logical contradictions leads at times to pointless statements. When we read that action and study are both *equally* "essential" and *equally* "fatal" to one another, he is hardly helpful and not particularly amusing (VI; Jan. 30, 1891). Elsewhere we are reminded that all thinking rests on analogies, and that all analogies are false (IV; Feb. 12, 1891): with one sweeping statement he has cut the ground from under the best of his helpful criticism. Again, action is thought "rendered into matter" (and *vice versa*), but he hastens to add that he knows not what thought is (II ; March, 1884). We are confronting here the maddening evasiveness of Humpty Dumpty and the Cheshire Cat. In every instance he is making the same point: in a monistic universe it is difficult to know where to take one's stand and that rough and ready judgments are therefore inevitable. In these abstractions, however, the point has become a tiresome trick.

Secondly, in these philosophic statements he is guilty of more than a degree of intellectual presumption, of an unwillingness to follow through on some of his sweeping claims. That, of course, as we said earlier, was the attractive feature for his admirers. Why should one expect systematic thoroughness from an avowed enemy of it? Butler was, after all, deliberately elusive. Elusive he was, but also incomplete. When he emphasized the reality of intelligence, defining intuitive thought as a fundamental component of being, Butler clearly moved in the direction of neo-Platonism (roughly so considered), by indicating at least a suspicion of the reality of transcendence (the unseen kingdom) beyond the graspable material world of "appearances." Nothing exists *qua* us, he said, "but what is thinkable" (IV; Oct. 17, 1890); and ideas, he pointed out, seem to have a life beyond the thinking individual: one's true life in fact was in one's effect upon others. Shakespeare and Handel were more alive in his day than when they actually lived, for their works were now affecting the minds and sinews of countless individuals.

Yet, neo-Platonism was a foreign land to him, nor would he have attempted to complete the journey. Despite his sense of an unseen kingdom, he drew back from its implications beyond the evolution metaphor. A "thing is a thing because we think it so"--the position of Berkeley and the German idealists who influenced Carlyle–but, he goes on, "we think it so because it is the thing that it is" (III; Jan. 1890), an obscure conclusion indeed. He did not try to decide the issue whether ideas and perceptions reflect an order of the real, or whether they are mere invention. His contempt for philosophic inquiry

44

was too strong, and no doubt he would have told us that resolving the question was irrelevant to the practical business of getting on.

His belief in the unity of mind and matter allowed him always to return to a safe positivist position where he felt free of troublesome metaphysics. That position, radically excluding all but the repeatedly verifiable, was more consonant with his temperament and expressed adequately his rejection of the supernatural foundations of the Christian faith. In his speculations he explored the positivist aspect of his theory, almost as if intent on avoiding the *odium theologicum* attaching to the more philosophical and theological critics of Darwin in, for example, his attempt to reduce thought to organic vibrations. In this sterile endeavor he came close to saying that what he believed was the primary cause of evolution was really the by-product of eternal matter; and in his critiques of the Darwinist position, though raising most astute objections, he did not fully confront its challenge even if he thought he had. In later life he once wrote that if a man sinned against the Holy Ghost and "made light of that spirit which the common conscience of all men, whatever their particular creed, recognizes as divine, there is no hope for him. No more there is" (VI; Apr. 4, 1900). In the same volume, the last, he also copied quotations from the materialist and atheistic philosopher Helvetius (and excerpts from Diderot's works) originally collected when a rebellious younger man in the early 1870's. These were, so it seems, useful for other moods, other battles; but he undoubtedly felt safer, more in his element as satirist with Helevetius' anti-metaphysical assertions than with the anti-Positivist humanism toward which his Lamarckism pointed.

This shrinking back is derived perhaps from that tendency to dismiss or else to trivialize so much, the art of the High Renaissance or Bach's music, for example. This tendency shows us the reverse side of his Fleet Street realism—he was too literal-minded to enter into the expansive and highly charged world of a Bach or Michelangelo, to see Wagner's genius despite his theatricalism, or in general to appreciate a symbolic expression and comprehension of life.[66] His views reveal a degree of *ennui*, of negation, the vice unfortunately of the professional satirist and critic. The danger of the satiric impulse is to become too corrosive, to see "through" too much and one thereby falls in the trap of believing empty pomp and pretension everywhere except of course in oneself. His attractive man-in-the-street norm often did harden into a dogma with all the characteristics of priggishness. It was his own brand of snobbery, paraded as a rebuff to the vanities of the

45

charmed upper circle of Victorian VIPs.

After these weaknesses are taken into account, we must remind ourselves that his outlook grew out of a specific context, and in that context it played, and still plays, its most relevant role. He looked for an unassailable position between two intellectual traditions because he desired, in an age of dogmatisms, to remain in a position of flexibility, in an attitude for all occasions, free of the intellectual and moral obligations demanded by fully defined systems. He worked out a common sense standard that would risk neither philosophical thoroughness nor intellectual anarchy. It had to remain at all costs the undefinable middle ground where he could be safe between warring factions, where doubt in all ultimate matters was highest wisdom. It was the necessary antidote in an age dominated by humorless Mr. Casaubons--by encyclopedic systematizers like Herbert Spencer, prophets like Ruskin and Carlyle, crusaders like T. H. Huxley and Dickens--who often did sound as if they had found the Newtonian laws underlying every department of human knowledge. Rather than meditate on Truth, he was content to cut the Gordian Knot of philosophic, moral, and theological subtleties by relying on an appeal to the universal sense of pleasure and profit. He chose the freedom of the jester, at once radical and conservative, one or the other as the occasion might dictate, conveniently disengaged, as a thorough-going skeptic must be, from all parties in order to be a gadfly to all in the name of good sense and kindliness. He wished to discomfit and unsettle the leading lights of his time, and hoped to set a better example himself: "I have chosen the fighting road rather than the hang-on-to-the-great-man road . . ." (IV; Apr. 24, 1893).

To account for his likes and dislikes as systematically as we have done, subject, verb, and accusative all in the right place, is not to overlook the reason for the appeal he continues to have to the common reader. One does not turn to his works, certainly not to the Note-Books, for great ideas but for the Butlerian spirit contained there. In fact, the best of Butler is what is freest of the immediate influence of his "finds." That is why, at the outset, we claimed he was really a philosophic wit. The casual variations on pet themes, bits of whimsey, anecdotes, and the epigrams where we find suddenly crystallized a striking and novel observation in refreshingly unpretentious, straightforward English are the most enduring elements of his work and least depend on our siding with him as disciple or devoté. We find there those little truths we tend to forget, the important unimportant things which cannot be trapped in an intellectual net: "Justice is my being allowed to do what I like. Injustice whatever prevents my doing so" (note 68); and a "man will feel money losses more keenly than loss even of bodily health so long as he can keep his money" (note 422). This is not the whole truth, yet he expresses here a very real state of affairs which our candor will not let us deny. Out of such materials the Note-Books are constructed and even in the pedantic, argumentative solemnity of his later book-length studies we find them embedded, pleasing us by a charm quite independent of the arguments into whose service they have been pressed. In such jottings we find the spirit he wished to set up against earnestness: let no unwary reader, he wrote early on in his career, "do me the injustice of believing in *me* . . . If he must believe in anything, let him believe in the music of Handel, the painting of Giovanni Bellini, and the 13th chapter of St. Paul's First Epistle to the Corinthians"--[67] in other words, in robust enjoyment, in the beauty and profundity of the commonplace, and, above all else, in charity, kindliness, *agape*.

His literary critics have rarely heeded the warning, but have been inclined to burden him with significance far too weighty for his modest contributions to bear, and to borrow his virtues from the achievements of men greater than himself. His essence is in his sense of humour which in any case inevitably plays with contradictions; and his laughter is that of the insignificant mocking the pretensions of the self-important, the growlings of the belly at the excesses of the striving spirit that is so useful in restoring balance and proportion. Butler's fancy that instincts are more trustworthy than acquired knowledge or tradition, that the majority of kindly, graceful folk are sounder about what matters than the influential and eminent is one of those comforting illusions erected on a half-truth which is reflected in much of the literature of the 19th century. To believe in it is the consequence of choosing sides too fiercely and of forgetting that men in all stations are limited creatures stumbling about an incomplete world. In his polemical battles, and even in *The Way of All Flesh*, Butler forgot this Christian principle; but he reminded himself and his imagined readers of its truth during his more unbuttoned moods and in his occasional remarks and witticisms. His best notes, consequently, ought be savored in this manner, not as the fruits of an original and sound system, but as makeshift guidelines, saving clauses, whimsical evasions, the occasionally necessary grain of salt we should resort to in the business of making up our minds if we are to retain healthy confidence in tending our garden by our own lights and to keep the proper distance from the deadening hand of abstract systems.

As for other notes--references, quotations, and memoranda--they reflect his passing interests and, as he says himself, record the quirks of his mind, and provide us with valuable details with which to reconstruct the period flavor of the Victorian era.

HP

NOTES

1 We are told he began to question the efficacy of infant baptism when he could not, while teaching a class of boys, distinguish the behavior of the baptised from that of the unbaptised (see Henry Festing Jones, *Samuel Butler, Author of Erewhon* (1835-1902): *A Memoir* (London, 1920), I, 60-61.

2 In 1865, after his return to London, he published (privately and anonymously) the results of his Biblical studies in a pamphlet entitled *The Evidence for the Resurrection of Jesus Christ as contained in the Four Evangelists critically examined.* It became the intellectual substance of *The Fair Haven* (see below).

3 The substance of "The World of the Unborn" and "Birth Formulae" in *Erewhon* are Butler's literary applications of the morality of "chance." The first was written shortly after his return from New Zealand in 1865 (see his autobiographical notes [1883], in Volume III).

4 He lost the greater part of his New Zealand earnings (some £4,000 after subtracting the investment borrowed from his father), by speculating, on the urgings of a fellow Johnian, Henry Hoare (see footnote to note 215), in various "rotten" companies, chiefly in The Canada Tanning Extract Company, based in Montreal. The Company went bankrupt in 1876, though Butler, as representative of its London directorship, travelled three times to Canada to try to salvage it. Since he had only reversionary interest to a goodly portion of Shrewsbury land by the will of his grandfather Dr. Samuel Butler, he thereafter remained dependent upon his father's money. After several appeals, Canon Butler did cut off the entail in 1883, ending his most pressing financial worries. During the late 1870's his finances were further strained by his insistence on returning money he had persuaded his friend, Charles Paine Pauli, to invest in these companies, and by continuing to provide him with a yearly allowance to help him out of his pretended financial straits. For full details, see Butler's account of their friendship in Volume III, and footnote to note 51.

5 Autobiographical notes [1883] included in Volume III.

6 Sometime after the appearance of *Erewhon* in 1872, when he enjoyed a brief period of lionization, Butler joined the Century Club (see footnote to note 442), and thus entered an intellectual world made up of positivists, political liberals and radicals. He rubbed shoulders with Leslie and Fitzjames Stephen, John Tyndall, W. L. Bright, Frederick Harrison, Lewis Morris, Walter Bagehot, and Edward Clodd. Clodd, banker and science advocate, because he admired *Erewhon* and *The Fair Haven*, invited Butler to his Sunday evening at-homes where he met Grant Allen, the astronomer Richard Proctor, and the radicals J. A. Picton and Mark Wilks. Even before 1872, shortly after his return from New Zealand, he flirted, it seems, with the Whig circle gathered at Crabb Robinson's Sunday breakfasts; and at Heatherley's art school in Newman Street (the "artists' quarter" of London in the 1860's and '70's) he probably met painters with Pre-Raphaelite sympathies (Rossetti, Millais, and Burne-Jones once attended the school). He was acquainted with the Chartist and freethinker George Holyoake, editor of the short-lived *The Reasoner*, which published Butler's "Mechanical Creation" (1865). But after 1879 or 1880 (significantly after his anti-Darwinist polemics *Evolution Old and New* and *Unconscious Memory* had been published), he left the Century becaue it was about to merge with the National Liberal Club; his estrangement from the art world had begun earlier. Clodd mentions that after the "deplorable attack" on Darwin in *Unconscious Memory*, Butler believed Darwinists to be in conspiracy against him,

and this made social intercourse with him difficult (Edward Clodd, *Memories* [London, 1916], p. 256.) In 1893 Butler wrote: "For my own part I confess my sympathies are rather with the mighty. I am afraid of liberalism—or at any rate of the people who call themselves liberals. They flirt with radicals, who flirt with socialists, who do something a good deal more than flirt with dynamite" (Correspondence, Vol. VIII, p. 265: letter of December 29 to Alexander Lean of Christchurch, New Zealand).

7 See General Note on the Text. He had started keeping notes more systematically from 1890 on: the first entry in Volume IV, the first unedited volume, is dated March 31, 1890.

8 Henry Festing Jones gathered much of his material for his biography from the Note-Books; he held back from the 1912 *Selections* all notes he planned to use in the *Memoir*.

9 See H. F. Jones's Preface to *Selections* (1912). Butler's correspondence with Miss Savage, his sister May, and, with his family have been published: *Letters between Samuel Butler and Miss E. M. A. Savage (1871-1885)*, ed. Geoffrey Keynes and Brian Hill (London, 1935); *The Correspondence of Samuel Butler with his Sister May*, ed. Daniel F. Howard (Berkeley, 1962), *The Family Letters of Samuel Butler, 1841-1886*, ed. Arnold Silver (Palo Alto, 1962).

10 Note-Books, II, Dec., 1886. Henceforth referred to by the volume number only.

11 IV; May 21, 1891. Nothing, he wrote (referring to his grandfather's literary estate), is so precious as unpremeditated opinion for inspiring further "fresh genuine opinion" (IV; April 11, 1891).

12 "How to Make the Best of Life," *The Shrewsbury Edition of the Works of Samuel Butler*, ed. H. F. Jones and A. T. Bartholomew (London: Jonathan Cape, 1923-26), XVI, 101. Henceforth referred to as *Works*. Butler would be familiar with examples of such humor as found, for instance, in *The Young Duke*.

13 See VI; Jan. 29, 1901.

14 Edward Clodd, *Memories*, p. 256.

15 For a full account of Darwin's various difficulties with his theory, see Peter Vorzimmer, *Charles Darwin, the Years of Controversy: 1859-1874* (London, 1972).

16 *Evolution Old and New* (1879; second edition, 1880), a summary of Darwin's forerunners, notably Lamarck, Buffon, and Erasmus Darwin; *Unconscious Memory* (1880), an account of the development of his own ideas, and reiteration of the *Life and Habit* theory (see below); *Luck or Cunning?* (1887), the bitterest attack on Darwin's logic and reputation. In Volume III, Butler quotes a letter in *Nature* (November 28, 1889) which reflects exactly his position: "Selection cannot be the cause of those conditions which are prior to selection (that is, changed conditions which generate variations); in other words, a selection cannot explain the origin of anything although it can and does explain survival of something already originated, and evolution consists in the origin of characters as well as of their survival."

17 In his copy of the *Origin* (6th edition) Butler wrote: "Mr. Darwin looks to plants and animals under domesticat[ion.] I look to the human mind." For a fuller account of Butler's ideas about machines and their relevance to a theory of evolution, see the editor's article, "Samuel Butler's 'The Book of the Machines' and the Argument from Design," *Modern Philology*, May, 1975, pp. 365-383.

18 The German zoologist August Weismann (1834-1914) introduced the distinction in his germ cell theory (*Keimplasmatheorie*): see note 1310 of this volume. Butler understandably rejected this theory that somatic reactions could not influence the germ plasm. In reviews of his evolutionary works, Butler was occasionally linked to von Hartmann since he had anticipated Butler's concept of unconscious memory.

19 See, for example, Walter Heitler, *Über die Komplementarität von lebloser und lebender Materie* (Zürich, 1976): here life is defined by teleological processes in which the laws of differential-causal determinism are slightly altered and even suspended.

20 An insignificant quarrel, regarded by Butler with unwonted seriousness, darkened his view of Darwin. On January 1880, in a letter to the *Athenaeum*, Butler challenged Darwin to explain how a veiled and prejorative reference to his *Evolution Old and New* came to be included in a translation of a German article on Erasmus Darwin when it had not been in the original published in the German journal *Kosmos*. For Darwin had vouched for the accuracy of the translation in a preface to it. On the advice of T. H. Huxley, Darwin did not reply even though he had drafted two letters (see Henry Festing Jones, *Charles Darwin and Samuel Butler: A Step towards Reconciliation* [London, 1911]). There was no malice on Darwin's part; the author, Prof. Ernst Krause, had taken the opportunity to revise the original, a common practice to which Darwin thought he need not call attention. See note 363 in this volume.

21 P. 426: "From beginning to end, our eccentric author treats us to a dazzling flood of epigram, invective, and what appears to be argument; and finally leaves us without a single clear idea of what it has all been driving at." Butler believed Allen had also written the unfavorable review in the *Examiner* that appeared on the same day. A. R. Wallace was much fairer (though negative) in his appraisal in *Nature* for June 12.

22 Clodd, p. 260.

23 See Darwin's *The Descent of Man* (1st edition), vol. I, pp. 152-3.

24 Clodd, p. 257.

25 In his copy of *Evolution Old and New*, Butler wrote: "And if any professional scientists reads this volume let him remember also that the consciousness of knowing much need not beget a confidence in his infallibility."

26 *Memoir*, I, pp. 50-51; see note 735. In a letter to W. E. Heitland (June 20, 1889) Butler confessed that at Shrewsbury he was a timid and physically puny boy, and that is why the "March temperament" of the Headmaster Dr. Benjamin Kennedy (the model for Dr. Skinner in *The Way of All Flesh*) was so distressing to him: When in an impulsive moment he came out of his shell, Dr. Kennedy always "touched my horns " (*Eagle, XXIV* [Easter term, 1913], p. 349).

27 Shaw approved Butler's debunking intentions in the anti-Darwinian *Luck or Cunning*; his review of it opens thus: "We are such an inveterately idolatrous people that it would perhaps be well for us if we could go back frankly to the cultus of the graven image, and leave our great men unworshipped" (*Pall Mall Gazette*, May 31, 1887, p. 5).

28 *Memoir*, II, pp. 98-99.

29 Butler walked off most paths in Kent, Surrey, and Sussex on weekend outings--in company either of his cousin Reginald Worlsey, Jones, or in the 1890's for a time with a Swiss acquaintance, Hans Faesch. He marked the paths he had walked on his ordnance maps, now in the library of St. John's College.

30 Philip Henderson, *Samuel Butler, the Incarnate Bachelor* (London, 1953), p. 177.

31 Bound with Volume VI (along with a collection of the improprieties mentioned below); numerous references to her and her talk are found also in the first three volumes. Her sayings have been published in *Butleriana*, ed. A. T. Bartholomew (London, 1932) under "Bossiana."

32 *Works*, IV, 1.

33 *Works*, IV, 61; 18.

34 Clodd, p. 257, in the letter referred to in footnote 6.

35 *Works*, IV, 249.

36   In the *Fair Haven* the narrator, who as we know from the introduction by his brother, is on the verge of going mad, concludes, after fully conceding the case of the historical critics of the Gospel (Friedrich Strauss's, for example), that Christ is really an Ideal, corresponding to our highest conceptions of spiritual good, and in its vagueness allows everyone to interpret it in his own terms. Butler meant this to be recognized as a typical sentimental face-saving of Victorian apologists—though not so far removed from his own compromise expressed in *Erewhon Revisited*; or indeed from the echoes of Feuerbach heard in Higg's debunking of Erewhonian deities (*Erewhon*).

37   Clodd, p. 263. It is of interest to note that *Life* and *Habit* was advertised as a work of "satire" and "imagination."

38   Raphael was not a "man" at all, Butler maintained, but a "worldling" interested in success; his reputation rested more on fashion than on the supposed purity of his sentiments (II; April, 1885).

39   He spent considerable time studying and gathering facts about the religious sculptures in the Ticino Canton and northern Italy, primarily to popularize the works of Gaudenzio Ferrari (1480-1547) and identify the forgotten Flemish sculptor who worked in northern Italy, Jean de Wespin (known also as Giovanni Tabachetti [1568-1615]). The results of his researches appeared in *Ex Voto* (1888).

40   Quentin Bell, *Ruskin* (New York, 1978), p. 50.

41   Butler's theory of evolution even is indebted to Bishop Joseph Butler's *Analogy of Religion* (1736) and William Paley's *Natural Theology* (1802); his ideas (on morality especially) link him to the empirical moralists of the 18th century, and his work carried him back to European philosophers and naturalists of that century, men like Helvetius, Diderot, Lamarck, and Buffon.

42   See note 1230. The eternity of matter, he wrote in his notes for a second volume on the *Life and Habit* theory (see General Note on the Text), is more than any other idea about it in harmony with our experience (folio 66 of the bound notes): this is the classic assumption of 19th century materialism which is no longer tenable today. Though the ideas discussed thus far were virtually fixed in his mind by 1878, he was influenced in his pantheistic monism by W. Stewart Duncan's *Conscious Matter* (London, 1881), which briefly mentions *Life and Habit* with approval; he copied out large excerpts, now bound with his miscellaneous notes. Duncan saw matter ultimately as coalesced force--bodies called atoms being inconceivable to him; thus mind was for him the effect of matter, that is of force: the active behavior of matter created the effective phenomena called subjective consciousness. This meant that there was only one substance though differentiated "locally, and physically conditioned by its property of force" (p. 93).

43   It is not unimportant to mention here that Butler took what should be called a "philological" approach to the real: he mentioned several times that man's *unconscious* expressions are his truest. The word "organ" indicates that our limbs are like tools which we manipulate and play; the phrase, "the mind's eye," reveals our awareness of the interchangeability of matter and mind; "peccant matter" (a medical expression) indicates our sense that, literally, something is "wrong." Chemicals, we say, "behave," and thus admit an element of choice to them; and machines "fulfill duties" and hence have built into them a purposive mechanism. In short, with such examples Butler indicated that even in our language we cannot eliminate the assumption of a directing intelligence.

44   In Volume II (March 1885) we read that it is common sense, not the Voice of the Lord, that makes men of one mind in a house. Here, however, Butler, in characteristic fashion, is disagreeing with a Biblical percept; a few pages further on clearly identifies common sense with the Voice of the Lord: this latter use of the concept is consistent with later references to common sense and the inner guiding principle.

45 In *Ex Voto* (1888) he wrote: "Let us have no more 'Lo here's' and 'Lo there's' in [respect to the beliefs of the future]. I would as soon have a winking Madonna or a forged decretal, as the doubtful experiments or garbled articles which the high priests of modern science are applauded with one voice for trying to palm off upon their devotees"(*Works*, IX, 24).

46 *Spectator* for February 15, 1902, p. 253.

47 Quoted in Etienne Gilson, *The Unity of Philosophic Experience* (New York: Scribner and Sons, 1938), p. 105.

48 Notebook for *Life and Habit*, Vol. II, folio 95.

49 See Valery Larband, *Samuel Butler: conférence faite le 3 novembre, 1920. à la Maison des Amis des Livres* (Paris: A.Monnier, 1920).

50 The emphasis on money is Butler's most bourgeois trait. In the context of his pragmatic morality, it links him to the prevailing Victorian attitude that poverty was in some real sense an avoidable failing: since the good swell (see note 114) is in his view nature's standard, it follows, though Butler never says so explicitly, that the poverty-stricken somehow do bear the stamp of nature's disapproval, and are to be avoided. Butler inverts thereby a dogma fundamental to Christianity.

51 Even atoms manifest freedom and necessity, and hence, a modicum of intelligence: free will "which comes from the unseen Kingdom within which the writs of our thoughts run not, must be carried to the most tenuous atoms . . . ." Yet necessity is just as present as free will: one can take either view and remain logically consistent, especially so since free will is quite real because it is one of the most consistent of our illusions. Life, consequently, is 8 parts cards, 2 parts play, and "the unseen world is made manifest to us in the play" (III; Nov. 1889).

52 *Works*, IV, 31.

53 On the backleaf of his copy of Darwin's *Variations of Animals and Plants*, vol. I (2nd edition, 1875), Butler wrote: "If I were asked what animal I would be if I were not a man, I would first find out what creature has varied least during the greatest number of ages and I should conclude that this was the one which on the whole found life easiest."

54 He called them his "finds." See IV, April 24, 1893; V; Nov. 26, 1894.

55 Butler's notes on the association of ideas and identity indicate that he had absorbed elements of Locke's *An Essay Concerning Human Understanding* (1690); in general, his remarks about the acquisition of ideas, and the force of habit and convention in knowing links him to Lockean pragmatism.

56 See Carlyle's "Characteristics."

57 *Sartor Resartus*, Book II, Chapter 9: Carlyle argues for a defeat of Byronic self-contemplation, for a defeat of "Self" as the means for recovering the Ideal *in* oneself and *in* practical work in the Actual, rather than in endless "Schwärmerei."

58 Julien Green, reviewing Valery Larbaud's translation of *Erewhon Revisited*, *Philosophies*, September, 1924; rpt. in Julien Green, *Oeuvres Completes* [Paris: Gallimard, 1972], Vol. I, 1017-18), points out that Butler's topsy-turvydom does not yield a new philosophy, nor can one call such play thinking: "Retourner les termes d'un principe est un exercise qui peut quelquefois donner le plaisir de la surprise mais qui ne coûte pas beaucoup à son auteur. Rien ne peut être vil comme un paradoxe; on s'en amuse un peu de temps, puis on revient à l'idée dont il est négation car *c'est d'elle qu'on a besoin et non de lui*" (italics mine).

59 *Analogy*, Introduction.

60 My analysis of Butler here is indebted to Chapter XII of Etienne Gilson's superb study, *The Unity of Philosophical Experience*, cited in n. 47.

61 For example, in a commentary on "By their fruits shall ye know them" he says that this depends on whether you are a judge of fruit, and how good a

one (note 193). Why, he asks, should the humble be exalted, for "they do not remain humble and meek long" once they are (IV, Oct. 17, 1980). Though clever, the witticisms reveals his limitations rather than that of the subject attacked.

62 *Le Carnets de Samuel Butler* (Paris: Gallimard, 1936), pp. 15-16.

63 Butler read Huxley's *Lay Sermons*, lent him by Clodd, to see if Huxley was the full-fledged materialist he suspected him to be. The book confirmed his judgment (Clodd, p. 260-1).

64 *Works*, XIX, 199.

65 The concept of vibrations Butler based on the German naturalist Karl Ewald Hering, and Herbert Spencer's *Principles of Psychology* (1880).

66 He was, he told Robert Bridges, unable to enter into the figurative side of art (*Memoir*, II, 321-322: letter of February 6, 1900).

67 From *Life and Habit* where he first justified his philosophic position (*Works*, IV, 35).

THE NOTE-BOOKS

Volume I

1874 - October, 1883

Revised

March, 1891 - February, 1897

These are the sayings of me Samuel Butler and of my friends--the prophecyings which my mother did not teach me at all, nor my father, nor any of my uncles and aunts, but altogether otherwise.

PREFACE

Copied from a note dated September, 1884 (April 4, 1891).

The following collection of notes was started at Montreal in the autumn of 1874.[1] I got a copying book then and began pressing my notes into it. These are now for the most part either used or destroyed.

I found the notes no use to me for want of an index. I had continually to look through my collection to see whether I had got such and such a note already, or to find one that I wanted, and as I did not write much at Montreal, I let the thing drop.

When I came back at the end of 1875, I had this book with some 30 or 40 pp. in it, and used it to press copies of the notes I had taken for *Life and Habit*,[2] which, however, I did not greatly use. I left considerable space between the last of my ordinary notes and the first page of the notes for *Life and Habit*, thinking that these would do for all the notes I was likely to take, and intending to press more *Life and Habit* MS. as the work went on. This, however, I did not do.

By and by I found I wanted a system of notes and the means of finding them, so I started an approximate index. On this I resumed the Montreal book, filled the blank leaves up to the *Life and Habit* notes and then went on to post them. This is how the handwriting of the notes comes to be so different on either side of the *Life and Habit* notes.

Since then I have weeded out and used many of the older notes and am now (September, 1884) about to weed them out again, so that very likely none will remain in the same small closely written handwriting as the *Life and Habit* notes-- but I leave these last untouched because I have referred to them in one of the opening chapters of *Unconscious Memory*.[3]

Now (April 4, 1891) having already begun to go through the collection again, I should like to say that as it grew larger I found the approximate index no use, and kept each letter in one or more envelopes that contained the slips, till a volume was full. I placed these slips in due order whenever I indexed, and the envelopes prevented their getting out of order so that the index was true while the volume was still growing.[4]

I greatly question the use of making the notes at all. I find I next to never refer to them or use them. Nevertheless I suppose they help to clear one's mind, and I have got into a groove of making them. I am aware that there are many of which I ought to be ashamed on a great variety of grounds, but as they came, so as a general rule I leave them--good bad and indifferent.

57

PREFACE NOTES

1   During his second journey to Montreal (August 5, 1874 to March 1875). He first went there in June, 1874, as representative of the London Board of Directors of The Canada Tanning Extract Company, returning about July 17, 1874; in September, 1875, he was forced to go again and remained until December. For an account of his attempts to salvage his investments in the Company, see A.W. Currie "Samuel Butler's Canadian Investments" *University of Toronto Quarterly*, 32 (Jan. 1963), 109-125.

2   He hit upon the cental idea of *Life and Habit* shortly after his arrival in Montreal in June 1874 (*Works*, VI, 18-22), and wrote these notes during his stay.

3   *Works* VI, 20-22. The "commonplace book" in which Butler kept these notes is no longer extant. Pressed copies of the first notes for *Life and Habit* referred to in *Unconscious Memory* (p. 21), some nineteen virtually illegible pages, were bound up with Volume VI of the Note-Books.

4   Butler's index has not been reproduced.

MAKING A BEAST OF ONESELF   1

Paton[1] said that total abstainers at any rate did not make beasts of themselves. I said that a man makes more of a beast of himself by not exceeding than by exceeding.

GOD   2

as per our bills of lading is a most pernicious kind of robber pirate or vermin.

HUXLEY'S FRENCH SOLDIER   3

See *Fortnightly Review*, Nov., 1874.[1] This man becomes a thief when in his abnormal states. I do not see why it should be less disgraceful to a man to have become a thief through having been wounded on the head after birth than from having been born with a bad head or having been unfortunately placed in childhood. I suppose because it is less common.

CHRISTIANITY   4

has been to the world on a larger and more disastrous scale, what Puritanism has been to the English nation. And yet it may be questioned whether Puritanism did not save the English nation at a very critical time.

SPOILED TARTS   5

Mrs. Brown at Shrewsbury[1] used to keep a tray of spoiled tarts, which she sold cheaper. They most of them looked pretty right till you handled them. We are all spoiled tarts.

NATURAL RELIGION   6

Whatever religion is not natural is unnatural. And yet whatever is, is natural.

MORAL CONSCIOUSNESS   7

A flea and an ugly servant girl both show that they have a moral consciousness by running away, if come upon unexpectedly: but the flea will jump all ways at random, while the servant girl will go as straight away as she can. So the servant has most moral consciousness.

OLD MEN'S DREAMS OF BOYHOOD   8

I once heard two elderly men comparing notes about the way in which they still sometimes dreamed they were being bullied by their schoolmasters, and that their fathers had come to life again.

These think they have a right to larger inheritance than the younger children as having had the energy to pester their fathers and mothers sooner than those who came after.[1]

ADAM AND EVE 10

Adam and Eve were naked in the garden of Eden and were not ashamed[1]-- but they were young and comely. I have seen German ladies at a *table d'hôte* capless, hairless, toothless, and not ashamed.

RELATIONS 11

I could stand my relations well enough, if they would only let me alone. It is my relations with my relations that I sometimes find embarrassing.

A LAWYER 12

is an artist whose art is conversant about clearness of expression.

Written about 1874   Copied March 23, 1891

SUBJECT--THE FLYING BALANCE 13

The flying balance. The ghost of an old cashier haunts a ledger, so that the books refuse always to balance by the sum of say £1.15.11--or find a more appropriate sum--no matter how many accountants are called in, year after year the same error always turns up. Sometimes they think they have got it right, and it turns out there was a mistake, so the old error reappears. At last a son and heir gets born and at some festivities the old cashier's name is mentioned with honour. This lays his ghost--next morning the books are found correct and remain so.

MYSELF AT DOCTOR'S COMMONS 14

A woman once stopped me at the entrance to Doctor's Commons and said, "If you please, sir, can you tell me is this the place that I came to before?" Not knowing where she had been before I could not tell her.

"Cant, as a means of prolonging life."

MORALITY AND CONTRADICTION IN TERMS 16

Every discovery is immoral, for it upsets existing *"mores."* Stagnation would be perfectly moral but that, if perfect, it destroys all *"mores"* whatever. So there must always be an immorality in morality, and in like manner, a morality in immorality. For there will be an element of habitual and legitimate custom even in the most unhabitual and detestable things that can be done at all.

IN ART 17

whatever has been once transcendent remains so, however such it be transcended later. All that is not transcendent dies and disappears--*exceptis excipiendis.*

CANADIAN JOKES 18

When I was there[1] I found their jokes like their roads--very long and not very good, leading to a little tin point of a spire which has been remorselessly obvious for miles without seeming to get any nearer.

WILLIAM THOMPSON[1] 19

The Maori chief (about 1863), on being told that General Cameron[2] was coming against him with big guns, said, "My big guns are night and storm."

THE MAORIS 20

About 1845 they burnt a town in the North Island called Russell. Cass[1] told me that during a truce a Maori said to him that he would shoot no more soldiers. Cass said he was glad to hear it, but asked why. The Maori said that it did not pay; the powder cost him thirteen shillings a pound, and if he did shoot a soldier the Queen could get another for a shilling. "Now," he continued, "it takes three years and a great deal of money to make a surveyor like you, and considering the price of powder, you are the kind of people whom I intend to shoot in future."

HEWLINGS[1] 21

the surveyor, of Canterbury, N.Z., was an old North Islander before he came down to Canterbury. He was asked how it was he came to speak Maori so well. He answered that he had taken his dictionary to bed with him for many years. He had some pretty half-caste daughters.

MISS RYDER   22

At Miss Savage's club[1] she said she should never marry--it was so degrading--and she tossed her little button of a nose. "But what will you do," said Miss Savage, "when some one falls in love with you?" ("I took care," she said to me, "not to say 'if' some one &c.") "He will never presume to tell me that he has fallen in love with me," replied Miss Ryder.

"But suppose you have fallen in love with him?"

"How dare you say such a thing as that to me?"

Enter old Miss Andrews, and others who are appealed to. Miss A flies into passion on hearing love abused and says she only wishes some one had fallen in love with her. The others chime in, and Miss Ryder finding she was getting the worst of it called them a parcel of old maids. Whereon the *mêlée* became general.

MORAL INFLUENCE   23

Every team of bullocks has a leader who exercises some tacit power of suasion. I am told a white bullock generally leads by night--perhaps because he can be seen farther. Old Ball used to lead mine. He was a large red bullock with a white face.

ERAS   24

The computation of time by the Christian era makes us see it as something that has been cut in half. The same may be said of any era, and indeed of anything that marks time. So if we wish to have as it were just intonation in the matter of time I suppose we should not have even clocks.

BULLOCKS   25

I observed in New Zealand that these know their names better than horses do.

MY THOUGHTS   26

They are like persons met upon a journey--I think them very agreeable at first, but soon find, as a rule, that I am tired of them.

A MAN ON HIMSELF   27

He may make as it were cash entries of himself in a daybook, but the entries in the ledger and the balancing of the accounts should be done by others.

FAMILIAR MISQUOTATIONS[1]   28

Prima dicte mihi summa dicende Mecaenas.[2]

*****

Sed revocare gradus, superasque revertere ad auras,
Hoc opus, hoc nigrum est, hoc tu Romane caveto.[3]
*****

And those who came to pray remained to scoff.[4]
*****

Nil admirari propre res est unica quae te recreare
Ter pure lecto poterit servare libello.[5]
*****

There is more truth in honest lies
Believe me than in half the truths.[6]

SILENCE   29

a storm or chorus of.

THE WORLD   30

may not be particularly wise. Still we know of nothing wiser.

IT IS NOT WHAT A MAN HAS DONE   31

that I much care about. If he has made it clear that he was trying to do what I like, and meant what I should like him to mean it is enough.[1]

MAN   32

is the only animal that can remain on friendly terms with the victims he intends to eat until he eats them.

Written 1874-1875   Copied April 6, 1891

HEREDITY   33

If a hundred men were taken, bred up for a hundred generations to the possession of £100,000 each; and if another hundred bred up for a hundred generations to the possession of £50,000, would the £100,000 men be appreciably different from the £50,000? I should think they would. If the figures were put at £200,000 and £20,000 I can hardly doubt that they would, and I imagine the £20,000 would be the finer men. (Edited)

will not be humbugged, and will tell the truth as near as they can. Thus if a painter has not tried hard to paint well, and has tried hard to hoodwink the public, his offspring is not likely to show hereditary aptitude for painting, but is likely to have improved power of hoodwinking the public. The germ-cells know what the parent meant perfectly well and will be a good deal more sincere than himself. So it is with music, literature, science, or anything else. The only thing the public can do against this is to try very hard to develop a hereditary power of not being hoodwinked. From the small success it has met with hitherto, we may think that the effort on its part can neither have been severe nor long sustained. Indeed all ages seem to have held that

> . . . the pleasure is as great
> Of being cheated as to cheat.[1]

(New note)

CONSERVATORIES   35

One of the main objects of a conservatory is to make believe that there is no such thing as death and decay. The man who attends to it should never be seen at work there. But he may be seen at work in the kitchen garden.

Copied April 5, 1891

A STARVED EXISTENCE   36

The young one was leading a starved existence; therefore he was sinning and nature hated him. His parents were not leading a starved existence, so she did not come down on them. Why should she? [for *Ernest Pontifex*] [1]

A STRONG HOPE OF   37

£ 20,000 in the heart of a poor but capable man may effect a considerable redistribution of the forces of nature. The disturbing effects of such a force may displace mountains. A little unseen impalpable hope sets up a buzzing vibrating movement in a nasty mess inside a man's head. This nasty mess shut up in a dark warm place undergoes a change of rhythm that none can note, and rings of rhythms circle outward from it, as from a stone thrown into a pond, so that the Alps are pierced in consequence.

the range of one man's influence over another was limited to the range of sight sound and scent; besides this there was trail, of many kinds. Trail unintentionally left is as it were hidden sight. Left intentionally it is the unit of literature. It is the first mode of writing from which grew that power of extending men's influence over one another by the help of written symbols of all kinds, without which the development of modern civilisation would have been impossible.[1]

Written 1874-1875   Copied and edited April 5 and 7, 1891

JOINING AND DISJOINING   39

These are the essence of change. A hedge is either for joining things (as a flock of sheep) or disjoining (as for keeping the sheep from getting into corn). These are its more immediate ends. Its ulterior ends, so far as we are concerned, and so far as anything can have an end, is the bringing grain meat or dairy produce into contact with man's stomach, or wool to his back, or that he may ride on horseback somewhere to converse with people and join his soul on to theirs, or please himself in some way. And his pleasure consists in the coming of something within the range of his senses or at least of his imagination.

Written 1874-75   Copied and edited April 7, 1891

SAY OF SOME VERY RESPECTABLE WORK ON MORALITY--THE BIBLE FOR EXAMPLE   40

"We shall have these crude and subversionary books from time to time, until it is recognised as an axiom of morality that luck is the only fit object of human veneration. How, and how far, a man has a right to be lucky, and hence venerable, at the expense of other people, is a point that has always been settled and always must be settled by a kind of higgling and haggling of the market."[1]

as far as his body is concerned, is only a piece of damp parchment with some holes in it, drawn over some bones and flesh. Curiously enough it is about the holes that the interest mainly centres--for eyes, ears, mouth, nose, must all be taken as holes, only that the eyes are glazed.

DEATH AND THE RESURRECTION   42

There are savages who have not yet come to believe in death. There are very able people who have not yet left off believing in the resurrection from the dead. Others again have got beyond believing in either death or resurrection.

FABBRICA ANCORA   43

An Italian told me once that his wife had borne him 14 children. I said, "Then she won't have any more." He replied, "Oh si, fabbrica ancora."[1]

Written 1874-1875   Copied and edited April 8, 1891

MONTREAL DIRECTORY   44

We found the steam had not been on at our offices[1] in Montreal during Sunday, and so everything was frozen hard on Monday morning. Quinn, the caretaker, kissed the Montreal directory in support of his assertion that the steam had been left turned on Saturday night.

JASON SMITH'S DREAM   45

He had rooms at the top of the central staircase in the New Court of St. John's.[1] One night he dreamed that he and his soul had become separated: he fancied himself lying in his bed bereft of soul and dead, and he was wondering where his soul could have got to. Suddenly he saw a thin shadowy figure at the bottom of the well of the stairs that led to his own room. "It is my soul," he exclaimed, "I know it, and it is coming back to me." He watched breathlessly as it glided up the stairs and finally stopped at his own door. "It will be with me," he cried, "in another second, I shall be alive again"--but the figure threw up its hands in despair and glided back again. It had forgotten its latch-key. Whereon Jason woke in terror.

This is recognised when we say of a sick person that there is something wrong with him. All is wrong that is not normal. Either very wrong or so right as to be wrong.[1]

SUBJECT FOR A SHORT STORY 47

A father wished to train his son to avoid speculation, and induced him to invest £5 in a company which he believed was rotten. The company succeeded: the son got £100 for his £5. So the father took it.

RIGHT AND WRONG 48

It is wrong to be too right. To be too good is as bad--or nearly so--as to be too wicked.

Written 1874-1875   Edited and recopied April 9, 1891

SUBJECT 49

A man saved from ruin by having invested in the invention of one whom as a boy he had always snubbed and misunderstood.

LAFLAMME[1] 50

the leading barrister at Montreal said to me once that I could not be too careful what I put on paper. "If I have," he continued, "three lines in the handwriting of any man I can get that man hanged."

PAULI ON THE COMMUNION OF SAINTS(IMPROPER) 51

Two men disputing what this meant referred to Pauli.[1] He replied that he had always understood it to mean "promiscuous intercourse."

SHAKESPEARIAN FRAGMENTS 52

"I say 'tis here, bring thy putty hither."
"Nay, but if it be not here I will eat both thee and thy putty."
Copied about 1858 or 1859 from a Newspaper account of a gas-explosion at Sheffield, and the inquest that ensued. I forget whether there was more or not, but I noted and copied the fragment just given.

It came out in evidence at a trial in New Zealand about 1863(?) [or] * 1864(?) of some very atrocious murderers, that a poor old man on the point of being murdered said, "If you murder me, I shall be foully murdered," and they murdered him.

In regard to this last note. Suppose this subject given out as an exercise for an imaginary dying speech--how few of those who tried to do it would hit upon anything like the real thing--and how the verisimilitude of nature would strike them at once when what had been really said was read to them.

CHRISTIANITY 53

People say you must not try to do away with Christianity till you have something better to put in its place. They might as well say that we must not take away turnpikes and corn laws till we have some other hindrance to put in its place. Besides no one wants to do away with Christianity--all we want is not to be snubbed and bullied if we reject the miraculous part of it for ourselves. At present I am obliged, for example, to keep out of English-frequented hotels in Switzerland and Italy, because I find that if I do not go to service on Sunday I am made uncomfortable. It is this bullying that I want to do away with. As regards Christianity I should hope and think that I am more Christian than not.

PAULI SAID ONCE 54

that people ought to be allowed to leave their cards at church instead of going inside. I have half a mind to try this next time I go to Switzerland.

SUBJECT 55

A youth who has sixpences and three penny bits saved for him till after some 20 years they have mounted up to £25--he spends it all and twice as much more in getting out of some abominable scrape, into which he never would have got but for the parsimony of his friends, and their little saving ways.

Written 1874-1875   Edited April 11, 1891

HEALTH BEFORE HONESTY 56

It is not the interest of honesty or talent or virtue, but those of health and happiness that should take the highest place. Honesty is made for happiness, not happiness for honesty.

here at Montreal if he refuses to believe in God and in a future state. Perhaps a day will come when they will refuse it if he believes in either the one or the other.[1]

HEAVEN 58

is the work of the best and kindest men and women. Hell is the work of prigs pendants and professional truth-tellers. The world is an attempt to make the best of Heaven and Hell.

HOGARTH'S IDLE AND VIRTUOUS APPRENTICE[1] 59

is an immoral work for it represents virtue and its consequences in a light nearly as odious as vice.[2] Those are best who are neither virtuous nor idle.

VIRTUE 60

She has never yet been adequately represented by any who have had any claim to be considered virtuous. It is the sub-vicious who best understand virtue. Let the virtuous people stick to describing vice--which they can do well enough.

FAITH 61

What is faith but a kind of betting or speculation after all? It should be, "I bet that my Redeemer liveth."[1]

A YANKEE SMILE 62

When a Yankee tells of some piece of smart dealing, there comes over his face a sweet far away smile as of one looking upon his child and being reminded by it of its dear dead mother. The man on the Grand Trunk railway[1] who promised us dinner at Richmond when he knew there was none, had just such a smile as this?

LIKENESS IN UNLIKENESS AND VICE VERSA (CONTRADICTION IN TERMS) 63

So leaves are like one another yet no two are alike. So are the small actions of kittens and puppies.

PAIN AND PLEASURE 64

are infectious. It depresses us to be much with those who have suffered long and are still suffering; it refreshes us to be with those who have suffered little and are enjoying themselves. But it is good for us to be depressed now and then.

is the custom of one's country and the current feeling of one's peers. Cannibalism is moral in a cannibal country.

GOOD SENSE   66

and right feeling are one and the same thing.

MAN   67

is conversant about superficies. It is his duty to be superficial--and in this respect he generally does his duty.

JUSTICE   68

is my being allowed to do whatever I like. Injustice is whatever prevents my doing so.

Copied and not edited April 12, 1891 and April 13, 1891

FROM A NEW ZEALAND NOTE BOOK OF MINE NOW DESTROYED   69

I copy the following verbatim from the copy I made when I went through my notes some years ago.

"I found the following in an old note book--dated April 1861. I keep it because it reminds me so strongly of New Zealand.

'It is Sunday. We rose later than usual. There are five of us sleeping in the hut. I sleep on a bunk on one side the fire; Mr. Haast,[1] a German who is making a geological survey of the province sleeps upon the opposite one; my bullock driver and hut-keeper have two bunks at the far end of the hut, along the wall, while my shepherd lies on the left among the tea and sugar, and flour. It was a fine morning and we turned out about seven o'clock.

The usual mutton and bread for breakfast with a pudding made of flour and water baked in the camp oven after a joint of meat. Yorkshire pudding only with no eggs. While we were at breakfast, [a robin] *perched on the sugar which was on the table and sat there a good while pecking at the sugar. We went on breakfasting with little heed to the robin, and the robin went on breakfasting with little heed to us. After breakfast Pey my bullock driver went to fetch the horses up from a spot about two miles down the river--where they often run: we wanted to go pighunting.

I go into the garden and gather a few peascods for seed till the horses should come up. Then Cook,[2] the shepherd, says that a fire has sprung up on the other side the river. Who could have lit it? Probably some one who had intended coming to my place on the preceding evening, and had missed his way, for there is no track of any sort between here [and] * Phillips's.[3] In a quarter of an hour he has lit another fire lower down and by that time, the horses having come up, Haast and myself--remembering how Dr. Sinclair[4] had just been drowned so near the same spot--think it safer to ride over to him and put him across the river. The river was very low and so clear that we could see every stone. On getting to the riverbed we lit a fire, and did the same on leaving it: our tracks would guide any one over the intermediate ground.

*****

Or again--I go out after breakfast to see the sheep: here is an event: among the groups of items that compose a day's existence I place this as a single circumstance, event, action, or what you will; but of how many actions is it not compounded! I take my cap, I get my stick and telescope, I unloose my dog. I could not find my telescope, and had to look for it. Here is an act. In looking for it I do twenty things. When I see it I move towards it which is itself an act containing a beginning middle and end. I take it, another act. I walk towards my dog-kennel--another act separable into acts for every step. At every step I produce an effect on countless pieces of grass or stone or earth. Each atom is affected, and the affection of each atom is an action containing a beginning, middle, and end. Where is this to stop? The actions are like the little fleas with smaller fleas upon their backs to bite them, and so *ad infinitum*.[5] We want an intellectual microscope to see them with.' "

Copied April 13, 1891

COMMUNICATION OF ALL KIND   70

is like painting–a compromise with impossibilities.

Written 1874-1875   Edited April 15, 1891

A HELL OF A PRICE   71

There was a man in New Zealand said to another, "How much do you want for that dog?" "Ten pounds" was the answer. "Ten pounts--that's a hell of a price." "Yes but he's a hell of a dog."

MY NEIGHBOUR JIMMY RAWLE   72

in New Zealand (for though he lived nearly twenty miles off he was almost my nearest neighbour) was urged by Tripp to get married--Tripp having lately got married himself. Rawle said, No, he should die like a pumpkin. "Why so," said Tripp. "Full of seed" was the answer.[1]

LOIS HEATHERLY[1]   73

was told that she looked as if butter would not melt in her mouth. So she tried, and found that it would--and it made her sick.

LADY HOLLAND[1]   74

spoke contemptuously of the order of the Bath, as "a thing that was got by deserving it." The garter came rather by birth.

MYSELF AND T.W.G. BUTLER   75

T.W.G. Butler[1] was one of the most brilliant fellows I ever met. Of course there was something wrong with him. He went mad ten or a dozen years ago, and when I last heard of him was in the asylum of some workhouse and regarded as incurable. He is the man whom I quoted in *Life and Habit* as having said to me that if he could think to me without words I should understand him better. He was no relation--I know every descendant of my grandfather's great-grandfather and relationship earlier than this does not count. Still we always used to think we could detect a family likeness.

One day at Heatherley's more than twenty years ago I foolishly said I hated God the Father and God the Son, and God the Holy Ghost. This was reported and some one taxed T.W.G. Butler indignantly with it a few days later. He said it was not he that had thus spoken. "Indeed," he added, "it could not be for I don't know one of them." Which of us, I wonder, is the one who ought to be in the workhouse asylum?

TOKAY AND CREAM   7(

See *Times* advertisement, September 13, 1877.[1]

"Dr. Druitt reports" on the Tokay. "A short ime since I was attending a gentle man nearly 80, who was dying of senile decay, and atrophy of the heart. . . . at las I suggested some Tokay. . . . In this case I also ordered a mixture of Tokay and Cream Such things may sometimes soothe a dying bed and enable an old man to forge the peevishness of suffering, and to bless his family tranquilly before he falls int his last sleep." I should think Tokay and Cream would be as likely to make on bless one's family as most things.

He places the current feeling of one's peers in close contact with whatsoever
ings are holy. "Whatsoever things are holy," he says, "whatsoever things are of
od repute." At least I think he does.[1]

Copied and edited April 17, 1891

SUBJECT: THE DIVORCE NOVELETTE   78

The hero and heroine are engaged against their wishes. They like each other
ry well but are each in love with some one else; nevertheless under an uncle's will
ey forfeit large property unless they marry, so they get married making no secret
one another that they dislike it very much.

On the evening of their wedding day they broach to [one] * another the subject
at has long been nearest to the heart of each--the possibility of their being divorced.

They discuss the subject tearfully, but the obstacles to their divorce seem in-
perable. Nevertheless they agree that faint heart never yet got rid of fair lady.
None but the brave," they exclaim, "deserve to lose the fair,"[1] and they plight each
her their most solemn vows that they will henceforth live but for the object of
tting divorced from one another.

But the course of true divorce never did run smooth, and the plot turns upon
e difficulties that meet them and how they try to overcome them. At one time
ey seem almost certain of success but the cup is dashed from their lips [and is] *
ther off than ever.

At last an opportunity occurs in an unlooked for manner. They are divorced,
d live happily apart ever afterwards.

CHRISTIANITY   79

true so far as it has fostered beauty, and false so far as it has fostered ugliness. It
therefore both very true and very false.

EXPRESSION   80

I have seen thoughts and fancies playing upon people's faces like the wind upon
oung heather.

"A raw snow-slushy morning with frightened hens cackling round a haystac and some one just going to kill a pig." It sounds like a reminiscence of our bacl yard at Langar.[1]

AN AMERICAN LADY 8

at Grindelwald[1] some years ago told me they had "laid the service on regular i twelve every Saturday."

NATURE'S GREAT LIE 8

That one great lie she told about the earth being flat, when it was round all th time--and again how she stuck to it that the sun went round us when it was we wh are going round her--this double falsehood has irretrieveably ruined my confidenc in her. There is no lie which she will not tell and stick to like a Gladstonian. Ho plausibly she told her tale, and how many ages was it before she was so much i suspected, and then when things did begin to look bad for her, how she brazened out and what a desperate business it was to bring all her shifts and prevaricatior to book.

A MAN BLOWING HIS NOSE IN THE BRITISH MUSEUM READING ROOM 8

He blew it six or seven times at pretty equal intervals--very loud--and it wi like the lowing of a cow coming home to be milked, on a soft February afternoor

Edited April 18, 189

I DO NOT KNOW WHAT THE FOLLOWING ALLUDES TO BUT FIND IT AND COPY IT, IN CASE I SHOULD REMEMBER 8

Far away beyond the first hilly region, there was a pianura of upland pastur I looked at her, her face faded away. She snapped a morsel of cheese from tim to time and was reading the *Daily Telegraph*.

WATER 8

is frozen steam, and ice frozen water.

These so far as I know consist of a page of rules for tuning the harpsichord--probably taken down by some one else, as embodying his practice. They are to be found prefacing a collection of Voluntaries "by the celebrated Mr. Handel" and among these are to be found the six little fugues--though whether they live there when they are at home, or whether they have been taken there from elsewhere I know not.[1]

"OUR FATHER WHICH ART IN HEAVEN"   88

There were two brothers who had quarrelled, and who had an old father who had quarrelled with both. One of them was heard by me to say that the only thing he now had in common with his brother was a wish to be able to repeat the first sentence of the Lord's prayer with literal accuracy.

SUNDAY   89

The great and terrible day of the Lord.

Edited April 25, 1891

EDUCATION OF SERVANTS   90

"I am sorry to say good housewives are almost always opposed to having servants well educated. . . . They must be taught like children and when they are children for any good to come of it. . . . The only school for servants I am acquainted with sent us the worst we ever had, and if it had not been for the very handsome fee it charged both us and her I should not have recognized it as an educational establishment at all." *Times,* April 1, 1880, p. 3.[1]

MISS SAVAGE   91

Writing to me she said the older she grew the more she hated society except that of the few she really liked. "Alas," she added, "time was that when even two or three were gathered together, no matter who, I longed to be in the midst of them."[1]

THE RESURRECTION   92

When I die at any rate I shall do so in the full and certain hope that there will be no resurrection, but that death will give me quittance in full.[1]

Who are these now? The clergy? hardly. Men of science? still less. The ordinary "good fellow," in the best of the more common interpretations of the words-he is the only one worth considering.

CHRIST AND THE CHURCH   94

If he were to apply for a divorce on the grounds of cruelty adultery and desertion, he would probably get one.

Written 1874-1880?   Edited May 5, 1891

HANDEL   95

I only ever met one American who seemed to like and understand Handel. How far he did so in reality I do not know, but *inter alia* he said that Handel struck ile with the *Messiah*--and that "it panned out well the *Messiah* did."

THE SEXUAL QUESTION   96

As regards the greater freedom which those who think as I do would allow the young of both sexes, with such precautions as the faculty may approve, we are met with pictures of the universal debauchery that would follow. This might perhaps have been true once, but the world is grown older and can be better trusted.

CATO AND THE YOUNG MAN   97

Cato saw a young man coming out of a house of ill fame and said, "macte virtute esto,"[1] in approval. Next day he saw the same young man coming from the same house, but he said nothing. The third day he saw him again and pulling him by the sleeve said, "Young man, when I said 'macte virtute' to you two days ago, I did not know you lived in that house."

THE PATRIARCH NOAH   98

Haycock[1] at Cambridge was fond of telling the following:
"The Patriarch Noah was seated one morning in the stern of the ark, when the devil came by in a light wherry. 'It's a hazy morning, Mr. Noah,' he exclaimed in a cheery tone, but the Holy Noah was deep in the second chapter of Obadiah,[2] and paid no attention. Again the devil said more cheerily still, 'Mr. Noah--it's a hazy morning,' but the second founder of our race buried himself still more deeply in the

page he was perusing. A third time the devil exclaimed with perhaps a shade of impertinence in his tone, 'It's-a-hazy-morning-Mister-Noah.' This time the righteous Noah could not restrain his indignation, so he said, 'You be damned! Shem[3], shut the window.'"

A LAWYER'S DREAM OF HEAVEN   99

Every man reclaimed his own property at the Resurrection, and each tried to recover it from all his forefathers.

THE RESURRECTION OF THE BODY

Yes! but how about the resurrection of the money? Shall the dead losses rise too?

WORDS GET LICHEN GROWN AND   101

crumble like stones in an old wall, but it does not do to build a new wall with old stones to make it look like an old one. Let the new work age if it will and gather picturesqueness in its own good time.

THE GREATEST HAPPINESS OF THE GREATEST NUMBER   102

This would require the immediate suppression of all the Greek and Latin classics. There can be little doubt that these, unless in good translations (Greek and Latin being taught as absurdly as they are), cause far more pain than pleasure.

Edited May 6, 1891

DARWIN, CHARLES[1]   103

It was said of some one in the last century that nothing but such parts could buoy up such a character, and nothing but such a character keep down such parts. Of Mr. Darwin it is at any rate true that nothing but such a character could buoy up such parts.

THE CHECKS AND COUNTERCHECKS OF SCIENCE   104

These are like those applied to clerks in a merchant's business--yet no matter how many checks there are one must in the end trust some one--and that some one-- even one's self may make mistakes.

as the unconscious cerebration, the conscience and verifying faculty of the race

GOD IS LOVE[1] 106

I like "Love is God" better.

HE THAT IS STUPID IN LITTLE 107

will be stupid also in much; and so with spite and everything else.

ARGUMENT 108

goes for very little with most people--assertion carries more weight generally.

CANADIAN RESTAURANTS 109

When the Canadians have a decent restaurant, they will be nicer people, and when they are nicer people they will have a decent restaurant.

GOD 110

The only people in England who really believe in God are the Peculiar people. Perhaps that is why they are called Peculiar. See how belief in an anthropomorphic God divides allegiance and disturbs civil order as soon as it becomes vital.

MIND AND MATTER 111

Moral gravitation is as patent as material. Probably each is a phase, mode, or function of the other.

PAULI, C. P., AT SAN FRANCISCO 112

A S. Francisco barman always used to press Pauli to have something whenever he saw Pauli coming into the bar-room. "Come, come," he used to say, "you must have something. You're the handsomest man God ever sent into [San Francisco] *, so help me God you are." Having known Pauli for nearly 30 years I should like to say that I believe the barman to have been right.[1]

ITALIAN MEDIAEVAL ROMANISM 113

mellowed with age. It is hard to think that modern Montreal Romanism or modern English dissent can ever become picturesque--but I suppose they will, for the Puritan has already become so.

SWELLS 114

People ask complainingly what swells have done or do for society that they

hould be able to live without working. The good swell is the creature towards which
ll nature has been groaning and travailing together until now.[1] He is an ideal. He
nows what may be done in the way of good breeding, health, looks, temper and
ortune. He realises men's dreams of themselves at any rate vicariously; he preaches
he gospel of grace. The world is like a spoilt child; it has this good thing given it
t great expense and then says it is useless.

ritten about 1876   Edited May 14, 1891

I'M A PUBLICAN   115

An old country clergyman declaiming against modern scepticism declared that
orality was all very well, but that it was not enough to keep men fairly straight.
Morality," he exclaimed, "may do for some people--it may do for Pharisees--but
am not a Pharisee. I am a Publican--thank God!"[1]

A YANKEE   116

n a steamer going up the Mississippi told the Captain he should go ashore at a small
wn where the steamer stopped for half an hour or so. "I wouldn't," said the Cap-
ain. "There is nothing to do there, the people are all asleep--it's only a one-horse
ttle place with no life stirring it." "Well," said the other, "I think I'll go ashore."
o he went.

He returned as the steamer was on the point of starting, and the captain asked
im what he thought of it. "Wall," he answered, "I went in--to the public market
lace, and I stole a pair of socks. I was arrested, tried, convicted, and publicly whip-
ed, all in the space of twenty minutes. You call it a one-horse little place. Now
call it rather a smart little place."

LOUIS BLANC ON OUR DAY OF HUMILIATION   117

t the time of the cattle plague said we were praying God to have mercy on those
oor cattle so that we might kill and eat them as usual.

ritten about 1876?   Edited May 21, 1891

HORSE AND POTATO-PARING

A horse harnessed in a cart straining after a potato-paring a little beyond hi reach upon the pavement--and his lips quiver towards it. Is this a piece of anima magnetism on the part of the potato--the potato attracting horses as a magnet doe needles? or is it chemical affinity? or is it proselytising instinct on the part of th horse? or how?

CONTACT BETWEEN THE WORLDS
11

There is some contact between us and any star that we can see. We are half i a place when we can see it.

AMERICAN DISHONESTY
12

Refer it to their Puritan ancestry.

ART COLLECTIONS
12

The two extremes of art collections are perhaps the Uffizi and Jones and Bo ham's auction rooms in Oxford Street.[1]

THE LETTER OF STRICT INACCURACY
12

I was explaining to Jones[1] that some eggs I was going to let him have were pe haps not quite so fresh as he thought. I said, "I don't often tell the truth but ther are times in every man's life when he departs from the letter of strict inaccuracy."

MADAME VIGNEAU[1]
12

at St. Leonard, in Lower Canada, had a mass said for our unfortunate Canada Tar ning Extract Company but it did not save it.

She was a half caste French Indian of the best stamp--one of the most remark able women I ever knew, and very good as long as you behaved well. She ruled ever one who had anything to do with her. She kept the inn at St. Leonard and I kne her well, and liked her very much. "Ah," she used to say, "in the old days the used to call me Colisse, but now they call me Madama Vigneau."

Written about 1876-1880   Edited November 21, 189

BEET ROOT AND MODESTY
12

The beet root is a better emblem of modesty than the rose. The colour is a ine; it conceals itself from the view more completely; moreover it is good to eat, and will make excellent sugar.

EVAPORATION 125

s an unseen heavenward waterfall.

MYSELF AND *THE FAIR HAVEN*[1] 126

What did I do in this book other than what the church does? She attacks reasonable conclusions under the guise of defending them, with a view to impose on those who have not wit enough to find her out.

THE NATURE OF THINGS IN THEMSELVES 127

A thing "*is*" whatever it gives us least trouble to think it is. There is no other '*is*" than this.

REPUTATIONS FOR ABILITY 128

I would rather lose twenty, than be at pains to keep one of them. Reputation s like a man's soul which he may find in losing, or lose in finding. It is like money, more easily made than kept.

CLASSICAL CLUB 129

There should be a classical club to translate the classics as the bishops in King ames's time revised the bible, and as the New Testament revisers are doing now.

CAMBRIDGE COOKING 130

There is a higher average of good cooking at Oxford and Cambridge than elsewhere. The dinners are better than the curriculum. But there is no chair of cookery: it is taught by apprenticeship in the kitchens.

JOUBERT 131

Matthew Arnold quotes him as saying "distrust in metaphysics words that have not been able to get currency in the world, and which are only calculated to form a special language." *Pall Mall Gazette*, April 13, 1880.[1]

OUR CONCEIT 132

He is a poor creature who does not believe himself to be better than the whole world else. No matter how ill we may be, nor how low we may have fallen, we would not change identity with any other person. Hence our self conceit sustains and always must sustain us, till death takes us and our conceit together so that we need no more sustaining.

are for the most part like bad sixpences, and we spend our lives trying to pass them on one another.

A MAN IS SHORN OF HIS STRENGTH   134

if he belongs to one set or to one woman.

LIFE AND VIVISECTION   135

The life of some people seems rather a vivisection than a life.

BODY AND CLOTHES   136

Instead of saying that such or such conduct will ruin a man body and soul, say it will ruin him body and clothes.

THE GREATEST HAPPINESS OF THE GREATEST NUMBER   137

will be best promoted by increasing the prosperity of those who are now best and comeliest.

THE KINGDOM OF HEAVEN   138

is the being like a good dog.

ART NOTE   139

A painter should find out what is the most important hundreth part of what he sees. If he can settle this justly he has painted his picture, to all intents and pur poses.

I WAS SICK AND YE VISITED ME[1]   140

I should say, "I was sick, and you were kind enough to leave me quite alone." Against this note I found Jones had written in pencil: "It must have been a reproach; H.F.J."

Written 1876-1880   Edited November 24, 1891

FROM GOD THE FATHER   141

to the parish beadle.

OLD MUSIC AND OLD PICTURES   142

Just as an old picture looks better in an antique frame, so old music gains in charm when heard with old fashioned accessories. Old editions of old books again help us to realise better the spirit of the author.

SAVAGES, CHRISTIANS, AND SCIENTISTS   143

There are savages who have not yet come to understand that we must all die. There are Christians who have not yet come to understand that no man can rise from the dead with his body. There are men of science who do not yet know that[1] absolute death is an impossibility.

FOLEY'S[1] THUMB MARK   144

We found it, very large and fat, on the padlock of the safe the morning after we had got rid of him. He said (I afterwards heard) that it was very mean of me to have had a new padlock put on so soon.

VIGNEAU   145

A very fine fellow--when he wanted to sign his name, used to take a piece of paper out of his pocket, and carefully copy his signature. I have often seen him do this; but he could not learn the signature by heart.

SENSIBLE PAINTING   146

like sensible law, sensible writing, or sensible anything else consists as much in knowing what to omit, as what to insist upon. It consists in the tact that tells the painter where to stop.

ART NOTE   147

There are three provinces of art. The what is; the what we should like to fancy as having been in the past; and the what we like to fancy as pure imagination. There should be no strict what was, or has been; this belongs to the antiquary and archae-ologist, not to the artist.

ILLUSIONS   148

We often hear it said that the world owes more to its illusions than to its reali-ties. But are not its realities based on, and do not they grow out of its illusions? If so, a reality is only an illusion so strong and so universal that no one can resist it.

Not only is nothing good or ill but thinking makes it so, but nothing is at all except in so far as thinking has made it so.

WALKING UPRIGHT   150

Walking upright was perhaps once as difficult as the feats of Blondin or Leotard[1] appear to ourselves. Perhaps it was thought wicked, perhaps it was only an imitation of a deformity, in flattery of some semi-simious chief who had lost his arms and could neither climb trees nor go on all fours. Perhaps it was developed by some vice, or perhaps it began as a mere piece of affectation. Anyhow until we take to flying we shall probably continue to walk as uprightly as we can if only to a cab or train.

A NEW PROFESSION   151

Portrait painting in words which people should pay for as they pay for their pictures.

PAULI   152

He was very ill one Passion week; he said he should go to bed on Good Friday and like a celebrated historical personage, rise again on the third day.

TITLE   153

Records of a mis-spent life.

STEALING WISELY   154

It is only great proprietors who can steal well and wisely. A good stealer, a good user of what he takes is *ipso facto* a good inventor. Two men can invent after a fashion to one who knows how to make the best use of what has been done already.

CANADIAN STEAM   155

The steam from a train on a frosty morning in mid-winter will hang on pine trees from ten minutes to a quarter of an hour.

SIN   156

Sin is like a mountain with two aspects according as viewed before it has been reached or after: yet both aspects are real.

Men are no more all equal before God than they are so before man. The sole element of truth in the contention lies in the fact that our bodies, not to say our minds, are built all upon one general plan.

ART NOTE   158

It is a nice question whether a consummate work of art, say Donatello's St. George or Tabachetti's sleeping St. Joseph,[1] can or cannot, in view of its longer lease of life and wider range of influence, further human spiritual welfare as much as a single well spent life can further it. My instinct, however, is in favour of the life. Yet is not Tabachetti's portrait of himself the outcome and record of a life?

Written 1876-1880   Edited November 27, 1891

MOTTO FOR WOMEN'S RIGHTS AGITATORS   159

I will exhibit a bill in parliament for the suppression of men. Merry Wives of Windsor.

FROM *WILD OATS* (AMERICAN COMIC PAPER)[1]   160

"Communication between the spirit world and the medium struck a snag." "Fifty years had skipped pretty lively over his apexed dome of thought."

POSTHUMOUS FAME   161

He who wants posthumous fame is as one who would entail land, and tie up his money after his death as tightly and for as long a time as possible. Still we each of us in our own small way try to get what little posthumous fame we can.

BY THEIR FRUITS YE SHALL KNOW THEM[1]   162

This depends on what sort of a judge of fruits you may happen to be--or, "Yes -if you are a judge of fruits."

THE ONE SERIOUS CONVICTION   163

that a man should have is that nothing is to be taken too seriously.

contained many of the elements of a Messiah.

MRS. THISTLETHWAITE[1]   165

Some one in Miss Savage's presence was questioning the sincerity of Mrs. T's repentance. "Oh, I assure you," was the answer, "her repentance is most profound. She had her portrait painted as a Magdalene last week."

SUBJECT   166

Bible stories for the use of little infidels.

SQUINTING   167

When a man who squints has a son who squints, this is a bad squint.

Written 1876-1880   Edited November 25, 1891[1]

PICTURES   168

are like the woman who washed Jesus' feet--they are saved much if they have loved much.[2]

INTELLECTUAL SELF-INDULGENCE   169

Intellectual over-indulgence is the most gratuitous and disgraceful form which excess can take, nor is there any the consequences of which are more disastrous.

McCULLOCH (GEORGE)[1]   170

He told me once that in drawing he "made a great many lines and saved the best of them."

THE LAWYER   171

Money should be to the solicitor, what souls are to the parson or life to the physician.

In front of my room at Montreal there was a verandah from which a rope was stretched across a small yard to a chimney on a stable roof over the way. Clothes were hung to dry on this rope. As I lay in bed of a morning I could see the shadows and reflected lights from these clothes moving on the ceiling as the clothes were blown about by the wind. The movement of these shadows and reflected lights was exactly that of the rays of an Aurora Borealis, less colour. I can conceive no resemblance more perfect. They stalked across the ceiling with the same kind of movement absolutely.

TIDAL WAVES OF AIR   173

Are there any or no? It would seem as though there should be, and yet I never heard of any even [in] * the upper atmosphere.

Written 1876-1880   Edited November 27, 1891

OH WHERE SHALL WISDOM BE FOUND[1]   174

The answer is all very well as far as it goes, but it only comes to saying that wisdom is wisdom. We know no better what the fear of the Lord is than what wisdom is, and we often do not depart from evil simply because we do not know that what we are cleaving to is evil.

T.W.G. BUTLER[1]   175

He admitted that we all want a certain amount of poetical pabulum--"but," he continued, "I get it, I have as much as is good for me. I read the *Royal Academy Catalogue* and take in the *Daily Telegraph.*"

EDMUND GURNEY[1]   176

I heard him say one night, in 1876, and he meant it, and saw no fun in it, there had been four great unselfconscious artists--Homer, Raphael, Wordsworth, and Nelly Farren. [2] [No wonder the poor fellow ended by taking his own life.]

HANDEL AND LECOCQ   177

I heard Edward Hall say on the same evening that after having known Lecocq, he really could not go back to Handel.[1] [No wonder the poor fellow failed for nearly half a million, only a few years afterwards.]

The Professor of Wordly Wisdom plucked a man for trying to tell people something they did not want to know.

GOD AS A MORAL RULER 179

The invention of God as a moral ruler was like the invention of him as a material creator--to save trouble to a dominant party--and no doubt for a long time it did save them a good deal of trouble.

MONEY 180

If a man is to die rich, he must go through the embryonic stages with his money as much as with his limbs.

Edited November 28, 1891

HENRY KINGSLEY[1] 181

I am told he has somewhere said that the Argus eyes of a small country town were good for boys.
This was not my grandfather's opinion.

MRS. DONCASTER[1] 182

said the porter was a very undermining person. There had been a fire and she said she had seen that "the element was very red."

SUBJECT 183

Fifteen mistresses applied for three cooks. Turn this into a little fairy story in which the mistress who thought herself nobody was chosen by the beautiful cook &c.

ULTIMATE TRIUMPH OF GOOD 184

When we say we believe in this, we mean that we are cock sure of our own opinions.

SUBJECTS 185

Reversions; scrapes; loss of reputation.

wanted to be buried in a vault at Brighton, but did not want her husband to be buried there. "Besides, my dear," she continued, "there is no room for him, the vault will only hold four, and five would crowd it inconveniently."

FASTS AND FEASTS   187

The Roman Catholic theory in this respect is based unconsciously on the practice of semi-civilised nations as forced upon them by seasons during which people could get very little to eat.

GEOLOGY   188

The father of [geology]* was he who seeing fossil shells on a mountain conceived the theory of the deluge.

Written 1876-1880   Edited and enlarged November 30, 1891

HANDEL AND DOMENICO SCARLATTI[1]   189

Handel and Domenico Scarlatti were contemporaries almost to a year both as regards birth and death. They knew each other very well in Italy, and Scarlatti never mentioned Handel's name without crossing himself, but I have not heard that Handel crossed himself when he heard the name of Scarlatti. I know very little of Scarlatti's music, and have not even that little well enough in my head to write about it, I retain only a residuary impression that it is often very charming and links Haydn with Bach, moreover that it is distinctly unHandelian.

Handel must have known and comprehended Scarlatti's tendencies perfectly well--his rejection therefore of the principles that lead to them must have been deliberate. Scarlatti leads to Haydn--Haydn to Mozart and hence, through Beethoven, to modern music. That Handel foresaw this I do not doubt, nor yet that he felt, as I do myself, that modern music means something, I know not what, which is not what I mean by music. It is playing another game, and has set itself aims which no doubt are excellent, but which are not mine.

Of course I know that this may be all wrong. I know how very limited and superficial my own acquaintance is with music. Still I have a strong feeling as though from John Dunstable,[2] or whoever it may be, to Handel the tide of music was rising, intermittently no doubt, but still rising, and that since Handel's time it has been falling.

Or rather perhaps I should say that Music bifurcated with Handel and Bach--Handel dying musically as well as physically childless, while Bach was as prolific in respect of musical disciples as he was in that of children.

What then was it, supposing I am right at all, that Handel distrusted in the principles of Scarlatti as deduced from those of Bach? I imagine that he distrusted chiefly the abuse of the appoggiatura, the abuse of the unlimited power of modulation which equal temperament placed at the musician's disposal, and departure from well-marked rhythm, beat, or measured tread, except on occasion and then not for long. At any rate I believe the music I like best myself to be sparing of the appoggiatura, to keep pretty close to tonic and dominant, and to have a well-marked beat measure and rhythm.

HANDEL AND BACH 190
[Written November 30, 1891]

Rockstro[1] says that Handel keeps much more closely to the old Palestrina rules of counterpoint than Bach does, and that when Handel takes a licence it is a good bold one taken rarely, whereas Bach is niggling away with small licences from first to last.

Written 1876-1880   Edited November 30, 1891

GOD 191

as now generally conceived of is only the last witch.

NO DRAGONS 192

People say that there are no dragons to be killed, nor distressed maidens to be rescued nowadays. I do not know but I think I have dropped across one or two nor do I feel sure whether it is I or they who have inflicted the most mortal wound

ENTERTAINING ANGELS 193

I doubt whether any angel would find me very entertaining. As for myself if ever I do entertain one it will have to be unawares.[1] When people entertain others without an introduction, they generally turn out more like devils than angels

MEMNON 194

I saw the driver of the Hempstead 'bus once near St. Giles's church. An old fat, red-faced man sitting bolt upright on the top of his bus, in a driving storm of snow, fast asleep with a huge waterproof over his great coat, that descended with sweeping lines on to a tarpaulin. All this rose out of a cloud of steam from the horses. He had a short clay pipe in his mouth, but for a moment he looked just like Memnon.[1]

THE SECOND CHAPTER OF OBADIAH 195

My sister said the servants would not understand it (there is only one chapter of Obadiah).[1]

READ *THE PENNY CHRISTIAN GLOBE*[1] 196

"Contains two powerful stories, and the largest amount of reading matter in any paper in the world." True advertisement.

FORTUNE AND HER WHEEL 197

In 1871 at Varallo, in Varallo Vecchio old Avondo shewed me a palazzo old and going to ruin over the door of which I observed a decayed fresco of Fortune and her wheel. I have looked for it once or twice since but never found it.

EATING GRAPES DOWNWARDS 198

Always eat the best first--for so every grape will be good. This is why Spring seems longer and drearier than Autumn. In Autumn we are eatings the days downwards, in Spring each one is "still very bad."

Written 1876-1880   Edited December 1, 1891

A GOOD TITLE 199

should aim at making what follows, as far as possible superfluous to those who know anything of the subject.

NATIONAL DEBTS 200

He only pays money who feels he pays it. National debts, then, are practically paid off as soon as the generation which is first taxed for the interest is either dead or has become accustomed to the burden. Still a nation should keep on paying its debt, for a time may come when a sudden effort is needed, and then the repayment of the debt may for a time cease, so that the pressure may be less felt.

"THE MOST ENERVATING KIND OF INTOXICATION" 201

comes from "full draughts of contemporary applause." *Times* Leader, March 10, 1876.[1]

When in doubt do as nearly nothing as you can.

TO LOVE GOD   203

is to have good health, good looks, good sense, experience, a kindly nature and a fair balance of cash in hand. We know that all things work together for good to them that love God.[1]

To be loved by God is the same as to love him. We love him because he first loved us.

THE PARABLES   204

The people do not act reasonably in a single instance. The sower was a bad sower; the shepherd who left his ninety-nine sheep in the wilderness was a foolish shepherd; the husbandman who would not have his corn weeded was no farmer &c. &c.[1] None of them go nearly on all fours, but halt so much as to have neither literary nor moral value to any but slipshod thinkers. Granted--but are we not all slipshod thinkers?

Written 1876-1880   Edited December 2, 1891

WE ARE HIS PEOPLE AND THE SHEEP OF HIS PASTURE[1]   205

We profess to accept with thankfulness the position of being God's sheep, yet few lambs are allowed to become full grown and it is not intended that any should die a natural death. A sheep's *raison d'être* is to be fleeced as often as possible, and then to have its throat cut.

Uriah the Hittite, if his own life had been spared would no doubt have sat down to the little ewe lamb which he carried so tenderly in his bosom, and dined off it with much satisfaction;[2] when, again, we see pictures of our Saviour with sheep behind him, and a lamb in his bosom, we should remember that the matter will not end here. If a shepherd caressing a lamb is a fair statement of the case, a cat playing with a mouse should be hardly less so. We may be asked to bless the grass, the sunshine and our fellow sheep, but can we reasonably be expected to bless the butcher? Is it not time to drop that metaphor?

OUT-CHRISTING CHRIST   206

comes to much the same as out-Heroding Herod.

Dr. Kennedy[1] told us one Sunday morning that God had communicated the art of making bread to Adam and Eve by a process of direct . . . I suppose he said "inspiration," but it came to much the same thing as "instruction." For years I seriously believed this. Jones, to whom I once laughingly repeated the fact, said that if God had taught Adam and Eve how to make buttered toast there would have been more sense in it.

ORGIES OF VIRTUE   208

Consecrations, ordinations &c.

Written 1876-1880   Edited December 3, 1891

ITALIANS AND ENGLISHMEN   209

Italians, and perhaps Frenchmen, consider first whether they like or want to do a thing, and then whether on the whole it will do them any harm. Englishmen, and perhaps Germans consider first whether they ought to like a thing, and often never reach the questions whether they do like, and whether it will hurt. There is much to be said for both systems, but I suppose it is best to combine both as far as possible.

MONEY AT THE LAST   210

If a man has as much money at the last as will enable him to die in comfort, he has as much peace at the last as he can reasonably expect.

MORALITY   211

Unless morality brings a man peace at the last, it is an imposture. Peace at the last is the *raison d'être* of morality. I have known very moral old men living with wives whom they have long ceased to love if indeed they ever loved them; fathers of sons whom they hate for having either distanced, or disgraced them, and of ugly disagreeable daughters whom they loathe in secret, but from whom there is no escape.

Is it moral for a man to have brought this upon himself? Is it moral of a man to have an old wife and ugly daughters at all? If this [is] * moral, what is immorality? Some one should do for morals what Bacon is supposed to have done for science.

THE SELFISHNESS OF WOMEN   212

They say it is so selfish of men not to marry; perhaps it is; but is it not selfish of women to insist on men's marrying them?

HOLLANDS[1] 213

reminds me always of the sound of the hautbois, perhaps because of its husky flavour, and because it begins with h.

MISS SAVAGE 214

Miss Savage said of one of her friends, that she had "the harmlessness of the serpent, and the wisdom of the dove."[1]

HENRY HOARE[1] 215

Pauli said he was like a wire fence--[meaning of course to huntsmen. I see Hoare has just filed a petition in Bankruptcy and is failing for £300,000 or £400,000--but I take the figures on hearsay.]

EUCLID 216

My cousin[1] said there was one touch of nature in him that always comforted him. It consisted in the words "which is absurd."

TRUTH 217

on any subject is the opinion which either has, or may come to have the whip hand.

SUAVE MARI MAGNO &c.[1] 218

Perhaps, but it is much more pleasant to be on the seashore when there is no shipwreck.

ELISHA AND THE BEARS[1] 219

One can understand why Elisha should have had a bear or two always, so to speak, on draught--and also that he should wish them to be fat. It will be remembered he was very bald.

WANTED: A SOCIETY 220

for the suppression of erudite research, and the decent burial of the past. The Ghosts of the dead past want quite as much laying as raising.

KNOWING A LITTLE MORE OR A LITTLE LESS THAN WE DO 221

We like those who know much about the same as we do, or much more, or much less; but we do not like them to know a little more or a little less. Jones says the same holds good with money.

WORSLEY, MY UNCLE PHILIP[1]
CONSCIENCE--PRANKS OF   222

He became a partner in Whitbread's brewery, but on conscientious grounds refused a partnership in a distillery. He drew the line at gin. What odd lines conscience does sometimes draw to be sure.

MARRIAGE AND HEAVEN   223

Marriage is distinctly and repeatedly excluded from heaven.[1] Is this because it is thought likely to mar the general felicity?

BIRD'S EGGS   224

Why do birds colour their eggs so beautifully for so short a time, and when it is not intended that they shall be seen by any but the parents? The sentimental turtle and the prosaic hen are alike satisfied to sit on a plain egg without going to the trouble and expence of colouring it. Why can a hedge-sparrow find no peace in anything short of tourquoise? We are tempted to exclaim, "To what purpose is this waste?"

HANDEL AND BACH   225

If you tie Handel's hands by debarring him from the rendering of human emotion, and if you set Bach's free by giving him no human emotion to render--if in fact you rob Handel of his opportunities and Bach of his difficulties the two men can fight after a fashion, but Handel will even so come off victorious. Otherwise it is absurd to let Bach compete at all. Nevertheless the cultured vulgar have at all times preferred gymnastics and display to reticence, and the healthy graceful normal movements of a man of birth and education, and Bach is esteemed a more profound musician than Handel in virtue of his more frequent and more involved complexity of construction. In reality Handel was profound enough to eschew such wildernesses of counterpoint as Bach instinctively resorted to, but he knew also that public opinion would be sure to place Bach on a level with himself, if not above him, and probably this made him look askance at Bach. At any rate he twice went to Germany without being at any pains to meet him, and once if not twice, refused Bach's invitation.[1]

TRUTH   226

I do not seek truth for her own sake: let her look to herself. I seek her for my own. It is true, I believe I like her, but I do so mainly because I know I can trust her--better at any rate than I can any one else. If I did not think this I would have nothing to do with her.

My uncles Philip and Sam[2] bribed him to eat a cock-roach for sixpence. He thought it all over, *more suo* very carefully and minutely. "The stomach," he said, "will be the worst part," but whether he swallowed the stomach for the sake of the sixpence or no the story does not say.

EXAMPLE   228

is not only the best way of propagating an opinion, but it is the only way worth taking into account.

KING THEEBAW   229

"The report of King Theebaw's death has not been confirmed but official intelligence has reach[ed] * India that he is suffering from some dangerous malady and that attempts are being made to stay the disease by sacrificing virgins." *Times*, April 25? 26? 1880.[1]

Written 1876-1880   Edited December 8, 1891

ART OF PROPAGATING OPINION   230

He who would propagate an opinion must begin by making sure of his ground, and holding it firmly. There is no more use in trying to breed from weak opinions than from other weak stock, animal or vegetable.

The more securely a man holds an opinion the more temperate he can afford to be; and the more temperate he is the more weight he will carry with those who are in the long run weightiest.

Ideas and opinions, like living organisms, have a normal rate of growth which cannot be either checked or forced beyond a certain point.

They can be held in check more safely than they can be hurried. They can also be killed; and one of the surest ways to kill them is to try and hurry them.

The more unpopular an opinion is the more necessary is it that the holder should be somewhat punctilious in his observance of conventionalities generally, and that, if possible, he should get the reputation of being well to do in the world.

Arguments are not so good as assertion. Arguments are like fire arms which a man may keep at home, but should not carry about with him.

Indirect assertion, leaving the hearer to point the inference, is generally to be preferred.

The one great argument with most people is that another should think this or that. The reasons of the belief are a detail that in nine cases out of ten are best omitted, as confusing and weakening the general impression.

Many, if not most good ideas die young--mainly from neglect on the part of the parents, but sometimes from over fondness.

Once well started, an opinion had better be left to shift for itself.

Insist as far as possible on the insignificance of the points of difference as compared with the resemblance to those generally accepted.

GOOD BREEDING THE *SUMMUM BONUM*   231

When people ask what faith we would substitute for that which we would destroy, we answer that we destroy no faith and need substitute none. We hold the Glory of God to be the *summum bonum* and so do Christians generally. It is a question of what is the Glory of God? It is here that we join issue. We say it varies with the varying phases of God as made manifest in his works; but that so far as we are ourselves concerned the Glory of God is best advanced by advancing that of man. If asked what is the glory of man, we answer "good breeding"--using the words in their double sense, and meaning both the continuance of the race, and that grace of manner which the words are more commonly take to signify.

The double sense of the words is all the more significant for the unconsciousness with which it is passed over.

HANDEL   232

is so great and so simple that it takes a professional musician to be unable to understand him.

Jones and I hammered this out between us.

Written 1876-1880   Edited December 10, 1891

RELIGION   233

Unless a religion can be founded on half a page of note paper it will be bottom-heavy, and this, in matters so essentially of sentiment as religion, is as bad as being top-heavy in a material construction. It must of course catch on to reason, but the less it emphasizes the fact the better.

DIFFUSENESS   234

sometimes helps, when the subject is hard: words that may be strictly speaking unnecessary still may make things easier for the reader by giving him more time to master the thought while his eye is running over the verbiage. So a little water may prevent a strong drink from burning throat and stomach. A style that is too terse is as fatiguing as one that is too diffuse. But when a passage is written a little long with consciousness and compunction, but still deliberately as what will probably be most easy for the reader, it can hardly be called diffuse.

The case of a woman now stands thus. Every one of her ancestors for millions and millions of generations has been endowed with sexual instinct, and has effectually gratified it. For a longer time than our imagination can realise there has been no link broken, and hence no exception. The instinct has been approved, confirmed and made stronger in each successive generation. Surely those in whom it has been thus sanctioned may claim the right to gratify it should occasion serve.

"No," says society to the unmarried woman very sternly. "Break the link, in your own person; stem the current of that passion to which both we and you owe our very being; run counter to the course of things that has led up to you, be indifferent to that which has ranked next to life itself in the hearts of every mother from whom you are descended. If you even attempt this more than Herculean task seriously, we will not honour you, but will laugh at you for an old maid; if on the other hand you are disobedient, we will chase you out into the streets and call you infamous."

And then we are surprised that women are not at all times exactly what we could wish.

ART NOTE--INARTICULATE TOUCHES   236

An artist's touches are sometimes no more articulate than the barking of a dog who would call attention to something without exactly knowing what. He is a great artist who can be depended on not to bark at nothing.

ART-NOTE--GIOTTO[1]   237

There are few modern painters who are not greater technically than Giotto, but I cannot call to mind a single one whose work impresses me as profoundly as his does. How is it that our so greatly better should be so greatly worse?--that the farther we go beyond him, the higher he stands above us? Age no doubt has much to do with it--for great as Giotto was, there are painters of today not less so, if they only dare express themselves as frankly and unaffectedly as he did.

CARPACCIO   238

No one can realise him till he has seen S. Giorgio dei Schiavoni at Venice.[1]

Written 1876-1880   Edited (or rather rewritten) December 18, 1891

ART NOTE--RELATIVE IMPORTANCES   239

It is the painter's business to help memory and imagination not to supersede them. He cannot put the whole before the spectator; nothing can do this short of the thing itself; he should not therefore try to realise, and the less he looks as f he were trying to do so the more signs of judgment he will show. His business s to supply those details which will most readily bring the whole before the mind along with them. He must not give too few, but it is still more imperative on him not to give too many.

Seeing, thought, and expression are rendered possible only by the fact that our minds are always ready to compromise, and to take the part for the whole. We associate a number of ideas with any given object, and if a few of the most characteristic of these are put before us we take the rest as read, jump to a conclusion, and realise the whole. If we did not conduct our thought on this principle, i.e. simplifying by suppression of detail, and breadth of treatment--it would take us a twelvemonth to say that it was a fine morning, and another for the hearer to apprehend our statement. Any other principle reduces thought to an absurdity.

He therefore tells best in painting, as in literature, who has best estimated the relative values or importances of the more special features characterising his subjects: that is to say, who appreciates most accurately how much and how fast each one of them will carry, and is at most pains to give those only that will say most in the fewest words, or touches. It is here that the most difficult, important, and generally neglected part of an artist's business will be found to lie.

The difficulties of doing are serious enough, but we can most of us overcome them with ordinary perserverance; these, however, are small as compared with those of knowing what not to do--with learning to disregard the incessant importunity of small nobody details that persist in trying to thrust themselves above their betters. It is less trouble to give in to these than to snub them duly and keep them in their proper places; yet it is precisely here that strength or weakness will be found to lie. It is success or failure in this respect that constitutes the difference between the artist who may claim to rank as a statesman, and one who can rise no higher than a village vestryman.

It is here, moreover, that effort is most renumerative. For when we feel that a painter has made simplicity and subordination of importances his first aim, it is surprising how much shortcoming we will condone as regards actual execution. Whereas let the execution be perfect, if the details given be ill chosen in respect of relative importance, the whole effect is lost; it becomes top heavy, as it were, and collapes. As for the number of details given, this does not matter; a man may give as few or as many as he chooses; he may stop at outline, or he may go on to Jean Van Eyck;[1] what is essential is that no matter how far or how small a distance he may go, he should have begun with the most important point, and added each subsequent feature in due order of importance, so that if he stopped at any moment there should be no detail ungiven, more important than another which has been insisted on.

Supposing, by way of illustration, that the details are as grapes in a bunch, they should be eaten from the best grape to the next best and so on down, never eating of worse grape while a better remains uneaten.[2]

Personally I think that, as the painter cannot go the whole way, the sooner he makes it clear that he has no intention of trying to do so the better. When we look at a very highly finished picture (so-called), unless we are in the hands of one who has attended successfully to the considerations insisted on above, we feel as though we were with a troublesome *cicerone*[3] who will not let us look at things with our own eyes, but keeps intruding himself at every touch and turn, and trying to exercise that undue influence upon us, which generally proves to have been the accompaniment to concealment and fraud. This is exactly what we feel in regard to Van Mieris, and, though in a less degree, with Gerard Dow--whereas with Jean Van Eyck and Metsu[4] no matter how far they may have gone, we find them essentially as impressionist as Rembrandt or Velasquez.[5]

For impressionism only means that due attention has been paid to the relative importances of the impressions made by the various characteristics of a given subject, and that they have been presented to us in order of precedence.

ART NOTE--SINCERITY   240

It is not enough that the painter should make the spectator feel what he meant him to feel. He must also make him feel that this feeling was shared by the painter himself *bonâ fide* and without affectation. Of all the lies a painter can tell the worst is the saying that he likes what he does not like. But the poor wretch seldom knows himself; for the art of knowing what gives him pleasure has been so neglected that it has been lost to all but a very few. The old Italians knew well enough what they liked and were as children in saying it.

[Written] * 1876-1880   Edited December 18, 1891

PICTURES THAT I NEVER PAINTED   241

Priest lighting his pipe from the fire of an itinerant tinker--Burial of Fidele (or Snowdrop)[1]--Nostradamus[2]--Seven Sleepers of Ephesus[3]--A sack race--Priest superintending alterations in the village fountain--Cat's meat man followed by cats-- Archway of my staircase (I did this but got tired and never finished it)--A puppy having a row with a large cock, (both afraid)--*Minga scuola* (Father carrying his truant son to school at Angera)[4]--An important industrial centre in the flint period- A fine horse in love with an ugly little old donkey--The unanswered challenge (a cock crowing at early morning to a wooden cock on a crucifix)--Women on trees at Fobello--Pigs sleeping in Piazza Gaudenzio Ferrari at Varallo.[5]

ART NOTE: EYESIGHT WILD AND TAME   242

If a man has not studied painting or at any rate black and white drawing, his eyes are wild; to learn to draw in light and shade tames them. The first step toward taming the eyes is to teach them not to see too much. Nothing tends so much to oversight as overseeing.* Half close the eyes, or look through black crape. By seeing with the half we know what we can best dispense with.
                              *Used in *Evolution Old and New*, p. 197.

ART NOTE--DETAIL   243

Another reason why it is as well not to give very much is that no matter how much is given the eye will always want more: it will know very well that it is not

100

eing paid in full. On the other hand no matter how little one gives, the eye will generally compromise by wanting only a little more. In either case the eye will want a little, but not much more: so one may as well stop sooner as later.

Written 1880   Rewritten February 17, 1892

FLUKES IN SHEEP   244

See quotation from a letter of Cobbett's, *Times*, April 29, 1880.[1]

STALLIONS AND BROAD MARES   245

should not, if there is anything in my *Life and Habit* theory, be allowed to do as little work as they do. They should be made to work as far as they can consistently with good condition.

MY COUSIN AND I ON THE HAPPIEST TIME IN OUR LIVES   246

We settled that we had never been much better off than at the (then) present time. My cousin added, "I should like a few more good theatres--and a Handel lub." So should I. Take it all round we thought we would not go back to any other time, and would compound gladly enough to have none better if we could be sure of having none worse. Afterwards my counsin was a little inclined to say he thought the time just after his divorce was that which he had enjoyed most, but he did not seem to care about changing. May 15, 1880. I have had a good deal worse since then. October 14, 1883. And I don't feel very well now. October , 1884; but since the end of 1886 I really do not see that I have had much to grumble about.[1] February 17, 1892.

MRS. BOSS[1]   247

aid that if Alice[2] meant bringing my cousin's children to tea she supposed she should have to grease her sides (for a curtsey).

MY THEORY OF THE UNCONSCIOUS   248

oes not lead to universal unconsciousness, but only to pigeon holing, and putting y. We shall always get new things to worry about.

MR. AND MRS. RUSH   24•

They kept the Plough at Eynsford.[1] Mr. Rush was very poorly. I saw Mrs
Rush in the kitchen making a pudding. I said I was so sorry to see Mr. Rush s•
ill &c. &c. She lisped slightly and said, "Yeth thir, and I'm tho poorly myself•
very poorly--we think it'th our liverth, thir."

THE LEVELLING OF THE BIBLE   25•

All men being equal before God &c.[1]--this is an unconscious recognition o
the vastness of our common universal history as compared with that of our mor
recent human civilisation. March 15, 1880.

ART NOTE   25

To impress a form on one's mind when one has nothing to draw with, trac
an outline on the palm of the left hand, with the right forefinger.

INSTINCT AND ORGAN   25•

are departments or details of mind and matter, and are functions of one another•
that is to say, there can be no variation in the one without corresponding variatio
in the other--as mind and matter generally are functions one of another.

COAXING GOD   25•

When we pray that God will be pleased to do with us according to his will
we are trying to coax him into having his own way.

NAME   25•

Charity Monk (from a tombstone).

SUBJECT   25•

The Psalms of David from a literary standpoint.

[THE] * GODS   25•

are those who either have money, or do not want it.

PAUL'S WILD BEASTS   257

at Ephesus.[1] They cannot have been very wild wild beasts. I do not believe he would have held his own against anything more alarming than a field mouse or a cock canary. He must have meant human wild beasts.

STREET PREACHER   258
(use in *Ernest Pontifex*)

Mr. Heatherley[1] once heard a man say, "I don't know a big A, mind you, from a bull's foot, but I can argue with any one about religion. What does this man mean who has been preaching to us about religion? Has he ever seen the bloke up there," pointing to the skies, "or the bloke down there?"--pointing downwards? cf. Ecclesiastes III:21.[2]

MAN IS A PARASITE   259

on the lower animals and on vegetables as much as the mistletoe is upon the oak. And the lower animals are the same. We live on one another's credit, and we do not know what it is all based on.

PROSELYTISING   260

We can only proselytise fresh meat. Putrid meat begins to have strong convictions of its own.

QUARRELING WITH ONE'S FATHER   261

A man begins to do this about nine months before he is born. He then begins worrying his father to let him have a separate establishment, till the father finds him a nuisance and lets him have his own way.

SUBJECT   262

On the art of leaving money.

COOLING OF THE EARTH'S CRUST   263

Is there any evidence that the earth's crust is now cooling? No doubt there is. I must look it up.

STOAT WITH BITTEN-OFF LEGS   264

In the window of 'Land & Water', Fleet Street[1], I saw for many weeks a stuffed stoat, that had bitten off three of its legs, in order to escape from traps in which it had been caught. Remember this *re* serpents--whose ancestors had legs.

to conceal her want of emotion.[1]

MRS. BOSS   266

She said she wished the horn would blow for her and the worms take her that very night.

HANDEL NOTES   267

Similarity between overture to *Jephtha* and "the monster Polyphe-eme."[1]--So also between "the goodly fellowship of prophets" *Dettingen Te Deum*, and "the muses singing round Jove's altar" in the Allegro and Penseroso.[2] So also between "then by god and man detested" in "Envy eldest born of hell" and "a man of sorrows" in "He was despised."[3]

LIFE AND SPONTANEOUS GENERATION   268

Unless we begin with life of some kind omnipresent throughout matter we must have spontaneous generation--*i.e.*, transition from absolutely non-living to absolutely living--somewhere. Yet the very men who are loudest in insisting on the impossibility of this insist at the same time on that which must either come to this in the end as regards their original form or forms of life, or rest on the omnipresence of low or potential life throughout matter.

So those who most deny the possibility of *a priori* knowledge, most insist on its existence, in instinct. See *Westminster Review*, April (?), 1880.[1]

[Change is only spontaneous generation made easy--it is hidden spontaneous generation, like hidden fifths in music. It seems to me that you must not begin with life or potential life everywhere, alone, nor with a single (or more) spontaneous generations alone, but you must carry your spontaneous generation or denial of the continuity of life down *ad infinitum*, just as you must carry your continuity of life, or denial of spontaneous generation down *ad infinitum*, and compatible or incompatible, you must write a scientific Athanasian creed to comprehend these two incomprehensibles.[2]

If, then, it is only an escape from one incomprehensible position to another-- *cui bono* to make a change? Why not stay quietly in the Athanasian creed as we are? I can give no answer to this as regards the unintelligible clauses, for what we come to in the end is just as abhorrent to reason and inconceivable by it as what they offer us; but as regards the intelligible parts--that Christ was born of a virgin died, rose from the dead--we say that if it was not for the prestige that belief in these alleged facts has obtained we should refuse attention to them. As it is, our of respect to the mass of opinion that accepts them, we have looked into the matter with care, and find the evidence break down.]

ART NOTES   269

Art has no end in view save the emphasizing and recording in the most effective way some strongly felt interest or affection. Where either interest, or desire to record with good effect is wanting, there is but sham art, or none at all: where both hese are fully present, no matter how rudely and inarticulately, there is great art. Art is at best a dress--important--yet still nothing in comparison with the wearer, and as a general rule the less it attracts attention the better.

ART NOTE 270

The mind accepts inconsistencies and inaccuracies in a picture as it accepts dreams--gratefully, if they are peaceful or amusing.

ART NOTE 271

When we go to pictures, we go for the most part to be taken both into common life and out of it.

Written in 1880   Revised February 19, 1892

ART NOTE 272

Wise execution in painting is a mode of wit, and consists mainly in truth and brevity.

ART NOTE 273

Truth in painting only means the nearest approach to truth that can be got with the most economical use of the resources at command.

ANIMALS AND VEGETABLES 274

are all more or less specialists, and only modify their species in virtue of having modified their special subjects of interest and study. Bodily form is the expression of organized opinion, and the one will vary as the other.

THICK ENOUGH ON THE TONGUE 275

I once heard a man say that some beer was not thick enough on the tongue for him.

HANDEL'S "TOTAL ECLIPSE"[1] 276

If I remember rightly the opening symphony that introduces the air is a five bar phrase--*i.e.*, a four bar phrase prolonged, to express the increase of distance which we all feel when groping after something in the dark.

Jones told me one day that he had seen a letter in the office: "Dear Sir—beg to send you the name of the solicitor of the young lady to whom I am engaged Her name is Agnes Merrifield of 26 J—— Street, Manchester: [my]* name is Jame Thompson of —— London." I said it reminded me of the opening bars of "Welcome Mighty King" in *Saul*:[1]

MONEY 278

is the last enemy that shall never be subdued. While there is flesh there is money—or the want of money, but money is always on the brain, so long as there is a brain in reasonable order.

Written November 14, 1880   Edited November 23, 1893[1]

DEATH AND CHANGE OF OUR OPINIONS 279

We retain our identity for two or three days after death quite as obviously as during the rapid changes that take place in our early embryonic development All the essentials of individuality continue for a time (and hence to some extent also for all time) as much after death as before it. The "we" is changed as it ha been changed many a time already, but it is not extinguished, except in so far a all change is an extinguishing. Death is indeed a great change in our opinions; when we are dead we shall no longer care for the things we now care for, but we shall care for some things. There is neither death nor life as we now understand these things; they are swallowed up each in one another.

SUDDEN DEATH 280

Those who die suddenly and without warning not only never die (in the sense in which no man ever dies to himself), but never even think they are going to die soon. A man knocked to pieces by a passing train while greasing wheel boxes does not even leave off greasing wheel boxes so far as he is himself concerned, but goes on greasing them for ever and ever for such an infinity of time as is practically no time at all. Or how about one who eats a good dinner and goes to sleep after it too near a charcoal fire of which he knew nothing?

I have never in my life succeeded in being this. Sometimes I get new clothes, and am tidy for a while in part, meanwhile the hat, tie, boots, gloves and under-clothing all clamour for attention and before I have got them all well in hand the clothes have lost their freshness. Still if ever I do get any money I will try and make myself really spruce all round for about a week, till I have found out as I probably shall--that if I give my clothes an inch they will taken an ell.

Written November 1880   Revised November 1893

WE SHALL SOON LEAVE OFF   282

growing anything that we can get made for us, and buy. In the end the only thing that will be grown within the womb of rich women is money. The poor will remain like the races of the lower animals, comparatively speaking, stationary.

MONEY   283

The last friend that shall not be subdued.[1]

REPRODUCTION   284

Its base must be looked for not in the desire of the parents to reproduce, but in the discontent of the germs with their surroundings inside those parents, and a desire on their part to have a separate maintenance.

ART NOTES   285

Knowledge of a man's other work and personal acquaintance with himself [is] * a great help to criticism.

A man's art work should be most conversant about that which he is most con-versant himself, *i.e.*, it should not go far afield except on a high day or a holiday.

A man should have a painting room not less than a mile from his living rooms. It was the not having this that choked me off--I mean the incessant interruptions, and temptation to go on with other work. But I suppose there was something more than this--and yet I do not know. If I had not the British Museum reading room which serves me as a studio away from home, my literary work would, I am sure, have been as great a fiasco as my painting, to which however I am continually long-ing to return. I gravitated down to that at which I found I could study fixedly and uninterruptedly away from home. If I had sold "Heatherley's Holiday," I should I feel pretty sure have stuck to painting.[1]

A man should begin to paint, or design a picture, on the day that he begins to study at all--and he should only study with a view to the subject he has decided to treat.

Study his 1787 water colours in our gallery,[1] and note that his drawings later were not at all like the places they represent.

Written November 1880   Edited November 30, 1893

THE FAMILY   287

I believe more unhappiness comes from this source than from any other--I mean from the attempt to prolong family connection unduly, and to make people hang together artificially who would never naturally do so. The mischief among the lower classes is not so great, but among the middle and upper it is killing a large number daily. And the old people do not really like it much better than the young.

HANDEL AND DICKENS   288

They buried Dickens in the very next grave, cheek by jowl with Handel. It does not matter, but it pained me to think that people who could do this could become Deans of Westminster.[1]

SEA-SICKNESS   289

or indeed any other sickness is the inarticulate expression of the pain we feel at seeing a proselyte escape us just as we were on the point of converting him.

SHALL I BE REMEMBERED AFTER DEATH?   290

I sometimes think and hope so, but I trust I may not be found out, if I ever am found out and if I ought to be found out at all--before my death. It would bother me very much and I should be much happier and better as I am. [This note I leave unaltered. I am glad to see that I had so much sense thirteen years ago. What I thought then I think now, only with greater confidence and confirmation.]

SUBJECT   291

On having a new tooth screwed in [I never had this, but I know people have them screwed in sometimes]. (Analogy between the artificial and the natural growth.)

ANTS   292

There are some that cannot stand refuse matter from the nests of other ants of their own species. See *Times*, May 24, 1880.[1]

His boots were hung over his charger, and the charger with the boots formed part of the procession. A little girl seeing this from a window said, "Mamma, when we die is there nothing left of us but our boots?"

ADAM AND EVE   294

A little boy and a little girl were looking at a picture of Adam and Eve. "Which is Adam and which Eve?" said one. "I do not know," said the other, "but I should know if they had their clothes on."

GLADSTONE AS A FINANCIER[1]   295

I said to my tobacconist that Gladstone was not a financier because he bought a lot of china at high prices, and it fetched very little when it was sold at Christie's.[2] "Did he give high prices?" said the tobacconist. "Enormous prices," said I emphatically. Now as a matter of fact I did not know whether Mr. Gladstone had ever bought the china at all: much less what he gave for it, if he did; he may have had it all left him for aught I know, but I was going to appeal to my tobacconist by arguments that he could understand, and I could see that he was much impressed.

ORGANIC AND INORGANIC   296

As people looked at glaciers for thousands of years before they found out that ice was a fluid, so it has taken them and will continue to take them not less before they see that the inorganic is not wholly inorganic.

EREWHONISM   297

See letter to *Times*, June 2, 1880, on the treatment of the insane.[1]

BORROMEO, COUNT GUIDO[1]   298

said of his descendants, "Tutti buoni, si, santi più." "May they be all good, but let us have no more saints." He had had two in his family, and they are, or at any rate have been, ruinously expensive.

Written November 1880   Edited December 1, 1893

PIERS PLOWMAN--SUBJECT   299

Write a complaint in this fashion of an over-educated English, middle class youth who finds himself steady, worthy in all respects, but unmarketable.

Dialogue between them on the night that Isaac came down from the mountain with his father. The rebellious Ishmael tries to stir up Isaac, and that good young man explains the righteousness of the transaction--without much effect.[1]

CARLYLE AND MIRABEAU   301

Carlyle must be a fraud (but of course he was) for he says in his *French Revolution* that Mirabeau loved his father who had treated him abominably and imprisoned him, and admires Mirabeau all the same.[1] Therefore Carlyle is more of either knave or fool than people can be allowed to be without being considered humbugs.

ISAAC OFFERING UP ABRAHAM   302

This I imagine would have been very wrong, no matter how plainly God told Isaac to do it. Fancy Abraham letting Isaac get him on to the mountain on such a ridiculous pretence as this.[1]

SUBJECTS   303

On the art of knowing what gives us pleasure. On the art of quarreling. Christian deathbeds. Literary struldbrugs. The limits of good faith . The third class excursion train or steam boat as the church of the future.

On the utter speculation involved in much of the good advice that is commonly given--as never to sell a reversion &c.

Tracts for children warning them against the virtues of their elders.

On making ready for death as a means of prolonging life.

[A] * *Porpoise* that knew it was to be stuffed and set up in a glass case after death, and said that it looked forward to it as a life of endless happiness.

Written November 1880   Rewritten Saturday, December 2, 1893

MY BACON FOR BREAKFAST   304

Now, when I am abroad, being older and taking less exercise, I do not want any breakfast beyond coffee and bread and butter, but when this note was written I liked a modest rasher of bacon as well, and have often noticed the jealous indignation with which heads of families who enjoyed the privilege of Cephas and the brethren of our Lord regarded it.[1] There were they with three or four elderly unmarried daughters, as well as old mamma: How could they afford bacon? And there was I, a selfish bachelor . . . . The appetising savoury smell of my rasher seemed to drive them mad. I used to feel very uncomfortable, very small, and quite aware how low it was of me to have bacon for breakfast and no daughters, instead of daughters and no bacon, but when I consulted the oracles of heaven about it I was always told to stick to my bacon and not to make a fool of myself. I despise myself, but have not withered under my own contempt so completely as I ought to have done.[2]

SUBJECTS 305

China lamb and shepherdess on public house chimney piece as against Madonna and child.

Earl Yniols. See the story in the original prose, and in Tennyson's poem.[1]

Art of propagating opinion. The habitual teetotaller. Essay on human misunderstanding. The irreligion of the future. Man and man, and man and woman.

Family prayers, a series of perfectly plain and sensible ones asking for what people generally do want without any kind of humbug.

A WOMAN CAME FROM NORTHUMBERLAND 306

to London to see her daughter who lived in some little backstreet in Whitechapel. She went out, lost her way, forgot the name of the street and had to go back all the way to Northumberland before she could hitch on to her connections again.

Written about November 1880   Edited December 21, 1893

ON BEING UNKNOWN 307

Lord Beaconsfield makes a character say: "But at any rate do not at present be discontented that you are unknown. It is the first condition of real power." *Endymion*, I, 331.[1]
I wonder how far this is true: not I imagine very far.

Written about November 1880   Edited December 21, 1893
                                      and September 27, 1894

CROESUS'S KITCHEN MAID[1] 308

She was part of him, bone of his bone and of his flesh, for she eats what comes down from his table, and being fed of one flesh are they not brothers and sisters to one another in virtue of community of nutriment which is but a thinly veiled travesty of descent? When she eats peas with her knife he does so; there is not a mouthful of bread and butter she eats, nor lump of sugar she drops into her tea but he knows it altogether though he knows nothing whatever about it. She is en-Croesus-ed and he enscullery-maided so long as she remains linked to him by the golden chain that passes from his pocket, and which is greatest of all unifiers.

True, neither party is aware of the connection at all, as long as things go smoothly. Croesus no more knows the name of, or feels the existence of his kitchen maid than a peasant in health knows about his liver; still he is awakened to a dim sense of an undefined something when he pays his grocer or his baker. She is more definitely aware of him than he of her, but it is by way of an overshadowing presence rather than a clear and intelligent comprehension. And though Croesus does not eat his kitchen-maid's meals otherwise than vicariously, still to eat vicariously is to eat; the meals so eaten by his kitchen maid nourish the better ordering of the dinner which nourishes and engenders the better ordering of Croesus himself: he is fed therefore by the feeding of his kitchen maid.

And so with sleep. When she goes to bed, he in part does so. When she gets up and lays the fire in the back-kitchen he in part does so. He lays it through her and in her though knowing no more about his action than we do when we wink or digest, but still doing it as by what we call a reflex action. *Qui facit per alium facit per se;*[2] and when the back kitchen fire is lighted on Croesus's behalf, it is Croesus who lights it though he is all the time fast asleep in bed.

If he discharges his kitchen maid and gets another, it is as though he cut out a small piece of his finger and replaced it in due course by growth. But even the slightest cut may lead to blood poisoning, and so even the dismissal of a kitchen maid may be big with the fate of empires. Thus the cook, a valued servant, may take the kitchen maid's part and go too. The next cook may spoil the dinner and upset Croesus's temper, and from this all manner of consequences may be evolved, even to the dethronement and death of the king himself. Nevertheless as a general rule, an injury to such a low part of a great monarch's organism as a kitchen-maid has no serious results. It is only when we are attacked in such more vital organs as the solicitor or the banker that we need be seriously uneasy.

It is certain as we have seen that when Croesus's kitchen maid lights the fire it is really Croesus who is lighting it, but it is less obvious that when Croesus goes to a ball the scullery maid goes also. Still this should be held in the same way as it should be also held that she eats vicariously when Croesus does so. For what he eats comes out in his requiring to keep a larger establishment--whereby the scullery-maid keeps her place as part of Croesus's organism and is nourished also.

On the other hand, when Croesus dies it does not follow that the scullery maid should die at the same time. She may grown a new Croesus, as Croesus, if the maid dies, will probably grow a new kitchen maid; Croesus's son or successor may take over the kingdom and palace, and the kitchen maid, beyond having to wash up a few extra plates and dishes at Coronation time, will know nothing about the change; it is as though the establishment had had its hair cut and its beard trimmed; it is smartened up a little, but there is no other change. If on the other hand he goes bankrupt, or his kingdom is taken from him and his whole establishment is broken up and dissipated at the auction mart, then even though not one of its component cells actually dies, the organism as a whole does so, and it is interesting to see that the lowest, least specialised, and least highly differentiated parts of the organism such as the scullery-maids and stable-boys most readily find an entry into the life of some new system, while the more specialised and highly differentiated parts such as the steward, the old housekeeper, or still more so the librarian or the chaplain, may never be able to attach themselves to any new combination, and may die in consequence. I heard once of a large builder who retired somewhat unexpectedly from business and broke up his establishment--to the actual death of several of his older employees.

So a bit of flesh or even a finger may be taken from one body and grafted on to another, but a leg cannot be grafted. If a leg is cut off it must die. It may however be maintained the owner dies too even though he recovers, for a man who has lost a leg is not the man he was.

Written about November 1880   Edited September 27, 1894

GOD, STATES, HOUSEHOLDS, INDIVIDUALS, AND THE CELLS OF WHICH INDIVIDUALS ARE COMPOSED   309

The extremes are unknown. If we would study them we must do so by the help of the means--with which we are more familiar.

ACCIDENTAL VARIATIONS   310

When Jones was ill at Cambridge he ordered a boiled rabbit smothered in onions. By some mistake they sent him a boiled fowl smothered in onions instead. This accidental variation was adopted by Jones, and from time to time he has repeated it.

Written about November 1880   Edited September 29, 1894

CONSCIOUSNESS AND HERBERT SPENCER   311

Herbert Spencer speaks of "the body of our consciousness"; he has tried as many others have done to articulate the skeleton of that body, but it does not seem to admit of very definite articulation--if such words may be pardoned.

A SENSIBLE CLASSIFIER   312

hould be like a sensible painter, and treat things broadly, considering rather how ew than how many distinctions he can draw.

113

I believe I just remember Dr. Butler. I had a vision of myself before a nursery fire with Dr. Butler walking up and down the room and watching my sister Harrie and myself. The nursery was not our Langar nursery; for a long time I thought thi must be fancy, but on finding from Archdeacon Lloyd that we were at Eccleshal at the end of 1838 I think it is probably true. My brother William died January 4, 1839 when I was 3 years and one month old. This I can remember distinctly My grandfather's death in 1839 (December 4) I remember vividly.[1] I was in the nursery--which became afterwards my mother's room--*i.e.* the first floor roon of the rectory that had one window looking East and two looking South. Mrs Watchorn had given me a little pot of honey as a birthday present, it being my birthday, and a string of bird's eggs. My father came in, told us grandpapa wa dead, and took the honey away saying it would not be good for me.

I was born in what was afterwards the best spare room, *i.e.* the westernmos first floor room on the left as you look towards the house. The room my brothe and I had, and which was always called the boys' room was the one next to thi with nothing but a thin partition between the two, and two windows looking North

A MONAD OF MIND   31

All the varied forms of thought and action are evolved as it were from a mona of thought and action--a sense of shock with slight consequent modification. Action descend with modification as much as organisms do, and change with change conditions.

THE BIBLE   31

may be the truth, but it is not the whole truth and nothing but the truth.

HANDEL AND THE WETTERHORN   31

When last I saw the Wetterhorn I caught myself involuntarily humming

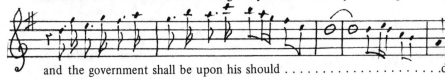

and the government shall be upon his should .d

The big shoulder of the Wetterhorn seemed to fall just like the run on "shoulder."

ART NOTES   31

Neither artist nor spectator ever see the same thing twice. *Masaccio's ow nose,* is I take [it] * the source of that peculiar type of nose which began with hi [?] and ran through Filippo Lippi, Filippino Lippi, Ghirlandajo, Pallaiuolo an others, coming to an end with Sandro Botticelli.[1]

We said we knew Blake was no good because he learned Italian at 60 in order to study Dante, and we knew Dante was no good because he ran Virgil, and we knew Virgil was no good because Tennyson ran him, and as for Tennyson--well he went without saying.[1]

CONVENIENCE AND TRUTH   319

We wonder at its being as hard often to discover convenience, as it is to discover truth. But surely convenience *is* truth.

Written about November 1880   Edited Friday, October 5, 1894

DISCOVERY   320

The contention now is not that he alone discovers who furnishes such proof as shall in the end convince, but that he alone discovers who popularises. So that no matter what a man has done, if the Cuviers, Huxleys, Tyndals, Darwins, Romanes and all such can snuff him out and then bring his discoveries forward as their own, it is they who have discovered, not he.

MIVART *RE* MAN AND THE LOWER ANIMALS   321

His contention that though the lower animals have been evolved from others still lower by descent with modification, yet man stands apart, and cannot have descended from any inferior type, is like saying that though the other planets are spheroidal, and revolve on their own axes round the sun, our own does not, for we see that its surface is flat, and that the sun goes round it, not it round the sun.[1]

MARY MAGDALENE AND THE 7 DEVILS[1]   322

There is an Indian tribe among whom a distorted version of this story is current. According to this, Christ was the devil's only begotten son whom he had sent into the world to save poor devils who were in distress. He found seven who were possessed by a Mary Magdalene and cast her off from them. But there took possession of them seven other Mary Magdalenes worse than the first.   [I need hardly say that I know of no such story.]

A. L. TAMPLIN   323

wrote a set of Messiah quadrilles.[1] I have never heard them but am told they are very funny.

The good book is almost every where prohibited.

*****

The desire of superstition is to make man stupid; her fear is that he become enlightened. Now to whom will she commit the care of making him a brute? To the scholastics, for of all the sons of Adam they are the most stupid and conceited.

*****

He who is falsely learned has by degrees lost his reason and has purchased his stupidity at too dear a rate ever to renounce it.

Helevetius, *Treatise on Man*, Engl. Trans., London, 1777, pp. 7, 8.[1]

WHAT IS BEING ALIVE?   325

If a man's body be photoed and his voice phonoed, in such quick succession of instants and for so long [that] * you may watch his minutest changes of tone and expression for half an hour, and if so many of the other phenomena of life and consciousness be given that the others go without either saying or being, in virtue of the fact that association accepts the part for the whole and jumps ever kangaroo-like to its conclusions--if moreover what he says is something which men are continually forgetting, and which may be repeated *ad infinitum* so that it be well put-- moreover if this man's other work is well known, and he is a power among men, as, we will say Shakespear, so that as we look upon him during the half hour that we can watch him and hear him we are wrapt up in him and hang upon his lips--is the man dead though he have been in his grave this twenty years? What is being alive but the presenting so many of the phenomena of life that the rest are taken for granted? And are not enough phenomena presented in this case to fulfill the conditions necessary for our thinking him alive? Surely at any rate, the man is more alive than dead, for there is neither sun nor moon, nor life nor death, any more than good or ill, but thinking makes it so.

Written about 1880   Edited October 6, 1894

WHAT IS BEING IN A PLACE?   326

Am I more in the Sistine chapel when I have first rate photographs before me of the frescoes it contains, and can study them at my leisure [not that I have the smallest wish to do so] or when I am in the Sistine chapel itself on a dull winter's day and pressed for time? The Sistine chapel is more in the autotype gallery in Rathbone Place[1] than it is at Rome.

So again he that is examining the moon through some great telescope is more in the moon than he is on earth.

It was a pet saying with him that men could not get rich by continually swapping knives.

LIGHTNING   328

does not descend in a perpendicular flash, but in a fine shower. See *Times* of May 18 and June 24, 1880.[1]

FIRE   329

I was at one the other night and heard a man say, "That corner stack is alight now quite nicely." People's sympathies seem generally to be with the fire so long as no one is in danger of being burned.

ART NOTE--COLOURISTS   330

A man cannot be a great colourist unless he is a great deal more. A great colourist is no better than a great wordist unless the colour is well applied to a subject which at any rate is not repellent.

A FRIEND   331

who cannot at a pinch remember a thing or two that never happned is as bad as one who does not know how to forget.

ST. MICHAEL   332

He contended with the devil about the body of Moses. Now I do not believe that a reasonable person would contend about this with any body or any thing.[1]

Written about November 1880   Edited Tuesday, October 16, 1894

CHRIST   333

He has been so important an organ in the world's body for so long a time that he must surely remain long as a rudimentary organ even when no longer actively employed.

SUBJECT   334

An essay on human misunderstanding. So McCulloch used to say that he drew a great many lines and saved the best of them.[1] Illusion, or mistake, or action taken in the dark, is one of the main sources of our progress.

These so far as I can see are the ones whose conduct is least likely to be un-natural.

QUI DIMIDIUM FACTI HABET BENE INCEPIT[1]   336

At any rate I have generally found that it was not till I had half done a book that I was quite clear what it was going to be.

THE IMPORTANCE OF LITTLE THINGS   337

This is all very true but so also is the unimportance even of great things--sooner or later.

THE EDITOR OF THE *TIMES*
NEGOTIATING MARRIAGES   338

See letter in *Times*, October 28, 1880 or a few days later, asking the editor whether it was true, as the writer had been given to understand, that the editor negotiated marriages, and if so what were his charges.[1]

ACTION OF ANTS   339

in enriching the soil, as also that of all insect life and of moles, mice &c.

SCIENCE AND RELIGION   340

are reconciled in amiable and sensible people but nowhere else.

TRUE LOVERS   341

are like sunsets and sunrises--more often written and talked about than actually seen.

HE THAT IS UNFAITHFUL IN LITTLE   342

will be unfaithful also in much.

Written about November 1880   Edited October 18, 1894

CONSCIOUSNESS   343

When consciousness has been reawakened about any matter, unconsciousness can as a general rule only be regained by beginning again at a very early stage, and repeating, in an abbreviated form, the earlier stages of experiment and failure. Man has resumed consciousness about some things in respect of which the lower animals are still unconsciously satisfied, as that self-interest is the main spring of ordinary action. Hence self-interest is less paramount with him than with them. Progress is impossible without a good deal of occasional resumption of consciousness. Such resumption is only possible as the result of accumulated capital which permits the necessary leisure.

THE DAMNATION OF UNITARIANS   344

Mr. Dally, the scripture reader at St. James's, Piccadilly, when I was working as a lay helper under Perring,[1] once said to me that "there were several things which would promote the damnation of Unitarians."

HABITUAL TEETOTALLERS   345

There should be asylums for such people. But they would probably relapse into teetotalism as soon as they came out.

MRS. HUDSON   346

I mean the wife of the once famous railway king.[1] In my young days she was the typical *nouvelle riche* and all sorts of stories used to be told about her. When I first knew her in 1864 she was very old and in very narrow circumstances. She was then living apart from her husband with whom she could not get on--or who could not get on with her, and I should say small wonder for she had an awful temper. She was always changing her lodgings and used to tell me dreadful stories about the landlady of every house she went into. She was very slow in speaking, and measured her sentences with great care to make them balance as she considered a well turned sentence should do. I only remember one, but it is typical of all I ever heard her say. It ran--"You see the world, and all that it contains, is wrapped up in such curious forms, that it is only by a knowledge of human nature that you can tell rightly what to do, to say, and to admire." I once told Jones of this and he said it was like an Academy picture.

DILATORY COURTSHIP   347

I heard not long since of a father who had long tolerated a visit from a young man, who while appearing to pay his addresses to a daughter of the house would not come to the point. At last he announced his intention of taking his leave-- on which his host looked at him severely and said, "You may go when you have proposed." What followed I did not hear.

CONTRALTO VOICE   348

My mother used to say that my elder sister[1] had a beautiful contralto voice. This was arrived at not through her ability to reach the low notes--which she could not do--but because she could not reach the high ones.

FAITH, THROUGH WANT OF   349

Through want of faith in any but natural means, a man may perhaps be able to remove mountains, but a good deal will depend upon the size of the mountain, and the kind of natural means in which the operator has elected to believe.[1] There is another adjunct moreover without which faith is ineffectual no matter how strong it may be. Faith without capital is like faith without works--dead being alone.[2]

If the natural means employed are the right ones, and they are backed sufficiently by capital, and if they are in the hands of competent people, and finally if the mountain is not too large, the mountain will be removed whether the one who sets the whole thing going has a strong faith or a weak one. Provided it is strong enough to remove the capital from the hands of its possessor to those of the work-people employed, it will be as strong as there is any occasion for it to be, and given the conditions already mentioned, it will remove the mountain.

WHAT HAPPENS TO YOU WHEN YOU DIE?   350

Jones was asked this question the other day, and answered by asking what happens to you when you are born? In the one case we are born and in the other we die, but it is not possible to get much further.

A ONE-SIDED MEETING   351

"I received your instructions to meet Mr. ------ at Putney on Friday morning: I did so but he was not there." My cousin Reginald saw this letter.

UNCONSCIOUS CEREBRATION   352

One morning I was whistling to myself the air "In sweetest Harmony," from *Saul*. Jones heard me and said, "Do you know why you are whistling that?" I said I did not; then he said, "Did you not hear me two minutes ago whistling 'Eagles were not so swift'?" I had not noticed his having done so and it was so long since I had played this air myself that I doubt whether I should have consciously recognised it. That I did recognise it unconsciously is tolerably clear from my having gone on to "In sweetest Harmony," which is the air that follows it.[1]

EREWHON REVISITED   353

They give commissions to such and such an eminent sculptor not to make a statue of the person they intend to honour. They subscribe the money, and pay the sculptor, who is expected to return the funds to the several subscribers. An impressive ceremony then takes place at the grave of the deceased, whose shade is invoked, and, on its appearing, is told to consider itself as having had a statue erected in its honour.[1]

There was a man who maintained that no man ought to let himself be made a martyr to his convictions. He held this opinion so strongly that, rather than give it up, he allowed himself to be burned alive--thus becoming after all a martyr to his convictions.

Written about November, 1880   Edited October 25, 1894

DREAM OF A GIANT   355

I saw him wet his thumb and put [it]* down on half a dozen men and women whom he thus picked up and brought close up to his eyes to sample them as a gardener samples small seeds.

CHRIST   356

He goes about as a roaring lion seeking whom he may devour.[1]

EAST LONDON AND RELIGION   357

See *Times*, September 29, 1880 (report of Church Congress), a speech by the bishop of Bedford on the indifference of East Londoners to religion.[1]

ANTS   358

See *Times*, September 30, 1880, and *Journal of [the]* Linnean Society* for September, 1880.[1] They have a language--live six years--and keep aphids' eggs all through the winter.

THE RIGHTEOUS   359

The psalmist says (Ps. 34) that the righteous shall not lack for anything that is good.[1] Should it not rather be that those who do not lack anything that is good find it easy to be fairly righteous? Or that they who do not lack &c. are generally taken as righteous?

COOPER'S[1] FUNERAL   360

Jones telling me about this said, ". . . and then a gentleman in a white surplice met us at the gate and announced himself as the resurrection and the life. A man looked down into the grave when the body was lowered, and said cheerfully, 'It seems to be a nice gravelly soil,' and then they all went away."

We being all members of God, it is He that eats his dinner in us, as much as we that eat it in Him, and when we say grace, it is really God in us thanking us for having eaten his dinner for him. Seeing then that we have to thank him for having been so kind as to select us as the vehicles of his dinner, and that he has to thank us back again for having conveyed it to him, there is a debtor and creditor account between him and us, the entries in which so nearly balance that, except as a matter of politeness, one hardly sees much use in entering either. God is not so punctilious as some people would make him out, and provided he gets his dinner fairly good, and fairly punctual, and fairly cheap, he will not make a fuss about want of napkins. Highly cultured people, being farther removed from the sources of God's grace, find it necessary to use more ceremony, but those who know God better understand that the only thing about which he is at all stiff is about having his dinner through you, and not through any one else. If you wish to get the credit of having eaten it for him, when all the time it was really somebody else that did so, there is no one who is less likely to be imposed upon, or more certain to mark his displeasure in ways about which there will be no mistake. The most sensible grace, if any, should be something like this: "I hope, O Lord, that you are going to have a good dinner, and that it will agree with me for you. Remember, O God, that at all times and in all places, whenever you have anything extra special which you would like to eat I shall always be delighted to eat it for you"; and then after dinner there might be an alternative grace congratulatory or otherwise, according as the dinner had been punctual, well cooked &c. or no.

Written about November, 1880   Edited October 29, 189[4] *

THE LOST BARREL ORGAN   362

Jones once saw the following advertisement on Eyre Street Hill: "Lost a barrel organ; plays the following tunes:--The Old Hundreth, Last Rose of Summer, They All Do It, Roaring Jelly, the rest unknown. The man is dark, about 5 ft. 6 in., was dressed in a round coat and wideawake hat, and flat-footed.

Any one meeting the man and stopping the organ will received £5 reward."

Written about November, 1880   Edited October 29 and 30, 1894

MISS BUCKLEY AND MR. DARWIN   363

About my quarrel with him (she is now Mrs. Fisher).[1] She had been to dine and sleep at Down (October, 1880) and I saw her in the Museum afterwards. She said Mr. Darwin had no idea that the last sentence of Dr. Krause's *Erasmus Darwin* was what it was. He knew nothing of what Dr. Krause had written, and was not responsible for it; he was just asked to write a preface, and that was all he had to do with the matter.[2]

My answer to this was, "Then why did not Mr. Darwin say this in his letter to me, and why did he not write to the *Athenaeum* and say so when I wrote to the *Athenaeum* in January, 1880. If he had done this, neither I nor any one else would have believed him, but we should have been bound to say we did, and I should have said no more."

Her second plea was that Mr. Darwin was at a complete loss to understand what my indignation was all about. "I am sure," said he, "that I must have done something very dreadful for he seems very angry, and if I only knew what it was I should be &c. &c." She quoted these as his words, imitating a plaintive tone as of an injured innocent.

Plea 3 was the nobleness and beauty of Mr. Darwin's character. He was not as other men are.

Plea 4 was that it was all a piece of personal pique on my part. "If," said she, "there is one thing which I detest and despise more than another it is a merely personal dispute. You cannot put up with anything that wounds your self esteem." What she meant by this last I do not know. She gave me the impression of wishing to go as far as she dared in the direction of saying that I had taken some private personal offence with Mr. Darwin of a nature quite different to that which I pretended in public, and that it was something to do with some wound my vanity had received. She did not say this outright but her manner was extremely angry, and the impression left upon my mind was that she was accusing me of private personal malice. I said, "Why Miss Buckley, it is not a private matter, it is a public one." "Who cares two straws about it?" said she fiercely--as though plea 5 were about to consist in the contention that Mr. Darwin was so strong and I so insignificant that it did not matter what he did.

Then she went on to say that I had to thank Mr. Darwin for having saved me from some very rough treatment at Dr. Krause's hands inasmuch as Dr. Krause had sent back his revised article to Mr. Darwin, with open attacks upon me of a very severe character (Crawley[3] had already told me this), and that Mr. Darwin had interfered, and had said, "No, this is not the place for an attack upon Mr. Butler," so all these passages were cut out, and I ought to be very grateful, but unfortunately the last paragraph was left.

This last constitutes plea 6. How it is reconcileable with plea 1--that Mr. Darwin did not know anything about what Dr. Krause had written--I do not quite see.

I was beginning to lose my own temper now, so I closed the conversation. A few days afterwards I met her again and tackled her. She was then more reasonable, and said nothing but h'm h'm, to all I said.

A few days after this, Miss Savage met her and Mr. Garnett[4] flirting down Berners Street (quite innocently but good square flirting). The postman was taking letters out of a pillar box, and as soon as the two had passed he put his thumb over his shoulder, and winked at Miss Savage--who told me this herself.

MOUSE IDEAS AND CAT IDEAS   364

There are some ideas which are like mice; no sooner have we stopped their holes in one place than they gnaw themselves new ones in another, turning up again and again *ad infinitum*. The only thing to do is to keep a cat idea, so to speak, which shall assimilate them, comprehend them, or more plainly gobble them up, as soon as they put in an appearance.

AURORA BOREALIS[1]   365

I saw one once in the Gulf of the St. Lawrence off the island of Anticosti. We were in the middle of it, and seemed to be looking up through a great cone of light millions and millions of miles into the sky. Then we saw it further off, and the pillars of fire stalked up and down the face of heaven like one of Handel's great basses. (I used this more or less in the Piora chapter of *Alps and Sanctuaries*.)[2]

TITLE   366

The treasury of unbelief.

PLEASURE, ON KNOWING WHAT GIVES US   367

People talk as though this were an easy matter, and so it is, in respect of things with which a person is well conversant; but where a subject is less familiar it is less easy,[1] and where it is completely new, no opinion can be formed at all. If i can, it will be found later that the opinion is unstable or that the subject was not really so new as it seemed.

People do not seem to know the importance of finding out what it is that gives them pleasure beyond in mere matters of eating and drinking, if, that is to say, they would make themselves as comfortable here as they reasonably can. Very few however seem to care greatly whether they are comfortable or no. At least one half of the misery which meets us daily might be removed, or at any rate greatly alleviated, if those who suffer by it would think it worth their while to be at any pains to get rid of it; that they do not so think, is proof that they neither know nor care to know, more than in a very languid way, what it is that will relieve them most effectually; or in other words that the shoe does not really pinch them so hard as we think it does. For when it really pinches, as when a man is being flogged, he will seek relief by any means in his power. So my great namesake said "Surely the pleasure is as great of being cheated as to cheat,"[2] and so again I remember to have seen a poem many years ago in *Punch* according to which a certain young lady being discontented at home went out into the world in quest to "Some burden make or burden bear, but which she did not greatly care." So long as there was discomfort somewhere it was all right.

To those however who are desirous of knowing what gives them pleasure but do not quite know how to set about it, I have no better advice to give than that they must take the same pains about acquiring this difficult art as about any other, and must acquire it in the same way--that is by attending to one thing at a time and not being in too great a hurry. Proficiency is not to be obtained here any more than elsewhere by short cuts, or by getting other people to do work that no other but oneself can do. Above all things it is necessary here, as in all other branches of study, not to think that one knows a thing before one does know it--to make sure of one's ground and be quite certain that one really does like a thing before one says one does. When one cannot decide whether one likes a thing or not, nothing is easier than to say so, and to hang it up among the uncertainties.

Written about November, 1880   Edited October 31, 1894

SCHUMANN'S MUSIC   368

I should like to like it better than I do; I dare say I could make myself like it better if I tried; but I do not like having to try to make myself like things; I like things that make me like them at once and no trying at all.

PALEY, THE REV. G. OF FRECKENHAM[1]   369

When I went there with my friend Paley, which I more than once did, I knew nothing about the former incumbent of Freckenham, Mr. Tillbrook, whose letters to my grandfather have since fascinated me.[2] Old Mr. Paley must have been a fellow of Peterhouse in Tillbrook's time and must have known him well. This however is not in the note that I am editing. That note was to the effect that when Henry Hoare was courting Miss Paley, he took an unconscionably long time in coming to the point. At breakfast one day he was talking and laying down the law about long engagements. "I do not like long engagements." said he. "Do you, Mr. Paley?" "No," was the answer, "nor yet long courtships."[3]

Written about November 1880   Edited November 5, 1894

WILD HOT WATER   370

A young student at Heatherley's[1] once asked me if New Zealand was not the place where the hot water grows wild.

125

The question whether such and such a course of conduct does or does not d
physical harm[1] is the safest test by which to try the question whether it is mor
or no. If it does no harm to the body, we ought to be very chary of calling it im
moral, while if it tends towards physical excellence, there should be no hesitatio
in calling it moral. Overwork is as immoral in the case of those who are not force
to overwork themselves (and there are many who work themselves to death for th
mere inability to restrain the passion for work which masters them as the cravin
for drink masters a drunkard)--overwork in these cases is as immoral as over-eatin
or drinking. This, so far as the individual is concerned; as regards the body politi
as a whole it is no doubt well that there should be some men and women so bui
as that they cannot be stopped from working themselves to death, just as it is u
questionably well that there should be some who cannot be stopped from drinkin
themselves to death, if only that they may keep the horror of the habit well in ev
dence.

IDIOTS   37

An idiot is a person who thinks for himself instead of letting other people thin
for him. He takes his own views of things and therefore not unfrequently differ
from his neighbours. Any person who differs considerably from his neighbours i
an idiot *ipso facto*.

A MAN   37

is a passing mood or thought coming and going in the mind of his country: he i
the twitching of a nerve, a smile, a frown, a thought of shame or honour, as it ma
happen.

MORALITY, THE STRIVING FOR A CODE OF   37

The English strive after a fixed immutable code of morality, as classifiers striv
after irrefragable definitions of species, or foreign nations after a written and un
questionable constitution.

GENTLEMAN   37

If we are asked what is the most essential characteristic that underlies this word
the word itself will guide us to gentleness, absence of browbeating or overbearin
manners, absence of fuss, and generally consideration for other people.

Written about November, 1880   Edited November 5 and 6, 189

A writer in the *Pall Mall Gazette*--I think in 1874 or 1875, and in the autumn months but I cannot now remember--summed up Homer's conception of a God as that of a "superlatively strong, amorous, beautiful, brave, and cunning man."[1]

This is pretty much what a good working God ought to be, but he should also be kind and have a strong sense of humour. After having said the above the writer goes on, "An impratial critic can judge for himself how far, if at all, this is elevated above the level of mere fetish worship." Perhaps it is that I am not an impartial critic but if I am allowed to be so, I should say that the elevation above mere fetish worship was very considerable.

Written about November, 1880   Edited November 6, 1894

ARGUMENTUM AD HOMINEM   377

So far from being a poor argument, this is one of the most powerful in the whole armoury of logic; there are few if any more justly cogent--provided always that it does not raise another argument about the *homo*.

Written about November, 1880   Edited November 6 and November 23, 1894

MY BOOK *UNCONSCIOUS MEMORY*   378

This has gone round the press to reviewers this day (November 5, 1880). I do not know whether it will help me to get the *Life and Habit* theory ventilated, but if I do get a hearing, it will be almost solely due to Mr. Darwin's blundering. If he had not done what he did in *Erasmus Darwin*, I might have written all my life to no purpose.[1]

I have let this note stand exactly as I found it, but it being now 14 years and a day since I wrote it, I cannot help wondering whether or not *Unconscious Memory* was or was not a wise move as regards the getting a hearing for *Life and Habit* -- which is the thing about which I was and still am most anxious. I do not know; but policy or no policy, Mr. Darwin having done what he did and having made no *amende* when his attention was called to it in the *Athenaeum*,[2] *Unconscious Memory* was inevitable. Such an attempt to ride roughshod over me by a man who was by way of being such a *preux chevalier* as Mr. Darwin set my back up, and I determined to place the whole story on more permanent record. I do not think it added much to the odium in which I already was: nothing could well do this; to have written *Life and Habit* at all was an unforgiveable offence, and *Evolution Old and New*,[3] though it could hardly make things worse, assuredly did not mend them. I was in for a penny and might as well be in for a pound.[4] This is what I suppose I felt, for it is now so long ago that I cannot say for certain how much of what I see now I did or did not see then. Anyhow, take it all round, I should do the same again if the occasion arose, and though I cannot see that *Life and Habit* has made much overt progress, I certainly see more and more signs of its becoming quietly, I might almost say, taken for granted. At any rate, whether *Unconscious Memory* has helped *Life and Habit* or no, there can be no doubt that it, and my other books on Evolution, have had a large share in making Huxley execute the *volte-face*, to use his own words, to which I have called attention. Vol. V, page 68 of these notes.[5]

Edited November 23, 189

A MORAL SEAGULL   37?

At the Zoological Gardens I once saw a big gull picking at the head of a smalle. one that was old and feeble. When it saw me looking it went away, but when I hac turned a corner it came back again. I shewed myself, and it turned round and wen away. I repeated this process two or three times always with the same result, and concluded that the seagull had a moral sense--for what else is a moral sense but a sense that teaches to avoid things which experience has taught us are in bad economy, or more briefly, mistakes?

HANDEL AND *THEODORA* AND *SUSANNA*   380

In my preface to *Evolution Old and New* I imply a certain dissatisfaction with *Theodora* and *Susanna*, and imply also that Handel himself was so far dissatisfied that in his next work *Jephthah* (which I see I inadvertently called his last) he returned to his earlier manner.[1] It is true that these works are not in Handel's usua manner; they are more difficult and more in the style of Bach. I am glad that Handel gave us these two examples of a slightly (for it is not much) varied manner, and am interested to observe that he did not adhere to that manner in *Jephthah*, but should be sorry to convey an impression that I think *Theodora* and *Susanna* works in any way unworthy of Handel. I prefer both to *Judas Maccabeus*,[2] which, in spit of the many fine things it contains, I like perhaps the least of all his oratorios. I hav played *Theodora* and *Susanna* all through, and most parts (except the recitatives) many times over; Jones and I have gone through them again and again. I have hear Susanna performed once, and *Theodora* twice, and I find no single piece in eithe work which I do not admire, while many are as good as anything which it is in m power to conceive. I like the chorus "He saw the lovely youth " the least of any thing in *Theodora* so far as I remember at this moment, but knowing it to have bee a favourite with Handel himself I am sure that I must have missed understandin it.[3]

How comes it, I wonder, that the chorale-like air "Blessing, Honour, Adoration is omitted in Novello's edition? It is given in Clarke's edition and is very beaut ful.[4]

Jones says of "With darkness deep," that in the accompaniment to this air the monotony of dazed grief is just varied now and again with a little writhing passage.[5] Whether Handel meant this or no, the interpretation put upon the passage fits the feeling of the air. (I found this note (such as it is) dated November 14, 1880.)

CHRIST   381

He had not been married to the church a twelvemonth before he began to flirt with a most respectable married woman, the wife of a man named Grundy, and he has continued in the most open adultery with her ever since.

Edited Wednesday, February 27, 1895

DR. BUTLER AND PINDAR   382

In Dr. Butler's adnotated (M.S.) copy of Pindar, now, if I mistake not in the library of St. John's Cambridge, I found the following after the seventh Nemean Ode: So ends this most detestably cramp and crabbed ode, of which Dissen says *'tanta est praestantia ut nunquam possit satis laudari'*, and of which I say, *'tanta est obscuritas ut vel nunquam scriptum vellem vel saltem deperditum.'* "[1] I think it is *scriptum* and *deperditum* but do not feel sure.

ONE TOUCH OF THE UNNATURAL   383

makes the whole world kin.

Written November, 1880   Edited Wednesday and Thursday,
                                                       February 27 and 28, 1895

MY VISITS TO CHARLES DARWIN AT DOWN   384

I went to Down[1] twice, the first time being a few weeks after I had published *Erewhon* in 1872.[2] Mr. Darwin was exceedingly kind and I enjoyed my visit very much. I could see, however, that he did not like *Erewhon*, in spite of the polite things he said. He did like the short "philosophical dialogue" referred to by me at the end of Chapter I of *Unconscious Memory*, and published I think in 1862 in the Canterbury *Press*. He wrote to me about this when I was in New Zealand. I do not know how he came to see it. I feel sure I did not send it to him. He wrote me that he considered it one of the best things that had been written upon the subject of his book, which was not saying much for the others.[3]

Almost immediately on my arrival Mr. Darwin praised this dialogue cordially, but I felt at once that he did not like *Erewhom*. Whether it was the machines or what I could not make out--at any rate I wrote the preface to the second edition to stroke him down, because I suspected the machine chapters to be the peccant matter.[4] He asked me if I had ever read much upon kindred subjects, and when I said "no," he added, "you have caught the terminology very well," and so it dropped.

He evidently bore a grudge against my grandfather, Dr. Butler. His brother Erasm
with whom I lunched (I think in 1874), heard Charles speaking more or less dispara
ingly of my grandfather to me, and immediately checked him and said, "I do n
think you should say so, Charles, Dr. Butler was always very kind to us."[5]

I think Charles Darwin smelt mischief with me from afar; Mivart's book *Th
Genesis of Species* had already been fluttering him not a little, and an uneasy co
science may have told him that I should be sure to get hold of it sooner or late
and that when I did I was just the sort of man who would go for him.[6] Howeve
he was very kind, and won my heart; when I went away I did so quite under th
impression that the visit had been a success.

I remember George Darwin[7] shocked me by saying he did not believe in "Natur
Selection" which I took then to mean "Evolution." I could hardly believe my ea
but his brothers stopped him from saying more, and the conversation was immediate
changed, nor did I think further of the matter for some time, but I am convince
now that the sons all of them knew what a fraud the *Origin of Species* really wa

My second visit was some months later. Frank Darwin asked me down.[8] H
father, to my great surprise received me with marked coldness--so much so that I w
on the point of asking Frank for some explanation, but I did not. All the Saturda
and Sunday forenoon I felt that I had made a great blunder in coming, but nev
found out what it was all about. I do not know that I was ever, in a quiet way, ma
to feel worse at ease. On Sunday after lunch I read some of the introduction t
The Fair Haven[9] to the sons, in the smoking room. Whether they told their fath
they liked it, and advised him to be careful, I do not know; the whole thing is st
a mystery to me; but at dinner Mr. Darwin's manner was changed; he was as friend
as he had before been the reverse, and he continued so to the end of my visit. I co
cluded, therefore, that he had been ill or tired the day before, and forgave him, b
I resolved never to go to Down again. Nor was I ever asked, but as I have said abov
I met Charles Darwin and Mrs. Darwin at Erasmus Darwin's. I think in 1874. I
was then quite friendly.

P.S. I feel pretty sure that what passed when Miss Buckley was at Down la
month, was much as follows.[10] Charles Darwin said, "You know Mr. Butler is rath
a strange person; his manners are very odd: when he had written *Erewhon* we aske
him here, in fact I believe he came twice, but somehow or other neither Mrs. Darw
nor myself were attracted by him. You know how many people I am obliged to ha
here, and with my health visitors are a strain upon me, so we did not ask him an
more. I am afraid Mr. Butler has been offended by this and attacks me in cons
quence."

In my account of what passed between Miss Buckley and myself I should ha
said that when she told me she had been staying at Down, and how delightful it ha
been, I said what a charming house it was to stay at--I too had been there. She w
silent in a manner that surprised me, so I repeated what I had said, but she was aga
silent. I did not put two and two together at the time, but feel tolerably sure th
I have now done so correctly. Her silence, however, may have simply meant th
whether Down was a pleasant place to stay at or no depended in great measure o
the state of Mr. Darwin's temper at the moment.

I may also add that on my first visit I met Woolner[11] the sculptor at Dow
I did not much like him.

On my second visit I heard Mr. Darwin say that the corrections of the press o
his last book (*The Expression of the Emotions*)[12] had cost him £160. No wond

e gets his work into such a muddle.

I had a letter from him in answer to one from myself which accompanied a opy of *The Fair Haven*. Very nice and kind. He told me he thought I should do vell to turn my attention to novel-writing. All scientific people recommend me to o this.[13]

Vritten November 1880   Edited Friday, March 1, 1895

GEORGE DARWIN AND *LIFE AND HABIT*   385

When *Life and Habit* came out I sent George Darwin[1] a copy. He hurried up by eturn of post with three lines to the effect that he had not had time to read it "but seems very interesting," and this was the last I ever heard of him.

WHEN FATIGUED   386

find it rests me to write very slowly with attention to the formation of each letter. am often thus able to go on when I could not otherwise do so.

SILENCE   387

There is none so impressive as that of a hushed multitude.

REGENERATION   388

The only true [one] * is re-creation; I do not want to be regenerated otherwise
nan by being refreshed and amused.

CONSCIENTIOUSNESS   389

a quality which it would be impossible to overrate if it had not been overrated.

HELL FIRE   390

If Vesuvius does not frighten those who live under it, is it likely that Hell fire
ould frighten any reasonable person?

SUBJECT   391

The battle of the prigs and blackguards.

POVERTY   392

I shun it because I have found [it] * so apt to be contagious. But I find my con-
titution more seasoned against it now than formerly.

131

So unaffected, so compos'd a mind,
So firm, yet soft, so strong yet so refined,
Heaven as its purest gold by torture tried
The saint sustained it, but the woman died.

SVEGLIARE   3S

To "unveil." This is the Italian for to "awaken."[1]

Written November 1800   Edited Saturday, March 2, 18S

A POEM ON THE NATIONAL DEBT   3S

My namesake T.W.G. Butler[1] told me many years ago that among the answe
to correspondents in one of the penny weekly papers he had seen "W.E.G. N
we should not recommend you to write an epic poem on the National Debt." Ca
W.E.G. have been Mr. Gladstone?

INTRODUCING A SUBJECT   3S

"My good man, would you be kind enough to direct me to Charing Cross ra
way station?"
"First turn to the left, second to the right and then straight; and, I beg you
pardon, Sir, but as you *have* introduced the subject I hope you will be pleased
assist me with a trifle, which I have not tasted a morsel of food since &c. &c."

PRODIGAL SON   3S

Introduce him somewhwere as still living in the wilds of Asia Minor, very ve
old, but always thrown into convulsions if any one mentioned veal in his presenc
Or let there b [a] * tribe with this unconquerable aversion to veal and let vario
little indications suggest to the reader that its members are descended from the P.S.[1]

SIGHT   3S

and all the other senses, are only modes of touch.

IMMORALITY   3S

Our instinctive repugnance to gross immorality is our unconscious sense of th
ills our fathers have suffered or are believed to have suffered in consequence of th
or that.

When I wrote to the Bishop of Carlisle, I was rather a humbug, and I suppose had excused myself to Miss Savage. She wrote back, "By all means make yourself iend with the Mammon of Righteousness, and if you *'exploiter'* that dear Bishop, know you will do it kindly."[1]

ELEPHANTS   401

ay a pretty fair third and Rhinoceroses a very fair fourth.

ASSOCIATION OF IDEAS   402

Going into my bed room I thought I saw and heard a few drops of water fall ı to the iron top of my stove. The floor shook a little with my step, and one of y eyebrows had got in front of my eye. I made the sound recur by moving my ʼot--it was exactly like a drop or two falling on the iron; on this my mind uncon- iously translated the hair into the visible object that should accompany the sound.

It is only rarely that two distinct things that have no connection synchronise ʼry precisely, but when they do it requires an effort to detach them. I only remem- ʼr two cases in point within my own experience. A gust of wind blew my hat off-- ıd a pig set up a loud squeal on the other side a hedge in absolute synchrony with y hat leaving my head. The first instinct was to assume that no two events could nchronise so exactly unless they were connected , and a very unpleasant mental jar as set up, which however of course immediately disappeared.

The other case was in Italy on a sultry thunderstormy day when the sun came ıt from behind clouds and went behind them again with almost incredible swift- ʼss. A man was knocking the spigot out of a cask of wine and the wine came spout- g out exactly as the sun came with a flood of light from behind a cloud.

No doubt ideas give and take in order to accommodate each other. No doubt ı the case given above the fact that I had an eyelash in front of my eye modified the ʼund I heard and made it more like rain, just as the sound modified the eyelash to falling drops.

VESUVIUS   403

A schoolboy asked what Vesuvius was answered, "Vesuvius was an architect ho lived at Naples and after whom the present volcano was called. He wrote a book ʼout the architecture of Herculaneum and Pompei and was suffocated in the first uption of the mountain which bears his name." (This is an invention of my own.)

ritten November 1880   Edited Saturday, March 3, 1895

From what my cousin and Gogin[2] both tell me, I am sure he is one of the be men we have. My cousin did not like to send Hyam[3] to him for a violin: he d not think him worthy to have one. Furber does not want you to buy a violin unle you can appreciate it when you have it. "He is generally a little tight on a Saturd afternoon; he always speaks the truth, but then it comes pouring out more." "H joints are the closest and neatest that were ever made." "He calls the points of fiddle the corners, Haweis[4] would call them the points. Haweis calls it the neck of fiddle, Furber always the handle."

My cousin says he should like to take his violins to bed with him.

Speaking of "Strad" violins Furber said, "Rough, rough linings, but they loc as if they grew together."

One day my cousin called, and Furber on opening the door before saying "ho do you do?" or a word of any kind, said, "The dog is dead" very quietly. The dog name was Rose.

My cousin, having said what he thought sufficient, took up a violin and play a few notes. Furber evidently did not like it. Rose was still unburied; she was la out in that very room. My cousin stopped. Then Mrs. Furber came in.

R.E.W. "I am very sorry, Mrs. Furber, to hear about Rose."

Mrs. F. "Well, yes sir, but I suppose it is all for the best."

R.E.W. "I am afraid you will miss her a great deal."

Mrs. F. "No doubt we shall, sir, but you see she is only gone a little while befo us."

R.E.W. "Oh, Mrs. Furber, I hope a good long while."

Mrs. F. (brightening) "Well, yes sir, I don't want to go just yet though M Furber does say it is a happy thing to die."

JONES WITH MLLE. DUBOIS[1]   4(

He had been ill, and was to go for a drive with Mlle. Dubois in an open carria at Hastings. He was the only available person to take her, and was to make himse particularly agreeable, &c. Jones began capitally, but after a little while he dropp off fast asleep, and slept peacefully almost all the rest of the drive.

Written November 1880   Edited, and typewritten by Alfred[1] March 20, 18(

GRADUATING   4(

An undergraduate was required in an examination paper to "graduate the Dani steel yard." His answer was: "Mr. ------ cannot graduate the Danish steel yard--plea Mr. Examiner graduate Mr. -----."

One night some years ago I was at the Globe Theatre, and the Prince of Wales me in. He was unpopular about that time in consequence of the Mordaunt Divorce se which was then on; it had come out in evidence among other things that Lady ordaunt had made the prince a pair of muffatees.[1] There was a little hissing when e came in, which subsided, and then a voice from the pit, near me, sang out, "How o you like your muffatees?" The prince smiled, and the feeling of the house at nce went round in his favour.

HAMLET DONE IN SUGAR 408

There is a shop in Exmouth Street where Hamlet may be bought done in sugar r twopence, holding a skull in his hand.

MR. DARWIN ON WHAT SELLS A BOOK 409

I remember when I was at Down[1] we were talking of what it is that sells a book. r. Darwin said he did not believe it was reviews, nor advertisements, but simply eing talked about" that sold a book. I believe he is quite right here, but surely good flaming review helps to get a book talked about. I have often enquired at y publishers after a review, and I never found one that made any perceptible in- ease or decrease of sale, and the same with advertisements. I think however that e review of *Erewhon* in the *Spectator* did sell a few copies of *Erewhon*, but then was such a very strong one, and the anonymousness of the book stimulated curio- y.[2]

UMBRELLA CATCHING IN A DRESS 410

X.Y.Z. first spoke to his subsequent wife through his umbrella accidentally catch- g in her dress as he was going along the street. He begged her pardon; she was then ung and pretty and she looked sweetly at him. The two soon squared matters; e became pregnant by him; he then married her and had several children by her whom two alone survived. She drank like a fish, spent all his money, dressed d powdered till she was a sight to see, but in the end went off with another man, d X.Y.Z. got a divorce. All this ten years or so of misery because an umbrella ojected a quarter of an inch further than X.Y.Z. thought it did.

GHOST 411

I saw one once near Bromley. It was in a barn, sitting on a beam from two to ree feet above my head. It was about 5 inches broad and 5 inches high, and nearly und. It had a wide flexible ⁓⁓⁓⁓⁓ gibbering mouth extending across its whole bstance. Two great socket eyes, which moved about with a quick sensitive motion, it contained no eyes. It had no nose, and no ears--the upper part of it was covered ith a soft silky yellow hair, the mouth was mousier, and the hair so short as to be rdly visible. There sat this object on the beam gibbering at Jones and my cousin d me--clearly at us, but we could not make head or tail of it at first. All three saw and felt that it was one of the most uncouth and weird looking objects which the human mind is capable of conceiving.

It was the nose of a horse--reaching its head up inside its stall, so that it cou
just get its nose on the beam and no more. Its head was a good deal above us, a
the rest of the horse was hidden.

SIR DE CALAMINES AGUOT   41

Many years ago I saw a pretty blue and white china vase with a spout to it
the bad part of Rathbone Place going into Newman Passage. It bore an inscripti
Sir de Calamines Aguot. Who, I wondered, was this man? He was a swell, this w
certain, his name was so aristocratic. He was probably a Knight Templar--a memb
of a brother-hood of which each man had a vase of his own to eat his soup out
or keep his water in, or something of that kind. For I presently saw two or thr
other vases of the same kind belonging to other "Sirs" with high sounding Norm
names. It was really very interesting. I was on the eve of an archaeological discove
which would make me celebrated &c. &c.

At length I discovered that "Sir" was short for Sirup, and that the vase wa
common chemist's and was for holding Sirup of Carraways.

LYING   4

has a kind of respect and reverence with it. We pay a person the compliment
acknowledging his superiority whenever we lie to him.

MORAL INFLUENCE, AND THE CARACAL   4

The Caracal[1] lies on a shelf in its den in the Zoological Gardens quietly licki
its fur. I go up and stand near it. It makes a face at me. I come a little nearer,
makes a worse face and raises itself up on its haunches. I stand and look. It jum
down from its shelf and makes as if it intended "going for" me. I move back; t
Caracal has excited a moral influence over me which I have been unable to resi

Moral influence means persuading another that one can make that other mo
uncomfortable, than that other can make oneself.

SYMPATHY AND IDENTITY   4

How closely they approach one another. A mother saw a window sash desce
upon her child's fingers and bruise them badly. She was in another part of the roc
but her own fingers were bruised as if they had been under the sash. I read this
Tuke's *Body and Mind*, or Carpenter's *Mental Physiology*--I forgot which.[1]

Volume I, Edition 2, p. 152 &c. These are passages dimly and confusedly resembling the theory of rhythms and vibrations which I have ascribed to Professor Hering *Unconscious Memory*.[1]
See page 190. He spoils it p. 191 close to the bottom[2]

KNOWING   417

implies something acted upon and something acting upon it. *Lib. cit.*, p. 152. This requires qualification.[1] The *ego* and the *non-ego* cannot be separated so sharply.

TASTE   418

comes near to eating, smell less near than taste, touch less near than smell, hearing less near than touch, seeing less near than hearing, but even "seeing" has some remains of eating with it. So "virtue sickens at the sight."

WORSLEY, R.E. AND *ST. JAMES'S GAZETTE*   419

My cousin said he did not like the conservatism of the *St. James's Gazette* so well as that of the *Globe*. "The *St. James's Gazette*, damn them, is open to reason, and the *Globe* isn't."

HERBERT   420

What an awful name it is. Sidney Herbert, George Herbert, Lord Herbert of Cherbury, Auberon Herbert, Lady Herbert of Lea, Herbert Spencer[1]--and a lot more cannot think of at the moment.
There is only one good man I know named Herbert, and he is Herbert Campbell of the Grecian Theatre.[2] When he says "H'm, you'd better take it about three times a day." "Are you living with your mother now?" "Have you got them all on?" "Ah, yes, it'll be a nice change for you," I feel that there are natures which even the name of Herbert cannot wreck, or even deteriorate. But probably Herbert Campbell's real name is not Herbert at all, but Charles or John or George or something of that sort.

WORSLEY, R.E. AT THE BUSKS   421

Alice[1] had with great difficulty got my cousin to go to an evening party at the Busks. He neglected society, she said, far too much, besides she wanted some one to take her, so my cousin was to go. But Alice had little gauged him my cousin's capacity for getting into scrapes. There were four musicians and who should be amongst them than that excellent violinist Silberberg[2]--Conductor at the Argyll Rooms? To him therefore did my cousin forthwith attach himself between the dances. Alice was very much ashamed of him.

PURSE, PERSON, AND REPUTATION   42

A man will feel money losses more keenly than loss even of bodily health as long as he can keep his money. Take his money away, and deprive him of the mean of earning any more, and his health will soon break up, but leave him his mone and even though his health breaks up and he dies, he does not mind it so much we think. Money losses are the worst, bodily pain is next worst, and loss of reputa tion comes in a bad third. All other things are amusements, provided money, health and good name are untouched.[1]

Written January or February, 1881   Edited March 21, 189

BODY A SMALL PART OF ONE   42

Though we think so much of our body, it is in reality a very small part of u a man's true life lies not in his body but in that which he does with his body. Befo birth we get together our tools; in life we use them, and thus fashion our true li which consists not in our tools and tool box, but in the work we have done wi our tools. It is Handel's work not the body with which he did the work that dra thousands of people on a winter's night from one end of London to the other; ar this is the true Handel, who is a more living power among us 122 years after h death than during the time he was amongst us in the body.[1] The body chang hourly--the work changes, but infinitely more slowly.

PLEASURE, ON KNOWING WHAT GIVES US   42

It is idle to say that this is easily known--it is the highest and the most neglected of all arts and branches of education.

WORSLEY, R.E. AND TEDDY   42

My cousin went to Clifton to see Teddy[1] who had Typhoid fever. My cousi was reading out of a book and came to a part which he said he thought might b skipped.
Teddy. "What is it about Papa?"
R.E.W. "It is something about self control."
Teddy. "Oh, that does not sound very nice."
So it was missed out. Teddy is now about ten.

DETECTIVE POLICE OFFICER WITH PRINCE OF WALES AND FRIENDS   42

The Prince was fond of going the rounds with the police, and did so once wi a few others, among whom there was a mere lad who nevertheless saw all that w

be seen. Before separating they liquored up, and the boy said to the detective
ho had gone round with them, "Now you think yourself a very sharp fellow, I
now."

"I don't know about that, but when I've seen a person once I generally know
iem again."

"I'll bet you, you don't know who I am."

"I beg your Ladyship's pardon," was the rejoinder.

NEXT BEST THING TO GETTING IN WITH NICE PEOPLE   427

I cannot often get in with the kind of people I like. The next best thing is to
lague those whom I do not like. This to a certain extent I do.

BUCKSTONE, J.B. AS FIRST WITCH IN *MACBETH*[1]   428

I am told that when the first witch opened her mouth the house knew Buck-
tone in a moment and burst into a roar of laughter, which kept breaking out from
me to time during all the rest of the performance. I wish I had been there, but
cannot even think of Buckstone as first witch without a burst of laughter, which
oes not subside readily.

VOUCHSAFE OH LORD   429

כ keep us this day without being found out.

WORSLEY, AMY,[1]   430

vhen at church with Alice (who is a Unitarian) makes a point of repeating, "I believe
ı God the father, and God the son and God the Holy Ghost," shaking them at Alice,
rho demurely holds her tongue. Amy all the while being a thorough little infidel.

CRUCIFYING CHRIST   431

If I had been born in the times of Jesus Christ, I trust I should not have been
mong his disciples. I hope I might even have been among those who crucified
im, but one must beware of spiritual pride. Who knows but what he himself might
ave been an Apostle if temptation had fallen in his way?

BODY A SMALL PART OF ONE   432

A man's real life is the life of which he knows nothing; he knows very little
f his present, so long as he is not out of gear; he forgets almost all his past, and the
reater part of the effect he produces (as the books of a writer) is wholly unperceived
y him.

CHRISTMAS CAROL AMENDED BY MISS SAVAGE   433

God rest you merry gentlemen,
May nothing you dismay,

Though Jesus Christ the Lord of all
Was born upon this day.

SOUL, TOO PREDOMINANT   43

"She looks as if her soul had got the better of her."

CUJUS   43

A man was asked in the little-go[1] what was the genitive of "qui"; he said "cujus.
--"Go on with the declension," said the examiner.--"cuja, cujum," said the undergraduate.

GIN, THE STRANGE   43

Mrs. Jones, a lodger of Mrs. Pillinger's[1] in the next house to my friend Jones's
went with the Pillingers and a few friends to the Grecian[2] one evening, and dance
While dancing she fell down, and excused herself by saying "it was the strange gin

MRS. BOSS   43

during the cold weather applied to the churchwarden for a ticket for coals. Th
churchwarden, who like every one else knows her exceedingly well, told her she wa
not a churchgoer. Mrs. Boss said she couldn't look him in the face and say she ha
been a *regular* churchgoer. (She had never been inside the church at all.)

GREATEST BENEFACTOR?   43

The man who invented the steam engine, or he who invented melted butter

Written early in 1881   Edited March 21 and 22, 189

PLEASURE   43

One can bring no greater reproach against a man than to say that he does no
set sufficient value upon pleasure--and there is no greater sign of a fool than th
thinking that he can tell at once and easily what it is that pleases him. A man ha
better stick to known and proved pleasures, but if he will venture in quest of ne
ones he should not do so with a light heart.

PAGET[1]   440

had to do an illustration of "Behold I stand at the door and knock" for *The Qui-ver*. He put Christ a glory round his head. The editor objected. Paget asked why. "Why?" was the rejoinder; "if I were to leave that Glory there the sale of the *Quiver* would go down one half." A little later they got him to do the disciples eating the corn on the sabbath day. Paget made some of them rubbing the corn with their hands, and blowing away the chaff. The editor sent it back saying he thought it better not to send him any but secular subjects in future--it was plain he did not understand the religious business.

MRS. PAGET ON GOTCH[1]   441

Miss Ross now studying painting in Paris has bad eyes and had to stay for many hours a day in a dark room. "It must be very lonely for her," said Jones, "are there any ladies she knows in Paris?" "Very few," said Mrs. Paget. "There's only Miss Broadbridge and Miss Yate, and" (here she looked wicked), "and--Mr. Gotch."

FLACK ON THE DEATH OF SAVAGE THE SENIOR WRANGLER   442

Savage had been senior wrangler January, 1855 and during my second term he was found dead in a ditch near Madingley.[1] Flack the bootmaker was measuring Fisher[2] for a pair of boots, and Fisher told him of how Savage had died. "Dear me," said Flack, "it's a very serious thing for the young man."

LIFE AND HABIT AND R.D. EYRE   443

At the Century[1] I was talking once with a man named Eyre (R.D., I think), who asked me why I did not publish the substance of what I had been saying. I believed he knew me, and said, "Well, you know, there's *Life and Habit*." He did not seem to rise at all, so I asked him if he had seen that book. "Seen it?" he answered. "Why I should think every one had seen *Life and Habit*, but what's that got to do with it?"

I said it had taken me so much time lately that I had had none to spare for anything else. Again he did not seem to see the force of the remark, and Macdonald who was close by said, "You know Butler wrote *Life and Habit*." He would not believe it, and it was only after repeated assurances that he accepted it. It was plain he thought a great deal of *Life and Habit*, and had idealised its author whom he was disappointed to find so very commonplace a person.

would be a good name for the author of a book of family prayers; Badcock, or Hitc cock--Bishop Badcock, Archdeacon Hitchcock, Canon Treadwell, or Canon Grou again, would be nice names. At Hornchurch I saw the name Grout on a tombstom Sancton would be a good name for a curate. There is a Mr. Sancton Wood,[1] ; architect and surveyor at Putney. Tabitha Pizzey.

ESSEX STREET CHAPEL, CLERK AT 4·

My Uncle Philip (Unitarian)[1] and family were at the opera near the front onc and saw the clerk singing in the chorus as a brigand. Next morning in chapel I saw them, and there was a guilty look between them.

ALEXANDER'S FEAST,[1] OVERTURE TO (HANDEL NOTE) 4·

describes the hurry and bustle of servants going to and fro with plates and dishes &

HOGARTH'S "LADY'S LAST STAKE"[1] 4∠

In this picture (now at the Academy) Gogin says there is a melon on the scree with a slice cut out--as though "a slice out of a cut melon" would not be misse I did not catch this when I looked at the picture.

HEATHERLEY[1] 44

told me a lady once said to him, "My daughter would have painted most beautiful in oil, but she did not like the smell of the varnish."

MISTAKE MADE BY PLANTS 44

See letter from Mr. Darwin in *Nature*, March 3, 1881.[1]

MRS. HENTY AND JONES 45

"Do you take an interest in astronomy, Mr. Jones?" "I take the deepest intere in it, I assure you; I am the only one of the family who does. You know perha the extraordinary influence which the Sun's atmosphere has upon the weather o the earth. Now when certain planets are in apogee, or perihelion, I forget which is called at this moment, they disturb the atmosphere of the Sun, and at these time we always have weather most prejudicial to animal life. If you remember last yea all the sheep were dying, I am sure that at Nazeing[1] the people lost their sheep by thousands. Jupiter was then in perihelion; he was very bright, every one was sayin how very bright he was. I looked at him through a telescope and he was a mos beautiful object. Next year it will be Jupiter or Uranus, I forget which, but it doe not much matter--all these things are perfectly well known now. People go abou the world looking at the eclipses, and they find out about the atmosphere of th Sun, and then they write and explain it to us in *Nature* &c. &c."

Subject for an article like those which Grant Allen has been writing on Evolution
ately in the *St. James's Gazette.* (March 6, 1881).[1]

LAYTON[1] ON *HAMLET*   452

He said he thought there was a great many deaths in *Hamlet.*

DERIVATIONS   453

All derivations are corruptions.

AMY WORSLEY[1]   454

ent with her father, my cousin, to Westminster Abbey. She had some sweetmeats
ith her. The Clergyman began, "When the wicked man turneth away from the
ickedness he hath committed and doeth that which is lawful and right"[2]--"Oh
pa," said Amy, "I hate it when it comes to lawful and right, don't you?" She
gan to hate it at a pretty early stage.

REASON   455

Our reason teaches us that the foundation of things is something abhorrent to
ır reasons: for it points to a self renewing motive power--that is to say, to perpetual
otion.

MISS SAVAGE   456

It was she who got a refuge put up in the middle of the street where Berners
reet debouches into Oxford Street. She wrote to the authorities and said it was
the direct route from Berners Street to the Houses of Parliament. She wanted
because her club is in Berners Street.[1] A friend of hers could see a certain tall
legraph post from her window, so she wrote to the proper people and told them
at it would be proper to them to put a weathercock on the top of it, and they did

MANZI (THE MODEL)   457

Armitage[1] had promised him sittings at the Royal Academy, and then refused
m on the ground that his legs were too hairy. He complained to Gogin.[2] "Why,"
id he, "I sat at the Slade School for the figure but last week, and there were five
dies, but not one of them told me my legs were too hairy."

ORGANIC AND INORGANIC   458

What we call inorganic is not so really--but the organization is too subtle for
ır senses, or for any of those applicances with which we assist them. It is deducible
wever as a necessity by an exercise of the reasoning faculties.

What tricks it plays. Thus if we expect a person in the street, we transform dozen impossible people into him while they are still too far off to be seen distinct] and when we expect to hear a footstep on the stairs--as we will say the postman--v hear footsteps in every sound.

CONSCIOUS MATTER (DUNCAN'S)[1]   46

The pith of his argument is this: "I feel and think; when I do this I am in psychical state; I act; when I do this then I am in a physical one--I am therefo alternately psychical and physical--and so is all matter."

Written April, 1881   Edited March 25, 18$

MEMORY, LOSS OF, AND DEGENERATION   4(

When a man's memory goes, it does so in the following order--"recent fac' ideas in general, sentiments, acts. In the best known case of partial dissolution (for getting of signs), the invariable order is--proper names, common names, adjectiv and verbs, interjections, gestures. In both cases the course is the same. Retrogre sion from the newest to the oldest, from the complex to the simple, from the volu tary to the automatic, from the less to the more organized.... The law is connecte with the physiological principle that degeneration first attacks the most recent form tion; and with the psychological principle--that the complex disappears before th simple, because it has been less often repeated in experience." *Mind*, April, 1881

TELEOLOGY, SIR J. LUBBOCK ON   4(

"But perhaps it will be said that I have picked out special cases;... that I ha put the cart before the horse; that the Ash fruit has not a wing in order that it m. be carried by the wind [or] * the Burdock hooks, that the heads may be transport by these animals, but the happening to have wings and hooks these seeds are th transported....

Let us take another case, that of plants in which the dispersion of the seeds effected by means of hooks. Now if the presence of these hooks were, so to sa accidental, and the dispersion merely a result, we should naturally expect to fir some species with hooks in all classes of plants.   They would occur for instan [among] * trees and on water plants. On the other hand if they are developed tha they might adhere to the skin of quadrupeds, then having reference to the habi and size of our British Mammals, it would be no advantage for a tree or to a wate plant to bear hooked seeds. Now what are the facts? There are about thirty Engli species in which the dispersion of the seeds is effected by means of hooks, but n one of these is aquatic nor is one of them more than four feet high. Nay I mig carry the thing further. We have a number of minute plants which lie below t vel at which seeds would be likely to be entangled in fur. Now, none of these ;ain, have hooked seeds or fruits. It would also seem as Hildebrand has suggested lat in point of time also, the appearance of the families of plants in which the fruits ' seeds are provided with hooks coincided with that of the land Mammals."

Fortnightly Review, April, 1881, pp. 444, 445.[1]

.. if seeds and fruits cannot vie with flowers in the brilliance and colour with hich they decorate our gardens and fields, still they surely rival--it would be im-)ssible to excel them--in the almost infinite variety of the problems they present • us, the ingenuity, the interest, and the charm of the beautiful contrivances which ey offer for our study and admiration." *Ibid.*, 455. This is teleology with a ven- ance.

NOT A PROFESSIONAL SCIENTIST   463

One great complaint against me is that I am not a professional scientist. It is)t shown that what I say is unsound, but it is contended that I cannot know the rticular matter on which I am writing because I have given no public proof that know all manner of other things which have no connection with it.

Written April, 1881   Edited March 27, 1895

TYNDALL, CARLYLE, AND DARWIN   464

"His (Carlyle's) opinions had for the most part taken their final set before the theory of man's descent was enunciated, or rather brought within the range of true :auses by Mr. Darwin. . . . To my own knowledge he approved cordially of certain writings in which Mr. Darwin's views were vigorously advocated, while a personal interview with the great naturalist caused him to say afterwards that Charles Dar- win was the most charming of men." *Times*, May 4, 1881. Letter from Tyndall[1]. See correspondence on vivisection a fortnight earlier, and letter from Hutton April 30(?)[2]

IDENTITY   465

To live a greatly changed life is near to living henceforward as somebody else; to live as somebody else is much the same as dying: indeed there is no other death than this. For even in the most perfect life there is something of death, and in the most perfect death there is something of life.

In the most dynamical state matter has something of a statical state and vice versa.

ATTRACTION AND REPULSION   466

At present the great power in nature is attraction, but the power of repulsion is not extinguished; if ever repulsion comes to be the predominating tendency there will yet remain a tendency towards attraction.

TURNIPS AND PRAYER 46

The turnips may say "our turnip which art in Heaven" &c. and "there is no even one man falleth to the ground but by the will of our heavenly turnip."

"MARIS" 46

Madame Devale said to my aunt Philip[1] quite seriously about husbands, "Ah je déteste les maris." I believe all women in their hearts do so--and most men to for the matter of that after a year or two find their wives more or less unsatisfactory

DUCKLINGS 46

A string of young ducklings as they sidle along through grass beside a ditch-- how like they are to a single serpent.

SCIENTISTS 470

Our Huxleys, Tyndalls &c. are the Albert Grants of human knowledge.[1]

RELATIONS 47

See article in *Times*, April 13, 1881.[1]

ACHIEVING TWOPENCE 47

A boy wanted to carry my bag for me on Rochester bridge. He said, "Can achieve twopence for you?"

PRAYERS AT SHREWSBURY 47

Our prayers contained the words "Oh Lord thou hast granted us more than either we desire or deserve." I used to say to myself as the Doctor[1] read these word --"not more than I desire, oh Lord."

Written May, 1881   Edited March 27, 189

"I KNOW THAT MY REDEEMER LIVETH" 47

Fancy singing this air,[1] and changing the word "know" into "think." "I thin that my Redeemer liveth."

"While I entirely share your feelings about Mr. Bradlaugh's publications and his rofessed opinions, it is part of my idea of Christianity that equal justice is due to 'hristian and Infidel, and it does not appear to me to be just to assert against one articular man (however bad he may be) a power in the House of Commons to test he sincerity of an oath which he offers to take in the manner prescribed by law y an extrinsic evidence of his actual belief or disbelief when no such power has ver been asserted or used against any other man, though other professed and notori-•us unbelievers have sat in the House of Commons, and perhaps may sit there still."
Times, May 11, 1881. Correspondence about Mr. Bradlaugh.[1]

ROBINET[1] ON THE UNITY OF NATURE   476

La nature n'est qu'un seul acte. Cet acte comprend les phenomènes passés,)résens et futurs; sa permanence fait la durance des choses.
Vue Philosophique de la Graduation Naturelle, p. 2. (Amsterdam, 1768)

IMAGINATION   477

vill make us see a billiard ball as likely to travel farther than it will travel, if we 1ope that it will do so. It will make us see people whom we want to see in all sorts)f impossible persons coming to us from a distance; it will make us think we feel ▲ train begin to move as soon as the guard has said "all right," though the train has ▲ot yet begun to move. If another train alongside begins to move exactly at this his juncture, there is no man who will not be deceived. And we omit as much as /e insert. We often do not notice that a man has grown a beard.

COMIC SONGS IN CONSECUTIVE HOURS   478

Why does not some one offer to sing 1000 comic songs in 1000 consecutive .ours?

TITLES   479

"Straws." "The defeat of death."

INTELLIGENCE, OMNIPRESENCE OF   480
(See Maupertuis and Diderot)[1]

A little while ago no one would admit that animals had intelligence. This is now onceded. At any rate then, vegetables had no intelligence. This is being fast dis-uted. Even Darwin leans towards the view that they have intelligence. At any ate, then, the inorganic world has not got an intelligence. Even this is now being enied. Death is being defeated at all points.

LEAVING MONEY   481

A sensible man in leaving money will think of who will do most good to the 1oney, as well as who the money will do most good to. For the person who will

do most good to the money, and make it breed most freely, or at any rate take th
best care of it, is he also to whom it will do most good.

Written in the spring of 1881

ERRORS OF SORROW   48

Our error often lies not in the having done things but in the being sorry tha
we have done them--and that too about things of which we were at one time terribl
ashamed.

MYSELF LIKE A SNIPE   48

My cousin says of me that I am like a snipe. When a subject is started, he say
it's no use agreeing or disagreeing with me, for at first I fly hither and thither i
contrary directions; he says he waits till I have begun to fly straight which after
while I do. Well--but this is what everybody does, is it not?

ALBATROSS   48

I was once compared to an albatross. I was crossing a mob of sheep over th
Rangitata on to my own run.[1] The sheep were tired with driving, there was an awfu
N. Wester on the riverbed, and a fresh was evidently about to come down. The shee
would not cross; nothing that we could all do would get them to face the river. I rod
over therefore to my own hut to get the assistance of two men who were putting u
my second hut--or I suppose I should almost call it my house. The river was sti
low, but I sent them down with my horse that they might cross it at once, while
got a mouthful of something to eat. Having got this I went down to the river on foo
and found these men by the side of the river funking. There was no excuse, seein
they had a horse, so I went straight into the river on foot and forded the first strean
Old Darby[2] describing it to some one else said, "and he went in--he went in--lik
an albatross."

SWAPPING KNIVES   48

Moorhouse[1] used to say that people cannot get rich by swapping knives. Ye
nature does go upon this principle. Everybody does eat everybody up. Man eat
birds, birds eat worms, and worms eat man again. It is a vicious circle, yet someho
or other there is an increment. I begin to doubt the principle *ex nihilo nihil fit*.

IMAGINATION AND "*EX NIHILO*" &c.   48

Imagination depends mainly upon memory, but there is a small percentage c
creation of something out of nothing with it. We can invent a trifle more than ca
be got by mere combination of remembered things.

[Animals and plants] * cannot understand our business, so we have hitherto de-
ied that they can understand their own. What we call inorganic matter cannot under-
and the animals and plants business, we have therefore denied that it can under-
and anything whatever.

SEASONS AND SPECIES   488

The Seasons are like species--there is only an artificial arbitrary division between
em. When two things present so many differences to us that we can easily take
ote of them, we call them different names, but strictly there is only one thing, one
ace, and one time.

CARLYLE AND PLATO   489

I don't like Plato, but I suppose I prefer him to Carlyle.

TYNDALL AND CARLYLE   490

See *Times*, May 4, 1881.[1] I am glad Tyndall explained all about light to Carlyle.

UNIVERSITIES   491

If a man is man enough to go to the University, he is man enough to begin his
rofession at once without any University.

DARWIN AND THE *EXAMINER*   492

When Miss Cobbe mauled Mr. Darwin last April in the *Times*, I expected to
nd some such paragraph as one that appeared in the *Examiner* Christmas, 1880,
 say that Mr. Darwin was very well, but the *Examiner* was very hard up at the
me when it put that paragraph in, and died soon after. At any rate it was dead
y April.[1]

JONES ON THE ALBERT HALL GALLERY   493

At *Israel in Egypt* we being in the Albert Hall gallery thought we saw a great
any very nasty looking people: I said I thought they might be better among the
ore highly priced seats. Jones said the only difference is that the people there are
iltured, and the people here want to be cultured.

BOSS   494

She said it was no use her trying to pass herself off as a maid--her son Tom was
 well known in the band (of the Volunteers who exercise in Gray's Inn Square).

See a letter from him in the *Times* on or about June 17, 1881 *re* the storag
of electricity.[1]

REVIEWER'S PUFFING   49

As an example of this see *Times*, May 26, 1881, an article on Dr. (?) Hunter
Indian Gazetteer.[1]

SWALLOWS IN SPRING OF 1881   49

When the long drought of May came to an end the swallows who had been stop
ped from building could get puddles to make mud with; I saw some on the mornin
after the rain, and they were tamer than I ever saw swallows before. They let m
come close to them, and I could see them getting the mud.

GRATITUDE   49

is as much an evil to be minimised as revenge is. Justice, our law, and our law cour
are for the taming and regulating of revenge. Current prices and markets and con
mercial regulations are for the taming of gratitude and its reduction from a publi
nuisance to something which shall at least be tolerable. Revenge and gratitude ar
correlative terms. Our system of commerce [is]* a protest against the unbridle
license of gratitude. Gratitude, in fact, like revenge, is a mistake unless under ce
tain securities.

AN OLD FOOL   49

I heard him laying down the law: "We've *no* words," he said dogmatically, "an
very few thoughts."

METHODIST CHAPEL NEAR WATFORD   50

"When God makes up his last account
Of Holy children in his Mount,
'Twill be an honour to appear
As one new born and nourished here."
We saw this cut in the stone over the door of a Primitive Methodist Chape
The windows were a good deal broken, and there was a notice of 10/s reward to any
one who should give such information &c. &c.[1]

EXCLUDING CHRISTIANS FROM PARLIAMENT   50

A day will perhaps come when it will be thought right to exclude any one fro
parliament who does not take a solemn oath that he does not believe in Christianit
and a personal God.

(Sunday School teacher who has mocked freethinkers becoming uneasy and having prickings of conscience lest he ought not to repent and be unconverted): "Alas! kind infidel, who shall rescue me from the body of this belief?"

"Young man," replied the unbeliever gently but firmly, "do you feel the want of infidelity? for if so, ere long you will surely find it &c.--"

This unbeliever was an unconscious Erasmus Darwinian.[1]

ARTIFICIAL FLIES, MINNOWS AND COCKCHAFERS 503

Can anything be meaner or more completely justify my contention that "when weakness is utter honour ceaseth?"

DR. KENNEDY[1] AND THOMAS 504
(a great overgrown neglected Welsh boy at Shrewsbury School.)

"Thomas," said Dr. Kennedy very solemnly, when catechising us in Chapel and preparing us for Confirmation. "Thomas," said the Dr., "repeat the fourth commandment."

Thomas replied in a strong Welsh accent, "You was remember keep holy Sunday." (He could hardly speak English.)

"Sit down Thomas," rejoined the Dr., "write out your catechism and bring it to me at 12 o'clock tomorrow."

ANTS 505

See article on, by Romanes in one of the monthlies for June 1881 (*Nineteenth Century*).[1]

THE PHILOSOPHER 506

He should have made many mistakes, and been saved often by the skin of his teeth: for the skin of one's teeth is the most teaching thing about one. He should have been, or at any rate believed himself, a great fool and a great criminal. He should have cut himself adrift from the society, and yet not be without society. He should have given up all, even Christ himself, for Christ's sake. He should be above fear or love or hate, and yet know all of them extremely well. He should have lost all save a small competence, and know what a vantage ground it is to be an outcast. Destruction and death say they have heard the sound of wisdom with their ears,[1] and the philosopher must have been close up to these if he too would hear it.

CHRIST 507

I dislike him very much, still I can stand him. What I cannot stand is the wretched band of people whose profession it is to hoodwink us about him.

There is a bourrée near the end of Handel's fifth violin Sonata; when Mrs. Bos
heard it she said, "Ah, that's me: that's the kind of woman I am, that is."

BOSS AND THE NEWSPAPER BOY   5(

She said he was such a pretty boy, she should like so much to kiss him. "God
morning, good morning, my dear, here's the penny for you &c."

CULTURE   5)

Some one said of another that he was cultured. "Yes," was the rejoinder--"no
to say manured."

MEANING WELL   51

Ted Jones, to tease me, said that von Hartmann meant well. I said I though
very badly of von Hartmann, but I should be sorry to think so ill of any one as t
believe he meant well.[1]

NAMES   51

Sibella Botibol, Mrs. Constable Midwife. Debaniah wife of Gregory Wright (i
Charlwood[1] Churchyard).

LITANY   51

From all them that travel by land or water, from all women labouring wit
child, from all young children and sick persons, Good Lord deliver us.

ASSIMILATION AND MORAL OR MENTAL GRAVITATION   51

There is a moral and mental gravitation whereby every particle of mind (!) a
tracts every other particle. Assimilation is the consummation of this mental grav
tation. It is seen faintly in suasion, and the way in which we get horses and dog
to work for us--more forcibly in a cat knocking all the will and sense out of a mou:
when playing with it, more forcibly still when the cat eats the mouse. Whoso eathet
his dinner is a missionary. But there must be a place found for repulsion.

HANDEL   51

left no school because he was a protest. There were men in Handel's time who
music Handel perfectly well knew who are far more modern than Handel. Hand
was opposed to the musically radical tendencies of his age, and as a musician w;
a decided conservative in all essential respects--though ready enough of course to g
any length in any direction if he had a fancy at the moment for doing so.

I think I have done this already.[1]

ROOTS SPROUTING   517

Near Sevenoaks I saw a beech root some eight feet in length and an inch in dia-
meter coming out of a bank and going into it again--the bank having fallen away.
ome half way down the exposed part, the root had sprouted.

Written Spring of 1881 or 1882

UNCLE JOHN[1]   518

wears no night shirt, considering them, as he says, an unnecessary expense. He stands
up against the back of a chair during family prayers. My cousin asked him why, and
was told that kneeling was very bad for the knees of the trousers, and caused them
o wear out much sooner.

RIGHT AND WRONG   519

Things can never be either very right or very wrong for long together. *Alps and
Sanctuaries*, 256, 257.[1]

GODS AND PROPHETS   520

It is the manner of Gods and prophets to begin "thou shalt have none other
God or Prophet but me." If I were to start as a God or prophet I think I should take
he line, "Thou shalt not believe in me. Thou shalt not have me for a God. Thou
shalt worship any d----d thing thou likest except me." This should be my first and
great commandment, and my second should be like unto it.[1]

CULTURE   521

A man should be just cultured enough to be able to look with suspicion upon
culture, at first, not second hand.

BUGS I MEAN   522

"Ever since the Chittern has been painted inside, on deck and below, and in
he cabins we have been free of vermin, so annoying to us and so very difficult to
get rid of if once on board, whereas before we were smothered with them, but now,
I mean bugs) are entirely free of them, because they cannot live where the indes-
tructibel paint is used." Copied from a M.S. letter in window of the Indestructible
Paint Co., Cannon Street.

Teddy (aged 10) was at tea, at my cousin's, and something was said about Dean Stanley: we said we hated him; Teddy said "why? he was a conservative wasn't he I thought Deans were always conservatives." We explained that though the instinct of a Dean would generally be on the right side yet that there were deans and deans "Well," said Teddy, "I did see that he gave some stodge to the working men the other day, and I thought that looked rather bad."

CLASSIFICATION   52

depends upon the shock to the mind which the perception of a difference occasions. The shock depends upon the amount of the differences. It is analogous to a man running up against an object and being suddenly stopped by it. Much depends upon the being prepared or unprepared for the shock. We cannot classify things, but we can classify the amount and character of the shocks which the sense of difference between them will cause to the average of mankind. See *Alps and Sanctuaries*, pp 35, 36.[1]

Written Spring or Summer of 1881

BEE IN A WINDOW PANE   52

When ninety-nine hundreths of one set of phenomena are presented while the hundreth is withdrawn without apparent cause, so that we can no longer do some thing which according to our past experience we should find no difficulty whatever in doing--then we may guess what a bee must feel as it goes flying up and down window pane. Then we have doubts thrown upon the fundamental axiom of life i.e., that like antecedents will be followed by like consequents. On this we go mad and die in a short time.

UNITY   52

When the steps between two extremes are so small as to cause very little perceptible shock at any stage, then the extremes are united, or made one. Everything can in the end be united with everything, by such easy stages, if a long enough and roundabout way enough is taken--the whole Universe, therefore, becomes united and made into one thing. See *Alps and Sanctuaries*, pp. 59, 60.[1]

OBJECT AND SUBJECT   52

It is said a thing cannot be both object and subject. I do not see how a line can be better drawn between object and subject than between "ego" and "non-ego."

I do not deny a separate existence in spite of unity, merely because I maintain nity in spite of separate existence. Neither factor should be lost sight of; the separate xistence factor is kept well in mind. The unity factor is generally ignored.

It may be well to consider what is the most convenient way of determining vhether a thing is to be regarded as a thing by itself or as a part of another thing.

CHILDREN, ON RESEMBLANCES   529

The first thing children want to know about anything which they are told of nd which is new to them is, what it will be like.

OLD MRS. PRING   530

My Aunt Philip's aunt Mrs. Pring[1] complained bitterly to my aunt of the parson f her village (of which she was squire) who had come to see her during a serious lness; "and you know, my dear," she said, "he read the bible to me, just as if I ad been any old woman in the village."

Her gardener Curtis had consulted her as to how and where some cabbages were o be planted. Later on the gardener came again with a suggestion which was obvious-y an improvement. "Curtis," said she, "if I tell you to plant the cabbages with heir leaves in the ground and their roots in the air you will be pleased to do so." And yet as she said to my aunt, she knew Curtis's way was much better, but she vas not going to have settled questions reopened, and she was going to be mistress n her own home.

Vritten in Autumn, 1881

MISS BUCKLEY[1]
What I said to her when Dean Stanely[2] died.   531

I said I was glad Dean Stanley was dead. I disliked his works and also he was y way of being lovable, whereas when I have been sketching in the Abbey I have een him going round with smaller people and behaving very rudely to them. His xpression was odious. Miss Buckley bridled up and said she was not at all glad. said, "Why I never knew such a person, you are never glad when any one is dead, ou were not glad when Tom Taylor, nor yet when George Eliot, nor Carlyle died." he bridled up at this still more. "I was glad," she said, "when Lord Beaconsfield ied."[3] She said this because she knew how greatly I admired him--on the whole t was a very pretty little spar.

DESTITUTION, MIDDLE CLASS   532

Write a book entitled "Middle class destitution."

These are the lowest of the condiments or spices, or relishes, just as agates are the lowest of the precious tones.

GAUDENZIO FERRARI   53
picture by, at Novara[1]

Top. Holy Family in middle; two angels holding the baby; and angel announcing to a shepherd, and some sheep in the background. A split annunciation on either side.

Below. Left. Peter and John. Middle, Madonna and child with Saint and angel. Right. Paul and a bishop.

A fresco on left hand side of a chapel nearly opposite the foregoing looked good but we could not see it well.

TOOLS AND ORGANS   53

The most incorporate tool, as we will say an eye, or a tooth, or the fist when blow is struck with it, has still something of the non-ego about it; and in like manner the most apparently entirely separated from the body, as the locomotive engine must still from time [to time] *, as it were, kiss the soil of the human body, and be handled, and thus become incorporate with man, if it is to remain in working order. Used in *Luck or Cunning*.[1]

ITALIAN NOTES   53
(not used in *Alps and Sanctuaries*)

The yellow dog at Faido.
Signora Bullo had lost 9 children (but had 10 still left).[1]
The old woman with a "gran mancamento di spirito."[2]
The places in which they cut their hay.
The way in which they conduct wood from high places.
The game at Morra.
Christ at Arto above Pella on the Lago d'Orta.
The death of Socrates at Civiasco.
Fabbrica ancora.[3]

Written October and November, 1881

GAUDENZIO FERRARI AT VERCELLI[1]   53

Church of S. Giuliano. Dead Christ with saints.
San Christoforo. Picture behind altar, and series of frescoes; the Magdalene under the table washing Christ's feet.

Santa Catarina. S. Eusebius and another saint, S. Nicolas, Joseph, John the ꞏaptist, and Sta. Caterina receiving ring.

S. Michele. Small fresco of Madonna and child and St. Anna (by Lanini).[2]

COPY OF A LETTER FROM TEDDY WORSLEY[1] 538

Bingfield October 16th (1881)

)ear Aunt Alice.

It is Miss Lewins birthday to day. We gave her a jam cover which held a jam ꞏot in. And Mrs. Enfield[2] gave her a book of Ruskins. The real Isoglaciarun was ꞏpen and there were flags all about the twon and there was a torch light proces-ꞏon. There was a great storm here and it blew chimneys and it blew down our when ꞏe were at drilling. Miss Lewin let us go to the swimming gala and the did all sorts ꞏf thing they eat a spunge cake under water and drank a botle of milk under the ꞏater. And he showed how to swim when you have got cramp and they had a boat ꞏnd a roughf man come in and he strugled and the poliseman came in and they stur-ꞏe and the all fell in.

Good by from Ted.

ELM (SWITZERLAND), THREATS DISREGARDED 539

Rocks continue to fall from the East side, the crevices are widening, and a great ꞏft extends from the top of the Risi Kopf to the bottom. The lower part of this ꞏection of the Ischingel is firm, but the upper part is inclining and moving toward ꞏlm, which the professor considers to be in as great danger as ever. Though the ꞏeople of the valley are fully aware of the danger with which they are threatened, ꞏnd most of them believe that the village is destined to utter destruction they cannot ꞏe persuaded to seek new homes. They think that the final catastrophe may perhaps ꞏot come to pass before the spring, and that when it does befall the watch they ꞏeep, sentinels being posted day and night on various parts of the mountain will ꞏnable them to escape in time.

Times, November 16, 1881[1].

LEGAL FICTIONS 540

A man who had to defend an action might be told that he was in gaol, or he ꞏnight be compelled to substitute himself for a non-existent Richard Roe. Any one ꞏvho wished to sell an entailed estate might have to begin by saying that it belonged ꞏo somebody else. A plaintiff who did not make at random a large number of asser-ꞏions in his bill was put to a serious disadvantage. A defendant gave sham bail for ꞏis appearance; and it was usual to put into pleadings mere random assertions, none ꞏf which might be true. To recover a horse or cow or to get an estate of which some ꞏne was in possession, it might be necessary to state the most egregious falsehoods. ꞏn order that one might sue upon a contract actually made at sea, it might be essential ꞏo say that it was actually made at the Royal Exchange. It sounds odd to be told ꞏhat "the wife is the daughter of the husband" or that "the mother and son are not

of kin".... But the fact is that when the history of these maxims is carefully scanne
[it appears that] they were generally modes of silently altering law at a time whe
above board reforms or innovations of any kind would have been stoutly resiste
When Acts of Parliament were rare or unknown; when law was regarded by uncritica
minds as of quasi sacred origin, and to say "it is written" is to say "it is immutable
these fictions were modes of acquiring jurisdiction and doing justice without offe
ing violence to deeply rooted feelings. *Times*, November 16, 1881.[1]

Written November, 1881

ROBINET, ON THE UNITY OF NATURE 54

The progress of Nature is effected by steps that are often imperceptible an
blend into one another with the utmost gentleness, hence all her productions a
linked in the closest possible sequence, though the accumulated divergences as see
at the extremities of the long lines of life of every kind, may raise some doubt as t
the existence of any links between the higher and the lower forms. Each has i
own individual existence, but none are isolated or independent. Each has relatior
nearer or more remote with all the others, and even the most extreme developmen
are still connected. The connection between them is so intimate and essential tha
each is sufficiently explained by the one that went before it, and is in its turn a suff
cient explanation of its successor. p. 2.[1]

MAUPERTUIS 54

See his *Venus Physique.*[1]

MAUPERTUIS AND DIDEROT 54

"In this work [*Système de la Nature*] Maupertuis combated the atomic theory
that of plastic and archetypal forms, and lastly that of germs boxed up one withi
the other. For all these hypotheses he substituted the universal sensibility of matte
He ascribed desire, aversion, memory, and intelligence to the primordial molecules
in a word he endowed them with all those qualities which we perceive in anima
and which the ancients comprised in the words 'living soul' .... Diderot accepts th
hypothesis with some reservations, which, however are more apparent than rea
and are rather by way of precaution than of objection."--Paul Janet, *Nineteent
Century*, April 1881, p. 697.[1]

LEIBNITZ[1] 54

He defined "substance" as that which is capable of action.

158

Mark Wilks[1] was falling foul of me the other night for my use of the word "mem-ry." There was no such thing he said as "unconscious memory"--memory was lways conscious and so forth; my business is--and I think it can be easily done--o show that they cannot beat me off my unconscious memory without my being ble to beat them off their conscious memory; that they cannot deny the legiti-acy of my maintaining the phenomena of heredity to be phenomena of memory, ithout my being able to deny the legitimacy of their maintaining the recollection f what they had for dinner yesterday to be a phenomena of memory.

BEAST, MARK OF THE   546

Surely the prophecy of Revelations XIII. 17, 18, is fulfilled in the universal dis-onesty complained of as existing among our commercial men. "And that no man ight buy or sell save he that had the mark or the name of the beast or the number f his name. Here is wisdom."

"MAN WANTS BUT LITTLE HERE BELOW"   547

ut likes that little good--and not too long in coming.

ACADEMIC SYSTEM AND REPENTANCE   548

The academic system goes almost on the principle of offering places for repent-nce, and letting people fall soft &c., by assuming that people should be taught how o do things before they do them, and not by the doing of them. Good economy re-uires that there should be little place for repentance, and that when people fall hey should fall hard enough to remember it.

SNAILS   549

There was a family that looked fat and healthy during a hard year when every ne else was pinched, yet no one knew how they lived. It was plain they had a horri-le secret--they were seen prowling about at unrighteous hours, and had the look f people who were doing something that would not bear daylight. It turned out hat they gathered snails, and ate them.

ADAPTIVENESS   550

Consider what this power postulates, and connect it with illusion, suasion, and ssimilation. See *Alps and Sanctuaries*, pp. 35, 36.[1]

SUDDENNESS   551

Consider what it is that constitutes suddenness in a change, or that makes us ble to call it gradual. Consider sudden changes of mind, or losses of memory, and radual ones.

The gratitude that parents claim from children is often no more reasonabl than it would be for a man of 40 to claim gratitude from a man of 30, because he once gave him 2/6 when he was at school. What horrible *liens* have some such people established over us?

FOUNDATION   55

I do not say that there is none, but only that there is none *qua* us--nothing about which we need concern ourselves; our business is with the thickening of the crust whereon we stand by extending our knowledge downward from above; as ice gets thicker as the frost lasts; we should not try to freeze upwards from the bottom

TRUTH, REALITY, AND EASY THINKING   55

Some things are more easily thought than others; a man at a high Church or Ritualistic English service may easily think himself in a Roman Catholic Church at the Royal Institution he may, with more difficulty, imagine himself in a church of some sort. A man sitting on the French side of the Mount Cenis tunnel by think ing hard enough may even imagine himself in Italy. The object of the tunnel is to make it easier for him to think this--to enable him to think himself in Italy so un interruptedly and with such complete absence of all jar and contradiction that h may be said to be actually there.

COINCIDENCE AND DESIGN   55

We can stand a single coincidence, or even two, and yet be satisfied that there is no connection between the two events, but we cannot stand half a dozen; if ther are many coincidences, and those such as we are not familiar with as being commo, forgeries of artistic people, there is no power which will hinder us from thinkin of design in connection with the effects produced. Thus if I see a piece of the *Ech* newspaper[1] lying on the ground, with a hole burnt through the middle of the C by a lucifer match, which exactly fits the white interior of the O without burnin the inked part I am apt to think that some one has amused himself by burning ou the hole carefully; if I find the white part inside the E similarly burnt, without th inky part's being touched, or without its being more touched than a little involuntar clumsiness on the burner's part would account for, I feel pretty sure that the burn ing was done purposely and for the amusement of an idle moment. If, however find all the white paper parts inside all the letters carefully burnt out, there is n earthly power will persuade me that the burning was not done on purpose.

FURBER[1]   55

said one day to my cousin, "I don't like Italian fiddles." "Well, but Furber, ther are Strads you know." "Yes, but they're too small most of them": then after a pause "The varnish is very fine."

On the leaving them off--gradually, on the evolution principle.

A PRINCIPLE OF MORALITY   558

It is more moral to be behind the age than in advance of it.

ART   559

All that is not pertinent in art is impertinent.

DENTISTS AND SOLICITORS   560

These are the people to whom we always shew our best side.

Copied from a paper sent by Ted
Jones--*I think* an American publication
called the *Index* (?) Dec. 10, 1874(?)

THE NEW SCRIPTURES ACCORDING TO DARWIN, TYNDALL, HUXLEY, AND SPENCER[1]   561

1. Primarily the unknowable moved upon Kosmos and begat protoplasm.

2. And protoplasm was inorganic and undifferentiated, containing all things in potential energy, and a spirit of evolution moved upon the fluid mass.

3. And the unknowable said, "Let atoms attract, and let their contact beget light, heat, and electricity."

4. And the unconditioned differentiated the atoms, each after its kind and their combinations begat rock, air, and water.

5. And there went out a spirit of evolution from the unconditioned, and working in protoplasm by accretion and absorption, produced the organic cell.

6. And cell by nutrition evolved germ, and germ developed protogene, and protogene begat eozoon, and eozoon begat monad, and monad begat animalcule.

7. And animalcule begat ephermeron; then began creeping things to multiply on the face of the earth.

8. And earthy atom in vegetable protoplasm [begat the molecules (?)] ; and hence came all grass, and every herb of the earth.

9. And animalcule in the water evolved fins and beaks, and on the land they sprouted such organs as were necessary, as played upon by the environment.

10. And by accretion and absorption came the radiata and mollusca and mollusca begat articulata, and articulata begat vertebrata.

11. Now these are the generations of the higher vertebrata, in the cosmic period that the unknowable evoluted the bipedal mammalia.

12. And every man of the earth while was yet a monkey, and the horse while he was a hipparion and the hipparion before he was an [osedon?] .

13. Out of the Ascidian came the Amphibian and begat the pentadactyle, and the pentadactyle by inheritance and selection produced the lobate, from which are the Simiadae in all their tribes;

14. And out of the Simiadae the lemur prevailed above his fellows and beg the platyrhine monkey;

15. And the platyrhine begat the catarrhine, and the catarrhine monkey beg the anthropoid ape, and the ape begat the longimanous orang, and the orang beg the chimpanzee, and the chimpanzee begat the "What-is-it?"

16. And the What-is-it went into the land of Nod, and took him a wife with th longimanous Gibbons,

17. And in the process of the Cosmic period were born unto them, and the children the anthropomorphic primordial types.

18. And the homunculus, the prognathus, the troglodyte, the autochthon, th terragon; these are the generations of primeval man.

19. And primeval man was naked and not ashamed, but bred in quadrumanov innocence, and struggled mightily to harmonise with the environment.

20. And by inheritance and natural selection did he progress from the stab and homogeneous to the complex and heterogeneous, for the weakest died and th strongest grew and multiplied.

21. And man grew a thumb for that he had need of it, and developed capaciti for prey.

22. For behold the swiftest men caught the most animals, and the swifte animals got away from the most men, whereby the slow animals were eaten, and th slow men starved to death.

23. And as types were differentiated the weaker types continually disappeare

24. And the earth was filled with violence, for man strove with man, and trib with tribe whereby they killed off the weak and foolish and secured the surviv of the fittest.

I added the following verses;

25. "This is the chronicle of the generations, as revealed unto Buffon the Scrib in the days of Louis king of France and George, king of England.

26. "After him there arose Erasmus Darwin also, and Lamarck, prophets (evolution. These men prophecied and wrote their prophecying in books which the delivered to our fathers that learning they might know and knowing might unde stand, and that they might teach their children the same.[2]

27. "But our fathers would not hear them, and reviled them and passed the by

28. "Till there arose Charles Darwin of the household of the prophets of Evol tion. The same was a wily man who threw dust in the eyes of the people.[3]

29. "He spoke not of them that had prophecied before him but concealed the words and delivered them as a new thing which the Unknowable[4] had shown direct to himself.

[30.]* "And the people who write in newspapers bowed themselves down an blew trumpets before him, for he was a man of substance.

[31.]* "And they arrayed him in a scarlet robe, and gathered themselves roun him crying, "Great is Darwin, woe unto him, whosoever shall gainsay the proph Darwin--

[32.]* "So that all men fall to the ground before him, and the earth is fille this day with the greatness of his glory."

162

See *Times*, July 18, 1881.[1]   Beef was best for them, and algae worst. I saw it
ated in the *Times* some time before this that neuter ants can be changed into queens
ʏ change of diet just as neuter bees can into queen bees.

ANTS   563

The honey making ants of S. America. See *Times*, September 20, 1881.[1]

ritten December, 1881   Edited February, 1896

DESIGN   564

There is often connection but no design, as when I stamp my foot with design
ᴀd shake something down without design, or as when a man runs up against another
the street and knocks him down without intending it.   This is undesign within
ᴇsign.
Fancied insults are felt by people who see design in a connection where they
ᴀould see little connection, and no design.
Connection with design is sometimes hard to distinguish from connection with-
ᴀt; as when a man treads on another's corns it is not always easy to say whether
ᴇ has done so accidentally or on purpose.
Men have been fond in all ages of ascribing connection where there is none.
ᴐ astrology has been believed in. Before last Christmas I said I had neglected the
asts of the Church too much, and that I should probably be more prosperous if
paid more attention to them: so I hung up three pieces of ivy in my rooms on Xmas
ᴠe. A few months afterwards I got the entail cut off my reversion,[1] but I should
ᴀrdly think there was much connection between the two things.   Nevertheless I
ᴀll hang some holly up this year.

APPETITE LESS AS WE GROW OLDER   565

Our gastric juices moreover are no longer so eloquent, they have lost that cogent
ᴜency which carried away all who came in contact with it. They are sluggish and
ᴀconciliatory. This is what happens to any man when he suffers from a fit of indi-
ᴇstion.

CHRIST A LIVING DEATH   566

Christ is equilibrium--the not wanting anything either more or less.   And so
Death, but Christ is a more living kind of Death than Death is.

My main wish is to get my books into other people's rooms, and to keep oth
people's books out of mine.

SEASONARIANISM 5(

does for time, what tidiness does for space.

HUMBUGS OF CHRISTENDOM 5(

I find it much harder to get seven good humbugs than seven good champio
There are scores of men whom all Christendom delights in justly, but there are fe
whom they unite after a long while in admiring undeservedly. Christ is certain
one of the two whom I have not named in *Alps and Sanctuaries*. Beethoven w
the other, but I did not dare stick to him:[1] I think I ought to have done so. I
has done some splendid things; so has Plato; still, take him all round he is a frau
and he is the musician by whom all the modern musical frauds swear.

"RESIST GOD" 5

said Jones, one day, "and he will flee from you."[1]

Written about December, 1881   Edited February, 18

BEES AT LANGAR DRAWING-ROOM PAPER 5

The paper at Langar was at one time of a pattern full of roses, red and whit
or camelias, I forget which. I have seen the bees come in on a summer's afternoo
and try flower after flower of them, going from sofa to ceiling and then down t
next row. They find it impossible in the presence of so many of the associated idea
to believe in the absence of the one they set most store by--honey.[1]

PERSONALITY, ONENESS OF, BETWEEN FATHER AND SON 5

At Charterhouse, if the son is flogged, the father is fined.

GOTHIC WOMAN 5

At Lewes there was a tall scraggy chambermaid; my cousin said she was a Goth
woman.

PREMATURE HATCHING OF SILKWORMS 57

When sent in baskets by trains, the jolting and unquietness generally haste
their development, and they hatch prematurely.

SHAKSPEARE 57

could be priggish sometimes in the way of business. Henry the Fifth's[1] speech "Bu
herein will I imitate the Sun &c" is both priggish and mean. His treatment of Falstaf

at the end is mean, and Shakspeare should not have allowed it.[2] However he
es promise to make him a competent allowance.

W. PHIPSON BEALE[1]   576

He is one of those men who must know everything; nothing must be shown
m with which he has not been long familiar. I showed him the prospectus of *Alps
d Sanctuaries* and he said at once, "Ah so you've got Fucine!" (and he called it
'u-cine" instead of "Fucine"). I shoved him quickly off this and made it plain he
ew not where Fucine was, so he said, "Ah yes, to be sure, I was thinking of Fu-
e."[2] There may be such a place but I do not know it.

One day he whistled me what he said was the slow movement in Beethoven's
Minor symphony. "Oh don't you know it?" said he. "It goes thus," and he whist-
l--yes--but what a different melody.

Sometimes he whistles or hums Handel to me. I have heard him rush at "Total
clipse" and "How Willing my Paternal Love."[3] He will rush at anything, if he
inks he can impress some one that he knows more than you do.

YOUNG PEOPLE, ADVICE TO   577

You will sometimes hear your elders laying their heads together and saying
hat a bad thing it is for young men to come into a little money--that those always
) best who have no expectancy and the like. They will then quote some drivel
om one of the Kingsleys[1] about the deadening effect which an income of £300
year will have upon a man. Avoid any one whom you may hear talk in this way.
ne fault lies not with the legacy (which would certainly be better if there were
ore of it) but with those who have so mismanaged our education that we go in
'en greater danger of losing it than other people are.

'ritten December, 1881   Edited February, 1896

SHAKSPEARE   578

If he had told us more about what he himself saw, said and did--what he thought
f the men and things of his day--what people he was fond of, what places he most
equented &c., and less even about *Hamlet* and *Othello*, it would have been better.

COMPLAINTS AGAINST ME   579

Some complain of me that they never know whether I am not laughing, and
thers that they are never sure but what I am in earnest.

MRS. DUDGEON[1]   580

aid to me that she and Dr. Dudgeon would be perfectly happy if it were not for the

children--some of whom were very troublesome and unmanageable. I said, "a
the children would be perfectly happy if it was not for you and Dr. Dudgeon." Sl
admitted it. I said what folly the family system was; the separation between paren
and children should be much more complete and begin much earlier than it doe
the children of rich and poor alike should begin at the lowest step of the social syste
and find their way up if they could; they would not feel this if they began youn
As it was the tie was generally alike painful and unprofitable to both parties. Sl
admitted this, but said it would be so unnatural that she could not bear to think
it, and yet she could be happy enough if it was not for the children.

STRENGTH AND MONEY 5&

Consider the analogies between physical and pecuniary strength or weakne:

HEAVEN 5&

It is in the essence of heaven that we are not to be thwarted or irritated. Tl
involves absolute equilibrium, and absolute equilibrium involves absolute unco
sciousness.

MORAL GUIDANCE 5&

We should turn for this not to foreign nations and to history, but to the low
animals also.

COUVADE[1] 5&

In the times of the Couvade there was a dangerous radical who opposed tl
custom, and broke his father's and mother's hearts by insisting that his wife shou
stay in bed for a day or two after her confinement, and obstinately refusing to l
put to bed himself.

EXTREMES MEET 5&

To be poor is to be contemptible; to be very poor is worse still, and so on, b
to be actually at the point of death through poverty is to be sublime. So "wh
weakness is utter, honour ceaseth."[1]

MADAME BERNIER 5&

(in Canada) did not suckle her child well. Dunn told her she was only fit for be

AN AMERICAN CANDIDATE 5&

during the war decried his opponent as one who had run away to Canada to avo
the conscription. "I," he exclaimed, "never shirked the fulfillment of a patriot
duty. I stayed at home and braved the terrors of the conscription. My name w
drawn. I paid for a substitute, and *his* bones are whitening the plains of Manassas

riting to Mr. Rae as though she did not know he was dead. The fitters singing under-
eath the priest's windows--"very bad men, very bad men," said Madame Vigneau.
In old days," said she, "they used to call me Colisse, but now they call me Madame
igneau."

M. MARQUIS   589

I had an interview with him (he was a priest) about a Church (R.C.) which was
anted or supposed to be wanted at Bulstrode,[1] and towards which certain R.C.
inds were to contribute. As I left him he patted me caressingly on the shoulder
id said, "You shall have your Church, yes, you shall have your Church."

DEATH   590

the nearest approach to a sin against the Holy Ghost for which there shall be no
pentance.[1]

PERSONA   591

The fact that we do not see people, but only the mouthpiece through which
iey speak and the mechanism through which they act is plain from our common
nguage; for we speak of people as persons, as masks, that is to say; for a person
nothing but a *persona* or mask. See *Alps and Sanctuaries.*[1]

PURSE--WHO STEALS MY, STEALS TRASH[1]   592

That just depends upon the amount I may happen to have in it.

PERMANENT FORMS OF MIND AND OF MATTER   593

As some bodily arrangements, say for example, a stomach are common to all
iose things that we generally call living, so there are some virtues and vices which
em as though they were permanently good or bad, certain conditions of mind
hich are no less universal among living beings than protoplasm.

PROTOPLASM OF MIND   594

Sense of shock bears the same relation to our more complex ideas, as an amoeba
ies to man.

CERTAIN PARALLELS   595

There is desire and power; there never can have been desire without some power,
id *vice versa*. Again there are faith and reason, consciousness and unconsciousness,
ind and matter, life and death, union and disunion. There must be always a dash
˙ the second even in the most extreme development of the first of any of these
ings.

may be, as I have said above, due to the naughtiness of the stiff-necked things th
we have eaten, or to the poverty of our own arguments, but it may also arise fro
an attempt on the part of the stomach to be too d----d clever, and to depart fro
precedent inconsiderately. The healthy stomach is nothing if it is not conservati
Few radicals have good digestion. See *Life and Habit*.[1]

LEDGERS 5?

are like the stars, or like our cells. There is neither speech nor language, but the
voices are heard among them, one day telleth another and one night certifieth an
ther.[1]

INCOGNITO 5?

The aim of the obscure is to become known, the aim of the most exalted p
sonages is very frequently to be incognito.

MORALITY, ELEMENTS OF 5?

Books on this subject are just as likely to be useful as books upon "polite lett
writing," "deportment" &c.

EREWHON, ADDENDUM TO 6(

"You are not guilty of the crime imputed to you, but you are unquestionab
guilty of another, which is not less heinous. You are guilty of the crime of bei
maligned unjustly and must take the consequences."[1]

DARWIN 6(

Frank Darwin[1] told me his father was once standing near the hippopotam
cage when a little boy and girl aged 4 and 5 came up; the hippopotamus shut l
eyes for a minute. "That bird's dead," said the little girl, "come along."

LION AT ZOOLOGICAL GARDENS 6(

I saw the lion snap up a piece of liver; a working man who was standing ne
me said it was like a flea going into Hyde Park.

GIRAFFE 6(

Another working man said to me about the giraffe that it must get up at 6
the morning if it wants to have its breakfast in its stomach by nine.

APPROPRIATE 6(

Whenever I see what I think to be an appropriate passage, I always suit the acti
to the word and appropriate it.

Why not a crusade against these? Fancy the amount of suffering they must
flict. There are as many epics enacted on a single summer's day in Switzerland
nong ants, as among the whole human race.

LEAF FROM TREE AND WOMAN FROM CONCERT ROOM 606

Consider the points of resemblance and difference between the mere dropping
f of a leaf from a tree, and the dropping off of guests from a dinner, or concert.

PAGANISM AND CHRISTIANITY 607

Paeans and Jeremiads.[1]

ritten about December, 1881   Edited February 24, 1896

A NEW SACRAMENT 608

I should like to add an eighth sacrament to those of the Roman church--I mean
e sacrament of divorce.

LOVE 609

mes to some men as the aftergrowth of young green leaves to city lime trees, but
is tells plainly of a previous blighting.

ART OF THE EARLY MASTERS 610

The art of these was as wild flowers; that of the culminating period was as beauti-
l flowers in a garden; our own art is for the most part like very clever waxwork
itation.

CHRISTIANITY 611

true in so far as it has fostered beauty, and false in so far as it has fostered ugli-
ss. It is therefore not a little true, and not a little false.

CHRIST 612

d indeed come to divide households and bring swords on earth,[1] and this is one
the reasons why I so much dislike him.

PAULI ON CHRIST'S SAYINGS 613

Pauli said Christ's sayings were like quack pills intended to be swallowed whole
ithout chewing, or knowing what they were made of, and they poisoned one.

She did not like my writing *The Fair Haven*, she wanted me to write a nove I justified myself and talked about the desirability of showing up the absurdit of our present beliefs and so forth. She laughed a little wickedly and then demure answered, "Have they not Moses and the Prophets?"

Written December, 1881   Edited February 24 and 25, 18

UNITY OF NATURE   6

I meet a melancholy old Savoyard playing on a hurdy gurdy, grisly, dejected, d ty, with a look upon him as though the iron had long since entered into his soul. is a frosty morning, but he has very little clothing; there is a dumb despairing lo about him which is surely genuine. There passes him a young butcher boy wi his tray of meat upon his shoulder. He is ruddy, lusty, full of life and health a spirits, and he vents these in a shrill whistle which eclipses the hurdy gurdy of t Savoyard. The like holds good with the horses and cats and dogs which I meet dai with the flies in window panes, and with plants, some are successful, or have nc passed their prime. Look at the failures *per se*, and they make one very unhapp sorry for them we must always be, but it helps matters to look at them in the capacities as parts of a whole rather than as isolated. I cannot see things round abo me without feeling that they are all parts of one whole thing which is trying to something; it has not perhaps a perfectly clear idea of what it is trying after, b it is doing its best. I see old age, decay, and failure as the relaxation of a musc in the corporation of things after effort, or as a tentative effort in a wrong directio or as the dropping off of particles of skin from a healthy limb; as for the sheddi skin, in the first place it has had its turn, in the second, it starts anew under fre auspices, for it can at no time cease to be part of the universe, and must always li in one way or another.

Written December, 1881   Edited February 25, 18

MY BOOKS   6

When anything in them is rather strange and *outré*, it is probably drawn straig from nature as close as I could draw it; when it is very plausible, there is probab no particular and especial foundation for it.

Jones being very ill for a long while (December, 1881) with all sorts of complications after scarlet fever,[1] said to me one day, "I have been thinking that this may possibly be my death bed, and if so I should like you to know that there is only one thing in my life which I seriously regret--one part of my conduct which I think has been distinctly wrong, and not what it should have been--I refer to my treatment of my mother. I have been much too good to her. If my life is spared I will endeavour to amend this in the future, and treat her more as she deserves." On this he laughed as heartily as he had strength to do.

BOSS 618

old my cousin that if any woman could live with him she could live with God Almighty.

MISCARRIAGES 619

We are all miscarriages, but some mis-carry sooner and more completely than others, some at three months after conception only, and some at 100 years after birth.

AUBERON HERBERT[1] 620

He and his wife resolved that they and the servants should henceforth dine together at one time and one table; they would thus diffuse sweetness and light over their whole household. This would have answered very well if the servants after a few days had not given warning *en masse*.

EUCLID AND FAITH 621

Even Euclid cannot lay a demonstrable premise; he requires postulates and axioms which transcend demonstration, and without which he can do nothing. His superstructure is demonstration, his ground is faith. And so his *ultima ratio* is to tell a man that he is a fool by saying, "which is absurd."[1] If his opponent chooses to hold out in spite of this, Euclid can do no more. Faith and authority are as necessary for him as for any one else. True, he does not want us to believe very much, his yoke is tolerably easy,[2] and he will not call a man a fool till he will have public opinion generally on his side, but none the less does he begin with dogmatism and end with persecution.

Written December, 1881   Edited February, 1896

I was completing the purchase of Queen's Villas, and had to sign my name
Mr. Needham merely seeing the name and knowing none of my books, said to m
rather rudely but without meanings any mischief, "Have you written any book
like *Hudibras*?"[1] I said promptly, "Certainly; *Erewhon* is quite as good a book :
Hudibras." This was coming it too strong for him, so he thought I had not hea
and repeated his question. I said again as before, and he shut up. I sent him a cop
of *Erewhon* immediately after we had completed. It was rather tall talk on my par
I admit, but he should not have challenged me unprovoked.

GOD, TO THE LEXICOGRAPHER   62

is simply the word that comes next to "go-cart," and nothing more.

MRS. GOUGH, HER NOSE   62·

Finetti, the waiter at Faido, was moralising, and holding forth about the beaut
of nature, and truth. "Tutto che è vero è bello,"[1] he exclaimed, rolling out his word
with fine fervid enthusiasm. "No, Finetti," said I, "Mrs. Gough's nose is true, bu
it is not beautiful." Finetti looked puzzled for a moment, and then left me, laugh
ing.

Written December, 1881   Edited February 26, 189·

DARWIN ON WORMS   62

He may, or may not be right as long as he keeps to what the worms actuall
do--I know nothing about them--I should like however to question his servants abou
all this sitting up at night, and going about in slippers &c. A very little of this may b
made to go a long way in capable hands. When he comes to "reflex actions," "ir
stinct," and "intelligence" he is not intelligible. See pp. 23; 24; 35; 64; 65; 91-96.[1]
I seldom read a greater muddle than that in the paragraph (in the pp. last re
ferred to) beginning with "As worms are not guided &c."[2] "A capacity for at las
suceeding" is bad enough; but he does worse than this, for he says first that ant
have no capacity for trying different ways and at last succeeding, and then a fe
lines lower down admits that they have such capacity, inasmuch as though the
are very stupid at first, after a time they generally act in a wiser manner.
On p. 98 there is a very characteristic passage. He says "we should remembe
what a mass of inherited knowledge[...] * is crowded into the minute brain of a work
er ant." But in the *Origin of Species* Mr. Darwin expressly denies that the instinc
of worker-ants could be due to inherited knowledge, and wonders that no one ha
yet adduced "this demonstrative case of neuter insects, against the well known do
trine of inherited habit, as advanced by Lamarck,"[3] and he declared that it woul
be a serious error to suppose that the instincts of neuter ants could be derived fror

xperience acquired in one generation, and transmitted to the next.[4]

I animadverted strongly on this passage in *Life and Habit*,[5] and am the more pleased that Mr. Darwin has come to a sounder opinion in his later works. The way n which Mr. Darwin shifts his ground is inimitable; there is no admission of error; imply in one place Mr. Darwin stands frowning at a certain idea, and warning people off it with what, for him, is severity, and in another we find him with his eyes upurned to heaven musing upon the wondrousness of the idea which he had before condemned.

The taking off his slippers was a great hit, and has touched the heart of more han one reviewer. "By night and by day," says a writer in the *Morning Post* (December 23, 1881), "has he watched them, sometimes spending hours in the dead of ight contemplating their creeping movements, and this in his stockinged feet in rder to avoid any undue vibration of the floor which might disturb them. That he result of such profound observation should be valuable is unquestionable, but ven Mr.[6] Darwin's staunchest friends, and his bitterest opponents must now coness that this remarkable book has surpassed expectation, and is exhaustive."[7]

****

"Mr. Darwin's last book is in every sense the equal of any one of its celebrated redecessors; charming in its style and fully evidencing profound learning, and full f evidence of the most patient and self-sacrificing observation. There is something ouching in the picture drawn by the thoughtful mind of one of the most learned nen of our age passing long hours in the dead of night (in his stockinged feet fearing est the vibrations caused by his shoes should disturb these sensitive animals) watchng the habits and mode of being of the[8] lonely, deaf, dumb, and blind worm."

****

I cannot tell whether the sensitive animals of the parenthesis are Mr. Darwin's hoes, or his stockinged feet, or whether again they are not the long hours in the lead of the night; at any rate it is clear that the taking [off] * Mr. Darwin's shoes has nade a deep impression upon the reviewer. So it would on Mr. Tom Pinch if Mr. 'ecksniff had taken off his shoes. I wonder this reviewer is not touched also by Mr. Jarwin's intimate acquaintance with technical terms. Mr. Darwin speaks of a stone loor as having "sagged," how charming is this unobtrusive little exhibition of famiiarity with other branches of knowledge than those which he has made more particularly his own. There is something infinitely touching in the use of this word in his particular place. It is true no builder would apply it as Mr. Darwin has done, he word is one which is used to express the bending of timber, and is never applied o stone by masons and builders; but this is of no importance; Mr. Darwin has shown hat he knows there is such a word, and this is very beautiful and very touching; vhether his use of it is right or wrong is a point about which sensible people will e indifferent. So they will be indifferent also as to whether Mr. Darwin has told hem all about worms which they might reasonably expect to find in a work which s declared to be exhaustive. The reviewer indeed does seem a little exercised upon he point:--

"It is certainly," he writes, "somewhat surprising that[9] Mr. Darwin has not menioned in his work the only known but mortal enemy of the worm, the slug, which

sucks him up and destroys annually an astonishing number. The reviewer havin
recently placed several earth worms on a plate covered with earth, and placed und
a glass bell, was able to observe the astonishing dread which the larger worms fe
in the presence of a single slug, who, however, passed unnoticed by the young
ones. It would seem that the little animals had no innate dread of their enem
and that the fear manifested by their elders was the result of experience. The fa
remains that the large worms expressed such terror of the slug as to speedily abandc
the earth on which that obnoxious animal was placed, and hide themselves und
another mound removed from the presence of their enemy, who on being transfe
red thither was greeted by an immediate exodus on the part of the old worms, '
fresh fields and pastures new and in a safer part of the plate. Not so the little one
they did not hesitate to creep even over the slugs, who however taught them tl
lesson of experience by seizing upon them and speedily devouring them." (*Mornin
Post*, December 23, 1881)

(I used a good deal of the above in Chapter XVIII of *Luck or Cunning.*)[10]

VITALITY OF CHRISTIANITY   6.

This is held to be an argument for its truth. Surely then the vitality of unbeli
should count for something, persecution has been tried against it in vain &c; it
always being supposed to be killed, but it always comes back again stronger th
before &c. &c.

Written about December, 1881   Edited February 26 and March 4, 18!

CHRIST'S SAKE, DOING ALL FOR[1]   6.

We say this just as much as the Christians--or if we do not say it in so man
words we mean the same thing. We say that a man should paint or write with I
eyes fixed not on his gross palpable reward, but on something higher and less tan
ble; on something which is seen with the eye of faith though not with the eye
reason. This is why I attack Darwin. Can it do me any good to attack him? Am
likely to get money or fame by doing so? I should not think so, not at least in m
own lifetime: he is too strong in possession and I am too unsupported. Any m
of sense must know that I should do better by keeping my opinion on evoluti
to myself and writing books like *Alps and Sanctuaries*. I think I took higher grou
by attacking Mr. Darwin as far as it was in the least possible for me to do so, a
therefore I attacked him, but the advantage[2] of exposing humbug is one which a
crues rather to the public than to the person who exposes it.

Written about December, 1881   Edited March 4, 18

Gogin[1] was one day going down Cleveland Street and saw an old lean careworn an crying over the body of his dog which had been just run over and killed by the d man's own cart. I have no doubt it was the dog's fault, for the man was in great stress; as for the dog itself, there it lay, all swelled and livid where the wheel had one over it, its eyes protruded from their sockets and its tongue lolled out, but it as dead. The old man gazed on it helplessly weeping for some time, and then got large piece of brown paper, in which he wrapped up the body of his favourite; tied it up neatly with a piece of string, and placing it in his cart went homeward ith a heavy heart. The day was dull, the gutters were full of cabbage stalks, and e air resounded with the cry of costermongers.

On this a Japanese gentleman who had watched the scene lifted up his voice d made the bystanders a set oration; he was very yellow, he had long black hair d was a typical Japanese, but he spoke English perfectly. He said the scene they d all just witnessed was a very sad one, and that it ought not to be passed over tirely without comment. He explained that it was very nice of the old man to be sorry about his dog and so careful of its remains, and that he and all the bystanders ust sympathise with this good man in his grief, to the expression of which sympathy oth with the man and with the poor dog he had thought fit with all respect to make em his present speech.

I have not the man's words, but Gogin said they were like a Japanese drawing; at is to say, wonderfully charming, and showing great knowledge, but not done in e least after the manner in which a European would do them. As for the bystanders, ey stood open mouthed and could making nothing of it; they liked it, and the panese gentleman liked addressing them. When he left off and went away, they llowed him with their eyes speechless.

THE PROPHETS STONING THE JEWS   629

The Jews would not have stoned the Prophets if the Prophets had not stoned e Jews first. Just as I am sure the literary and scientific people of to-day would t dislike me as much as they do if I had not shewn my dislike to them pretty openly st. "We hate him, because he first hated us." This is what they would say, and ey would be quite right.[1]

OLD MRS. PANTON   630

I sent her to try and sell some of my studies. I wanted 15/-- for one very fair udy of a girl's head. Mrs. Panton did not succeed with the dealers. "One dealer," e said, "liked it very much, but when I told him I wanted 15/--for it he said, 'Oh ar me no, no such money.' " The poor old woman said this very dramatically, ting up her eyes and throwing up her hands, and repeating it more than once; then e munched her toothless old jaws, and folded her arms waiting for further orders-- I gave her the studies to get rid of her and them.

LOVING GOD   631

How can we love him if we fear him, and how can we not fear him if he is the ute which theologians have represented him?

The reason why words recall ideas is that the word has been artificially int
duced among the associated ideas, and the presence of one idea recalls the othe

HEBREW WRITERS AND EXAGGERATION   6:

We must remember that we are dealing with people to whom 36 hours we
good for 72. Christ could not have been dead more than 36 hours, yet the ear
christians call this three days and three nights.[1] Discount what they tell us by o
half all round, and I dare say it is right enough. Christ half died upon the cross, a
half ascended into heaven &c. As for God, if a thousand years to him are but as ye
terday,[2] he is an unaccountable person with whom the less we have to do the bett

THE GRAFTED THUMB   6:

An old man three hundred years ago had his thumb grafted on to a boy's han
the boy's thumb having been amputated; that same thumb has been cut off a
grafted anew for many generations, and it is said, is still living.

MISS BUCKLEY ON PEMMICAN   6:

Miss Buckley, Mr. Garnett,[1] and I were talking together about some book s
was writing, of which she had this or that much done. I said that if she had so mu
she would probably find it swell whether she liked it or not to the required siz
she did not seem to understand, so I explained that when I had about done a bo
and not seen it for a few weeks I found myself wanting to add paragraphs here a
there pretty freely. She said, "Oh that is the way you work, is it? Now I do ju
the opposite; I write a good deal more than I want and then make pemmican
it."

CLOVEN HOOVES   6:

Show the cloven hoof indeed? He showed himself to be a centipede, and eve
one of his feet a hoof, and each hoof cloven.

Written January, 1882   Edited March 5, 18

KATTY JONES   63

Mrs. Jones says of Katty[1] (a heavy lumbering gowk about 30, whom she h
never been able to get off her hands) that she "would have fallen before a great man

SENSITIVE PLANTS   63

I take it that all plants feel, but some make more fuss about their feelings th
others.

more generally known and appreciated than when I was a boy. At Littlehampton
ıst November (1881) I saw a bill in a green grocer's window announcing the coming
f a comic singer who was to sing a song of which the refrain was "Handel, Moses,
ulius Caesar, Timothy, Titus, Bartlett, Coutts." When Handel is as familiar to the
ıultitude as Moses, on the one hand and the Baroness Burdett Coutts and her hus-
and[1] on the other, his admirers should [be] * fairly well contented.

WORKING ON IN THE DARK   640

When we have eaten a piece of a cow it has to go on working in the dark for some
me before it gets to understand us, just as I am now working rather in the dark
ith double entry.

HALOS AT LITTLEHAMPTON   641

Jones and I, walking from the Beach Hotel towards the sea, just after the moon
ad risen, the moon being on our left hand, were accompanied one foggy night by
vo haloes on our right hands which formed complete circles and seemed about ten
ards off; they went as we went, each could see his own halo, but neither could see
ıe other's.[1]

UNITY OF NATURE   642

We can never quite get rid of the oneness of things with others that are distinct
nd separate from them, nor of the distinctness and separateness of things that never-
ıeless appear to be one.
When do we commonly consider a thing as one, and when commonly call it part
f another thing?

SPECIALISM AND GENERALISM   643

Woe to the specialist who is not a pretty fair generalist, and to the generalist
ho is not also a bit of a specialist.

PECKSNIFF AND DARWIN   644

I do not see how I can call Darwin the Pecksniff of science, though this is exactly
hat he is; but I think I may call Lord Bacon[1] the Pecksniff of his age, and then a
ttle later say that Mr. Darwin is the Bacon of the Victorian Era. This is like passing
ne item through two different accounts as though I had made Pecksniff Dr. to
acon, and Bacon Dr. to Darwin instead of entering Pecksniff Dr. to Darwin at once.

IMMORTALS TO OURSELVES   645

I said in *Alps and Sanctuaries* that we were mortals *quâ* others and immortals
uâ ourselves.[1] This is true, but it has its converse side, for it may be said that we
re mortal to ourselves inasmuch as we die to our own work, and know nothing of

the pain or pleasure it may be giving, and immortal *quâ* others, inasmuch as ou
work lives to them, though it is dead to us and we to it.

THWARTED, ON NOT BEING 64

Not only should a man have had his own way as far as possible, but he shoul
avoid commerce with things that have been stunted or starved. He should not eve
eat such meat as has been overdriven or underfed, or afflicted with any disease, ne
will he touch fruits or vegetables that have not been well grown.

NINEVEH BULLS 64

I said I was glad I had said in *Alps and Sanctuaries* that the fossil of a meg
therium bored us.[1] "Yes," said my cousin, "and the Nineveh bulls bore us. How
it that I pass them twice every day going to and coming from my dinner and nev
want to go 50 yeards out of my way to see them? If I want my dinner I don't wa
the bulls, and when I've had my dinner I want them less. I don't mind looking int
Bryce Wright's shop window. What I do enjoy is a pilgrimage to Furber's."[2] Even
the bulls were in Bryce Wright's window we should soon want them changed fo
something else.

THE ELECTRIC LIGHT IN ITS INFANCY 64

I heard a woman in a bus boring her lover about the electric light; she wante
to know this and that, and the poor lover was helpless. Then she said she wante
to know how it was regulated; at last she settled down by saying that she knew it w
in its infancy; the word "infancy" seemed to have a soothing effect upon her, fo
she said no more, but leaning her head against her lover's shoulder composed herse
to slumber.

THE BIBLE AND THE POOR 64

The Bible is like the poor; we have it always with us,[1] but we know very littl
about it.

REFORMS AND DISCOVERIES 65

are like offences; they must needs come, but woe unto that man through who
they come.[1]

LYING 65

People should learn to lie as they learn anything else--from very small beginning

A MAN WHO WISHED HIMSELF YOUNG AGAIN 65

There was a man who wished this, and a fairy took him at his word. He w
not long before he begged and prayed to be as he was before.

A man who has gone out and got some way from home, finding that he has left his purse behind him, and has no money is more than half paralysed.

MY RANDOM PASSAGES 654

Emmanuel at the Century Club[1] very kindly and hesitatingly ventured to suggest to me that I should get some friend to go over my M.S., before printing it; a judicious editor would have prevented me from printing many a bit which it seemed to him was written too recklessly and offhand. The fact is that the more reckless and random the passage is the more carefully it has been submitted to friends and considered and re-considered; without the support of friends I should never have dared to print one half of what I have printed.

MIS-QUOTATION 655

"Now in this month of roaring daffodils" from Tennyson's introduction to the *Nineteenth Century*, No. 1 (it is "roaring month of daffodils"[1]). Miss Savage gave me this, she made the mis-quotation in a room full of ladies and then innocently said she wondered why Tennyson had called daffodils "roaring." Lots of reasons were forthcoming and no one suspected guile.

H. E. CLARKE,[1] MY LYING LETTER TO 656

He wrote me a congratulatory note about *Alps and Sanctuaries*, saying how glad he was to see it had reached a second edition. I knew he disliked me and was humbugging, and he picked some holes, and came the humble, and generally I do not like him, so I replied with a letter crammed with lies about the way the book was succeeding, and the effect it had had upon the sale of my other books (not a copy of one of which has been sold so far as I know this two or three months past). I said I was afraid I ought to confess that the book's reaching a second edition so soon was due to the Americans who had helped me off with 200 copies. They never took a copy, and the fact that any second edition got out is due to nothing but a mistake on the part of the binder. We printed 1000 copies and had "second edition" put upon the second 500.[2] The actual sale so far has been about 200 (January 15, 1882).

GUARDS 657

always ride with their faces to the engine; they find the fatigue very greatly lessened thus.

WORDS AND IDEAS 658

These two things act and react upon one another like demand and supply, desire and power, faith and experience; but it is impossible to say which came first if the signification of words be extended so as to embrace every expression of an idea.

We know of no absolutely unchangeable environment, and of nothing which does not change with a changing environment. Everything is sensible of something. But how monotonous is the greater part of the existence of the atoms of the earth's crust. We see the flints sticking out of the edge of a cliff; these are subject to many kinds of change, but how slowly do the flints live that are fifty feet inside the cliff and fifty feet below the surface of the ground.

January, 1882   Edited March 6, 1896

MRS. BOSS   660

She says she can't abear to see Ivens now; she's got the water nearly right up to her heart, and a polly punch upon her head.

EREHWON, ADDENDUM TO   661

or a brief allusion to some other country where every one is expected to be more or less mad, and sanity is considered madness. The lawyers try to get people off on pleas of sanity. And people who are too sane are sent to Asylums where they are initiated into folly so far as they are found capable of it.

GRACE AND GOODNESS   66ℤ

There is no true gracefulness which is not epitomised goodness.

SUDDEN ACCESSIONS OF WEALTH   66ℤ

It is upon the evolution principle that these are so often fatal. The jump is too sudden. I heard the other day of a man who was at the Mart by accident and heard a very valuable freehold public house put up for sale. It was let for £75 a year to the Brewer's Company, the lease being about to run out in four or five years when the rental would be vastly increased. The Brewer's company were about to bid but mistook the time by an hour, it was also an extremely wet day. The property was put up at £1000 and the man offered this sum without any idea of getting it. It was knocked down to him, but five minutes afterwards he was offered first £1000 and presently up to £3000 for his bargain. It so turned his head that he took to drinking and died shortly. So with people who win prizes in lotteries.

RELIGION   66ℤ

Is there any religion whose members can be pointed to as distinctly more amiable and trustworthy than those of any other? If so this should be enough. I find the nicest and best people generally profess no religion at all, but are ready to like the best men of all religions.

One reason why we find it so hard to know our own likings is because we are
o little accustomed to try; we have our likings found for us in respect of by far
ne greater number of matters that concern us: thus we have grown all our limbs
n the strength of the likings of our ancestors, and adopt these without question.

MISS BUCKLEY[1]   666

She said to me the other day, "Why don't you write another *Erewhon*?" I said,
"Why Miss Buckley, *Life and Habit* was another *Erewhon*." They say these things
o me continually to plague me, and make out that I could do one good book, but
ever any more.

THE OLD MASTERS   667

If they had been able to do all they tried and wanted to do perhaps some of
nem would stand less high now than they do. This as regards the second best of
nem only.

HOSTILE REVIEWS   668

A perception of the value of a hostile review is as old as Paul's Epistle to the
hilippians I.15-18.[1]

DEMAND   669

imperious, supply suppliant.

IMAGINATION   670

I read once of a man who was cured of a dangerous illness by eating his doc-
or's prescription, which he understood was the medicine itself. So Moorhouse[1]
nagined he was being converted to Christianity by reading Burton's *Anatomy of
Melancholy* which he had got by mistake for Butler's *Analogy*,[2] on the recommenda-
on of a friend. But it puzzled him a good deal.

THEIST AND ATHEIST   671

It is hard to say which we ought to admire and thank most--the first theist or
he first atheist.

SLEEPY PEARS   672

I had a pear which was rotten in the middle. Some one asked me whether I
ked sleepy pears. I said I did not mind them sleepy but this one was snoring.

181

I was once sent to examine a school at Bolton,[1] just after I had taken my degree. I was to have my travelling expenses paid, and was going to charge second class fare, when Mr. Jacques, the Head Master, hearing of my intention said to me rather sternly, "Young man, there are two classes of people in this world: there are those who prey, and those who are preyed upon; never you belong to the latter." So I charged first class fare, and travelled second.

METEORIC SHOWER   674

On the morning after the last great display of shooting stars I asked our old servant Ann whether she had seen them. "No," she said, "I did not see them myself but Job Heathcote was driving round and he saw them. He said he'd seen them a many times before, but he never saw them so bad as they were last night."[1]

FAITH AND INNER LIFE   675

"Without faith an inner life is impossible." This should be translated, "without cheating oneself one cannot [retain] * all one's early teaching."

THE PRAYER BOOK   676

According to the prayer book theory we are like our table cloths, which must go to the wash once a week, inasmuch as they are sure to have got more or less dirty. But surely there should be a form for those who after a great many years find that they do not require quite so much rubbing and scrubbing, as when they were younger.

H.F. JONES ON EUCLID   677

Jones says Euclid would never have done for the staff of the *Daily Telegraph*. But one never can tell.

BUDDHISM   678

seems to be a jumble of Christianity and *Life and Habit*?

MISS BUCKLEY   679

She is the sort of person who if she had known Shakspeare would have said to him when he wrote *Henry the IVth*, "Ah Mr. Shakspeare, why don't you write us another *Titus Andronicus*, now that was a sweet play, that was." And when he had done *Anthony and Cleopatra* she would say that her favourite plays were the two *Henry the VIths*.[1]

PARIS EXHIBITION OF 1867   680

There was one department there set apart for what were announced as the "produits religieuses, de la France." I entered it, and found bleeding waxwork saints with choppers in their heads and red sealing wax smeared about them, pulpits, reading desks &c.

Jones, my cousin, and I were in the antechurch while service was going on; we came in just as the clergyman had intoned the words, "The Lord be with you," and the choir had answered, "And with thy spirit." My cousin turned round to me and hummed the bit from *Pinafore* which says, "You're exceedingly polite,

And we think it only right

To return the Com-pli-ment."[1]

PEERS AND KINGS AND RICH PEOPLE 682

do virtually now live in alternate generations. The peer's son gets married, then sickens of waiting for the peerage, dies, and the grandson inherits.

WHEN I AM DEAD 683

Do not let people represent me as one who suffered from misrepresentation and neglect. I was neglected and misrepresented: very likely not half as much as supposed, but nevertheless to some extent neglected and misrepresented. I growl at this sometimes, but if the question was seriously put to me whether I would go on as I am or become famous in my own life time, I have no hesitation about which I should prefer. I will willingly pay the few hundreds of pounds which the neglect of my works costs me in order to be let alone and not plagued by the odious people who would come round me if I were known. The probability is that I shall remain after my death as obscure as I am now; if this is so the obscurity will be probably merited, and if it is not a fact, my books will not only work as well without my having been known in my lifetime, but a great deal better; my follies and blunders will better escape notice, to the enhancing of the value of anything that may be found in my books. The only two things I should greatly care about if I had more money are a few more country outings and a little more varied and better cooked food; nicer things, and more expensive things to eat and drink.

P.S. March 5, 1896. I have long since obtained everything that a reasonable man can wish for.

February, 1882 Edited March 8, 1896

PATTY ROSCOE AND MY UNCLE ON EVOLUTION 684

Amy heard Patty Roscoe talking to my Uncle about Mr. Wicksteed's sermon;[1] he had preached on evolution. Patty Roscoe said that his remarks had been very sensible; she really did not see where the line was to be drawn, and supposed that after all we must admit intelligence and reason as having a place among the higher mammals. My Uncle passed all this, and so the matter was settled, and intelligence and reason are now let in among the higher mammals; here, however, we really will draw the line; nothing shall induce us to admit intelligence and reason among the lower mammals.

The man who can do nothing right.

DIVERSION AND CHANGE   686

The diversion or change of mental images is clearly pleasant, for we have come to use the word as the equivalent for being amused and pleased.

THOUGHT AND BUDDHISM   687

All that we are is the result of what we have thought; it is founded on our thoughts; it is made up of our thoughts--Buddhist saying. *Times*, February 1, 1882.[1]

PRIESTS, AN ARGUMENT FOR (not serious)   688

Is man capable of doing for himself in respect of his moral and spiritual welfare (than which nothing can be more difficult and intricate) what it is so clearly better for him to leave to professional advisers in the case of his money and his body, which are comparatively simple and unimportant?

PRAYERS   689

I dropped saying them suddenly without malice prepense, once for all. It was the night I went on board ship to start for New Zealand September 29, 1859. The night before I had said my prayers and doubted not that I was always going on to say them, as I always had done hitherto. That night I suppose the sense of change was so great that it shook them quietly off. I was not then a sceptic. I had got as far as disbelief in infant baptism, but no further.[1] I felt no compunction of conscience, however, about leaving off my morning and evening prayers--simply I could no longer say them.

WIT   690

There is no professor of wit at either University. Surely they might as reasonably have a professor of wit as of poetry.

A RECALCITRANT BLACKSMITH   691

A new Curate was explaining to the village blacksmith the nature of miracles The blacksmith was docile and accepted the story of Jonah in the whale's belly As the Curate put it, he said he saw no difficulty in it and was ready to believe it The Curate then went on the Shadrach, Meshach, and Abednego in the burning fier furnace.[1] "Now the furnace," said the Curate, "was many times larger and hotte than your forge." This riled the blacksmith; he was proud of his forge which ha been his father's before him. Besides he could realise a furnace to himself. "No, he said, "I don't believe it, and I don't believe the b---y fish story either." And s the matter dropped.

Compare these things more closely.

BEETHOVEN LAUNDRY 693

Near Walton (and Hersham) there is a cottage with "Mrs. T. May Beethoven aundry " on it.

GOD 694

is a respector of persons--no one more so.

MEN WITH TAILS 695

Many men still grow tails--small ones. Jones knew a boy at Radley[1] with one; he could not move it, it lay close in between his buttocks, but it could be seen when he bathed, and I am assured that quite an appreciable percentage of men examined for the army are dismissed as unfit in consequence of their having a small rudimentary tail.

THE ATTEMPT TO GET AT FOUNDATIONS 696

is trying to recover consciousness about things that have passed into the unconscious stage; it is pretty sure to disturb and derange those who try it on too much.

AGRIPPA AND AGRIPPINA 697

Mr. Latham, of Trinity Hall,[1] has two ravens, named as above. Mr. Latham throws Agrippa a piece of cheese, he takes it, hides it carefully and then goes away contented; but Agrippina has her eye upon him, and immediately goes and steals it, hiding it somewhere else. Agrippa however has always one eye upon Agrippina, and no sooner is her back turned than he steals it and buries it anew. Then it becomes Agrippina's turn, and thus they pass the time making believe that they want the cheese, though they neither of them really want it. One day Agrippa had a small fight with a spaniel, and got rather the worst of it. He immediately flew at Agrippina and gave her a beating. Jones said he could almost hear him say, "It's all your fault."

February, 1882   Edited March 10, 1896

MY LETTERS 698

I hope no one will ever collect them, and publish them. I don't believe I ever wrote a letter in my life, which I would allow to be published if I could help it.

As it is we know very little of what is going on in ourselves, and are conscious of what we do only very broadly so long as nothing goes wrong with us. We are more conscious of others, and others are more conscious of us, than we are of ourselves; how much more thought has been turned upon Handel and Shakespeare than Handel or Shakespeare can have ever turned upon themselves. In how many do not these men live who never saw them? The part, therefore, of one who has lived much in and for others, that death destroys, is only a very small one. Shall we complain that we shall one day come to know ourselves a little less even than we do at present? How small is the life we live in our fingers as compared with the life we live in that which our fingers may have written?

CHRIST AND THE DEVIL IN THE WILDERNESS   700

The devil tempted Christ; yes; but it was Christ who tempted the devil to tempt him.[1] Then was the devil led up into the wilderness to be tempted of Christ.

MRS. BOSS   701

always calls Chester Terrace, where my uncle lives, "Chester Rents" or "the rents," partly out of spite because she hates my cousin's people almost as much as he does, and partly because she used to live in Chichester Rents, Chancery Lane.[1]

SAMENESS, IDENTITY, UNITY   702

"Bishop" and "evêque" are the same word, and they are not nearly the same word.

"SHOCK" AND "DIVERT"   703

Our use of these words is very suggestive. We show that we hate any great change introduced too suddenly, and like almost any change which does not startle.

THE EXPERIENCE OF OLD MEN   704

can hardly become hereditary, for few old men, and no old women, have children. Later average age of reproduction will not only tend to longevity, but also to more hereditary good sense.

CATHOLICS--HOW CAREFUL WE SHOULD BE ABOUT LYING   705

In *Alps and Sanctuaries* I implied that I was lying when I said Handel was a Catholic;[1] but he was a Catholic, and so am I, and so are all well disposed people It shows how careful we ought to be when we lie--we can never be sure but what we may be speaking the truth.

THE INVISIBLE CHURCH   706

Is there not somewhere something about "the holy invisible church"? There ought to be. The true church will ever be invisible.

HERBERT SPENCER ON RHYTHMS AND VIBRATIONS   707

See *Principles of Psychology*, p. 152 &c. and p. 190, 225; he spoils it p. 191. He confounds ego and non-ego p. 147. See §13 of his *Principles of Biology*.[1]

EATING, AND ALL THE SENSES   708

They are all a kind of eating. They are all touch, and eating is touch carried to the bitter end.

NERVOUSNESS AND IMPOTENCY   709

As confidence begets power, and power confidence, so nervousness increases impotence, and impotence nervousness.

METAPHYSICS   710

There is no such metaphysics as physics in the hands of a scientist who goes too far for his facts.

CONSCIENCE-JABBERING   711

When I was a small boy I used to be made to recite a poem about conscience. I forget it, but it came to this--that if one did not take very great care, one's conscience would leave off talking. I think one's conscience had better not speak at all than be always jabbering, as some men's do.

PAULI AND THE CHURCH OF ROME   712

When I began to make friends with the Church of Rome, Pauli asked me to find out from Father (or brother?) Gabriel (Mr. McWalter) what was the least thing they would take--what in fact were the cheapest terms on which they would have him--what was the smallest article in the way of Romanism that was in the market.

TWO STORIED HOUSES IN HOLBORN   713

There are still two left, next to Brett's distillery,[1] nearly opposite Chancery Lane. I mean houses with nothing but a shop and one floor above them (and that not high) with a red tiled roof. Relics almost of the suburban days of Holborn. April 2, 1882.

Extremes meet. Loving everybody is loving nobody; and God everywhere practically God nowhere, so that the difference   [is]* between + and -0. But fc many reasons the +0 is to be preferred.

CHANGE   71

There is no such change as changelessness under changed surroundings.

AN AMERICAN FUNERAL   71

A man was being buried and a woman standing near the grave was weeping bitte ly--so much so as to attract the attention of the bystanders; on this the widow wer up to her and said, "Look here, stranger--air you running this funeral or am I?"

Written April, 1882   Edited March 10, 189

HINDOO ENGLISH   71

"When Sir George was Lord of Belvedere he pretended to be *summum bonur* and triton among the minnows. He was indeed the *cactus grandiflorous* of Benga and also flouted native gentlemen with contumelious pranks. But though he flaunte himself, clothed in gaudy tinsel, it was not for ever and a day, for the House of Con mons have torn off every rag and tatter, and exposed his *cui bono* in all its nake hideousness."[1]

ON THE DEATH OF AN AIMABLE YOUNG LADY[1]   71

"Had she been protracted to a distant old age, where after diffusing her life an light upon those immediately around her, she would have sunk beneath the wester horizon--had she been favoured with this blessing we are now at a loss to compr(hend what an inesteemable boon she would have been to the world.... Without know ing the alpha and beta of the science of music, too frequently did she pour forth th burden of her soul in heart stirring songs and hymns without the least reserve, thoug in company with her dear elderly relatives."

* * * * *

"His first business on making an income was to extricate his family from th difficulties in which it had lately been enwarped, and to restore happiness and sur shine to those sweet and well beloved faces on which he had not seen the soft an fascinating beams of a simper for many a grim-visaged year.
"He departed this life on the 17th of August 1871 A.D. of paralysis and ruptur of a blood vessel, leaving four issues two male and two female.

188

"Drs. Payne, Fayrer, Nilmadhub, Mookerjee, and others ... did what they could
to, with their puissance and knack of medical knowledge, but it proved after all
as if to milk the ram! His wife and children had not the consolation to hear his last
words, he remained sotto voce a few hours, and then went to God about six p.m.
The house presented a second Babel or pretty kettle of fish; all wept for him and
whole Bengal was in lachrymation; and more I shall say that even the learned judges
of the high court heard sighs, and closed it on its appellate and original sides." *Times*,
April 11, 1882.

Review of *The Memoir of the late Honourable Justice Onocool Chunder Mooker-
ee by Chindronauth Mookerjee* ... author of the "Effects of English Education upon
the Native Mind." Calcutta, Thacker Spink and Co.[2]

DEATH OF C. DARWIN   719

"The time has gone by when it was conceived possible to extinguish a scientific
hypothesis by authority.

* * * * *

"In France, though official science still struggles against it, the attitude of independent workers is rather that of accepting Mr. Darwin's views while giving as much
as possible of the credit of them to the Frenchman Lamarck. [1]

* * * * *

"There never was a more honest man. Not only was he superior to the ordinary
pettinesses and jealousies of the disoverer--as is shown by the well known story of
his conduct with regard to Mr. Wallace's simultaneous statement of the evolution
hypothesis, but he was incredibly scrupulous in verifying all his facts, in listening
to every objection, in balancing every consideration that was brought before him.

* * * * *

'--and lastly that marvellous book on earthworms which he published only last winter." *Times* leader, April 21, 1882.[2]

* * * * *

"On April 19, 1881, all the civilised world held its breath at the news of the
death of Lord Beaconsfield; not less must be the effect upon the most civilised part
of the civilised world, when the announcement of the death of Charles Darwin flashed
over that earth whose secrets he has done more than any other to reveal. (!)

* * * * *

"Simplest habits ... the simple, but intensely interesting ... his manners were childlike simplicity ... his simple readiness to listen, suggest and help ....

* * * * *

"We need not here enter into the delicate distinctions, which exist between the developmental theories of Erasmus, which were prematurely sown in unfruitful and unprepared soil, and those of his greater grandson, which have revolutionised research and thought in every department of human activity.

"His habits and manners were of childlike simplicity, his bearing of the most winning geniality, and his modesty and evident unconsciousness of his own greatness almost phenomenal. In sending a letter or contribution to a journal he asked for its insertion with a doubting hesitancy rare even in a tiro.

* * * * *

"Of course Mr. Darwin's originality has been assailed. Kant, Laplace, Buffon, Erasmus Darwin, and of course Lucretius, have been brought forward as the real originators of the fertile idea which has taken its name from Mr. Charles Darwin. Give these old world worthies all the credit which is justly their due, and it is not little; let it be granted that Darwin received the first initiative in his fertile career of research from a study of what they had done by his predecessors (sic); and yet how comes it that these old theories fell comparatively dead, and bore no substantial fruit?"

(I may interrupt to answer this question thus. The French Revolution stopped Buffon and Erasmus Darwin. Poverty, want of social influence, and the reaction against the French Revolution stopped Lamarck. The *Vestiges*[3] was not stopped, but was widely read and had made a large number of converts long before 1859. The *Origin of Species* succeeded so rapidly, firstly because the older writers had been smouldering a long while and a spark would have been enough to set the evolution theory blazing; secondly, the French Revolution and 1830 scares had been well recovered from, and the world was beginning to take up the position as it had been left by such men as Gibbon[4] and the free-thinking philosophers of the last century--these two main causes were supplemented by the fact that Mr. Darwin was a rich man, and played his cards socially remarkably well. He courted all rising men and litterateurs, just as he courted me after I had written *Erewhon* and, as under the pretext of ill health and literary business he only showed very little (keeping mainly to his private study where visitors were not allowed), he could be at his best when seen, and be easily idealised by young green horns who like myself were at first flattered by being noticed by him. But, as I found on my second visit, he could be brutally uncourteous when he chose, though why he chose to be so on this particular occasion I cannot imagine. His urbanity, childlike simplicity, unselfishness and mock modesty were about as genuine as those of Mr. Pecksniff.

"Mr. Darwin's great theory in some of its parts may require modification; he himself latterly, we believe, did not seek to maintain it in its original (want of? integrity. (dishonesty?) (Then why did he not tell us what parts he wished to abandon, and which to keep!) As has been suggested, (!) some greater law may yet be

190

ound which will cover Darwinism, and take a wider sweep; but whatever development science may assume Mr. Darwin will in all the future stand out, as one of the
giants in scientific thought, and scientific imagination.

"Between 1844 and 1854, he published through the *Ray* and other societies
various monographs which even his greatest admirers admit do not do him the highest
credit as a minute anatomist." (This is the first I have seen of this in any paper.
These monographs should be looked to.)[5] *Times*, Obituary Notice, April 21, 1882.[6]

The *Morning Post* claims Mr. Darwin as the great Apostle of design. It complains that Mr. Darwin who, as it says, has insisted on design in nature more than
any other man should have been reckoned among the upholders of anarchy.[7]

As for me, I have already returned my corrected proofs of the appendix to *Evolution Old and New* more than a week, and cannot now recast what I had written,
but I suppose I must write a preface to say how sorry I am Mr. Darwin is dead.[8]
I see Mr. Gladstone signalised the anniversary of Lord Beaconsfield's death two days
ago by giving a dinner party. I certainly should avoid the anniversary of Mr. Darwin's death if I wanted to give a dinner party, but it goes rather against my grain
to eulogise him merely because he is dead. April 21, 1882.

"How long the era he opened will last none can tell. Veins of thought supposed
to be of inexhaustible wealth sometimes fail. It is still less possible to predict that
a larger law may not sooner or later embrace and merge that of evolution itself.
But it is no rash assertion that the facts must survive, and something more than the
facts, which Darwin spent his happy life in collecting. He accumulated facts and he
will have taught posterity how to accumulate them. Should the theories which he
inferred from facts as he knew them ever become subordinate or obsolete, it will
be in virtue of discoveries made through the method he used and enthroned." *Times*,
April 26, 1882.[9]

I wish I could find out what this method was. The great method which Darwin
used was personal social influence and a plausible manner--but this is not a new discovery. If it is to this however that the *Times* refers, it does well to continue [that]*
"no increase in the facilities for observing nature or enlargement of the range of
physical knowledge is likely to disprove the value of his method.

"He found a great truth, trodden under foot, reviled of bigots and ridiculed
by all the world; he lived long enough to see it, chiefly by his own efforts, irrefraga-
bly established in science, inseparably incorporated with the common thoughts of
men, and only held and feared by those who would revile and dare not." Huxley
in *Nature*, April 27, 1882.[10]

This is more near the truth. We all know that Mr. Darwin has been the greatest
populariser of Evolution; but he did not find Evolution so "trodden under foot"
as Huxley says, nor as I for decency's sake have pretended in my Preface to the second
edition of *Evolution Old and New*.[11] It was all ripe for dropping into the mouth
of any one who opened his mouth for it.

The *St. James's Gazette* writes:

"On the other hand there is a kind of over curious criticism which, in opposition to the first popular impression seeks to exaggerate the importance of Mr. Darwin's fore-runners, and of those parts of the doctrine which are not peculiarly his
own, and to disparage the value and novelty of his work. This kind of criticism is
doubly and trebly suspicious, both in itself and with regard to its probable motives;
nevertheless it has been urged with much persistence, and in one case by a competent naturalist." *St. James Gazette*, April 24, 1882.[12]

This is meant partly for me, and I should think the insinuation of unworthy motives is intended entirely for my benefit: if so, the writer is discreet in not writing so that I can lay hold of him, and in not giving his name. When people dare not come out and fight and yet cannot refrain from innuendo, I think we may guess which way the battle has begun to go.

This writer is likely enough the one whom I challenged in this very journal in my letter of December 8, 1880, but who did not venture to reply.[13] Greenwood[14] knows the facts very well and should not have allowed the foregoing innuendo to appear in his paper.

The *St. James's Gazette* continues: Mr. Darwin "was not ambitious of popular fame, still less did he trouble himself about the questions of priority which too often raise unseemly strife between men of science." It is true there was no quarrel between Darwin and Wallace,[15] but it is admitted by Darwin himself that he hurried up the bringing out of the *Origin of Species* because he was told that Wallace was on the same track.[16] If he did not "trouble himself about questions of priority," why this trouble to be if possible prior to Wallace?

I do not blame Mr. Darwin for wanting to get his work out before that of a rival--only don't let every one say that he was above all such considerations. This very reviewer continues that Mr. Darwin's "hand was amicably forced, so to speak, by Mr. Wallace having independently reached, and being ready to publish, closely similar conclusions."

The reviewer says Mr. Darwin "was anxious to be understood, and minded to make his own position completely clear to those who were willing to understand him." If ever there was a writer whose aim was to seem clear without being so it was Mr. Darwin.

BISHOP OF CARLISLE'S SERMON ON DARWIN   720

I see almost at the beginning of his sermon he said "De mortuis nil nisi bonum." He might almost as well have said at once that he had a bad opinion of Mr. Darwin. As things go now there is hardly any way of vilifying a man much worse than to say of him "De mortuis &c." as soon as he is dead.

But I am glad they buried him in Westminster Abbey. The Bishop made a hit when he said that in France Mr. Darwin could not have been buried in a church but that if he had been so buried no man of science would have been present. Anything is good which makes either side more tolerant of the other.

MY LETTERS TO MARRIOTT   72

Marriott--now the Rt. Honble Sir William--and I were of the same year at St John's and were intimate.[1] I do not know which of us was more profoundly convinced of his own abilities and importance. From New Zealand I wrote him many long foolish letters which he kept. Many years afterwards when we had had some at any rate, of our nonsense taken out of us, we met, and he told me he had my old letters and that they were very funny. Hoare[2] told me so also--by "funny" meaning laughable on account of their conceit. Marriott was evidently keeping them for no other purpose than to laugh, and make others laugh at me, so I called on him one day and begged the loan of them. He made me swear I would give them back but when I read them I was so much ashamed that I burned every one of them. The following extracts were copied by me, I think for use in *Ernest Pontifex*, in case

-wrote that novel. Jones says that I am not to destroy them--so I leave them for
1 my shame that I should have written them. March 11, 1896.

"I am now a confirmed grazier; little enough, is it not? for all one's high aspira-
ons to end in? Once upon a time I believed in myself; I believed I was destined
) exercise an influence upon my generation; that I should be wanted--I knew not
hat for, but for something--and that when wanted, I should be found all there.
does not look very like it now, does it?

"I think I am a unitarian now, but don't know and won't say; as for the Trinity
cannot make head or tail of it, and feel inclined to agree with a negro who was
eard in church here the other day to repeat the response in the Athanasian Creed,
he father impossible, the son impossible, and the Holy Ghost impossible: so there
re not three impossibles but one impossible'."

"I do not mean half the arrogance which I express. Hoare[2] gave me rather a
1arp wigging for a letter I wrote him not long since--just a few days before I came
) see that the death of Jesus Christ was not real. He says I swore at the articles.
his certainly I should not have done; but please think that I am not so conceited
s some of my friends suppose. I feel strongly, and write as I feel, but I am open
) conviction, and that I can take in more sides of a question than one is proved
y the many changes my opinions have undergone.

"For the present I renounce Christianity altogether. You say people must have
)mething to believe in. I can only say that I have not found my digestion impeded
nce I have left off believing in what does not appear to be supported by sufficient
vidence. As for going to Church I have left it off this twelvemonth and more, not
ecause I think it wrong to go to Church, but because I do not like going, and do
ot feel any good effects from having gone. When I went last I made a few notes,
nd on returning wrote a short account of what I had seen heard and felt. I wrote
without either humour or exaggeration, but tried to put down bona fide what
assed within and without me."

Written June, 1882   Edited March 15, 1896

CRABBE ROBINSON'S BREAKFASTS[1]

I was asked to one of these once but I was not a success. I forget who were ther except my cousin Dick, George Scharf, J. Pattisson and Street the Architect.[2] I used to go to my uncle's often on a Sunday evening when I first came back fro[m] * New Zealand, and Crabbe Robinson went there too, every third Sunday for years till he was 90 or over. He was not nice, nor were the people I met at his break fast. They did not like me better than I them--for I never was asked again. I only accepted the invitation to please my uncle.[3] When the old man died, he left my uncle a copy of Roger's *Italy*, and my uncle and aunt, considering how many years they had borne his often repeated stories, thought it was rather shabby of him.[4]

MERIT-TRIUMPHING: DARWIN AND BACON

It is all very well to say that merit triumphs in the end, but look at Bacon. H treated Roger Bacon much as Charles Darwin treated his grandfather.[1] Yet th credit remains his to this day. Had there been reviews in his day, when he died the would have contained nothing about his taking bribes and being dismissed fror the Chancellorship. If anything was said about the matter at all, it would have bee to the effect that he took them out of the guileless innocence of his heart, becaus "it never occurred" to him that there could be any harm in "so usual a practice, or that it was done due to "an oversight." His critics would lay the greatest stres on his simple-mindedness and contempt of money; upon his wonderful straigh forwardness of character, and perhaps most of all on the gratitude he showed t all who had helped him towards advancement. As for Roger Bacon--well--perhap there was such a person, but his works have an interest only to those who curiousl study prophecy.

MRS. GELDART AND BECK[1]

When the living of St. Edward's fell vacant--one of the parish churches of Cam bridge, Trinity Hall being patron--Mrs. Geldart said to Beck: "Now you know, M Beck, we must have some one who believes in the Trinity." "You can only hav the pick ma'am, of what there is in Cambridge" was the rejoinder.

MRS. GELDART AND YOUNG DICKENS[1]

At one of her freshmen's parties a son of Dickens was there. She made littl notes beforehand of what she was to say to each undergraduate, and talked to eac one with her note book in hand. To Dickens she said, "So Mr. Dickens, I hear yo are a son of the man who writes those dreadful books; dear, dear, I can't think ho any one can read them."

GLADSTONE

should be treated in exactly the converse way to Enoch and Elijah. He should b carried down to the lower regions without dying.[1]

"A damsel belonging to Barclay's establishment being here, I thought it right
to try and do her good', so I asked her after many unsuccessful questions, if she
ad not heard of the Lord's coming into the world. 'Why,' she said, 'I may have
one so, but I have forgot it.' 'But surely you must have heard your Master read
out it [2] at School and Church and Chapel.' 'Very likely I have,' said she placidly,
ut it has quite slipped my memory'--and this uttered with a lamb-like face, and
mild blue eye."

DARWIN'S BOOK ON WORMS   728

There was a review of this by F.A. Paley, I think in *Frazer's* during the early
rt of 1882, the reticence of which was noticeable.[1] In the *Monthly Journal of
ience* for June, 1882, there is also a first article which blows on Darwin quietly
good deal.[2]

MY FATHER'S THEMES   729

I heard my Aunt Mrs. Bather[1] many years ago (she died in 1853 or 1854) say
at my father as a boy had to write a theme upon silence. He began, "Silence is
virtue which renders us agreeable to our fellow creatures"--he was not intending
be satirical. He had to do another on inconsistency. This one began, "Incon-
stency is a vice which degrades human nature and levels man with the brute." I
t both of them into *Erewhon*--but I changed "inconsistency" into "consistency."[2]

BURMAH, HOW I WAS SAVED FROM GOING INTO THE   730

I paid my passage for New Zealand in this ship, and was only dissuaded from
ing in her at the last moment by the advice of my cousin Dick[1] who was at some
ouble in the matter. I remember it was sorely against my will (and I think against
y father's will too), that I recovered my passage money and went in the *Roman
nperor* which followed her instead. The *Burmah* was never heard of again.[2]

BUFFON, JUDGMENT, SENTIMENT   731

When Buffon says that there is more sentiment in animals than judgment,[1]
says virtually that their unconscious is vaster than their conscious memory.

ASSOCIATED IDEAS   732

How children dislike any failure in this respect--unless indeed they like it. I
ed to dislike Soda water, because I could not understand where the bubbles came
om; but we like the failure sometimes as in conjuring tricks, or agreeable surprises.

C. DARWIN   733

I have praised him in my books much more than I like, and not said one half
much bad of him as I believe, but I suppose this is all right.

PROPER PSALMS   7

We sometimes see these announced. "Are there," Jones asks, "any improp psalms?"

HOW I GOT TO KNOW THAT I LIKED HANDEL BEST   7

As a boy, from twelve years or so, I always worshipped him; at Cambridge wh Sykes[1] began to play Beethoven I would leave the room: I did not like him; lit by little I began to like him, and then I played him, and Bach, and Mendelssoh *Songs Without Words,*[2] and thought them lovely, but I always liked Handel be Little by little, however, I was talked over to placing him and Bach and Beethov on a par as the greatest, and thought I did not know which was the best man. O night when I was about thirty, I was at an evening party at Mrs. Longden's,[3] a met an old West End Clergyman of the name of Smalley.[4] I said I did not kn which was greatest, Handel, Bach, or Beethoven; he said, "I am surprised at th I should have thought you would have known." "Which," said I, "is the greatest "Handel " was the answer. I knew he was right, and have never wavered since. suppose I was really of this opinion already, but it was not till I got a little tou from outside that I knew it.

GREAT MEN AND LIFE   7

It is only those who die great (whether known or not) who are ever really bo at all. The others are still-born. But the great ones are only embryos during li Their true life is the life after death, and of which they seem to be unconscio

THE GREAT CHARACTERS OF FICTION   7

live as truly as the memories of dead men. For the life after death it is not necessa that a man or woman should have lived.

EVOLUTION AND SENSE OF CHANGE   7.

The great principle that underlies evolution is the desires of the animals th vary.

The great principles that underlie desires turn mainly upon food, reproducti and self-defence.

What is the principle that underlies these three desires? Dislike of change, te pered by desire for change.

Under this there lies continued sense of identity (for which some change is nec sary, inasmuch as without sense of change there is no sense of identity, nor inde any sense at all), and under this again Memory. Beyond which I cannot go.

Kant says (and Rosmini? see Davidson's *Rosmini*, p. 10)[2] that all our knowledge founded on experience.   But each new small increment of knowledge is not so ιnded: and our whole knowledge is made up of the accumulation of these small ιv increments not one of which is founded upon experience.   Our knowledge, εn, is founded not on experience, but on inexperience; for where there is no novelty, ιt is to say no inexperience, there is no increment in experience.   Our knowledge really founded upon something which we do not know--but it is converted into perience by memory.

It is like species, we want to know the cause of the variations where accumula-ιn results in species.   Any explanation which leaves this out of sight ignores the ιole difficulty.   We want to know the cause of the effect that inexperience pro-ιces on us.

INFINITE SUBDIVISION OF ATOMS   740

Query whether this in the end does not come to no subdivision at all?

IGNORANCE OF OUR OWN EXISTENCE   741

We are absolutely unaware of our own existence, and indeed are quasi non-istent unless when exercising some faculty.

MATTER AND MIND   742

People say we can conceive the existence of matter, and the existence of mind. ιdoubt it.   I doubt how far we have any definite conception of mind: nor yet of ιatter pure and simple.   What is meant by conceiving of a thing or understanding ι?

When we hear of a piece of matter instinct with mind, as protoplasm for example, ere certainly comes up an idea, a picture before our closed eyes, which we imagine bear some resemblance to the thing we are hearing of, but when we hear of matter apart from every attribute of matter (and this I suspect comes ultimately to "apart om every attribute of mind") we get no image before our closed eyes--we realise ιthing to ourselves.   Perhaps we surreptitiously introduce some little attribute, ιd then think we have conceived of matter pure and simple, but this I think is as ιr as we can go.

The like holds good for mind: we must smuggle in a little matter before we ιt any definite idea at all.

PHILOSOPHY   743

a general rule is like stirring mud or not letting a sleeping dog lie.   It professes appease our ultimate "why?"   In truth it is generally the solution of a *simplex ιotum* by a *complex ignotius*.[1]   This at least is my experience of everything that ιs been presented to me as philosophy.   I have often had my "why's?" answer-ι with so much mystifying matter that I have left off pressing them through fatigue,

197

but this is not having my ultimate "why?" appeased. It is being knocked out time.

BOSS

When my cousin has said something to her that she does not like, she repli "never mind, it's only lent," meaning that she will pay him out for it some d

JONES ON DICKENS

I said of Dickens that he was vulgar. "He's worse than vulgar," said Jones. "H moral."

CHERUBS AND R.E. WORSLEY

He said the Cherubs on Amy Nesmyth's grave at Cobham, near Woking, w like illegitimate children of George the Fourth.

A FREETHINKER

I once asked a man if he was a freethinker: he said he did not *think* he w

SAMENESS

If a man is not the same that he was five minutes ago, it follows that he m be a little the same as somebody else--for he certainly is a little the same man t he was five minutes ago.

ILLUSION AND PROGRESS

A fertile source of the first of these, and therefore of the second, is the f that the absence of one (or sometimes even of a good many) of the associated id does not count. A broken letter, for example, or an undotted i in a printed wo does not count; the idea is raised as much as though all the associated ideas had be present.

PITY--WHO MOST NEED IT

Not the dead; nor the truly living; nor yet the dying; but those who can hard be called alive or dead or dying.

WANT

If we want very much, we need not think much about the way: the want itse if genuine, will suggest the way better than anything else--provided of course t there is a way.

BOSS 752

id that when young Watkins died, his poor dear skin was like alabaster.

INEQUALITY 753

High and progressing nations vary more than low, and so middle-aged men in
ll power vary more than children and old people. Progress goes from the simple
the complex. *Times*, June 2, 1882.[1]

C. DARWIN 754

See *Atlantic Monthly, Monthly Journal of Science*, and *Contemporary Review*
r June, 1882.[1]

JONES AND ST. MARK'S, VENICE 755

Jones knew an old lady who said she had been to Venice and seen St. Mark's. It
is so beautiful. "It is made of all the different kinds of architecture; there's Bis-
ntine, and Elizabethan and Gothic, and perpendicular, and all the different kinds
d Mr. Ruskin says it's lovely."

SUBJECT 756

On running up against old friends.

SOLICITORS 757

A man must not think he can save himself the trouble of being a sensible man
d a gentleman by going to his Solicitor, any more than he can get himself a sound
nstitution by going to a doctor; but a solicitor can do more to keep a tolerably
ll meaning fool straight than a doctor can do for an invalid.

DANS L'ANIMAL IL-Y-A PLUS DE SENTIMENT QUE DE JUGEMENT[1] 758

So we call a man sensible more often than we call him judicious.

INOCULATION 759

There should be inoculation for marriage, as well as for speculation.

BALLOONING 760

There was an article in the *Times* (early in June? 1882) which convinces me
at the navigation of the air must be near at hand. When the *Times* dismisses a
bject so contemptuously as this, it is generally on the point of succeeding.[1]

if you follow it far enough always leads to conclusions that are contrary to reasc

ROME, THE CHURCH OF 7

It is not its doctrines, but its intolerance that we object to--the way in whi it claims that it must be right and every one else wrong.

SERMONS 7

I heard of an old clergyman who died, and after his death his sermons were s(at ninepence a barrow load.

INOCULATION 7

or a hair of the dog that's going to bite you--this principle should be introduc in respect of marriage, and speculation.

THE BODY OF CHRIST 7

Father Lockhart[1] wants to prove the resurrection by asking what became Christ's body on the assumption that he was not carried up to heaven. But (1) question, "what became of the body?" does not touch the resurrection; it has do with the Ascension and with nothing else. (2) They might as well ask what beca of young Grey and the woman he is supposed to have run away with, or what came of the murderers of Lord Frederick Cavendish and Mr. Burke.[2] They sho show that all the natural ways in which Christ's disappearance might be account for are out of the question before they want me to accept a supernatural expla tion.

BOSS 7

said that Mrs. Honor would drink everything she could stand upright and pay I money for.

SATISFACTORY 7

Nothing could be satisfactory even for a short time if anything could be so very long.

ARTIFICIAL FLOWERS 7

There are real artificial flowers and artificial artificial flowers. A nursery gard is a place where they make real artificial flowers (by creating new varieties &c.) a yet there is something to be said for the view that real flowers are artificial artific flowers.

Who are the men who do this? Not the experts, but the public who though
ey do not know enough to be experts, yet know enough to decide between them.

ritten June, 1882   Edited March, 1896

ORDER   770

Note the double sense of the word "order" as something commanded and "a
nsequential arrangement."

HOLY GHOST IN HAT   771

I was with my Aunt Worsley at the National Gallery once, and we were before
an Eyck's picture of John Arnolfini and his wife[1] (if the picture is indeed this).
y aunt mistook it for an annunciation, and said, "Dear, dear, what a funny notion
put the Holy Ghost in a hat."

SUBJECT   772

A Grammar of dissent, or primer of unbelief (for the use of men like Father
ockhart).[1]

FATHER LOCKHART AND ECCLESIASTES   773

I called on Father Lockhart at Ely Place,[1] and he was showing me that the dis-
iction between men and animals was not arbitrary, but was founded on something
sential, immutable &c. "So, the bible," he continued, "says that the soul of a
an goeth upwards, and the spirit of a beast goeth downwards."
"No," said I, "let us have the whole passage." So he turned to the Vulgate and
und "*Quis novit si* &c.": "Who can say that the soul of a man goeth upwards,
d the spirit of a beast downwards?" See Ecclesiastes III. 21.[2] Our English ver-
on is wrong; it has "who knoweth the spirit of man that goeth upwards, and the
irit of a beast that goeth downwards to the earth?" The context shows that the
lgate is right in rendering the question as one involving scepticism concerning our
owledge on these points. Father Lockhart was much scandalised. He said he
d not think he had ever read the passage before. I don't think he had.

NIRVANA   774

Men's common expressions and actions show that the balance of evil, in their
es, is on the side of movement and exertion.

told me he should like to know more of my opinions as a free-thinker: he had talke
with few or none except myself and Davidson (who wrote a book on Rosmini).
He said, "It is my profession to know these things." I thought it might be his pr
fession, but it was not his performance.

WORDS AND ACCOUNTS   77

Fighting about words is like fighting about accounts, and all classification
like accounts. Sometimes it is easy to see which way the balance of convenien
lies; sometimes it is very hard to know whether an item should be carried to or
account or to another.

TIME   77

A woman who was going to take one of my houses in Atwell Road told n
she had a house for the time being in Oglander Road. "But I've only taken it," sl
said, "for a time. I've taken it for a temporary time."

FATHER LOCKHART   77

He told me the external evidences for the miracles were incontrovertible.
said I did not think so, and gave some reasons: a nugatory talk followed, at the en
of which he said, "Well, I can only say I find it absolutely impossible to conceiv
how any one can be in your frame of mind." I found it difficult, though not in
possible, to understand how an able and amiable man like Father Lockhart can thir
as he does--but I did not say so. However this may be, Father Lockhart or his su
cessors will have to get to understand how people can think as I do; for there ar
a good many of us.

A PARADOX CONCERNING PRINCIPLES   77

They say we can build no superstructure without a foundation of unshakab
principles; there are no such principles; there is no certainty; we cannot get beyor
a strong "I think"; there is no irrefragable "I know"; nevertheless we have got
fairly stable superstructure. A good working "I think," is enough for practical pu
poses.

FORESIGHT AND ETERNITY   78

The idea of Eternity is incompatible with that of a foresight which foresa
all future time from a beginning, for it involves a beginning, and an end (in the wor
"all future time"), whereas the essence of eternity is that there is neither beginnir
nor end, but it is not incompatible with the idea of a foresight which sees a litt
way ahead, and a good long way behind--a cornet shaped foresight--such as I suppo
to have controlled the development of plants and animals.

This is what my sisters say when I tell them the subject of any new book which has made a stir, such as *The Revolt of Man*.[1] What they mean in a quiet way is, "I could make a very amusing book upon this subject. I don't happen to have done so because I have so many other things on hand, but I see perfectly well how it could be done--and you will therefore please to consider that to all intents and purposes I have done it--but I don't think you could."

RISTORI'S QUEEN ELIZABETH 782

I went to see this and admired it very much. I sat next a low Irish family who came in with an order. "Look, look," said the paterfamilias, "now she's taking off Queen Elizabeth," but the most amusing thing was to see Harry Nichols, with whom we are so familiar in burlesque parts, playing the part of a Courtier and offering Mary Stuart's death warrant to Elizabeth. "What have you here"? said the Queen. "Mary Stuart's death warrant," said Harry Nichols very grumpily; he looked altogether out of his element. A few nights before I had seen him as Mrs. Sinbad, Sinbad the sailor's mother, and he had been saying, "I could do with a kidney, just to stay my stomach till I get back to Europe."[1]

MRS. PROSSER[1] WROTE 783

some fables which I was told in Shrewsbury were considered superior to Aesop's. There's more point in them," said my informant.

I dare say there is, I have not read Aesop for a long time, and I have never read Mrs. Prosser at all, but I remember her very well. My sister Harriet was at School there and I once went and had tea with the girls. I was very young at the time. The idea of Mrs. Prosser on one pinnacle and Aesop on another as the two great fable writers of the world rather tickles me.

OLD BOYS' SONGS 784

At the opening of the new school buildings[1] there was a concert, the boys sung and played remarkably well, and looked a very good lot. One boy had written a comic song and sung it--it was extremely clever and he sung it excellently. It was to the tune of that song in *Patience* where there comes in the line, "Oh what a most particularly pure young man this pure young man must be,"[2] and contained a suggestion that the old boys present should subscribe handsomely to the new chapel, which was then standing still for want of funds; apropos of this there was a line which ran so near as I can recollect:
"What a singularly pleasant link between the past and present a chapel thus built will be."
I told my sisters of this maliciously, for I knew they would be scandalised at chapel being introduced into a comic song--at least they would not feel sure that they ought not to be scandalised--and yet as it was done with Mr. Moss's[3] sanction it must be all right; they received it in judicious silence and refused to commit themselves.

PRAISE YE THE LORD   78

I had to go to service at St. Mary's and for the first time for a good many yea
I heard a considerable part of the beautiful liturgy of the Church of England. Nothin
particularly struck me, except that when the clergyman says, "Praise ye the Lord,
the reply is, "The Lord's name be praised."[1] This is a little cold. It seems to say
"We are not quite sure about it, we will pass it; since you insist upon it we will rais
no hindrance, but we had rather leave it an open question as far as our own actio
is concerned."

CHIEF JUSTICE MAY[1] AT THE OPENING OF THE
NEW SHREWSBURY SCHOOL BUILDING   78

There was one boy whom he remembered and particularly wanted to see, an
this boy particularly wanted to see him. They sat next each other for an hour, bu
did not know each other till chance led to an explanation. (The other boy was Cano
Hornby.)[2]

THE BISHOP OF MANCHESTER AT THE SHREWSBURY OPENING   78

He complained that parents now said, "Teach our boys something that wi
make them able to earn money. Teach them how to build bridges, or to make the
way in mercantile pursuits &c."[1] The more sensible in fact a parent seemed to be
the more the Bishop disapproved of him. But then he has no children of his ow

MR. ROTHERY AND DARWIN   78

Next day a Mr. Rothery, a County Court judge somewhere in South Wales, an
I believe also Commissioner of Wrecks,[1] called on my father and said what a beaut
ful sermon the Bishop had preached. He eyed me evidently with disapprobatio
and was barely civil. He said he had been staying at Darwin's a few months befor
Darwin had died, and fell to lauding Darwin in a way which rightly or wrongly
thought was directed at me. He had evidently heard Darwin's version of our quarre
but what that version was I know not.

NEWSPAPER BOY'S CRIES   78

In the station they cry the papers with melodies which are very like old ecclesi
stical responses. This I suppose is because the responses were founded upon th
natural cadences of the human voice when crying anything loud:

Even--ing pa--per
We praise thee oh Lord
The Lord be with you

Dai--ly Tele---graph   Dai--ly Telegraph
And with thy spirit.

HANDEL AND MICHAEL ANGELO AND LEONARDO 790

There has been no Handel of painting. Michael Angelo and Leonardo wrote
onnets. Fancy Handel writing a sonnet. Leonardo left countless, and as useless
s countless, measurements of every part of the body. Handel's rules for tuning are
suppose authentic. They begin: "1st chord. In this chord tune the fifth pretty
lat, and the third considerably too sharp." This was near enough for Handel.[1]

Written August, 1882   Edited March, 1896

G. DARWIN AND KANT 791

G. Darwin[1] seems to have a good notion of taking after his father. First Pro-
essor Ball (I think it was) led the claque with an article in *Nature* about the tides
nd the moon, I think somewhere about November, 1881;[2] for this we were all to
ow down and worship G. Darwin. Then comes a letter to *Nature* from some German
o say that this theory ought to have been known to Englishmen as Kant's, and Kant's
vords were given. To this replies Professor Huxley saying that he had been calling
eople's attention to Kant--and, as it seems to me, blowing on G. Darwin by his
ilence (but I have not seen the letter for months and am writing from recollection).[3]
here was no reply however from G. Darwin. To prig and, when you are found
ut, pay no attention, seems characteristic of that family, and Englishmen seem
o like them for it.

LUINO, BERNARDINO'S PICTURE OF NOAH AND HIS SONS IN THE BRERA[1] 792

At lunch I was talking of this with Jones just after we had seen the picture;
ve had had some remarkably good Barbera and it had warmed me about as much
s half a glass over a pint of bitter would do. I said I was very glad I was not one
f Noah's sons--I was sure I should have been Ham. Jones rejected this promptly.

"You," he said, "would not have been any of the sons--you would have been Noah.

JONES AND MY KNOWING THE MOON 79

The first time Jones came abroad to me, I had not seen much of him, and ha had no idea of his joining me abroad. He wrote to me however in 1877 proposir to join me, and I let him come.[1] He was to join me at Varese. I was on my be behaviour, and Jones was still untainted. We had dinner at the Riposo, and the sat outside under the verandah of the house opposite to smoke our cigarette. Jon asked me if I knew much about the stars. "No," said I a trifle sternly--for I am lik Marcus Aurelius Antoninus and am thankful to say that I have never troubled myse about the appearance of things in the heavens.[2] Then seeing that Jones was a litt. frightened, I said more softly, "I know the moon," and so the matter ended. I neve heeded it, but Jones told me this summer (1882) and we both laughed.

CANDID 79

When they opened the New Law Courts they knighted Jones's friends Mr. Pair and Mr. Roxburgh.[1] Jones got me to write his congratulatory letters for him. In on place I began a sentence "Candidly," but I corrected myself at once and said, ' hate the word so much that I will not use it even when I am lying."

Written September, 1882   Edited March 20, 189

MISQUOTATIONS 79

"I do not wear my coat upon my sleeve." (H.F.J.)

TAME SWALLOWS 79

The tamest I ever saw were near Gravesend; they let me get within five or si feet of them; it has been a long dry spring and they had not been able to get mu to make their nest with: there had come a shower and made some puddles, and the were so busy getting mud that they let me come almost close to them.

PIGEONS SOMETIMES SIT IN WATER 79

I saw some, 3 or 4, in the little stream you cross near a few houses just wher the road branches off to Thames Ditton from the Portsmouth Road about 1½ mile from Surbiton; they were standing in water 1 inch or 1½ inches deep and some wer sitting right down in the water. I saw pigeons do the same at Verona during th inundations[1]--they were squatting in very shallow water, and evidently enjoyin themselves very much. They do so in Clifford's Inn. I have seen them from m windows.

A man is as much alive when he is dead as at any other time for aught I can see. 〈H〉e is either never alive at all, or he is always alive.

C. DARWIN 799

Mem.: his letter to a student at Jena (?) about immortality. See *Pall Mall Ga-tte*, September 23, 1882. (I have utterly forgotten what it was).[1]

MY BOOKS 800

It may conceivably matter to some one else whether he has read my books or 〈n〉, but it does not matter to me.

TEDDY WORSLEY ON MARRIAGE 801

He said to his father, "I don't think I shall get married, papa, when I grow up." 〈"W〉hy not Teddy?" said my cousin. "Well, you see you did make such an awful 〈m〉uck of it, didn't you?" This was not said chaffily, but reflectively. He knew his 〈fa〉ther had made a mess of it, and saw no reason to think he was likely to do better 〈hi〉mself.[1]

ARS EST CELARE ARTEM[1] 802

This is one of those maxims which all preach, but few practice.

AMY WORSLEY[1] AND DOGS IN HOT WEATHER 803

When she was a little girl, she saw the dogs going about with their tongues out. 〈Sh〉e did not know it was their tongues, but thought it so odd that all the dogs that 〈the〉y were running about with a little bit of ham in their mouths. Why, she wondered, 〈di〉d they not eat it at once, and how odd that they should all have ham at the same 〈tim〉e. Who could have given it them? &c.

〈W〉ritten October, 1882   Edited March 21, 1896

SINOCOPE 804

A man told Jones that his father had died that morning. "What did he die of?" 〈sai〉d Jones. "Sīnŏcōpe" was the reply.

EATING OVERDONE MEAT 805

People think there is a certain amount of goodness in the meat which if stewed 〈ou〉t of the meat is still stewed into the gravy. This is true up to a certain point, but

ere long the mind of the meat and of the gravy is so changed that there is no doi
anything with it; it cannot understand sufficiently to be capable of conversion.

EATING, AND SITTING QUIET AFTERWARDS 8(

This is akin to not walking about during service so as to distrub the congregatio
We are catechising and converting our proselytes, and there should be no row. *
you get old, you must digest more quietly still.

EATING AND LOVE 8(

We are fond of what we eat. So a nurse tells her child she should like to e
it. Eating is a mode of love, and *vice versa*.

SKETCH–THE CHUCK UNDER THE CHIN 8(

Going from Arona towards Milan I sat next to a very nice young man who look
down in the mouth about something. Perhaps he had drawn a bad number and w
going to serve a long term of military service. An old man sat opposite him, pr
sumably his father, and he was down in the mouth too. Now and again the old m;
bent forward and chucked the young one under the chin with his fore-finger: tl
young one just smiled and that was all.

AMATEUR OR PROFESSIONAL 8(

Be one or other, but do not try and mix them.

THOUGHT AND WORDS 8

When we think consciously we do so in words; it is for this reason that we (
not realise to ourselves the way in which the lower animals think. Before we cou
speak we used to think as the lower animals think, but we have forgotten that.

THE WEALTH OF THE WORLD 8

The way in which a later age profits by the works of the great men that ha
gone before is like the way in which most able and well conducted people gr(
richer as they grow older.

EATING AND COOKING 8

A little cooking is good because it unsettles the meat's mind and prepares it f
new ideas.

UNITY AND MULTITUDE 8

We can no longer separate things as we once could. Everything tends towar
unity: one thing, one action, in one place at one time; on the other hand we c;
no longer unify things as we once could; we are driven to ultimate atoms, each o
of which is an individuality; so that we have an infinite multitude of things doi

n infinite multitude of actions in infinite time and space, and yet they are not many ⁣ings but one thing.

ritten December, 1882   Edited March 23, 1896

AMY WORSLEY AND OLD MRS. TAYLOR'S MONEY   814

She said to my cousin, she supposed old Mrs. Taylor would settle her money ⁣n her daughter Anna, my cousin Phil's wife--"but do you know, papa, I hope she ⁣on't, because if she does Uncle Phil will not be able to lose it all." Amy is now ⁣early 15.[1]

THE LADY OF THE LAKE[1]   815

Call it somewhere the woman of the pond.

A SPECULATION -- AND GREAT WESTERNS   816

A man urged me to buy Great Westerns in November when they were about 49. He said he knew for a certainty that Rothschilds had been buying some--of ⁣ourse, it might be mere chance, but those people did not generally buy without reason: they were going to build a fleet of steamers to start from Milford Haven ⁣or America, and if so they would take all the Liverpool traffic. They would do all ⁣nat London and North Western had done, but I had better be quick for they were ⁣oing up fast and indeed--so I rather gathered-- I ought to take a cab and go up into ⁣ne city and buy at once or there would not be any left. When a man talks to me ⁣a this way I know that I had better wait till his bull account is closed before I buy. ⁣did not buy Great Westerns: they have never been so high since, and there are still ⁣lenty in the market.

MEMORY AND ASSOCIATION   817

We can remember a great many things if we want to do so, but we can only want one or more of the associated ideas has come across us to put us in mind of want- ⁣ag--till a wave (perhaps) of similar characteristics has run into a wave already feebly ⁣oursing in our brains. If we try to remember "something" or "anything" indefinite, ⁣ve remember nothing. If a man says to himself "now I will remember something" ⁣without knowing what, his first effort is to find something which shall suggest some- ⁣hing to him to remember.

McCULLOCH[1] AND TALL THOMAS   818

McCulloch took me to lunch one Sunday, some years ago, at tall Thomas's. ⁣was very much bored, met odious people, and had a very insufficient dinner. Mc- ⁣ulloch says that when I had left the house a few minutes I turned to him and said ⁣ather sternly, "McCulloch, this must not occur again."

209

If "a little dose of judgment and reason" enters into the most instinctive action, so a little dose of unreason and instinct enters into our most deliberate ones.

TRÜBNER[1] AND MYSELF   82

When I went back to Trübner after Bogue[2] had failed I had a talk with hir and Mr. Edwardes his partner. I could see they had lost all faith in my literary pro pects. Trübner told me I was a *"homo unius libri,"*[3] meaning *Erewhon.* He sai "You are in a very solitary position." I said I knew I was, but it suited me. I sai "I pay my way; when I was with you before I never owed you money, you fin me now not owing my publisher money, but my publisher in debt to me. I nev owe so much as a tailor's bill; beyond secured debts, I do not owe £5 in the wor and never have (which is quite true); I get my Summer's holiday in Italy every yea I live very quietly and cheaply, but it suits my health and tastes, and I have no a quaintances but those I value. My friends stick by me. If I was to get in with the literary and scientific people I should hate them and they me. I should fritter awa my time, and my freedom without getting a *quid pro quo*: as it is, I am free an give the swells every now and then such a facer as they get from no one else. (course I don't expect to get on in a commercial sense at present; I do not go th right way to work for this, but I am going the right way to secure a lasting reput tion, and this is what I do care for. You cannot have both--a man must make up h mind which he means going in for--I have gone in for posthumous fame, and I se no step in my literary career which I do not think calculated to promote my beir held in esteem when the heat of passion has subsided."

Trübner shrugged his shoulders. He plainly does not believe that I shall succee in getting a hearing: he thinks the combination of the religious and cultured worl too strong for me to stand against. If he means that the reviewers will burke n as far as they can, no doubt he is right; but when I am dead there will be other r viewers, and I have already done enough to secure that they shall from time to tin look me up. They won't bore me then, but they will be just as odious as the prese ones.

SAMENESS   82

Same is as same does.

MYSTIFICATION   82

There is the mystification of absolute ignorance, and the mystification of fogge science.

BOSS'S MOTHER &c.   82

She was a pretty woman though Boss said so herself: she had a splendid mou of teeth--it was a sin to bury her in her teeth.

She debated about wearing a wedding ring. Tom[1] wanted her to but she wou not.

Worsley[2] abused her in some way. "Ah, you would not have said that if you ad known me when I was sweet seventeen."

Frank, a fellow lodger, came upstairs very drunk. Boss lay in wait to run him. Take your boots off, Frank," said Boss. "But why did you tell him to take his oots off?" "Oh, to stop him wanting to go out again and get more drink."

Frank *loq.*: "Didn't I know your boy's father, and didn't I play with your bro-hers...." "Now take care Frank, mind what you say, Jenny is in the room." Boss vanted to make out that Frank was going to make advances to her.

MYSELF AND THE COCK   824

I went into Fleet Street one Sunday morning last November '82 with my amera (lucida),[1] and looked at the gap where it stood, it was rather pretty, with an ld roof or two behind and scaffolding about, and torn paper hanging to an exposed arty-wall, and old fireplaces &c., but it was not very much out of the way. Still would have taken it if it had not been the Cock. I thought of all the trash that as been written about it, and of Tennyson's plump head waiter[2] (who by the way sed to swear that he did not know Tennyson, and that Tennyson never did resort o the Cock), and I said to myself, "No--you may go. I will put out no hand to save ou."

JONES AND A MISQUOTATION FOR TENNYSON   825

Jones says,

"Tis better to have loved and lost
Than never to have lost at all."

r you might have it:

"Tis better never to have loved
Than to have loved and never lost."[1]

JONES AND THE PRAYER FOR THE CHURCH MILITANT   826

He says he likes that part where it says, "We also bless thy Holy Name for all hy servants departed this life."[1]

SUBJECT   827

On Memory as a key to the phenomena of assimilation.

EATING   828

An animal which refuses to let another eat it has the courage of its convictions, nd if it gets eaten, dies a martyr to them.

211

To forbid all mannerism is to forbid form and insist on everything's being though
out afresh *de novo*.

MY FATHER AND HIS WOODSIAS   83

When I was a boy we used to get woodsias on Snowdon and Glyder Fawr
There were four plants left on Glyder still when I was young, and William Williams
swore that there were none others. My father would get a plant and take it hon
and put it in the green house: of course it died: but his other ferns were kept in th
green house, so this must be kept there too. I had a plant which I found in a hithe
to unsuspected place, where there were many plants. I brought its own stones an
its own earth, enough to fill a pot; knowing that the woodsia likes growing whei
water can flow on it in heavy wet weather from some swollen rill. I made a litt
syphon and occasionally let the water run on to it for two or three hours as from
miniature waterfall. My woodsia lived for years. I remonstrated with my fath
about keeping this high mountain fern all the summer in the green house but it w
no use. Years afterwards I brought him some very fine woodsias from the Cantc
Ticino,[3] and brought their own stones and earth, and planted them and set the
where they would occasionally be dripped on by water from a gutter, but it was n
use. Next time I went to Shrewsbury, there they were in the hot bed with the oth
ferns. This is my father all over.

Written January, 1883   Edited March 25, 189

SPEECH OF ANIMALS   83

See *Journal of Science* for January, 1883.[1]

ART NOTE   83

That all the most permanently interesting pictures show signs either of havir
been laboured at very much, or of not having been laboured at all.

MRS. FRENCH AND THE NATIONAL GALLERY   83

She keeps a ham and beef shop in Fetter Lane.[1] She told me once that sh
did not hold with the pictures in the National Gallery.

WHITTAKER AT THE NATIONAL GALLERY   83

I had not seen him for many years. Then I saw him copying at the Nation
Gallery, but though we looked at one another we did not speak. He was a bo
at Heatherley's,[1] but I knew nothing particularly against him. Next time I was
the Gallery I saw him again. He came up to me and said, "I do not know wheth

you know me. I have been in disgrace--some letters I wrote to my mother--I do not like speaking to people, for I do not know whether they know about it or not, or whether they would wish to recognise me." I knew nothing, but was sorry for him and rather liked the outspokenness with which he owned to having been in disgrace. I said I had heard nothing, but went and saw his work and encouraged him. I have since been told he had had ten years penal servitude for threatening to murder his mother. I don't think I shall cut him.

BODY AND MIND   835

We shall never get straight till we leave off trying to separate these two things. Mind is not a thing at all, or if it is, we know nothing about it. It is a function of body. Body is not a thing at all, or if it is we know nothing about it. It is a function of mind.

ART NOTE   836

"Insist again on doing the first thing that comes. No matter how small a thing you see, if you see anything, attend to that." This is all wrong. It should rather be, "Never do anything till you are sure that it is the most important thing as yet left undone."

MISQUOTATION (H.F. JONES)   837

"The Assyrians came down like a--like a--like a thousand of bricks and have done with it."[1]

CATHOLICISM   838

I do not presume to be a judge of Catholic doctrine, but I do presume to be as good as a judge as other people of the way in which the cat is jumping. I hold it is jumping away from Catholicism; if I thought the Catholics were permanently in the long run on the winning side I would join them tomorrow.

MYSELF AND CHÂTEAU LAFITTE (CLARET)   839

When I was a boy I used sometimes to taste claret at my father's dinner table when there was a party, or guests in the house. I got the taste well into my head. I never tasted claret again for years, but when I did I found it quite different; much more like weak port wine; I could not make it out, and supposed my memory was at fault, but a few years ago I was dining with Jason Smith[1] and after dinner there was some wine which I at once recognised as the claret of my infancy. There was no mistake about it. I asked Jason what the wine was. He said it was Château Lafitte and very fine. I have no doubt my father, when I was a boy, was finishing up my grandfather's cellar, for he has never had any Château Lafitte since. At least he has never given me any (January 7, 1883) and so I was brought up on 1834 port and never taste anything like port now.[2]

We want some corresponding expression for times when some sudden unexpecte(good fortune comes upon us. "He was going to be taken up the precipice in a lift, or something of that kind.

THE ROSSETTI EXHIBITION[1] 84

I have been to see it and am pleased to find it more odious than I had even dare(to hope. I met Rossetti once at Wallis's;[2] there were three besides myself. I dislike(them all very much, but Rossetti the most.

WITH THE TEMPTATION &c. 84?

I suppose that when people pray that with the temptation there may be a way also for them to escape, they mean a way for them to escape being found out.

MISQUOTATION 84?

Make some one speak of the holy gruel instead of the holy grail (Jones).

MY FATHER AND TOM[1] 84(

When I was last at Shrewsbury my father said of Tom my brother, "I don' care about knowing where he is, so long as we hear of his death."

THE OLD YACHTSMAN 84!

There was an old gentleman I heard of the other day who owned a yacht whicl he kept for years but never went near. The captain made a home of it, kept hen on board, and had everything his own way. One day he received a letter saying tha the owner was coming, and was in despair because he guessed that all his good time were now to come to an end as the owner was probably going to say that he woul(keep the yacht no longer. By and by he came and went round the ship. "Very nice very nice," he said to everything. "And how long, pray, have you been in my ser vice now?" "Fourteen years, Sir," said the Captain. "Dear, dear me, fourteen years well, well, it must be time you had your wages raised." So he raised them and wen away. The captain lived on his raised wages ten years longer, and when he died the old gentleman then sold the yacht.

Written January or February, 1883   Edited March 31, 189(

TURNER AND TINTAGEL 84(

When at Tintagel by way of making myself pleasant to the old woman who showed the place I said, "I suppose you don't know where Turner's picture waaken from?"--which by the way I suppose he took pretty much [from] * his own ancy.[1] "Turner, sir?" was the answer. "No, sir, I never heard of the gentleman."

WORDS AND IDEAS, INTERACTION OF   847

These things are like desire and power, or mind and matter, which come up ogether out of things too small for us to notice them and act and react upon one another.

JONES AND MY BOOKS   848

Jones helps me with them very much, so much that I say he writes them for ne. Still I wrote three books in which Jones had no voice whatever--*Erewhon, The ʼair Haven* and *Life and Habit*.

CHILTERN HUNDREDS AND CHEVIOT HILLS   849

"He took the Cheviot Hills, you know, or whatever it is that people take when hey leave parliament."[1]

LITTLE CART SUCKING THE BIG ONE   850

When I was a boy that used to be a saying at Langar if any one saw a wheel-ɔarrow under a cart in a shed or barn. I always say it now of the Metropolitan Rail-vay Station at Charing Cross underneath the main station.

NILE--CROCODILE   851

She went up the Nile as far as the first crocodile.

ANDREW WILSON   852

ιas been writing a book on evolution and running Darwin. I see he has also been unning Pear's Soap in the Christmas number of the *Graphic*.[1]

LOGIC AND PHILOSOPHY   853

When you have got all the rules and all the lore of philosophy and logic well nto your head, and have spent years in getting to understand at any rate what they nean, and have them at command, you will know less for practical purposes than ɔne who has never studied logic or philosophy.

SUNDAY SCHOOL TEACHER   854

Mr. Ward, the fishmonger in Leather Lane, told me of a Sunday School teacher τ Southgate, who got tipsy at the school treat, stole 25 pieces of cake and made mproper proposals to the curate.

Poor dear little Miss Johnson,[1] whenever I go to see her work says, "I'm s, glad you like the picture," or, "I'm so glad you think I am on the right track," bu I have not said I like the picture, nor that I think she is on the right track; I hav only said as little as I could beyond what common charity required.

Written January or February, 1883   Edited July 15, 189

MYSELF AND GARNETT[1] IN THE BRITISH MUSEUM   85

I called on Garnett one morning in his den, which is a room arrived at by th King's library, and told him among other things that I had begun a series of Londo subjects, with the Camera Lucida. As we were talking he took me through the King' library on our way back to the reading room, and we passed the collection of view of London which have been lately acquired by the Museum. "Exactly," said "every one of these things is valuable, and we are much obliged to the man wh did it: here is a way in which a man with no very unusual power may make himsel enjoyed long after he is dead, and that too with no great strain upon himself--I sha certainly go in for it." Then I blew on historic and imaginative pictures generally and upon imaginative literature--at any rate, as compared with the sympathetic an intelligent rendering of what we see every day round about us. "If Shakespeare, I added, "had gossiped more about himself, told us where he dined, what he had fo dinner, what men he knew and liked and why, and what he thought for exampl of his fellow dramatists--surely we could have spared one or two of the minor plays." I knew this was going as far as it was safe to do, and indeed it proved so, for Garnet said at once, "Perhaps, but I think it would be rather a difficult task to say whic plays you would sacrifice." I thought to myself that *Hamlet* or *Othello* would d very nicely, but I did not dare to say so, so I acquiesced and let the matter drop as, alas! I soon did my collection of London sketches.

"ABSOLUTE KNOWLEDGE": "IS"   85

We have no concern with "is"; our only concern is with the way of considerir and expressing things which the main part of capable and reasonable men will fin most convenient for or within the next few years; anything more than this is ridin the desire for security into full cowardice.

EATING AND CANNIBALISM   85

If after death the cells retain a faint memory of their having entered into organi combinations, and show this by way of greater aptitude for re-entering into soci life--then there is a good deal to be said for Cannibalism. For man's flesh shoul need less education by man than that of any other animal.

The balance against them is now over £350. How completely they must have
een squashed unless I had had a little money of my own. Not one of them would
ave been written, at any rate I should never have been able to continue the battle
·ith Darwin beyond *Life and Habit*. Is it not likely that many a better writer than
am is squashed through want of money? Whatever I do I must not die poor--these
xamples of ill-requited labour are immoral. They discourage the effort of those
·ho could and would do good things if they did not know that it would ruin them-
·lves and their families; moreover, it sets people on to pamper a dozen fools for
ach neglected man of merit, out of compunction. Genius, they say, always wears
·n invisible cloak--these men wear invisible cloaks--therefore they are geniuses-- and
: flatters them to think that they can see more than their neighbours. The neglect
·f one such man as the authors of *Hudibras*[1] is compensated for by the petting of
dozen others who would be the first to jump upon the author of *Hudibras* if he
·ere to come back to life.

Heaven forbid that I should compare myself to the author of *Hudibras*, but
till, if my books succeed after my death--which they may or may not, I really know
othing about it--anyway if they do succeed, let it be understood that they failed
uring my life for a very few obvious reasons, of which I was quite aware, for the
ffect of which I was prepared before I wrote my books, and which on consideration
found insufficient to deter me. I attacked people who were at once unscrupulous
·nd powerful, and I made no alliances--I did this because I did not want to be bored
·nd have my time wasted and my pleasures curtailed. I had money enough to live
·n, and preferred addressing myself to posterity rather than to any except a very
·ew of my own contemporaries. Those few I have always kept well in mind. I think
·f them continually when in doubt about any passage, but beyond those few I will
·ot go. Posterity will give a man a fair hearing, his own times will not do so if he is
·ttacking vested interests--and I have attacked two powerful sets of vested interests
t once. What is the good of addressing people who will not listen? I have addressed
·he next generation, and have therefore said many things which want time before
·hey become palatable. Any man who wishes his work to stand will sacrific a good
·eal of his immediate audience for the sake of being attractive to a much larger
·umber of people later on. He cannot gain this later audience unless he has been
·earless and thoroughgoing--and if he is this, he is sure to have to tread on the corns
·f a great many of those who live at the same time with him, however little he may
·ish to do so. He must not expect these people to help him on, nor wonder if for
time they succeed in snuffing him out. It is part of the swim that it should be so--
·nly as one who believes himself to have practised what he preaches, let me assure
·ny one that it is much better fun writing for posterity and not getting paid for it
if you have money of your own to live on) than I can imagine it being to write
·ke, we will say, George Eliot and make a lot of money. January 29, 1883.

"YE SUFFER FOOLS GLADLY"[1]   860

·ays the Apostle. "Why no Paul," I feel inclined to answer, "not exactly gladly."

217

in anything like luxury is one of the most expensive things a man can indulge himsel
in. It costs a lot of money to die comfortably unless one goes off pretty quickly

Written February, 1883   Edited July 15, 189

MY BROTHER[1] AND *QUIVIS*   86

He was asked in the *viva voce* part of his little go examination to decline *quivis*
He thought a little, and said, "*Quivolo, quivis, quivult.*"

OPEN MATRIMONY   86

A man was moralising at the life class one night about the purity of youth &c
I said, "It's all very well for you to talk--you know you are living in open matrimon
yourself."

AMSTERDAM CANAL[1]   864

It was twisted awry by a tornado of private interests.

MY COUSIN SUPPOSED TO BE DYING   865

When he was a child he was very delicate. My Aunt said to him once, "Yo
need not be afraid about dying my dear, Grandmamma and Aunt Nora (who wer
dead already) will take care of you."

PEOPLE LIKE BIRDS IN THE HEDGES   86

The people we see going about are like the birds we see in the hedges--they loo
all right, but for the most part they are hard up, or nearly so.

SPEECH   86

is a kind of mean proportional between thought and action.

PARENTS AND CHILDREN   86

I am sorry to have to admit it, but I do not observe that even gross cruelty an
selfishness on the part of parents towards their children is followed by any ver
bad effects upon the parents. Parents may make their children very unhappy with
out having to suffer anything that makes them unhappy in return.

218

MISS CORNELIA KNIGHT[1]   869

When Pius VI was confined in the Castle of S. Angelo, they would not let him
ave any communication with his friends, who at last got permission to send him
ome transcripts from the Manuscripts of Herculaneum by way of amusement. These
ranscripts were in fact an account of what was going on, written by Miss C. Knight
a very good Greek. (M.S. note among Dr. Butler's papers).

SMOLLETT IN *RODERICK RANDOM*   870

ays his grandfather had a natural loathing for any creature that was in distress--
nd that a coward works out his own salvation with fear and trembling.[1]

FATHERS   871[1]

Those who have never had a father can at any rate never know the sweets of
sing one. To most men the death of his father is a new lease of life.

"DO ANYTHING BUT TALK"   872

It has been said of some animals that they can do anything but talk; I know
eople of whom it may be said that they can talk, but that this is the only thing
ey can do.

GEORGE ELIOT   873

She cribbed her chapter on machines in *Theophrastus Such* from *Erewhon*. I
ught to be highly flattered. In one year I made Mr. Darwin write a book (*Erasmus
arwin*), and George Eliot crib a chapter.[1] Some years ago when Lord Lytton and
wrote books anonymously about the same time, I do not think I got the worst
f it.[2] I see myself cribbed from continually, but never named, and my books, I am
ld, can hardly be mentioned in scientific circles without making people lose their
mper. I know I ought to be ashamed of myself for caring what such people as
eorge Eliot, Charles Darwin, Lord Lytton &c. do or do not do--or for paying any
ttention to what may or may not be said about me, but I am afraid I do care and
o pay attention.

GOD AND PHILOSOPHY   874

The very slender rewards which God has attached to philosophy make it evi-
ent that he does not set much store by it nor wish to encourage it.

BOSS AND ROBERT   875

She said some one had a "haricot vein." Robert[1] said he had a kind of "harris-
iss" in his nose.

THOU HAST DONE ALL THINGS WELL[1]

87•

Jones said that "some things well" would be nearer the mark.

DRURY LANE VIEW OF ELIZABETH'S REIGN

87'

The bills of the pantomime sum up her reign thus: Mary Queen of Scots, Si
Walter Raleigh, potatoes, tobacco, Shakespeare. February 1, 1883.[1]

CRUCIFYING CHRIST

87\$

Christ was only crucified once and for a few hours; think of the hundreds o
thousands whom Christ has been crucifying in a quiet way ever since.

ART NOTE

87\$

On drawing from memory as exemplified by drawing a policeman's hat.

A LITERARY MAN'S TEST

88(

Molière's reading to his housemaid has I think been misunderstood as thoug▌
he in some way wanted to see the effect upon the housemaid and make her a judg▌
of his work.[1] If she was an unusually clever smart girl this might be well enough
but the supposition commonly is that she was a typical housemaid and nothing more
If Molière ever did read to her it was because the mere act of reading aloud put hi▌
work before him in a new light, and by constraining his attention to every line mad▌
him judge it more rigorously. I always intend to, and generally do, read what I writ▌
aloud to some one--any one almost will do, but he should not be so clever that I ar▌
afraid of him. I feel weak places at once when I read aloud where I thought as lon▌
as I read to myself only that the passage was all right.

MATTER AND MIND

88]

We have, or at any rate think we have, a fairly definite idea before us when w▌
talk of matter, but I don't think we ever think we have any definite idea about ou▌
own meaning when we talk of mind.

MORALITY

88\.

turns on whether the pleasure precedes the pain or follows it (provided it is sufficient)
Thus it is immoral to get drunk because the headache comes after the drinking, bu
if the headache came first and the drunkenness afterwards, it would be moral to ge
drunk.

FOUNDATIONS OF MORALITY

88\:

are like all other foundations; if you dig too much about them the superstructure
will come tumbling down.

The Ancients attached such special horror to the murder of near relations because the temptation was felt on all hands to be so great that nothing short of this could stop people from laying violent hands upon them. The fable of the Erinyes was probably invented by fathers and mothers and uncles and aunts.

WHAT MUCK *HAMLET* IS AFTER THIS   885

At the Strand Theatre in *Champagne*, Penley came on as a lugubrious knight in armour with a great coat and umbrella, and was very funny.[1] I turned instinctively to my cousin and said, "What muck *Hamlet* is after this." It was in that piece Marius[2] sung the song, "Some girls do and some girls don't" which I changed into "some breeds do and some breeds don't" and introduced into *Life and Habit*.[3]

Written February or March, 1883   Edited December, 1896

WANTS AND CREEDS   886

As in the organic world there has been no organ, so in the world of thought there is no thought, which may not be called into existence by long persistent effort. If a man wants either to believe or disbelieve the Christian Miracles, he can do so if he tries hard enough; but if he does not care whether he believes or disbelieves, and simply wants to find out which side has the best of it--this he will find a more difficult matter; nevertheless he will probably be able to do this too if he tries.

MYSELF AND DANTE   887

I see Mr. Gladstone has been lately writing to the effect that he owes no small part of his success to the study of Dante. I am of opinion that I owe no small part of whatever small success I may have obtained to the fact that I have ignored Dante.

RUBENS AND ANTWERP[1]   888

Jones was at dinner the other night and heard a clergyman raving about Antwerp. "You feel," he said, "under the spell of a certain painter--Rubens, for instance. As you go about the street you feel as though you might meet him at every corner." The hostess said, "Ah, when we were there we went about in the trams."

"CLEANSE THOU ME FROM MY SECRET SINS"[1]   889

I heard a man moralising on this, and shocked him by saying demurely that I did not mind these so much, if I could get rid of those that were obvious to other people.

If he had known a great deal of what passes for music now, he would perhap have been glad not sorry that the combinations and permutations of musical sound were at any rate limited somewhere.[1]

TO MAN, GOD'S UNIVERSAL LAW   89

"gave power to keep his wife in awe" sings Handel in a comically dogmatic little chorus in *Samson*--but the universality of the law must be held to have failed in the case of Mr. and Mrs. McCulloch.[1]

MISQUOTATIONS   89

Dulce et decorum est desipere in loco; and suppose "Batten on this Moor" t have some connection with *Othello*.[1]

Written February or March, 1883   Edited December 16, 1896

WOMAN SUFFRAGE   89

I will vote for it when women have left off making a noise in the reading roo of the British Museum, when they leave off wearing high headdresses in the pit of theatre, and when I have seen as many as twelve women in all catch hold of the str or bar on getting into an omnibus.

MY MOST IMPLACABLE ENEMY   89

from childhood onward has certainly been my father. I doubt whether I could n make a friend of my brother[1] more easily than I could turn my father into a cordi genial well-wisher; and yet I do not for a moment doubt the goodness of his intentio from first to last.

SMALL MATTERS   89

We may decide these for ourselves: important ones, *e.g.* our death, and, if v must marry, our wife, our profession, place of residence &c., we had better lea as far as possible to God, or, which is the same thing, to the course of events (use in *Alps and Sanctuaries*).[1]

WHAT TO LEARN   89

Never try and find out anything, or try to learn anything till you have four the not knowing it to be a nuisance to you for some time. Then you will rememb it, but not otherwise. Let knowledge importune you before you will hear it. O schools and Universities go on the precisely opposite system.

OUR HIGHEST "IS"   89

is still only a very strong "may be"; .9999 of the truth.

This is instinctive because in so many past generations we have feared death. ut how did we come to know what death is, so that we should fear it? The answer ▸ this is that we do not know what death is, and that this is why we fear it.

UNCONSCIOUSNESS AND THE TWO MOST IMPORTANT THINGS   899

The two most important things a man has are his body, and his mind. The unani-ous verdict of those best qualified to form an opinion is that the less ninety-nine ndredths of us know about either one or the other, the better. The more important thing is the more important it is that we should know nothing about it. (See *Alps d Sanctuaries*, p. 141).[1]

BEING IN A PLACE, SEEING, AND HEARING   900

What is being in a place? If I see the moon, so far, I am in the moon. Which is ost true--for a man who has spent hours and hours nightly looking into the moon rough the most powerful known telescope, to say that he has been in the moon?-- for one who passed through Rome at night fast asleep in a Pullman Car to say at he has been at Rome?--or for an ascetic Catholic priest to say that he has ever een in this world at all?

Which again has heard the C Minor Symphony best? Beethoven who was stone-eaf when he wrote it, or some listener whose ears were perfect, but had no knowledge hatever of music?

Which sees a picture best? An old painter gone blind to whom another painter xplains it, or an unfortunate school boy who has been dragged to see it as a show, nd whose heart is all the while in the cricket field? (See "What is being alive.")[1]

UNCONSCIOUS ACTIONS   901

The things we do with most unconsciousness are those which we die quickest f] * if we do not do.

DORMANT, OR UNCONSCIOUS, MEMORY   902

Nothing will waken this except something which bears a real or fancied resem-lance to the original circumstances.

MELCHISEDEC[1]   903

as a really happy man; he was without father, without mother and without des-ent. He was an incarnate bachelor. Jones says he was "a born orphan."

THE REPRODUCTIVE SYSTEM OF HABITS   904

Every habit seems to come from some other habit, as much as *omne ovum* comes x *ovo*;[1] and every habit seems to have a reproductive system, for the mere fact of ur having done a thing once inclines us to do it again, provided it has not positively urt us.

223

How closely these run into one another. Next to having actually done a thin
oneself, the strongest incentive to doing it is to see some one else do it. If five spa:
rows sit on a balcony, and one flies off, the chances are that the others will do s
whether there is reason or no, and I have read of a woman whose fingers were bad
bruised by merely seeing a window shut down upon the fingers of her own chil
(in Tukes's *Body and Mind*, but I hardly believe it.)[1]

IDENTITY WITH ONE'S ANCESTORS, AND CONTEMPORARIES   90

We are so far identical with our ancestors and our contemporaries that it is ver
rarely we can see anything that they do not see. It is not unjust that the sins of th
fathers should be visited upon the children,[1] for the children committed the sin
when in the persons of their fathers; they ate the sour grapes before they were born
true, they have forgotten the pleasure now, but so has a man with a sick headach
forgotten the pleasure of getting drunk the night before.

OUR WICKED CELLS   90

The best way of exterminating the wicked cells that we may have in our bodie
is to encourage the good ones. They will kill the others better than we can. So wit
mind and habits.

Written about March, 1883   Edited December 18, 189

UNNATURAL   90

Men misuse this word as they do the word "spontaneous"--as though anythin
which is a part of nature could be "unnatural." Whatever is, is natural. Instead o
saying "unnatural" they should say "unintelligible to myself," "disgusting," or wha
not.

FOOD AND POTENTIAL ACTIONS   90

When I see food in a shop window I see latent, or potential, action.

MISS M. AND *THE FAIR HAVEN*   91(

Miss K. (I suppose to see how much flattery I could swallow) told me that Mi
M. had said *The Fair Haven* would never die. I said I did not see how it well coul
for it had never yet lived.

MISS POTTER AND POOR PEOPLE   91

Miss Potter who works a good deal among the poor in Seven Dials[1] asked me a *conversazione*, rather abruptly, if I liked poor people. I said I did not, and there the conversation ended.

INTELLECTUAL RATTLESNAKE   912

I know a man, and one whom people generally call a very clever one, who, when his eye catches mine if I meet him at an at home or an evening party, beams upon me from afar with the expression of an intellectual rattlesnake on having espied an intellectual rabbit. Through any crowd that man will come sidling towards me, ruthless and irresistible as fate; while I, foreknowing my doom, sidle also himwards, and flatter myself that no sign of my inward apprehension has escaped me.

MATTHEW ARNOLD ON RIGHTEOUSNESS   913

According to Mr. Matthew Arnold, as we find the highest traditions of grace, beauty, and the heroic virtues among the Greeks and Romans, so we derive our highest ideal of Righteousness from Jewish sources. Righteousness was to the Jew what strength and beauty were to the Greek, or fortitude to the Roman.[1]

This sounds well, but can we think that the Jews taken as a nation were really more righteous than the Greeks and Romans? Could they indeed be so if they were less strong, graceful, and enduring? In some respects they may have been; every nation has its strong points; but surely there has been a nearly unanimous verdict for many generations, that the typical Greek and Roman is a higher, nobler person than the typical Jew--and this referring not to the modern Jew, who may perhaps be held to have been injured by centuries of oppression, but to the Hebrew of the time of the old prophets, and of the most prosperous eras in the history of the nation. If three men could be set before us as the most perfect Greek, Roman, and Jew respectively, and if we could choose which we would have our only son most resemble, is it not likely we should find ourselves preferring the Greek or Roman to the Jew? And does not this involve that we hold the two former to be the more righteous in a broad sense of the word?

I dare not say that we owe no benefits to the Jewish nation, I do not feel sure whether we do or do not, but I can see no good thing that I can point to as a notoriously Hebrew contribution to our moral and intellectual well being, as I can point to our law and say that it is Roman, or to our fine arts and say that they are based on what the Greeks and Italians taught us; on the contrary, if asked what feature of post-Christian life we had derived most distinctly from Hebrew sources I should say at once "intolerance"--the desire to dogmatise about matters whereon the Greek and Roman held certainty to be at once unimportant and unattainable. This, with all its train of bloodshed and family disunion, is chargeable to the Jewish rather than to any other account.

There is yet another vice which occurs readily to any one who reckons up the characteristics which we derive mainly from the Jews--it is one the word for which we have derived from a Jewish sect, and which we call "Pharisaism." I do not mean to say that no Greek and Roman was ever a sanctimonious hypocrite; still, sanctimoniousness does not readily enter into our notions of Greeks and Romans, and it does so enter into our notions of the old Hebrews. Of course, we are all of us sanctimonious sometimes. Horace himself is so when he talks about "*aurum irrepertum et sic melius situm &c*";[2] as for Virgil, he was a prig pure and simple; still, on the whole sanctimoniousness was not a Greek and Roman vice, and it was a Hebrew one.

True, they stoned their prophets freely, but these are not the Hebrews to whom M[r] Arnold is referring; they are the ones whom it is the custom to leave out of sigh[t] and out of mind as far as possible, so that they should hardly count as Hebrew[s] at all, and none of our characteristics should be ascribed to them.

Taking their literature, I cannot see that it deserves the praises that have bee[n] lavished upon it. The Song of Solomon and the Book of Esther are the most interes[t] ing books in the old testament, but these are the very ones that make the smalle[st] pretensions to holiness, and even these are neither of them of very transcenden[t] merit. They would stand no chance of being accepted by Messrs. Cassell and Co or by any biblical publisher of the present day. Chatto and Windus[3] might tak[e] the Song of Solomon, but with this exception I doubt if there is a publisher in Lor[n] don who would give a Guinea for the pair. Ecclesiastes contains some fine thing[s] but is strongly tinged with pessimism, cynicism, and affectation. Some of the pro[-] verbs are good, but not many of them are in common use. Job contains some fin[e] passages, and so do some of the psalms--but the psalms generally are poor, and fo[r] the most part they are querulous, spiteful, and introspective into the bargain. Mudie[s] would not take thirteen copies of the lot if they were to appear now for the firs[t] time--unless indeed their royal authorship were to arouse an adventitious interes[t] in them, or unless their author were a rich man who played his cards judiciously wit[h] the reviewers. As for the prophets--we know what appears to have been the opinio[n] formed concerning them by those who should have been best acquainted with them I can form little idea about the merits of the controversy between them and thei[r] fellow countrymen, but I have read their works, and am of opinion that they wi[ll] not hold their own as against such masterpieces of modern literature as we will sa[y] *Pilgrim's Progress, Robinson Crusoe, Gulliver's Travels* or *Tom Jones*. "Wheth[er] these be prophecyings," exclaims the Apostle, "they shall fail,"[5] on the whole should say that Isaiah and Jeremiah have failed.

I would join issue with Mr. Matthew Arnold on yet another point. I understan[d] him to imply that righteousness should be a man's highest aim in life. I do not lik[e] setting up righteousness nor yet anything else as an aim of life, a man should hav[e] any number of little aims about which he should be conscious, and for which h[e] should have names, but he should have neither name for, nor consciousness concern[-] ing, the main aim of his life. Whatever we do, we must try and do it rightly--thi[s] is obvious--but righteousness implies something much more than this--it conveys t[o] our minds not only the desire to get whatever we have taken in hand as nearly righ[t] as possible, but also the general reference of our lives to the supposed will of a[n] unseen but supreme power. Granted that there is such a power, and granted tha[t] we should obey its will; we are the more likely to do this the less we concern our selves about the matter, and the more we confine our attention to the things imme diately round about us which seem, so to speak, entrusted to us as the natural an[d] legitimate sphere of our activity. I believe a man will get the most useful informa tion on these matters from modern European sources; next to these he will get mos[t] from Athens and ancient Rome; Mr. Matthew Arnold notwithstanding, I do not thin[k] he will get anything from Jerusalem which he will not find better and more easil[y] elsewhere.

McCULLOCH'S EXTRAVAGANZA 91[.]

He[1] showed me his pictures the other day and said of one, "I mean to call this 'an extravaganza in psychology'." He was quite serious, and was rather pique[d] at I did not at once fall to admiring the title. As a matter of fact I wished him ood morning then and there.

THOUGHTS ON VICE AND VIRTUE 915

Virtue is something which it would be impossible to overrate if it had not been verrated. The world can ill spare any vice which has obtained long and largely nong civilised people. Such a vice must have good which cannot be well spared ong with its deformities. The question, "How if every one were to do so and so?" ay be met with another, "How if no one were to do it?" We are a body corporate s well as a collection of individuals.

As a matter of private policy, I doubt whether the moderately vicious are more nhappy than the moderately virtuous. "Very vicious" is certainly less happy than tolerably virtuous"--but this is about all. What pass[es] * muster as the extremes f virtue probably make people quite as unhappy as extremes of vice do.

The truest virtue has ever inclined toward excess rather than asceticism; that e should do this is reasonable as well as observable, for virtue should be as nice calculator of chances as other people, and will make due allowances for the chance f not being found out.

Virtue knows that it is impossible to get on without compromise, and tunes erself, as it were, a trifle sharp to allow for an inevitable fall in playing. So the salmist says, "If thou Lord, shouldest be extreme to mark what is done amiss,"[1] nd by this he admits that the highest conceivable form of virtue still leaves room or some compromise with vice; so again Shakespeare writes "they say best men are oulded out of faults and for the most become much more the better for being a ttle bad."[2]

EPICURUS REVERSED 916[1]

Epicurus held that there are gods but they are careless about human affairs.[2] I old that there is a God, but that human beings should be careless about him.

A DRUNKARD 917

ould not give money to sober people. He said they would only eat it, and buy othes and send their children to school with it.

UNCONSCIOUS THOUGHT 918

Most of our thought, like most of our action, is now unconscious--but must we ot think that during the beginnings of thought, all thought was conscious? Or as there always a mass of unconscious thought to a trifle of conscious?

BREVITY THE SOUL OF WIT[1] 919

This hold good quite as much for painting as for writing.

CONVENIENCE AND THOUGHT 920

We have to consider not what things are, but what it will give us least trouble

in the long run to think they are: what is the way of looking at them which w
be most convenient to ourselves as "coming together with" and fitting in with oth
conceptions on which we have so based our action and invested our money that
change of value would materially and prejudicially affect us. We have to consid
how we shall run least risk of running up against ourselves and hitting ourselves
some other place by and by, and how, when we do hit ourselves, we shall do so wi
least unpleasantness.

Hit ourselves somewhere we are bound to do: no idea will travel far witho
colliding with some other idea. Thus if we pursue one line of probable convenien
we find it convenient to see all things as ultimately one; that is, if we insist rath
on the points of agreement between things than on those of disagreement. If v
insist on the opposite view, namely on the points of disagreement, we find ourselv
driven to the conclusion that each atom is an individual entity, and that the uni
between even the most united things is apparent only. If we did not unduly insi
upon--that is to say, emphasize and exaggerate--the part which concerns us for tl
time, we should never get to understand anything: the proper way is to exaggera
first one view and then the other, and then let the two exaggerations collide, b
good temperedly and according to the laws of civilised mental warfare. So we s
first all things as one, then all things as many, and in the end, a multitude in uni
and a unity in multitude.

Care must be taken not to accept ideas which, though very agreeable at fir
disagree with us afterwards, and keep rising on our mental stomachs, as garlic do
upon our bodily.

A PICTURE MADE OF BUTTERFLIES AT THE BARLEY MOW, ENGLEFIELD GREEN[1]   9:

As an example of how anything can be made out of anything or done with an
thing by those who want to do it (as I said in *Life and Habit* that a bullock can tal
an eye lash out of its eye with its hind foot[2]--which by the way I saw one of n
bullocks in New Zealand do), I saw at the Barley Mow a picture of a horse and d
talking to one another made entirely of butter flies' wings--it was very well and spir
edly done too.

There was another picture done in the same way of a greyhound running aft
a hare, also good but not so good.

JONES ON BACH'S MUSIC   9:

He says it puts him a little too much in mind of those moving pictures und
which you see written "put a penny in the box and the figure will work."

JONES AND TWO MIS-QUOTATIONS   9:

Is it not Wordsworth who has so pathetically said, the man is father of the child

"Oh God, that men should put an enemy into their brains to steal away the
hearts." (Used in *Ex Voto*.)[2]

228

Painting is only possible by reason of association's not sticking to the letter of bond--so that we jump to conclusions.

ASSOCIATED IDEAS   925

When we are impressed by a few only, or perhaps only one of a number of ideas ich are bonded pleasantly together, there is hope; when we see a good many ere is expectation; when we have had so many presented to us that we have ex- cted confidently, and the remaining ideas have not turned up, there is disappoint- nt. So the sailor said in the play, "Here are my arms, here is my manly bosom, t where's my Mary?"

WE HAVE ALL SINNED   926[1]

 d come short of making ourselves as comfortable as we easily might have done-- rather, as it now seems to us that we easily might have done.

ASSOCIATED IDEAS   927

I once saw a lot of brilliant blue Christmas roses growing in a garden at Wey- dge. I was very much surprised and pleased, for I thought we had a new flower. looked more closely, however, and we saw a little spot of blue sticking to a leaf. e owner of the garden had painted his Christmas roses.

AUNT ANNA[1]--SALT   928

My Aunt Anna did not dare to do naughty things herself, but she used to egg mother on to do them; and my mother was always ready. One day she said, anny, pull about the salt," and my mother at once pulled it about and got punish-

PROCTOR--SPACE "PRACTICALLY" INFINITE   929

The *Times*, March 24, 1882 reports R.A. Proctor as having said that space was actically" infinite. I think he went on to say that time was also "practically" inite.[1]

DON'T BE FASTIDIOUS, CHILD   930

There was an old woman in Ludlow who gave her servant the key of the house or to unlock the tea caddy. The maid remonstrated, but her mistress said, "Don't fastidious child--take the key I give you."

SUN GOING ROUND THE EARTH   931

A child asked the same old lady whether the earth went round the sun or the n round the earth. "Lor', child," she said, "what questions you ask to be sure. hought it all over yesterday and I can't think it all over again to-day; what I thought

then I think now; sometimes one and sometimes the other." (No. This old lad
was old Mrs. Hughes, mother to Thomas Smart Hughes and to Mrs. Monk, wife ↑
the Bishop of Gloucester.[1]

Written April, 1883   Edited December 23, 189

ORGANS AND TOOLS   9:

A man should see himself as a kind of tool box; this is simple enough! T♦
difficulty is that it is the tools themselves that make and work the tools.

PARASITIC WORMS   9:

The small parasitic worms that infest our systems only come out at night--♦
at any rate, come out much more by night. See *Times*, February 28, 1883.[1]

TRAINS AS ORGANS OR TOOLS   9:

We say a man "takes" the train.

THE POSTULATES   9:

A boy was asked in examination what were the postulates; he replied, "The♦
are three postulates: the first is that things which are equal to the same are equ♦
to one another; the second, that things which are greater than the same are great♦
than one another; the third, that things which are less than the same are less th♦
one another."

HEREDITY IN THE *ATLANTIC MONTHLY*   9:

At the very end of March, 1883, I was saying to Jones that it was a long tim♦
since any of the Magazines had said anything about Evolution, and it was time som♦
of them had something on the subject. The very next morning I saw the *Atlant♦
Monthly* advertise an article on Heredity. "Here," thought I to myself, "there m♦
be something about *Life and Habit*," so I went off to Mudie's at once. I could n♦
find the article for a good long time, but at last did so on page 507. It began:
A soldier of the Cromwell stamp
With sword and prayer book at his side
At home he lived in church and camp
Austere he lived and smileless died.
and ended three stanzas later by saying that the subject of the poem had a cool ar♦
reasoning brain and a quick unreasoning heart. The wretch's name was Thom♦
Bailey Aldrich.[1]

See *Times*, April 4, 1883. "The gardener said it went very mad."[1]

PROVIDENCE ITSELF   938

)uld not be more absolutely improvident.

ritten March, 1883   Edited December 23, 1896

IF I BREAK DOWN PREMATURELY   939

1d I often think I shall, it will have been due partly to the severity of my bringing
p; to overwork and continual pressure put upon me when I was young; partly to
1e Christian religion which led my people to set me on almost every wrong track
1 which I could be set; partly to the years of very great pain which I passed be-
veen, we will say, the years 1862 and 1872, and hard work all that time, partly to
1e very great anxiety about money which I have been in until the last year or two,
1 anxiety which though lessened is not removed; partly to the hard work which
1y books have cost me, and the completeness of the failure which has attended
1em; the chorus of sneer and the heavy debt against them, at this moment nearly
400--truly Charles Darwin is revenged; partly to want of that rest which, if I had
1ore money, I could take, but which even in my holidays I do not get, for the ever
resent anxiety about money weigh upon me at all times; I never see my way safe-
᾽ for a good time ahead; I get through, but it is always by the skin of my teeth;
1t if I break down, it will be due I think more than anything else to the sense of
1e relations which exist, and always have existed, between me and my father. March
383.[1] [For the last ten years I have had nothing that I have any wish to complain
f. December 23, 1896.][2]

MY FATHER AND MYSELF   940

He never liked me, nor I him: from my earliest recollections I can call to mind
ɔ time when I did not fear him and dislike him; over and over again I have relented
wards him, and said to myself that he was a good fellow after all; but I had hardly
ɔne so when he would go for me in some way or other which soured me again. I
1ve no doubt I have made myself very disagreeable: certainly I have done many
ery silly and many very wrong things; I am not at all sure that the fault is more his
1an mine; but no matter whose it is, the fact remains that for years and years I have
ever passed a day without thinking of him many times over as the man who was
1re to be against me, and who would see the bad side rather than the good of every-
1ing I said and did. He used to say to his nurse, so my aunt, Mrs. Bather,[1] said,
'll keep you: you shan't leave; I'll keep you on purpose to torment you," and I
ave felt that he has always looked upon me as something which he could badger
ith impunity or very like it, as he badgered his nurse. There can be no real peace
1d contentment for me until either he or I are there where the wicked cease from

231

troubling. An unkind fate never threw two men together who were more natural uncongenial than my father and myself.

MYSELF AND THE RETURN OF THE JEWS TO PALESTINE[1]   94

A man called on me last week (March 20, 1883) and proposed to me grave that I should write a book on an idea which he had hit upon, which should lead the return of the Jews to Palestine; he said he had called on me because of my litera reputation; he said he knew how to get the poor Jews back; but that the difficul lay with the Rothschilds, Oppenheims &c.; still with my assistance it could be dor I was much flattered, but declined to hear the scheme on the ground that I did n care twopence whether the Rothschilds went back to Palestine or not. This was f to be an obstacle, but he began to try and make me care, and then I had to get r of him.

Written April, 1883   Edited December 30, 189

KARMA   94

When I am inclined to complain about having worked so many years and take nothing but debt, though I feel the want of money so continually (much more doub less than I ought to feel it), let me remember that I come in free *gratis* to the wo of hundreds and thousands of better men than myself who often were much wor paid than I have been. If a man's true self is his "karma," the life which his wor lives, but which he knows very little about and by which he takes nothing, let hi remember at least that he can enjoy the karma of others, and this about squar it--or rather far more than squares it.

THE MOUTH   94

goes thus

I HAVE NAMED TWO PIECES OF MUSIC   94

the names to which will I think stick. The first is Handel's great fugue in the fourt of the first set of the suites, which I called the "three o'clock fugue." The secon is the last of the six great fugues, which I call the "old man fugue"; the subject is lik an old man's epitaph on himself, and life, and things.[1]

They say the sex is not determined till the embryo is in a very advanced stage;
ιt for months after birth we still speak of a baby as "it."

POST-NATAL GROWTHS   946

Babies grow their clothes and their food: they pay for neither: they grow their
ɔots almost as much as they have grown their hair and eyes, and the milk which
aintains them makes them almost as much one person with their mothers after
rth as before.

ALL GROWTH OR NOTHING GROWTH   947

You may have all growth, or nothing growth, just as you may have all mechanism,
 nothing mechanism, all chance or nothing chance, but you must not mix them;
ιd having settled this, you must proceed at once to mix them.

CLOTHES AND HABITS   948

Remember that a habit is still used for a riding dress, and that the French call
ɔthes "habits."

PALM ON PALM SUNDAY   949

Last year we brought back some Palm on Palm Sunday;[1] we were regularly
·sieged as soon as we got into the street, and had it begged off us before we got
ɔm Waterloo Station to the middle of Waterloo Bridge. We had no idea that peo-
·e cared about it. This year we brought back a lot to be able to give away, but we
ɖ not reach town till dark, and were not asked for any.

ritten April, 1883   Edited December 30, 1896

THE VENTILATORS ON THE THAMES EMBANKMENT   950

They are making a great outcry about these, just as they made a great outcry
ɔout the Griffin.[1] They say the ventilators have spoiled the Thames embankment.
 hey do not spoil it half so much as the statues do--indeed I do not see that they
 ɔil it at all. The trees that are being planted everywhere are, or will be, a more
·rious nuisance. Trees are all very well where there is plenty of room, otherwise
 ιey are a mistake; they keep in the moisture, exclude light and air, and their roots
 ιsturb foundations; most of our London Squares would look much better if the
 ees were thinned. I should like to cut down all the plane trees in Clifford's Inn
 ιrdens, and leave the smaller ones.

REFUSING TO FIGHT   951

They say a man cannot refuse a challenge with impunity. What nonsense. Look
 ·t Mr. Gladstone and the Kilmainham treaty; look at Mr. Parnell;[1] look at Mr. Darwin
 ιnd myself. The fiction is a wholesome one, but it is a fiction none the less.

Lord Chesterfield says there were only two things a man of honour must n●
do: he must not cheat at cards, and he must not refuse to fight. What Charles Da●
win did to me was very like cheating at cards, and he certainly refused to fight.

ALPS AND SANCTUARIES   95

I took up a copy from the tray on Mudie's[1] counter, and found that in t●
passage where I had said that Tennyson had written "there is more doubt in hone●
faith, believe me &c.," some one had carefully corrected the passage and transpose●
.the "doubt" and the "faith"; if they go through my books correcting the misquot●
tions when I say I am quoting from memory, they will have their work cut out. ●
may say here that whenever I say, "I quote from memory," it means "I am misquo●
ing on purpose."[2]

PAULI AND THE SALVATION ARMY   95

He met the Salvation Army and eyed them with disgust. A prig of a you●
high church curate stood near, and seeing Pauli look very well done all round as ●
always does, vented a few ejaculations about its being "awful" &c. Pauli hated hi●
nearly as much as he hated the Salvation Army, and woman-like wanted to tea●
him. His quick wit suggested a two-edged blow, and he smiled pleasantly as he sai●
"They do look bloody fools, don't they"?

CLOTHES DRYING ON HINDHEAD   95

On Hindhead this Easter we saw a family wash hung out to dry. There we●
papa's two great night shirts, and mamma's two lesser night shirts, and then t●
children's smaller articles of clothing and mamma's drawers, and the girls drawer●
all full swollen with a strong North East wind, but Mamma's night shirt, or one ●
them, was not so well pinned on, and instead of being full of steady wind like t●
others, it kept blowing up and down as though she were preaching wildly. We stoo●
and laughed for ten minutes. The housewife came to the window and wondered ●
us, but we could not resist the pleasure of watching the absurdly life-like gestur●
which the night shirt made. I should like a holy family with clothes drying in t●
background.

MY LETTERS   95

I hope no one will publish them after I am dead: they were always hasty, ofte●
insincere, and never intended for the public eye. Then there is my New Zealan●
book.[1] The only good these things can do is to shew that a man may be a very gre●
fool for a very long time, and yet do better things sometimes. Then there is t●
editing of these notes--so carefully dating them. As I look back at the earlier on●
I cannot conceive what made me think it worth while preserving them. Howeve●
there they are, and I will not throw good trouble after bad by troubling further wit●
them.

He sent a turbot from Grove's[1] for my Christening dinner, but my mother's cook
skinned it.   Mr. Brooke of Colston[2] told me that when my grandfather saw what
had been done he turned to my mother and said, "Good God, Fanny, it's skinned."
These were the *ipsissima verba*.[3]   He, Mr. Brooke, was sitting on the other side of
my mother.

DOMENICO SCARLATTI[1] AND HANDEL   958

Domenico Scarlatti never mentioned Handel's name without crossing himself.

MY FATHER AND SCIENCE   959

Because my father has made a collection of plants people may perhaps say I got
my taste for biological study from my father.   I do not think it was so.   My father
never to the best of my belief gave me the smallest encouragement in this respect,
nor does he care about the study of living forms.   He cares only about making a
complete collection, but what he cares most about is the strapping of the specimens
down with little strips of paper.

REFLEX ACTIONS   960

Reflex actions: ordinary actions; instinctive: reasoned.

MEMORY AND PERSONAL IDENTITY   961

See an article in the *Modern Review*, April, 1883.[1]

CHARLES DARWIN AND *LIFE AND HABIT*   962

Romanes in the reprints from *Nature re* Charles Darwin lauds him for having
been so prompt to examine and encourage any new views of evolution.[1]   He never
that I know of paid the smallest attention to *Life and Habit*.   They all kept pretty
mum about it.

ritten May, 1883   Edited December 31, 1896

MEMORY AND ORGANISM   963

The offspring in the womb grows organisms which it will not want to use for
many years.
    It does this because it remembers having made the corresponding growth at the
corresponding period of its development.

But (bearing in mind the dropping out of intermediate memories) how came my ancestor to remember so much of a later stage at so greatly an earlier period as to make provision for it?

This must have come about step by step. The use of the organ cannot originally have been so long subsequent to the provision for it, and there is in all memory recollection of a little on either side the actual thing mainly remembered, but this wants attention.

ART NOTE 96

When one is painting from nature, one remains quiet for a long time, so that the birds and wild animals, if there are any about, become used to one and come out. So do children. At Westminster the boys (very good fellows) got quite used to me, and so do village children.

THE BISHOP OF GIBRALTAR AND MONACO 96

He has been blowing on Monaco. Yet he makes his own money by pretending to possess the faculty of spiritual generation. See a letter, *Times*, April 3, 1883. See also a letter from Mr. Wright, April 25, 1883.[1]

DARWIN AND HIS TRADUCER 96

See article in the *Monthly Journal of Science* for April, 1883.[1]

NO PLACE TO PUT HIS BREAD AND BUTTER IN 96

After the Crimean War, when people took to wearing beards and moustaches I heard of one little girl who would not kiss a friend of her mother's whose mouth was hidden by his moustache--because, as she said, she could not love him; he had no place to put his bread and butter in at.

MRS. PAULI AND MRS. GREY 96

Pauli's mother[1] always liking a scene and to dwell upon the detail of her death which she believed to be (as it then was) far off, desired Mrs. Grey to lay her out. One day she called Mrs. Grey aside and began very solemnly giving instructions as usual, when Mrs. Grey interrupted her: "Oh no Mrs. Pauli, I won't hear of it; if you think you are going to be buried in that beautiful lace night gown, you are very much mistaken. I mean to have that night gown myself."

RENAN 96

There is an article on him in the *Times*, April 30, 1883, of the worst *Times* kind and that is saying much. It appears he whines about his lost faith, and professes to wish that he could believe as he believed when young.[1] No sincere man will regret having attained a truer view concerning anything which he has ever believed. And then he talks about the difficulties of coming to disbelieve the Christian Miracles as though it were a great intellectual feat. This is very childish. I hope no one will say I was sorry when I found out that there was no reason for believing in

eaven and Hell. My contempt for Renan has no limits. (Has he an accent to his
ame? I despise him too much to find out.)[2]

AN OLD MAN CARRYING A REJECTED PICTURE 970

I saw an old painter carrying his rejected picture in Newman Street with a great
ross on the frame. He was bearing his cross, and looked very sad.

SUBJECT 971

An embryo--its component cells fearing birth as we fear death; some say there
s a life beyond it; others say no; all would prefer to remain as they are; none see that
ey always have been in one life or other, and always will be.

ABNORMAL DEVELOPMENTS 972

If a man can get no other food, it is more natural for him to kill another man
nd eat him than to starve. Our horror is rather at the circumstances that make it
atural for the man to do this, than at the man himself. So with other things the
esire for which is inherited through countless ancestors; it is more natural for men
o obtain the nearest thing they can to these even by the most abnormal means if
he ordinary channels are closed, than to forgo them altogether. The abnormal growth
hould be regarded as disease, but nevertheless as showing more health and vigour
han no growth at all would do. I said this in *Life and Habit* when I wrote, "It is
ore natural for a man that he should eat strange food and his cheek so much as
nk not, than that he should starve if the strange food be at his command." Chap-
er III, p. 52.[1]

A BULL GIVING SATISFACTION 973

My cousin found among Whitbread's[1] papers a letter from a farmer's wife ac-
nowledging payment for a bull. She said she hoped he "gave satisfaction."

SKETCHING FROM NATURE 974

s very like trying to put a pinch of salt on her tail. And yet many manage to do it
ery nicely.

DARWIN, CHARLES, AND THE ACCEPTATION OF EVOLUTION 975

I remember hearing Charles Darwin say that when he began to write on evolu-
ion he did not find a single man who accepted it; he spoke emphatically: "There
as not one," he said, "of my friends who accepted it." All I can say is that he
ust have been very unfortunate in his friends. With seven or eight editions of the
estiges[1] sold already, there were plenty of believers in Evolution if he had chosen
o look for them. True, the doctrine was generally rejected, but if the public had
ot been ripe to receive it, the *Times* would never have backed him up from the
utset as it did. If the *Times* and a few other leading papers had not backed him,
e might have written till now and made very little impression.

I remember meeting my Aunt's uncle Edgar Taylor[1] some years ago at Tavito Street, and hearing him say he once saw and spoke to Porson.[2] I was intereste and asked him about it. The old man prosed a long while how he was on a visit t Cambridge and there was a gentleman sitting in a window who it seems was Pr fessor Porson, "and he said to me, 'Where have you been at school'?" and this wa all.

My mother's sister, Aunt Bessy,[1] is what they call a person of weak intellect her intellect may be weak, but if she wants one thing and every one else anothe it is the every one else who has to yield, not she. Once she was a Taviton Stree and my Aunt Philip[2] had fairly fled, leaving Alice[3] as mistress of the house. It wa Summer, and after dinner the desert was not to Aunt Bessy's liking. The nervou twitching motion in her head showed that she was much displeased, and at last sh spoke. "If your mother had been here (twitch), Alice (twitch), there would ha been strawberries: there would have been strawberries (twitch), Alice (twitch), your mother had been here (twitch). I am your Aunt (twitch), and it is not righ it is not respectful, Alice (twitch), that there should not be strawberries. It is th time for strawberries, Alice (twitch), and if your mother had been here" &c. N one could say a word, and she hammered away with a persistence that the stronge intellect might envy.

She lived 40 years with a Miss Evans at Tavistock, and the two got on very we but a few months ago Miss Evans was taken ill and was evidently going to die. Au Bessy has a great fear of death, so she insisted that the connection should end a once, and she came up to my Uncle's at Chester Terrace pending other arrangement She insisted that she should not be told if Miss Evans died. She said to Amy,[4] " is much better for me, Amy, that I should not know if Miss Evans is dead," and n one dared tell her when she did die--which she did soon after Aunt Bessy had gon

In the course of her life she had accumulated household gods to the exten of one box and a whatnot. In this she keeps her doll and her toys. She is about 7 now, but believes herself to be pretty. "I hope they will say, Amy, that the prett lady (twitch), the lady with the pretty brown hair, Amy (twitch), has been here. When she went to Clifton she sewed up £8 in her petticoat. (She died I think la year (1895) aged about 85. She said it was very uncomfortable to make a Will, s she died intestate whereby I took some £700 which I should never have receive otherwise.)

Written May, 1883   Edited January 1, 18 [97]

CROSSING ONESELF 97

The three desiderata for a cross are: 1. that it shall not be too wide; 2. that shall be wide enough; 3. that the thing with which one crosses oneself shall be goo

its kind. It is hard to say what is too wide, what is wide enough, and what good
its kind. Reason is apt to make mistakes on all these heads, and so is inclination.
 mixture of reason and inclination is the safest guide.

IT AMUSES ME AND HURTS NOBODY 979

A woman at Heatherley's did a singularly funny picture of the night model, an
rab--on the same canvas with her study of the day model, a young woman in a red
elisse. The two had no connection, and their juxta-position was very droll. She
id it amused her and hurt nobody else. I said to Sadler,[1] "If it doesn't hurt her
certainly amuses every one else."

H.E. CLARKE'S SONNET ON COROT 980

He wrote a sonnet on Corot and read it to Mr. Elder.[1] When he had done Mr.
lder said, "And pray where is Corot?" taking Corot for the name of a place.

BOSS AND ILLEGITIMACY 981

Boss's son Tom is illegitimate: but he has himself committed bigamy first with
opsy and now with Phoebe--or Phebe, as Boss calls her without sounding the second
Boss was not married quite enough. Tom is married a little too much. She was
ying one day that illegitimacy did not matter much, and was much pleased when
y cousin explained to her that all the animals were illegitimate.

YESTERDAY, TOMORROW AND TUESDAY 982

The little Maldens[1] can get so far with the days of the week but no farther as
t.

MARRIOTT AND MY LETTERS[1] 983

Marriott, now member for Brighton, had kept a lot of my old letters written
 Cambridge and from New Zealand. I knew they were very silly, and he used to
it me with them, saying I had said this and that; about a year ago I determined
 get them off him and called at his chambers taking him unawares. We found a
x full of old letters and picked out mine, I alleging that I wanted them for my
vel. I promised faithfully that I would restore them; but first I burned one, and
en another, and then little by little the whole lot. I met him in the street the other
y, but instantly began praising him for his conduct in the House; this interested
m, so he forgot all about my letters, but I shall catch it some day.

THE MODERN SCHOOLMASTER 984

es not aim at learning from his pupils, he hardly can: but the old masters did.
e how Bellini learned from Titian and Giorgione who came to study in his school
hen he was 63 years old, and they each 15. All Bellini's best work was done after
is time.[1]

I came upon Miss Buckley talking to Mr. Garnett[2] in the British Museum a
joined them. Miss Buckley told me I ought to read the *Life of Lord Lawrence*
he was such a grand man &c. I never will forgive him for having opposed Lord Be
consfield's Afghanistan policy (I think he did, but it doesn't matter); any way,
was not going to have him; but Miss Buckley would not have nay, so I screwed
my face and said that my Aunt Sarah had known him--as though that was final.
knew very well that neither she nor Mr. Garnett knew who my Aunt Sarah w
but it made Garnett laugh, and the mystery of the thing staunched Miss Buckle

DICKENS'S HOUSE   9

On one of our Sunday walks Jones and my Cousin and I were at Gad's Hill:
American tourist came up and asked if that was Charles Dickens's house, pointi
to it. I looked grave and said, "Yes--I am afraid it was," and left him.

IRRATIONAL RATIONALISM   9

"An then he finishes his book with one of the saddest, most eloquent and mc
pathetic passages I ever read, in which he bitterly deplores the result to which (as I
imagines) his reason had conducted him. He confesses that he had much great
satisfaction and happiness in his old[1] belief, but in obedience, as he supposes,
inexorable logic he throws over belief, and announces himself an atheist." *Scien
and Faith.* Goodwin (Bishop of Carlisle), p. 227, 228, *re* a work called *Examin
tion of Theism* by Physicus (who was that ass Romanes).[2]

MYSELF AND POSTERITY   9

Posterity will not have imagination enough to tell it what a fool I am, and it
dangle enough works before it, it may be caught by some of them. Why I shou
wish to trouble posterity--what harm it has done me for which I would punish i
what good for which I would reward it--I know not; all I know is that I mean catc
ing posterity if I can.

SON BUONA PER LA VORARE LA TERRA   9

A poor woman once declined to look at a picture I was painting at Prato.[1] S
said, "Son buona per lavorare la terra, ma per la geografia non son capace."[2] She w
so scared she would not even look.

BIRDS AND BEASTS COMING OUT OF BRITISH MUSEUM   9

I came one morning in May, 1883, and found the steps of the main entran
all covered with stuffed birds and beasts on their way to South Kensington. It w
very droll and very pretty. They looked like the creatures coming out of the ar

MARK'S "ST. FRANCIS PREACHING TO THE BIRDS"[1]   9

This picture, a very dull one as it appears to me, was sold at Christie's a few yea ack at the same time as O'Neil's "Death of Raphael"[2]--some time I should think 1876, 1877, or 1878; it fetched over £1100, and much about the same price as e O'Neil. I don't know which picture is the duller, and was pleased to see them tch so nearly the same price, but sorry that the price should be so considerable.

RICHES   992

How hardly do they that have riches enter into the kingdom of Heaven.[1] Yes, ey take longer in dying than other people do.

ART NOTE. ACCURACY   993

After having spent years in striving to be accurate, we must spend as many more discovering when and how to be inaccurate.

DIFFERENCES OF KIND AND NOT DEGREE   994

We often say that things differ in degree but not in kind, as though there were fixed line at which degree ends and kind begins. There is no such line. All differnces resolve themselves into differences of degree, being the accumulation of a umber of differences of degree. Hence to the metaphysician everything will become ne, being united with everything else by degrees so subtle that there is no escape om seeing the universe as a single whole. This in theory, but in practice it would et us into such a mess that we had better go on talking about differences of kind s well as of degree.

GHOSTS AND COINCIDENCES   995

As an example of a coincidence which with a little more might easily have become ghost story, see *Times*, May 21, 1883, letter from Grove of the Crystal Palace, Papé the clarionet player.[1]

DARWIN AND EVOLUTION   996

Darwin's *claqueurs* are continually crying out that he should have the credit f having discovered evolution--not because he discovered it, but because he popuurised it. He ought to have the credit of having got people to believe in it, though e got them to think they believed in a distorted and impossible form of it. He ound a discredited truth, which he so manipulated that it became an accredited allacy. This is what he did, and this is all he should be credited with.

CITIES, COLONIES, AND PLANETS   997

We see cities throw off colonies as the sun threw off planets, as hives throw ff swarms, or we ourselves offspring; how far does this parallelism go?

THOUGHT IN THE WORLD   998

The accumulation of matter shews itself in a growing visible heap: the accumulan of thought shows itself in changed habits and appearances. Thought cannot be hoarded otherwise. There was not so much thought in the world 200,000 year ago as there is now, but all the makings of the thought were there.

GRAVITY AND LIVING BEINGS 99

My cat throws himself on his back, and as soon as he gets nearly asleep, gravit asserts itself (just as our heads nod when we nap), and makes him get into an u comfortable position. I watched him shift himself half a dozen times over, so as t get into a position which the force of gravity should not disturb as soon as he fe asleep.

MYSELF AND ORIGINAL RESEARCH 100

The contention against me is that I have made no original researches, but ha as a general rule taken my facts at second hand. Perhaps, but what are the Darwi Huxley, and Tydnall people good for it we cannot rely upon their facts and procee to make deductions from them?

FAMILY PRAYERS 100

When I was last at Shrewsbury[1] I noted that the prayers began, "Oh God, wh art always more ready to hear than we to pray." Is it not rather impertinent t tell God this?

I knelt next to my elder sister and repeated the responses to the Lord's praye but perfunctorily: not enough for her to be able to lay hold of--but perfunctoril as one who meant to do the lot but then forgot a bit, and then woke up a bit; I don know whether she noticed, and I took care she should not be able to think it wa intentional.

"THEY DAUBED IT WITH SLIME"[1] 100

This is one of the few verses in the bible that I used to like when I was a chil

FAITH 100

I heard it defined the other day as the power which enables us to believe thing that we know to be untrue.

GABRIEL GUSTAV VALENTIN 100

See Obituary notice in the *Times*, May 28, 1883.[1]

IRVING AND GARRICK[1] 100

We know what nonsense Irving's admirers talk about him. How far, I wonde was Garrick much better?

IMAGINATION 100

If through preconceived opinion or some accident we have misread a word, th

242

nagination will supply another if another is wanted to complete the sense. One
ay I was poorly and reading the *Times* lazily. A paragraph was headed "The French
Madagascar." I read this, "The French call it Madagascar." Feeling that there
ould be no such heading I looked again and saw my mistake. I had read "in" as
it"; and as "The French it Madagascar" would not make sense, I had supplied the
earest verb that lay to hand and for the moment actually saw it, though there was
o such word printed.

PAULI AND ENTWISTLE *RE EREWHON* 1007

Pauli has done more to shape me than any other man. I have often cribbed
rom his good sayings; several of them are in *Erewhon*, and indeed in every book
hat I have written there is something of his. Entwistle[1] told him that he was sure
e wrote *Erewhon*. Pauli said he did nothing of the sort. "Well then," said Entwis-
le, "you talked to be beggar who did." "I've talked to you often enough," rejoined
'auli, "but you never wrote *Erewhon*, nor never will." Not that *Erewhon* is much
o have written. For my own part I find it the only one of my books which I can
o longer read. Such as it was however, I believe I am responsible for it except in
espect of a few good things by way of detail, such as every one gets from friends
i talking with them about his work.

HANDEL AND MYSELF 1008

Pauli shaped me more than any man I have ever known, but of all dead men,
Iandel has had the largest place in my thoughts. In fact I should say he and his music
ave been the central fact in my life ever since I was old enough to know of the
xistence of either music or life. All day long–whether I am writing or painting
r walking–but always–I have his music in my head, and if I lose sight of it and of
im for an hour or two, as of course I sometimes do, this is as much as I do. I be-
ieve I am not exaggerating when I say that I have never been a day since I was 13
/ithout having had Handel in my mind many times over.

A. MARKS AND MYSELF *RE* ROBESPIERRE[1] 1009

Alfred Marks[2] had been talking furious radicalism and calling Lord Beacons-
ield a ----------- Jew, and a lot of nonsense of that kind. I told him his own name
nd the cast of his own features marked him as quite as much of a Jew as Lord Bea-
onsfield was (they don't, but he has a Jewish tinge). I said, "You are just the kind
f man who was responsible for the terror during the French Revolution. You are
ke Robespierre in every respect but one--that you are not incorruptible." We are
till excellent friends.

MYSELF AND LESLIE STEPHEN[1] 1010

I had not seen him for years; we had dropped each other by mutual consent.
till I believe I owed him a call which had remained some eight or nine years unpaid.
he other day I saw him in the Museum, went up to him and apologised, saying
ow long and often he had been upon my mind, and explaining that the great break
n my life caused by my long visit to America must be my best plea. Then I compli-
nented him upon his work on Ethics,[2] and said I had got it from Mudie's and that

243

I was sure it was a very valuable contribution to the literature of the subject. H
said rather impatiently that he hated all his books as soon as he had finished then
the only pleasure of a book was the writing it; the moment it was published he bega
to loathe it; he asked me if I did not feel the same. I hm'ed and ha'd a little, sai
I did not--and added laughingly that on the contrary I liked my books very mucl
So I do continually read them again, and find very little need of substantial alter
tion though I should like to alter plentifully in small matters. I think a man mu
be an ass if he hates his book as soon as he has written it. He should not hate
unless it is full of mistakes, and if it is full of mistakes he should have found out mo
of them before he published. We met therefore, but as usual, we found ourselv
on different sides immediately.

MY SISTERS AND MY PAINTING   101

One of my sister's amenities is to call my painting, "drawing." If I say I a
painting such and such a picture they reply that they are glad I am "getting on wi
my drawing"--they never call it painting; they know the difference very well, the
don't make the mistake to Edith Hall; it is intended as a way of cheapening wha
I am doing. If it pleases them, it does not hurt me.

THAT WOULD BE VERY NICE   101

Another trick that my elder sister has, when I play her anything on the pian
is to say, "Oh yes, yes, I can see that would be very nice"--meaning of course, "
it was properly played, but you play it so damned badly that I can only see it woul
be very nice."

OYSTER BITS AND MRS. REEVE[1]   101

My cousin's aunt Mrs. Reeve, mother of the present Editor of the *Edinburg*
Review, once found him as a small boy struggling with the back of a fowl. She too
him in hand, and explained to him how he should eat it.
"These my dear," she said, "are called the oyster bits; you should take the
out like this--they will come off quite easily," and she took them off.
"Then, you know, you should pepper them and salt them--not too much--b
just a little pepper and a little salt," and she peppered and salted them.
"And then, my dear, you should eat them--like this"--and she ate them, leavir
him to get on with the rest of his bone as well as he could.

SUBJECT   101

A letter to the Christian evidence society.

Written June, 1883   Edited January 5, 189

244

There are some men so ignorant of what gives them pleasure that they cannot be said ever to have been really born as living beings at all. They present some of the phenomena of having been born; they reproduce, in fact, so many of the ideas which we associate with having been born that it is hard not to think of them as living beings--but in spite of all appearances the central idea is wanting.

FRANK DARWIN AND MYSELF, *RE LIFE AND HABIT*   1016

Soon after *Life and Habit* came out, Frank Darwin asked me about the bit of song quoted on page 201 as having been altered.[1] I have given it as

"Some breeds do and some breeds don't,
Some breeds will but this breed won't,
I tried very often to see if it would,
But it said it really couldn't and I don't think it could."

He wanted to know what it was in the original. I told him it was

"Some girls will and some girls won't" &c.[2]

He said, "Oh," and looked very much scandalised.

FRANK DARWIN AND MYSELF AS REFERRED TO IN
UNCONSCIOUS MEMORY   1017

The friend referred to on page 33 of *Unconscious Memory*[1] was none other than Frank Darwin himself. He and all of them very well know that the *Life and Habit* theory is the right one, but they won't say so.

ADVERTISMENT   1018

The following has appeared lately: "Mrs. Smith having cast off clothing of every description invites inspection."

HANDEL AND THE PONTIFEX NOVEL   1019

It cost me a great deal to make Ernest play Beethoven and Mendelssohn--I did it simply *ad captandum*; as a matter of fact he played none but early Italian, old English music, and Handel--but Handel most of all.[1]

HANDEL'S SHOWER OF RAIN   1020

The shower in the air, "Thus cheers the sun" in *Joshua*[1] is I think the finest description of a warm sunny refreshing rain that I have ever come across, and one of the most wonderfully descriptive pieces of music that even Handel ever did.

in one of her coarse letters to my friend her son, when he was out of employment and looking for work wrote, "Surely it cannot be your intention to ask your sisters to keep you."

ASSIMILATION AND PERSECUTION   1022

We cannot get out of persecution: if we feel at all we must persecute something the mere acts of feeding and growing are acts of persecution. Our aim should be to persecute nothing but such things as are absolutely incapable of resisting us.

MYSELF AT THE MUSEUM   1023

I never leave the Museum without leaving a little heap of torn M.S. behind me. The attendants must think I go there to tear up my writing, not to write.

HERBERT DRAPER[1] AND MYSELF   1024

I met him in Fetter Lane not long since. He is one of the men who are very civil to me when they think I am up, and not so civil to me when they think I am down. At present I am certainly unpopular and he knows it.

"What are you preparing for our instruction now?" said he quite civilly--but still there was a doubtful tone about the question, and I know him so very slightly that he had no business to ask. I smiled, made a slight grimace, and said, "Oh I suppose I'm writing something." He said, "I saw your last book, *Alps and Sanctuaries*." He didn't say he liked it, and was wanting me to ask him whether he did or didn't. Of course I was up to that. "Ah," said I, "that's been out about a year and a half now," and turned the conversation, so he didn't get his little fling.

SHE DOES GIVE OUT SO   1025

Dinah--Mrs. Jones's[1] old servant--said to Jones the other day that his mother couldn't stand hot weather. "You know Master Harry," she said, "your Ma's very large now, and she do give out so," meaning perspire.

BLACK PUDDING LUCY   1026

or the Hallelujah Dredger is a heroine in the Salvation Army.[1]

HE'S STILL DEAD   1027

A fussy old man met a young one. "How are you, how are you my dear fellow--and how is your dear father?"

"Oh, my father is dead--he has been dead this two years." The old gentleman retreated, but forgot all about it.

Some time afterwards the two met again.

"How are you &c.--and how is your dear father?"

The young man replied, "He's still dead, thank you."

Arthur Malden[1] showed his little girl an illustrated *Pilgrim's Progress* in which there was a picture of Apollyon. Next day she said, "It frightened me so much that I very nearly dreamed about it, and if you please, may I take my pink doll to bed with me tonight to protect me?"

GROWING TEETH OUTSIDE THE WOMB   1029

We are taking to do this more and more through our dentists who make us artificial teeth.

SCIENCE AS AN AVOCATION   1030

Why, I wonder, may Mr. Spottiswoode, Sir J. Lubbock, and Mr. De La Rue follow science, "not as a vocation, but as an avocation," and why may not I? See *Times,* June 28, 1883.[1] They may, but I mustn't. I suppose it is because they are rich.

Written June, 1883   Revised January 6, 1897

HANDEL AND THE BRITISH PUBLIC   1031

Rockstro[1] says the English people loved Handel and treated him well &c. I don't see that. The Court treated him well and gave him pensions amouting to £600 a year, which he held for many years. But for this income he would have been at times absolutely penniless. In the last ten years of his life he made a few thousands, but till he was 64, he was in continual difficulties and worried nearly out of his life. If he had died at 64, he would not have left a penny behind him. They worried him into a fit of paralysis in 1737, and if they could they would have killed him outright long before he had written his best works. It was only the Court that made him possible.[2]

AUNT SARAH[1] AND PRETTY FOWSES   1032

Aunt Sarah says there is only one story of her childhood extant; that, she considers it to her credit, and tells it accordingly. My great-aunt Mrs. Hutchings,[2] asked her which she liked best, cakes or flowers. "Oh, fowses, pretty fowses," replied Aunt Sarah immediately: then reflecting a little she added, "Cakes is very nice."

MR. GARNETT[1] AND ASTROLOGY   1033

I have several times mentioned him in these notes and sometimes half, as it might seem, disparagingly. I do not mean this. He is one of the very best men I ever knew--never tired of doing good natured things for students--none of whom can be more indebted to him than I am. We should find his loss irreparable if he were to leave the Museum. His sense of humour is very keen and there can be no question about his learning and his general ability. At the same time I cannot accept him as a critic. He ran *John Inglesant*[2] hard, and did not like to hear me speak disparagingly of it. Also he believes in astrology and when I was a good deal out of sorts this spring and summer (1883)[3] told me gravely that he was not surprised, for that if I was born in the latter half of the day (December 4, 1835) on which I was actually born, Saturn at the present time was exercising a malignant influence upon me. He was quite serious. I wrote and asked my father at what hour I was born as near as he could remember, but he could remember nothing about it[4]--so Mr. Garnett will, I doubt not, settle it that I was born in the latter half.

TWINS AND THINGS DONE SYNCHRONOUSLY   1034

If I write "Mrs. Doncaster

Mrs. Doncaster" twice over without any thought the two hand writings will be as like as twins generally are. If I waited a day or two between the two writings they would not resemble one another so clearly.

GUILTY INNOCENCE   1035

Montesquieu says somewhere--in a novel of which I forget the name--something like the following:
"I received my pardon--I retained my innocence--alas! without the hope of becoming ever guilty."

BOSS--AND MY COUSIN'S BREAKFASTS   1036

She said, "I get him eggs and bacon and he don't like that, and then I get him a bit of fish and he don't like that, or else it's too dear, and you know fish is dearer than ever; and then I get him a bit of German (sausage) and he says it rises on him and hits him in the eye. Oh, it takes me to a perfect shadder, because I fret inwardly; I go home and wander in my room and cry for hours all about them paltry breakfasts."

MYSELF   1037

I have written so much about myself because I am the subject on which I am the best informed.

GUANO, THE SMELL OF   1038

Going down the river to Sheerness I heard a man say as we passed the Belvedere Guano Works[1] that the guano made the workmen who had to do with it smell very badly. "There's no woman will marry them," he said, "not unless she's been brought up in a cat's meat shop."

He continued with a story about the sailors on a ship in which he had sailed, and how they had had a row with some Maltese. The Maltese had sold them some beautifully coloured birds with which the sailors were delighted, but "after they had left Malta a few days the birds was wrong." He said this mysteriously and looked very grave--meaning that they had been painted. To me it seemed that it was not the birds that were wrong. It was the people who sold the birds that were wrong.

DOING THINGS FOR THE WORKING CLASSES   1040

It is only our conceit--as though our way of living and looking at things must be so much better than other people's--which makes us want "to do things for the working classes."

MISS SAVAGE AND THE SELF HELP CLUB   1041

She said they were called the Self Help Club, because they helped themselves, and they were the only people whom they did help.

Written July, 1883   Edited January 8, 1897

G.H. DARWIN AND THE TIDES[1]   1042

First came Professor Ball's two papers in *Nature*, November 24, and December 1, 1881.

On January 5, 1882, there appeared a leader by George Darwin "On the Geological Importance of the Tides"; it concludes with a sentence which admirably illustrates the tendency of ancestral characteristics to reappear in offspring, though sometimes at an earlier age. The sentence runs:

"In conclusion I wish to add that in my first paper I probably attributed too much of the changes in the configuration of the earth and moon to the effect of bodily tidal deformation of the earth's mass. The evidence is strong that such tides are now but small, or even scarcely sensible in amount, and accordingly in all probability the later part of the changes must be attributed almost entirely to the effects of oceanic tidal friction, whilst in the earlier part the tides of the solid or semi-solid matter constituting the planet were the most important."[2]

How like this is to the passage I animadverted on in *Life and Habit* and *Evolution Old and New*, in which George Darwin's father wrote (though at a later age than that at which George Darwin did so): "In the earlier editions of this work I underrated as now seems possible, the frequency and importance of modifications due to spontaneous variability. But it is impossible to attribute to this cause &c." See *Evolution Old and New*, pp. 358, 359.[3]

How Charles Darwinian also is the "probably," "in all probability," "almost entirely," "small or even scarcely sensible." The same desire to leave as many loop-

holes for escape as possible is noticeable in the work of both father and son. Eac
has to beat a retreat, but each leaves it very uncertain how far they admit themselve
to be wrong and how much of what they thought when they first wrote they thin
still. The same heavy lumbering unperspicuous build of sentence is common to bot
father and son.

But the similarity is not confined to characteristics of style and thought. It
found also in the external surroundings of both, inasmuch as each has got a we
developed *claque* to back him; the great development of this organ on the part o
the father has, it would seem, been transmitted to the son. It seems hardly fair t
press heredity so far as to make it involve a man's inheriting things that were be
gotten by others who were no relation to him; but there are always people read
enough to hang on; it is the power to attach these that I suppose hereditary and t
be characteristic of both the Darwins.

What Huxley has been to Charles Darwin, that Professor Ball now is to Georg
Darwin. He writes:[4]

"A great scientific theory is generally the outcome of many minds. To a certai
extent this is true of the theory of tidal evolution. It was Professor Helmholtz wh
first appealed to what tides had already done on the moon. It was Professor Purse
who took an important step in the analytical theory. It was Sir William Thomson'
mathematical genius which laid the broad and deep foundations of the fabric. Thes
are the pioneers in this splendid research, but they were only the pioneers. Th
great theory itself is chiefly the work of one man. You are all familiar with th
name he bears. The discoverer of tidal evolution is Mr. G.H. Darwin, Fellow of Trin
ity College Cambridge."

How exactly this resembles the tone with which Charles Darwin's *claque* bi
Buffon, Erasmus Darwin, and Lamarck stand aside, and proclaim Charles Darwi
as the real discoverer of the fact that all animals and plants have a common origi

Not only do the characteristics of the father reappear in the son as regards styl
the having to retreat, the mode of retreating, the developments of a *claque*, the wa
in which the *claque* discharge their functions, but they also reappear in respect o
the fatuousness with which both father and son deceived themselves into believin
that they were discoverers.

In *Nature* (January 5, 1882, p. 127) I find a letter signed A. Dupré,[5] in whic
the main points of what Professor Ball calls George Darwin's theory are shown t
have been insisted upon by Kant, not a single important detail being omitted, eithe
in respect of fact or argument in support of the fact. M. Dupré, however, speak
of Kant's work as having been "almost universally overlooked."

In the next number (January 12, 1882)[6] appears a letter from Professor Huxle
to say that he, at any rate, had not overlooked Kant's work, and had devoted a con
siderable portion of his anniversary address on Geological Reform for the year 186
to an attempt to do justice to Kant's work. He reprinted his address in his *Lay Se
mons*, "and therefoe," he continues, "I have reason to know that a considerabl
portion of the reading, or at any rate book buying public, has no excuse for ove
looking Kant's work."

Professor Huxley does not seem to like to see any one burlesqueing with the so
the role which he had himself played with the father. As for George Darwin himsel
he completes the resemblance to his father by keeping silence under circumstance
in which one does not understand how a fair man could do so. On the 16th of Febru
ary he writes about Jupiter's atmosphere as though nothing had happened.[7]

The foregoing is an example of what I mean by saying that the young Darwins appear to me to be examples of descent with singularly little modification.

As if to crown the resemblances between parent and offspring in this case, a Dr. Haughton writes January 19, 1882, to wave Kant aside exactly as Professor Ball had waved the other earlier workers in the field which G. Darwin has chosen.[8]

"The claim," says Dr. Haughton, "for priority on behalf of Kant, by the metaphysicians, must be set aside, as Kant's statement was not based on sound dynamical principles."

It was not the metaphysicians, but Professor Huxley, who had stood up for the value of Kant's work. Besides, as far as I can see, Kant bases his statements on exactly the same "dynamical principles" as George Darwin himself. Certainly those who read M. Dupré's account of what Kant maintained (*Nature*, January 5, 1882) will see that it is not based upon anything in the least approaching metaphysics. Kant however happened to write about metaphysics, and we none of us know much else about him, so Dr. Haughton picks up "metaphysics" as the cheapest stone he can find, and flings it at Kant's head.

There is nothing which men like Professor Ball and Dr. Haughton enjoy so much as toadying some one. They know that Charles Darwin stood at the top of the tree, and I dare say would have gone for him if he was not already surrounded by such a host of admirers that there was little room for them. George Darwin, if not the rose, was at any rate very near the rose, and by running him they might become members of the inner circle--so they chose him as the one whom they should hang on to. It is a purely personal matter, and science has nothing whatever to do with it; having, so to speak, laid their money on him, they do all they can to damage the others who are in the field.

There are no actual highwaymen about England now, but literary and scientific highwaymen are not lacking.

INHERITANCE OF ACQUIRED CHARACTERISTICS 1043

See an excellent example contributed to *Nature* for July 21, 1881, by Charles Darwin--about a man who had thumbs of which the skin was badly cracked from exposure to cold.[1]

PUMPING MACHINES FOR ALL DUTIES 1044

I see this announcement made over a shop which I pass on my way to Cannon treet railway station. It attributes a moral responsibility to machines, and shows how completely in the expressions which we use unconsciously we regard them as living beings.

Written August 1883   Revised January 9, 1897

OLIVER MADOX BROWN[1] 1045

I saw an article about him in the *Athenaeum* for one of the last weeks in July,

251

1883.[2] It said he was comparable only to Chatterton. I know nothing about Chatter
ton, but think it very likely that he was comparable only to Oliver Madox Brown
I knew him (O.M.B.); he used to come up to my rooms and bore me very much by
insisting on reading me extracts from *Gabriel Denver* and other M.S.S. I told him
did not like them: they were not in my line, but he was a pertinacious young bore
and I suffered a good deal from him. He was, I should say, very dull, without any
but the vulgarest, crudest notions of effect--with no idea of drawing from nature
and reproducing, as closely as he could, what he saw and heard. At the same time
he was quite square, not ill-natured, and I could have done with him well enough
if he would have stayed a quarter of an hour instead of coming to sit for hours til
I had smoked myself silly, and had to take and turn him out in self-defence. I do
not believe he had any growth in him, and have pigeon-holed him as a harmless
not ill-natured young fellow, who was at the same time irretrievably commonplace
and bent on posing as a genius.

AN EGG FOUND WITHIN ANOTHER EGG   104

When things get off their beat what pranks they play. Look at all kinds of mon
strosity. In the *Monthly Journal of Science* for August, 1883, there is an account
of an egg which being of abnormal size was opened and found to contain another
complete egg, shell and all, inside it.[1]

UNCONSCIOUS HUMOUR AND HOME   104

"I have always observed within my experience that *the men who have left home
very young* have *many long years afterwards* had the tenderest love of it." Letter
by C. Dickens to the Honble Mrs. Watson, quoted from *Charles Dickens and Rochester*, by Robert Langt[on].* Chapman & Hall.[1]

MY COUSIN AND GOTHIC   104

At Sheerness the other day he paused before a minute corrugated iron chapel
very small and as bald as it could possibly be. Then he said, "How I do hate Gothic."

CONTINUATION OF EXTRACTS FROM PAPERS ON DEATH OF
CHARLES DARWIN[1]   104

"The first edition of this remarkable production (the *Origin of Species*) appeared
in 1859, and no competent physicist now doubts that--whatever may hereafter modi
fy, complete, enlarge, or even correct, the main theories of its author--the book it
self was 'epoch-making' and must ever remain &c." *Daily Telegraph*, April 21, 188
(Leader).[2]
"Whether his (Charles Darwin's) theory will meet the fate of those which pre
ceded it, or become a more enduring part of the scientific doctrines than did the
dreams of Lamarck, or the 'Vestiges of Creation,' it is difficult to say" (Obituary
Notice). *Standard*, April 21, 1882.[3]
"Whatever may be our opinions about the ultimate vitality of the doctrines
Natural Selection and the Survival of the Fittest, it is impossible for any one wh
aims at &c." *Standard* Leader, April 21, 1882.[4]

If it tends to thicken the crust of ice on which, as it were, we are skating, it is
ll right. If it tries to find, or professes to have found, the solid ground at the bottom
of the water, it is all wrong.

HANDEL AND "TYRANTS NOW NO MORE SHALL DREAD"   1051

The music to this chorus (in *Hercules*)[1] is written from the tyrant's point of
iew. This is plain from the jubilant defiance with which the chorus opens, but
becomes still plainer when the magnificent strain to which he has set the words
"all fear of punishment is o'er," bursts upon us. Here he flings aside all considera-
ions save that of the gospel of doing whatever we please without having to pay
or it. He remembers himself, however, shortly, and becomes almost puritanical
over "the world's avenger is no more." Here he is quite proper.

From a dramatic point of view Handel's treatment of these words must be con-
lemned for reasons in respect of which Handel was very rarely at fault. It puzzles
he listener, who expects the words to be treated from the point of view of the vanquished slaves and not from that of the tyrants. There is no pretence that these parti-
ular tyrants are not so bad as ordinary tyrants, nor these particular vanquished slaves
ot so good as ordinary vanquished slaves, and unless this has been made clear in some
vay, it is dramatically *de rigueur*, that the tyrants should come to grief, or be about
o come to grief. The hearer should know which way his sympathies are expected to
o, and here we have the music dragging us one way and the words another.

Nevertheless we pardon the departure from the strict rules of the game, partly
because of the welcome nature of good tidings so exultantly announced to us about
ll fear of punishment being over, and partly because throughout the music is so
nuch stronger than the words that we lose sight of them almost entirely. Handel
probably wrote as he did from a profound though perhaps unconscious perception
of the fact that even in his day there was a great deal of humanitarian nonsense talk-
d, and that after all, the tyrants were generally quite as good sort of people as the
anquished slaves. Having begun on this tack, it was easy to throw morality to the
vinds when he came to the words, "all fear of punishment is o'er."

MIND AND MATTER--A BLUSH   1052

They say that all phenomena may be expressed in terms of mind or in terms
f matter which ever we please. If so, mind and matter should be two names for
he same thing, but I do not know what they mean when they say this.

Is a blush, for example, matter affected by mind without the aid and instru-
nentality of other matter?

CONSCIOUSNESS   1053

Nothing can look more unconscious than an egg or seed, which may lie for twenty
ears and yet germinate, consciousness making its appearance little by little, till from
eing imperceptible it becomes the main thing that can be perceived.

All the consciousness which we know of comes up insensibly from things which looked to us at one time unconscious, and after a certain time they become unconscious again.

Nothing conscious remains conscious for long.

Unconscious things may remain unconscious for a long time, but they can also be kindled into consciousness by proper treatment. Comminute granite, add water and a little well manured soil, and you can convert your granite into a plant, and through the plant into an animal. True, you must change such a substance as vitriol or coal tar before you can make it conscious; but you can change it; and I am not sure how far this power does not involve as a necessary consequence the presence of intelligence and a low reasoning faculty in all matter.

GALLIUM   105

melts at 85 $^\circ$, and when melted remains liquid long after it ought to solidify again unless reminded, as it were, of solidity by being touched by a little solid Gallium on which it solidifies at once.

BEER AT 4D A POT   105

I heard a man say to another at Abbey Wood, "I went to live down there just about the time that beer came down from 5d to 4d a pot. That will give you an idea when it was."

SCIENTISTS AND PROPHETS   105

"How many more victims must be sacrificed before wrongheaded vestrymen will obey the teachings of science?" *Globe*, about November 17 or 18, 1878.[1]

Here we have exactly the spirit of the Hebrew prophets.

SUBJECT   105

A girl played upon by a ritualist parson tries to get her father to make a will in her favour, to the exclusion of her younger brother, intending to leave the money to the church. She dies a day or two before her father.

THE REVD. ORBY SHIPLEY ON HIS JOINING THE CHURCH OF ROME   105

He says his going over was the result mainly of "a silent gradual and steady growth of many years in religion. I have long held, I have long taught nearly every Catholic doctrine not actually denied by Anglican formularies, and have accepted and helped to revive nearly every Catholic practice not positively forbidden. In short intellectually and in externals, so far as I could as a loyal English Clergyman, I have believed and acted as a Catholic.

"All this I have held and done as I now perceive on a wrong principle, *viz.*--of private judgement. When I became convinced that the right principle of faith and practice of religion was authority; when I saw clearly that it is of less moment what one accepts, and does, than why one accepts and practices, I had no choice as to my course. The only spiritual body which I could realise that actually claimed to teach truth upon authority, and that visibly exercised the authority which she claimed was e Church of Rome. For the last time I exercised my right of private judgement, as every person must exercise that gift of God in some way and to some extent, nd I humbly sought admission into the communion of the Catholic Church." *Times*, November 26 or 25, 1878.[1]

The weak place in Mr. Shipley's position is his acknowledgement that his opinion concerning authority is based ultimately on his private judgment. He admits the principle of private judgment. How much then? and under what circumstances?

A SUDDEN START 1059

The start we give on seeing an unexpected toad is an example of the fact that so habit can be changed abruptly without disturbance, and is closely connected with the sterility of certain wild animals in captivity and also with that of hybrids.

MEN TO LOOK TO 1060

The Marquis of Worcester, and Roger Bacon.[1]

THE EYE, CREDULOUS: ART NOTE 1061

Painters may remember that the eye as a general rule is a good simple credulous organ--very ready to take things on trust if it be told them with any confidence of assertion.

ART NOTE 1062

If a student is to do any good, his development will epitomise the history of painting.

MENDELSSOHN'S *SONGS WITHOUT WORDS*[1] 1063

Jones said it was a mercy they had no words.

KNOWLEDGE AND CONVENIENCE 1064

We should not aim at knowledge--this is beyond our grasp. We should aim at that way of looking at things which will give us least trouble, as fitting in most harmoniously with our other ideas.

BELLINI, PESARO[1] 1065

Mem.: Go to Pesaro and see the Bellini there.

CLASSIFICATION, UNITY, ORGANIC AND INORGANIC 1066

I think I have in M.S. somewhere a note of the way in which no sooner do we think we have got a *bonâ fide* barrier, than it breaks down again. The divisions between varieties, species, genus, all gone; between instinct and reason, gone; between animals and plants, gone; between man and the lower animals, gone; so ere long the division between organic and inorganic will go.

255

KNOWLEDGE AND CONVENIENCE   106

There is nothing you cannot wrangle about. The thing to do is to find som
few general propositions which sensible people will not think it worthwhile to wrar
gle about, and are not likely to think it worthwhile for some time to come. Yo
can wrangle about Euclid's axioms if you like, but sensible people won't like. Wha
is wanted for philosophy is a few axioms and postulates like Euclid's which, righ
or wrong, the people whom we have to deal with will accept without further fus
We can put those who reject these into mad houses.

MOTTO FOR MYSELF   106

I should like "*Quaerenda pecunia primum est*" or "*Virtus post nummum*" c
something of that sort.[1]

MOSS AND MY BOOKS   106

When I was at Shrewsbury last August year,[1] Moss said something about m
books, so I asked him if he would like them for the head room library; he said h
should be very glad to have them; I said he had better look at them first, as *Th
Fair Haven*, for example, might not be exactly the sort of thing he would like t
give his boys. At any rate, I was to send the books, which I did at once. At th
end of May last I was at Shrewsbury and wanted to know whether my books wer
put into the library; I called on Moss and he said he had not yet had time to loo
at them. I have not thought it prudent to return to the subject.

MY UNCLE JOHN AND THE COCK-ROACH   107

It was a cock-roach and not a cock-chafer of which my uncle John said tha
the stomach would be the worst part.[1]

SENSE AND SCIENCE--MOTTO   107

"Men of Science have to find arguments for men of sense to weigh and judg
of." Sir Edward Backet Denison, in a letter to the *Times*, August 13, 1883.[1]

COPERNICUS, AND KNOWLEDGE AND CONVENIENCE 107

It is not true that the sun used to go round the earth until Copernicus's tim
but[1] it is true that we had certain ideas which could only fit in comfortably wit
our other ideas when we came to consider the sun as the centre of the planetar
system.

ATOMS, UNITY, THE UNIVERSE   107

The idea of an indivisible ultimate atom is inconceivable by the lay mind.
we can conceive an idea of the atom at all, we can conceive it as capable of bein
cut in half: indeed we cannot conceive of it at all unless we so conceive of it. Th

nly true atom--the only thing which we cannot subdivide and cut in half is the universe. We cannot cut a bit off the universe and put it somewhere else: therefore he universe is a true atom, and indeed is the smallest piece of indivisible matter which our minds can conceive; [1]and they cannot conceive of it, any more than of he indivisible atom.

SONGS WITHOUT EITHER WORDS OR MUSIC   1074

That is what I want to write.[1]

SUBJECT   1075

On the formation of opinion. Take the subject of free trade and see how opinions iffer about it; but how does opinion come to be formed on such a matter? Priestraft arises from men's desire to have their opinions formed for them. This desire ; like nature: you may expel it with a fork, but it will always return.

HOTEL AT PARIS   1076

Gogin[1] says "Hotel de Nice," 4 bis Rue des beaux arts, Paris.

INVOLVED SENTENCE   1077

The longest and most involved sentence which I can call to mind at this moment in a letter to the *Times* of August 16, 1883, about forest fires in America.[1]

LIFE AND HABIT AND UNITY BETWEEN SUCCESSIVE GENERATION   1078

In *Life and Habit* I insisted on the unity existing between two successive generaions. How would it be to insist rather on the want of unity which exists between he several moments in the life of the individual, and run this as hard as I ran the ther?

DEATH AND LIFE   1079

You can no more cut anything wholly off from life than you can from the material universe.

THE ABBÉ AT CAEN AND BAYEUX   1080

I sat next an Abbé at the *table d'hôte* at Caen, and knew he was like some one ithout being able to recollect exactly who. At Bayeaux I happened to sit next to] * him again: I bowed: he acknowledged it with more or less of a smile, but when e smiled I knew who he was like. It was Sophy Larkin[1] as I had seen her at the audeville a few nights before. He was like her as she was saying, "Oh Lucretia-- appy girl," and later on he looked just as she looked when she said, "Shocking laria, shocking," or when she said, "I've said it again." I half think it must have een Sophy Larkin in disguise.

257

We commonly know that we are going to die, but we do not know that we are going to be born. Is this so? We may have had the most gloomy forebodings on this head and forgotten all about them. At any rate we know no more about the very end of our lives than about the very beginning. We come up unconsciously and go down unconsciously.

NATURE MEAN 108

Nature is essentially mean, mediocre. You can have schemes for raising the level of this mean, but not for making every one two inches taller than his neighbour and this is what people really care about.

September, 1883   Revised January 13, 189

TRUTH AND PERPETUAL MOTION 108

The search after truth is like the search after perpetual motion or the attempt to square the circle. All we should aim at is the most convenient way of looking at a thing--the way the most sensible people are likely to find give them least trouble for some time to come.

THE FINEST MEN 108

I suppose an Italian peasant, or a Breton, Norman or English fisherman is about the best thing Nature does in the way of men--the richer and the poorer being alike mistakes.

BIRTH AND DEATH 108

We come in time to know that we have been born, but not that we have died. Is this so?

CRITICISM BY JUDGE AND JURY 108

Critics generally come to be critics not by reason of their fitness for this, but of their unfitness for anything else. Books should be tried by a judge and jury as though they were a crime, and counsel should be heard on both sides.

POST-NATAL AND PRE-NATAL ACCIDENTS 108

When I say that a man's pre-natal accidents are more important to him than his post-natal, I only say what Darwin has insisted on when he said that the nature of the seed is more important than soil and climate--of course within reasonable limits.

The world will always be governed by self interest: we should not try and stop
is: we should try and make the self interest of cads a little more coincident with
at of decent people.

SUBJECT: ARLETTE   1089

I suspect it was Arlette and not Matilda who did the Bayeux tapestry--see her
ory in Bradshaw's guide to Normandy.[1]

PHYSICS AND METAPHYSICS   1090

There is no drawing the line between physics and metaphysics. If you examine
ery day facts at all closely, you are a physicist; but if you press your physics at
l home, you become a metaphysicians; if you press your metaphysics at all home,
)u are in a fog.

For example, we say such and such a thing is so and so. But what is "a thing"?
rictly speaking there is only one thing–the universe; all other things are called
› through arbitrary classifications like species, and tend to vanish as "things" if
:amined with any closeness.

The difficulty is to know where to stop in what direction. There is so much
› be got by study within due limits, and so much to be lost by going beyond them;
id so often an enquiry which at first seems very profitless has developed great re-
lts. Where is the line to be drawn? That is just what every one must settle for
mself, and be a fool or otherwise according as he has settled it well or ill. There
n be no rule given for drawing lines. As material things prove all to be connected
id parts of one thing, as the pebble at our feet and the most remote and profitless
:ed star are still united, so "does it rain, my dear?" and the most dreary metaphysi-
l enquiry are still closely connected.

POEM   1091

Oh Critics,
Cultured critics who will praise me after I am dead,
Who will see in me both more and less than I intended,
But who will swear that whatever it was it was all perfectly right,
You will think you are better than the people who, when I was
Alive swore that whatever I did was wrong,
And damned my books for me as fast as I could write them;
But you will not [be] * better : you will be just the same, neither better nor worse
And you will go for some future Butler as your fathers have gone for me.
Oh! how I should have hated you!

But you nice people,
Who will be sick of me because the critics thrust me down your throats,
But who would take me willingly enough, if you were not bored about me,
Or if you could have the cream of me, and surely this should suffice,
Please remember that if I were living I should be upon your side,
And should hate those who imposed me either on myself or others;

Therefore, I pray you, neglect me, burlesque me, boil me down, do whate
you like with me,
But do not think that if I were living I should not aid and abet you.

There is nothing that even Shakespeare would enjoy better than a good burlesq
of *Hamlet*.[1]

PETER'S MOTHER-IN-LAW   10

One of the strongest proofs of Christ's personal influence over his followers
to be found in the fact of Peter's remaining on friendly terms with him notwit
standing his having healed his mother-in-law.[1]

I said this to my cousin and he repeated it to an old General at whose house
goes to fiddle. "Yes," said he, "but you know, the Saviour was always a lady's man

SIGNORA BULLO[1] AND THE DOLL   10

Coming downstairs one morning at Faido, I surprised the *padrona* dressing
little pink leather doll for her grandchild. The doll as yet had no clothes on a
was lying on a seat near her. When the *padrona* saw me, she snatched it up wi
a face of horror and hid it under her dress, as though it were a human being. I cov
ed my face with my hand and said, "Oh! oh! oh! come son scandalezzato." For
rest of the day the *padrona* could not meet me without blushing and laughing.

WATCH SNAPPING   10

I heard of an old gentleman who used to snap his watch loudly in church,
a sign to the parson that he should bring his sermon to an end.

OFFSPRING   10

A man's waste tissues and excrementa are to a certain extent offspring. T
molecules have a greater aptitude for organization for their having been connect
with him.

"I DID NOT EXCEED LAST NIGHT"   10

When Mr. Sam Carter[1] resigned his connection with the Midland Railway, l
friends gave him a dinner. Next day he went to the Apothecary and said, "I do n
feel very well this morning. I did not exceed last night, but I should like you
treat me as if I had exceeded."

CHRIST   10

He is like species. He has descended with modification.

NAMES SEEN BY ME IN CHURCHYARDS   10

Jane Dolding, David Welstead, Martha Pippett, Phoebe Knock, Edward Budd
Josiah Chockery (Cioccari?), Gilbert Golder, George Griggs, Robert Bubb, Lyd
Luck, Thomas Truss, Rebecca Weekling, Sarah Skittlethorpe.

I said to an old woman at East Grinstead that I thought owls were rather nice ⸱eople. "Oh do you think so," she replied hurriedly, "I'm sure I don't, I think they're ⸱iteful."

DEAF IN ONE EAR   1100

My cousin said to a man once that he was a little deaf in one ear. "Never knew ⸱married man who wasn't" was the rejoinder.

SNOW BONES AND MONEY BONES   1101

When the snow bones lie, it is said there will come more snow to bury them. ⸱nd after a great money calamity, if the money bones lie, there will come more ⸱oney.

OVERDRIVEN MEAT   1102

They say beasts should not be overdriven before they are killed, as it hurts the ⸱eat &c. This may be so, but our ancestors for countless generations have been ⸱unters, and must have driven their meat pretty hard before they killed it; yet it ⸱es not seem to have disagreed with them. And most of the wild animals hunt ⸱eir prey.

⸱eptember, 1883   Revised January 21, 1897

FASTS AND FEASTS   1103

The Roman Catholic theory is the best—alternate fasts and feasts, and the same ⸱ade movable so as to avoid too great regularity.

PHOTOGRAPHING AND PHONOGRAPHING AND DEATH   1104

If a man is photographed and phonographed enough, can he be said to be dead death?

MRS. McCULLOCH[1]   1105

She smiled sweetly at McCulloch and said, "Do you wish you were not married ⸱y dear?" The poor wretch writhed inwardly but at once said "no" as was required ⸱ him.

LOHENGRIN[1]   1106[2]

⸱as a prig. In the bedroom scene with Elsa he should have said that her question

261

put him rather up a tree, but that as she wanted to know who he was he would te
her, and would let the Holy Grail slide.

INSISTING ON BEAUTY 110

When a certain kind of person insists on this or that as very beautiful, it is onl
his way of trying to insist upon his own beauty.

THE SNOW KEEPS OFF QUITE NICELY 110

One sweltering hot day in June I saw a man in a railway carriage look wistfull
up at the sky. "The snow," he said, "keeps off quite nicely, don't it?"

DANGEROUS KNOWLEDGE 110

There are certain things quite [1]incontrovertible, and quite worthy of bei
known and considered, yet a mere knowledge of which will turn most men in
dangerous characters.

CHRIST 111

was born B.C. 4, rose from the dead and ascended into heaven (according to th
scriptures) A.D. 34, and was set to music by G.F. Handel in 1742.[1]

FLYING FROM THE WRATH TO COME 111

A man at the Hotel Monte Generoso was complained of to me by a lady wh
sat next [to]* me at the *table d'hôte* as being a nuisance because he practised on t
violin. I excused him by saying that I suppose some one had warned him to fly fro
the wrath to come[1] (meaning that he had conceptions of an ideal world, and w
trying to get into it. I heard a man say something like this many years ago, and
stuck by me).

DRINKING WATER 111

Is drinking water a reminiscence of the time when we actually were water?

FIRE AND LIGHTNING 111

Fire must always burn something or go out. Lightning is fire: what is the ligh
ning burning?

TRIBAL RIGHTS 111

are a souvenir of the compound animal.

BLÉ AND *TÊTER* 111

Blé is "blade"; Buffon spells it "bled." *Têter* is "to taste, to suck the teats

GOD'S MESSAGES 1116

God gives different and sometimes contradictory versions of the same story to fferent people; or else they, being different, catch different points in the story and ve different versions of it.

GAINING ONE'S POINT 1117

It is not he who gains the exact point in dispute who scores most in contro-rsy, but he who has shown the better temper.

ART NOTE 1118

The young painter when he goes out to sketch from nature: the mistakes he akes.

SHADE, COLOUR AND REPUTATION 1119

When a thing is near and in light, colour and form are important. When far and shadow, they are unimportant. Form and colour are like reputations, which when ey become shady are much of a muchness.

HANDEL'S BIG CHORDS 1120

These I used in *Erewhon*, or the jig in the second set of suites[1]--one feels them the diaphragm. They are, as it were, the groaning and labouring of all creation availing together until now.[2]

SUBJECT--A FREETHINKING FATHER 1121

A freethinking father has an illegitimate son (which he considers the proper ing) and finds this son taking to utterly immoral ways. He turns Christian, be-mes a clergyman and insists on marrying.

TITLE FOR THE ART BOOK 1122

The complete pot-boiler--what to paint and how to paint it.

THE SHORTEST POEMS 1123

at I know are:

February Filldyke, and March many weathers.

e next is:

The kangaroo ran very fast
I ran faster--Kangaroo!
The kangaroo was very fat
I ate him--Kangaroo! Kangaroo!

BONNET ON IRRITABILITY 112

"Every muscular fibre contracts itself on the touch of any body, whether sol: or liquid, and immediately resumes its position. This has been termed irritability."

Contemplation of Nature (translation, London, 1766, Pref., p. xiv.

Does not everything contract or expand the moment it comes into contac with anything else? And do muscular fibres or other things return immediately to the status quo? I should think not.

BONNET ON NUTRITION OF MIND 112

He says that the senses prepare the mind's food as the stomach does the body' or as the roots of plants turn earthy particles and water into sap.[1]

FATIGUE AND MIND 112

He says the mind is fatigued by attention as the body by exertion. But "ho should fatigue reside anywhere but in the organs?" &c. See *Contemplation of N ture*, London, 1766, Preface, p. xxxv.[1]

MEMORY 11:

He says, "The soul never has a new sensation but by the interposition of t senses. This sensation has been originally attached to the motion of certain fibre Its reproduction or recollection by the senses[1] will then be likewise connected wi the same fibres." *Ibid.*, p. xxxvi.

See Huxley as quoted by Clifford in his article on Right and Wrong. *For. nightly Review*, n.s., Vol. 18, p. 780? 795?[2]

BONNET ON MEMORY 11:

He has some further remarks on this subject in the preface to his *Contemp. tion of Nature*, pp. xxxvii-xliii. But they do not seem to me to come to much. I declares the simplest form of memory to be the continuation of pain or pleasu after the immediate cause has ceased.[1]

BONNET ON IMMUTABILITY AND AGAIN ON MUTABILITY 11:

See *Contemplation of Nature*, London, 1766, Vol. I, p. 26, p. 31, p. 34, p. 5(but the passages are hardly worth turning to.[1]

SENSITIVE PLANT AND POLYPUS 113

See Bonnet, *Contemplation of Nature,* London, 1766, I, 39.[1]

HATING   1131

It does not matter much what a man hates provided he hates something.

CHAIRS AND CAMPSTOOLS   1132

e seats under domestication. Wild seats are seldom comfortable.

MUSH AND MUCH   1133

e both derived from "*mucchio*," a heap.

ptember, 1883   Revised January 27, 1897

THE LANGUAGE OF ANIMALS   1134

I put out my hand to a sub-alpine cow; she came to me and licked it. Then she
rned away and there was an expression upon her face which said as plainly as any
ords could do, "As you did introduce the subject, I thought it possible you might
ve had such a thing as a pinch of salt about you, but I see you haven't. Good after-
on."

MIND AND BODY   1135

From man to the amoeba special organs drop off, and so do special senses.
But organization drops off faster than mind does. The amoeba has more mind
proportion to its body than man has in proportion to his.
Between the highest intellect of the most enlightened nations and that of the
vage, or even of the agricultural labourer, there is a great gap; but there is no equi-
lent gap in organisation.
There is more mental difference in propotion to organic difference between the
lest European and the lowest Australian savage, than there is mental difference
proportion to organic difference between man and the amoeba.
In the one case intellect has dropped off while organisation has not; in the other
ganisation has dropped off while mind has not dropped off proportionately.

CHRONIC AND TEMPORARY   1136

Both are derived from time, but one means a long time and the other a short
e.

MAX MÜLLER   1137

What an odious man he must be. See his letter to the *Times*, September 25
26, 1883.[1]

Working all night. See *Times*, March 7, 1879.[1]
Warehouseman and Draper's Journal, February 15, 1879.[2]

EATING A BUNCH OF GRAPES   113

To eat the worst first is tempting providence to kill one before one comes t
the best. Always eat downwards, not up; for when the best has been eaten, there
none better with which to compare the next best, and each grape will seem goo
down to the very end. If you eat the other way you will not have a good grape
the lot. People should live on this principle more than they do, but they do live o
it a good deal; on the whole from, say, fifty, we eat our days downwards.

AUTUMN SEEMS BETTER THAN SPRING   114

because we are eating the days downwards instead of upwards.

MYSELF AND WASHING UP IN NEW ZEALAND   114

In New Zealand for a long time I had to do the washing up after each meal.
used to do the knives first, for it might please God to take me before I came to th
forks, and then what a sell it would have been to have done the forks rather tha
the knives.

LIFE AND HABIT   114

One aim of this book was to place the distrust of science on a scientific basi

PHONOGRAPH FOR A BAD SLEEPER. MY FATHER'S SERMONS   114

A bad sleeper should have a phonograph to lull him to rest by preaching, w
will say, my father's sermons. If I survive my father I will keep some of his sermon
for this purpose. The machine should be placed on a high shelf to imitate a pulpi

GALL-MAKING PLANT LICE   114

alternate generations of. See *Times*, March 12, 1879.[1]

BESTIA!   114

Italian children often say this to one another, meaning "you fool," rather tha
"you beast."

ART NOTE: EMBRYOLOGY OF PICTURES   114

All things in nature grow up from small beginnings, and so should pictures. The
should epitomise the history of painting, they should be rehearsed in little, and
possible should be begotten of some other picture which has suggested them.

"Perhaps," he said, "transubstantiation may not be true, but if you tell these mple people this, it is telling them that they may re-open the fundamental ques- ons of morality."

"Well and good," said I, "I admit this is an evil, but on the whole it is the least vil."

THE ELEMENTS   1148

If they get into one kind of company they become one thing; if into another, nother.

MAWLEY SAID   1149

f a man, "he's worked his way up you know. I don't like men who work their ay up."

IS LIFE WORTH LIVING?   1150

This is a question for an embryo, not for a man.

MY LIFE   1151

I have led a more virtuous life than I intended, or thought I was leading. When was young I thought I was vicious. Now I know that I was not, and that my un- onscious knowledge was sounder than my conscious. I regret some things that I ave done, but not many. I regret that so many should think I did much which I ever did, and should know what I did in so garbled and distorted a fashion, as to ave done me much mischief; but if things were known as they actually happened, I elieve I should have less to be ashamed of than a good many of my neighbours-- nd less also to be proud of.

BELONGING TO A FIDDLE   1152

My cousin met a man once in Furber's[1] shop and asked who he was. "Oh," id Furber, "he belongs to that Amati over there."

"DON'T YOU THINK IT WOULD BE VERY NICE?"   1153

My aunt used to send my cousin [on]* errands with this preface: "My dear, n't you think it would be very nice if you were to go and post these letters"-- what not?

STOMACH   1154

One's stomach is one's internal environment.

He writes--of course ironically--"These people are all over black, and have such
flat noses that they are hardly to be pitied."[1]

WILD ANIMALS AND ONE'S RELATIONS   115

If one would watch them and know what they are driving at, one must keep
perfectly still.

TED JONES'S[1] BESETTING SIN   115

The headmaster at Radley[2] used to ask the boys what was their besetting sin
and they had to tell him one. Ted Jones said his besetting sin was inattention at
Chapel--especially during the psalms. A few days afterwards the headmaster asked
after the sin and Ted said it was better; so they got along quite nicely.

MONDAIN[1]   1158

Use this word in connection with men of science.

THE UNKNOWN   115

is the as yet no part of the swindle.

MAX'S HEAD OF CHRIST   116

"To noblemen, gentlemen, and exhibitors. For sale, at No. 2 Liverpool Street
that wonderful painting of Christ with the apparently moving eyes, suitable for private sanctuaries, chapels, gift to church, or exhibitions. No reasonable offer refused."
Times, advt. September 23, 1878.[1]

METEORIC STONES   116

I took three Italian painters over the British Museum. They admired the Elgin
marbles, but they were much more fetched by the meteoric stones.

TITLE FOR THE ART BOOK   116

On the imitation of Nature.

BOSS AND HER SON   116

She said to him, "I don't know the meaning of the word but you are a nasty
sot."

A SIMPLE PALETTE   116

Explain this, and draw attention to Rembrandt's palette in his portrait of himself in the Louvre.

We may and must have some, but the work itself will give many more and make hem much more definite. I did not see my way clearly with *Life and Habit* when I began to write it. I knew I was close on to a big thing, but I should never have got well hold of it if I had waited till I understood myself before I began to write it.

LUCKY OR UNLUCKY   1166

A sensible man commonly knows no more whether his life on the whole has been lucky or unlucky, than whether he is plain or handsome.

September, 1883   Revised January 29, 1897

ALCOHOL   1167

The question is whether our ancestors have been so long accustomed to alcohol hat it is easier now to go on with it and make the best of it, or whether the habit s so recent that it can be broken easily and without disturbance. I think decidedly he first of these two alternatives is the right one.

SUBJECT: PORTRAIT PAINTING IN WORDS   1168

A new profession for literary men. Go and stay with a man and describe him-- ay in fact what a beast he was--if he was one.

IT'S MUCH TOO EARLY   1169

A man asked another to take a nip. "No," was the answer. "It's much too early--besides I've had one already."

WHOSO HATETH HIS BROTHER   1170

s a murderer[1]--but not whoso hateth his sister. Christ perhaps had sisters of his own.

FLATTENING THE TRUNK OF A LIME   1171

You can do this by pollarding it early on two sides, leaving it to grow upon he other two only. See some limes in the Vicarage garden at Shoreham in Kent.

SUBJECT   1172

A spurious Archbishop's charge.

as the devil said of the ten commandments.

THE SIMPLICITY OF NATURE   117

This is due to her not being so clever and prescient as people try to make out Unless an idea is pretty obvious, it will seldom occur to any either animal or plant

THE LITTLE WOOLLY PIG OF GOD   117

There was an inland African tribe in a country too hot for sheep, who had there fore no definite idea about a lamb. The missionary who converted them brough the idea somewhat nearer to their comprehension by calling Christ "the little wool ly pig of God."

HEZEKIAH HOLLOWBRED   117

He was landlord of the Harrow public house at Bulphan and was a good ol man. He called houses "housen." He said South Ockenden was a nice place, ther were three public housen in it. He said he liked gentle company, he did.

IMAGINATION   117

At Ivy Hatch[1] while we were getting beer in the inner parlour we heard a con fused melee of voices in the bar amid which I heard a man say, "imagination wil do any b---- thing almost." I was writing *Life and Habit* at the time and was muc tempted to put this passage in. Nothing truer has ever been said about imagination Then the voice was heard addressing the barman and saying, "I suppose you wouldn' trust me with a quart of beer would you?"

R.E. WORSLEY ON HIS FATHER[1]   117

He said there were two things which stamped him. One, that he liked the stick jaw stocking end of a roley poley pudding without the jam in it; the other, that h liked sleepy pears.

R.E. WORSLEY AND OLD SAM WHITBREAD[1]   117

One day when my cousin was a boy at the Brewery having come to see his father old Sam Whitbread caught him, and asked him who was Solomon's son. My cousin to my uncle's horror, did not know, but Mr. Whitbread was delighted, and whe my cousin grew older made him his accountant at a salary of £20 a year, whicl place my cousin kept till old Mr. Whitbread died.

EDGAR ROSCOE[1] AND OLD SAM WHITBREAD   118

Also at the brewery little Edgar Roscoe saw old Sam at lunch eating oysters and shocked his elders and his good little brothers and sisters by asking for some. M Whitbread was much pleased and he scored more than any of the others.

Dr. Parkes wrote a book on health,[1] and said that physiology proved the bible ght in all it said about marriage, which was the natural condition of man. My uncle id, "What a fine man he must have been! How much I should have liked to have nown him!" R.E.W. "Is he dead?" "Yes." "How old was he?" "About 40." What did he die of?" "Decline." "Had he any children?" "No."

LIFE AND THE POWER TO MAKE MISTAKES   1182

This is one of the criteria of life, as we commonly think of it. If oxygen could istake some other gas for hydrogen and go wrong and then not mistake it any ore, we should say oxygen was alive. The older life is, the more unerring it becomes respect of things about which it is conversant--the more like in fact it becomes to ch a thing as the force of gravity, both as regards unerringness and unconscious-ss. Query, is life such a force as gravity in process of formation, and was gravity ce--or rather were things once liable to make mistakes about such a matter as avity?

THE AUTHOR OF *THE VESTIGES OF CREATION*[1]   1183

In his preface to the edition of 1853 he writes concerning his book:
"It never has had a professed adherent, and nine editions have been sold. Oblo-y has been poured upon the nameless author from scores of sources--and his lead-g idea, in a subdued form, finds its way into books of science and gives a direction research. Professing adversaries write books in imitation of his, and, with the nefit of a few concessions to prejudice, contrive to obtain the favour which was nied to him." p. ix.
He was himself not only a plagiarist, but a bad plagiarist, and had no right to mplain.

eptember 1883   Revised February 1, 1897

CONSCIOUSNESS, VISIONS, AND PERCEPTIONS   1184

Savages saw in their dreams visions of men, and concluded that the actual body the person dreamed of had been in some way before them, or that if not the actual dy yet some emanation therefrom had been really seen. By degrees it became knowledged that there had been nothing present save in the mind of the dreamer. uery whether other phenomena, and indeed all phenomena, will not have to go the ay of ghosts and be recognised as subjective only.

UXLEY'S PROPOSITIONS CONCERNING CONSCIOUSNESS AND ACTION 1185

I think I got the following from one of the monthlies about the year 1879, but ve made no memorandum.[1] The propositions are:

271

I.   The brain is the organ of sensation, thought, and emotion; that is to sa'
some change in the condition of the matter of the brain is the invariable antecede
of the state of consciousness to which each of these terms is applied. (There nev
was consciousness without change. Query is there ever change without consciou
ness? S.B.)
II.   The movements of animals are due to the change of form of the muscle
which shorten and become thicker, and this change of form in a muscle arises fro
a motion of the substance contained in the nerves which go to the muscle.
III.   The sensations of animals are due to a motion of the substance of the nerv
which connect the sensory organs with the brains.
IV.   The motion of the matter of a sensory nerve may be transmitted throug
the brain to motor nerves, and thereby give rise to a contraction of the muscles
which these motor nerves are distributed; and this reflection of motion from a se
sory to a motor nerve may take place without volition, or even contrary to it.
V.   The motion of any given portion of the matter of the brain excited by t
motion of a sensory nerve leaves behind it a readiness to be moved in the same wa
in that part, and anything which resuscitates the motion gives rise to the appropria
feeling. This is the physical mechanism of memory.

NATURE OF ORGANISM MORE IMPORTANT THAN CONDITIONS OF EXISTENCE (WITHIN LIMITS)   118

Darwin insists on this, but it amounts to saying that the experience of mar
past generations is more potent than the accidents of a single life.

HEARING OR READING   118

other people's criticism of a book or picture or piece of music before forming a
opinion.
Some say we should not do this; I maintain we should do it as much as ever w
can--unless of course when there is no doubt.

DUMB BELLS   118

Regard them with suspicion as academic.

THE THIEF   118

once committed beyond a certain point should not worry himself too much abo
not being a thief any more. Thieving is God's message to him. Let him try and
a good thief.

BUFFON ON THE MENINGES   119

There is flippancy in the way in which Buffon says that if the seat of sensatic
must be placed in the head it had better be in the meninges.[1]

We cannot do this much either in writing or painting. We must do something oughly as near as we can, and then cut it about and rearrange it.

HUXLEY ON *EVOLUTION OLD AND NEW*   1192

Miss Buckley[1] told me she had told Huxley that I was at work on Buffon, Dr. . Darwin and Lamarck. Huxley said, "He could not have got hold of three men nore likely to mislead him." The fact being that Huxley, at any rate then, knew othing about any one of the three. I have reason to think Huxley wrote the arti- le on *Evolution Old and New* in the *Saturday Review*,[2] but not enough to warrant ne in saying so. I pitched into him in *Unconscious Memory* to pay him out whether e wrote it or no.

SENSE OF TOUCH   1193

All the senses resolve themselves ultimately into a sense of touch. There is but ne sense, "touch," and the amoeba has it. When I look upon the *foraminifera* I ook upon myself.

"GOD IS GOOD, BUT IS KEERLESS"   1194

An American pressed his friend to take an umbrella, the friend repeatedly de- lined. "Well," said the American, "I'd take it if I were you; God is good, but he's eerless" (careless).

CRABBE ROBINSON   1195

ored my uncle and aunt at Taviton Street every third Sunday for a dozen years nd more during his extreme old age. I often used to meet him there and he talked ncessantly, telling the same old stories and swaggering as rich, stupid, vain old men lo. He left them two volumes of Batty's (?) *Italy*, and they thought it was shabby f him. I see I have got this already.[1]

"HAVE YOU GOT TWOPENCE"   1196

I heard a man say this to another at Reading Station. "Yes I have," was the nswer, "and father and mother both living too."

BOADICEA OR ANNE BOLEYN   1197

A barman at St. Albans told me that a queen once used to live there "but whether t was Boadicea," he continued, "or whether it was Anne of Bow Lane I don't remem- er at this moment."[1]

AWKWARD   1198

neans in a dangerously violent temper. I heard a man at St. Albans say that his nare had been troublesome in the night either from toothache, or "orkardness," and at Thames Ditton[1] I heard a woman summon a man to help her with another woman who she said was "orkard."

BUFFON

in passing through Isidore Geoffroy[1] and Mr. Darwin, had to descend with a good deal of modification before he reached the British public.

WORDS

are not as satisfactory as we should like them to be, but, like our neighbours, we have got to live with them and must make the best and not the worst of them.

LIFE AND SENSE

Leaving aside the question how they are so for the present, we should confine ourselves to the following--how they act now, how they have acted so far as we can get at the facts, whether there is reason to think they ever acted differently, and what millions of years of such action would be likely to result in.

THE FIRST GOOD FRIDAY

Jones said there was a crucifixion on, that night.

RUDIMENTARY ORGANS

Two things are equally plain: i. that most of our organs are so well adapted for their purpose that they present all the phenomena of design; ii. that some of our organs are no less clearly useless than the others are useful. This has baffled evolutionists and will baffle them till they take the line I have taken in *Life and Habit, Evolution Old and New* and *Unconscious Memory*.

SETTLING A QUESTION

All one can do is to shut one's adversary up, to bring about in one way or another that he shall not wish to pursue the subject further. When there is a general consent to drop a question either from weariness or any other cause, it is settled but not till then.

ANDROMEDA[1]

The dragon was never in better health and spirits than on the morning when Perseus came down upon him. It is said that Andromeda told Perseus she had been thinking how remarkably well he was looking. He had got up quite in his usual health &c. When I said this to Ballard,[2] and the other thing I said about Andromeda in *Life and Habit*,[3] he said he wished it had been so in the poets. I looked at him and said that I too was "the poets."

THE CRAMMER[1] 1206

Pauli says he is the only honest schoolmaster at present.

ST. GEORGE OF DONATELLO[1] 1207

He is only an amoeba that did not know when to stop, a huge overgrown excre-
cence, the outcome of disordered imagination.

THE FUTURE WEALTH OF ENGLAND 1208

, in good workmanship, and academies, however plausibly disguised, are the last
ource from which good workmanship will come.

GRANT ALLEN ON DARWIN 1209

Grant Allen is among the meanest of our many mean pseudo-scientists, but that
e should formally cut the Darwinian view of evolution for the Lamarckian is a
gn of the approaching end of Natural Selection's reign. True, Grant Allen calls
he Lamarckian view the Spencerian, but that is only to be expected. See his arti-
le "Idiosycrasy," *Mind*, October, 1883.[1]

TRUTH 1210

Any fool can tell the truth, but it requires a man of some sense to know how
) lie well.

MAN 1211

God's highest present development. He is the latest thing in God.

SIGHT 1212

a long arm. Do we not shoot out as it were immaterial pseudopodia which embrace
l that is in the field of vision?

HYACINTH ROOT 1213

I had one in a shallow saucer-like pot which grew up into the air; finding itself
the air it began to imagine itself a leaf; it turned greenish, and finally uncurled
self and became distinctly leaf-like. For aught I know it may then have grown
self a small bulb, and all through a blunder, because the pot happened to be too
allow.

PRIG 1214

There is no prig like an old one.

The same skill which now guides them and me in arts and inventions was one time exercised upon the invention of these very organs themselves. The lig ments which bind the tendons of our feet, or the valves of our blood vessels a the ingenious enterprises of individual cells who saw a want, felt that they cou supply it, and have thus won themselves a position among the old aristocracy of t body politic.

BIRTH AND DEATH   121

We rarely see either of these. We see people, as consciousness, between t two extremes.

BROAD CHURCH AND PAGANISM   121

Let the broad church sail as near, not philosophical stoicism, but good rollic ing Paganism, as it dare; just as the ritualists do with Romanism. I think it wou then draw.

TENTATIVE BANKRUPTCY ACTS[1]   121

These afford good illustrations of the manner in which organisms have be developed.

THE VOKES FAMILY   121

were at a cricket match, and there was a little form about 18 inches high in fro of them; both Victoria and Rosina declared they could not get over it, and insist on its being removed. Those who do not know the Vokes family may be told th they are among the most agile dancers on the stage.[1]

RUDIMENTARY EXPRESSIONS   122

Most men's expressions are rudimentary--i.e. cant.

SCOTCH CHRIST AS GOOD SHEPHERD   122

In a stained glass window in an episcopal church near John of Groat's house Christ is represented as the good shephered--in a tartan plaid.

MASSACRE OF ST. BARTHOLOMEW'S AND REVOCATION OF THE EDIT OF NANTES[1]   122

I do not know that we have gained much by those French Huguenot famili that have settled among us--Martineau's, Romilly's &c.

CLEANLINESS   122

is almost as bad as Godliness.[1]

There are only two--those who teach too much and those who don't teach at
.l. All teachers do one or the other.

MISS SAVAGE   1225

eing asked, in the game where you have to name your favourite authors &c., what
ere her greatest faults, replied, "lying and covetousness." The company were a good
eal scandalised.

BUTLER, THE AUTHOR OF *HUDIBRAS*   1226

He was almost as much an immoral spectacle for dying poor and prematurely
roken down in a garret,[1] as Charles Darwin was having achieved a renown which
e so little deserved. If matters go no better with me than they are doing, there will
ave been two Samuel Butlers dying within half a mile or so of Covent Garden under
ircumstances which leave a good deal to be desired. October 13, 1832.[2] Assuredly
 ever man was prematurely weakened in power by want of money and unfair treat-
ent, I am so now--and yet all may come so easily right, or might still come if the
ick is not too long in turning. I fear, however, that it will turn just a trifle too
te.

THE LORD GAVE   1227

nd the Lord hath postponed the taking away. Blessed be the name of the Lord.[1]

SOUNDS AND ECHOES   1228

A man may begin as a bad sound, or even as a bad echo, but he is to be distrusted
he begins as a good echo.

ctober, 1883   Revised February 2, 1897

MY NOVEL *ERNEST PONTIFEX*[1]   1229

Mr. Heatherly[2] said I took all the tenderest feelings of our nature, and having
read them carefully over the floor, stamped upon them till I had reduced them to
 indistinguishable mass of filth, and then handed them round for inspection. I
 not take this view of the matter myself.

THE ETERNITY OF MATTER   1230

That something should have come out of nothing is inconceivable; we may state
ich a proposition in words, but the words will convey no ideas to us.

The only alternative is that something should not have come out of nothing and this is saying that something has always existed.

But the eternal increateness of matter seems as troublesome to conceive, as it having been created out of nothing. I say "seems" for I am not sure how far it really is so. We never saw something come out of nothing, that is to say, we never saw beginning of anything except as the beginning of a new phase of something pre existent. We ought therefore to find the notion of eternal being a familiar on to us, as indeed being the only conception of matter which we are able to form nevertheless, we are so carried away by being accustomed to see phases have their beginnings and ends that we forget that the matter of which we see the phase begin and end, did not begin or end with the phase.

Eternal matter permeated by eternal mind, matter and mind being function of one another, is the least uncomfortable way of looking at the universe; but as it is utterly beyond our comprehension, and cannot therefore be comfortable, sens ble persons will not look at the universe at all except in such details as may concer them.

GOD   123

proposes, but it is through man, and therefore man who commonly both propose and disposes.

MEETING IN THE WAXWORKS   123

I saw an account of a man committed for trial for murder. On leaving the dock he turned round to the people in court, and said, "Farewell dear friends--next time you see me it will be in the waxworks."

HOUR HAND OF THE CLOCK   123

Educated men are getting to the age at which they understand pretty readily that the hour hand of the clock really does move.

MODEST COMPETENCE   123

I have taken [vows] * of modest competence, but alas! I seem on the high road to break them.

SINNERS   123

came into the world to save Christ Jesus.[1]

Written October, 1883   Revised February 5, 189

278

s becoming a rudimentary organ, but the third class railway train on a Sunday morn-
ng is something of a church.

NECTARIES OF PLANTS   1237

See *Times*, April 18, 1879.[1]

LIFE   1238

s a superstition, but superstitions are not without their value.

LUCRETIUS ON EVOLUTION   1239

It comes to very little, but see V.853.et.segn.[1]

GOD   1240

helps them who help themselves. Yes, because he and they are one.

PRETENCE OF KNOWLEDGE   1241

I was nearly 40 before I felt how stupid it was to pretend to know things that
did not know, and I still often catch myself doing so. Not one of my schoolmas-
ers taught me this, but altogether otherwise.

"HAVE I BEEN TO ROME MY DEAR?"   1242

Jones heard an American lady ask her daughter this at the Hotel at Stresa.[1]
"Oh yes, mamma dear," was the reply. "Don't you remember, that's where we
bought our striped stockings."

UNCLE SAM ON HIS WIFE'S DEATH   1243

I was sent for to Chester Terrace in order that Uncle Sam might have a scratch
at me.[1] I had to go, but I knew very well what it would be; he is a spiteful old man,
who lost his eyesight fifty years ago and more, and has lived upon flattery ever since
from every quarter except one--and that one was an exception with a vengeance--
his wife, my Aunt Ellen. My Uncle and I had long dropped each other by mutual
consent, and I was rather surprised at being sent for to come and see him, but I
couldn't very well say no, or thought I couldn't, so I went. He was nasty the whole
time without intermission. He said, "And now Sam I wish you would explain to me
what all this is which you have been saying in your new book" (*Life and Habit*). I explained, and when I had done he said in his most unpleasant manner, "Ah--it appears
to be a resuscitation of the old Pythagorean notion." Of course I said nothing--but his
manner was rude and was meant to be rude. I do not suppose he had listened to a
word of what I had been saying; he just wanted an occasion for a scratch, and got it.
Then he said about the death of his wife, "I had very kind letters from Wilderhope,
and Harrie wrote most kindly"--(you never wrote, you wretch). "I had much pleasure

in sending them a few little mementoes of your Aunt which she desired they should have when she was on her death bed"--(you see you got no memento). After a while he said, "I suppose you having given up drawing." Like my sisters, he would not call it painting. May wrote to me that he wrote "quite simply" about his wife's death. He does not seem to have prevaricated about mere facts.

SIR ANTONIO PANIZZI   1244

and the Duke of Modena. See *Times*, April 9, 1879.[1]

WATER CANARIES   1245

Gold fish.

PARTING   1246

"It will be for years, and (rubbing his hands) it may be for ever."

TED JONES[1] AND HIS MAMA   1247

"And then mamma did me the honour of coming to see me in the dining room and told me she did not think I was behaving quite nicely--not quite like myself. 'You know my dear,' she continued, 'if I had had any idea you had set your heart on it I should have said *no* at once.'"

SOCIETY AND CHRISTIANITY   1248

The burden of society is really a very light one. She does not require us to believe the Christian religion, she has very vague ideas as to what the Christian religion is--much less does she require us to practise it. She is quite satisfied if we do not obtrude our disbelief in it in an offensive manner. Surely this is no very grievous burden.

LAMARCK'S DOCTRINE NEVER PROVED   1249

This is one of the stock cant arguments which reviewers fling at my head. It has been proved quite as much as evolution at all is proved--that is to say sufficiently for reasonable people.

PROFESSIONS   1250

All forms of animal and vegetable life are professions.

ACCIDENTAL MODIFICATION   1251

When Jones was ill at Cambridge he ordered a boiled rabbit smothered in onion sauce. By some mistake they brought him a boiled fowl smothered in onion sauce. Since then he has stuck to boiled fowls instead of boiled rabbits. Many a modification comes about in this way.

SELF-MADE PEOPLE   1252

All organisms are self-made people.

SMALL CHURCH   1253

There is a very small church on a hill side a little east of Alfriston.[1] Jones said
was smaller than all the other little churches put together.

OH FOOLS AND SLOW OF HEART   1254

ɔ believe *all* that the prophets have spoken.[1]

LITTLE E-WEE-LAMB   1255

A boy at Radley pronounced "ēwe" thus when reading the passage in chapel.[1]

AND DAVID DID EAT[1]   1256

Another boy laid the emphasis on the *did*.

October, 1883   Revised [February] * 11, 1897

AVOID ALL APPEARANCE OF EVIL   1257

By all means.

JONES'S OLD COUSIN JOSEPH   1258

ᵣrites a kind of Queen's speech letter to Jones's mother once a year and always
ᵥinds up, "I have made an arrangement with my servant for another six months
ᵥithout any addition to her wages." Last year, 1879, detailing as usual the condi-
ion of all the invalids among his friends, he wrote, "Miss------, the lady whose father
ɔok her to Temple Bar to see Lord Nelson's funeral, is still in a very precarious
tate."

DEATH   1259

only a greater modification than any after which we have been able to remember
ᵤrselves.

MY COUSIN AND MYSELF   1260

At Lewes during a Christmas outing I had changed the water cans outside our
ed room doors to get the one I thought hottest and largest--and I had helped myself
ᵣst to milk at breakfast, thus getting the cream that had risen in the night, and

then I complained to Jones of my cousin's wanting something at breakfast whic[h] clearly did not belong to him. Commenting on this I said, "He had been treate[d] perfectly fairly hitherto–so far as he knew."

ART NOTE. THE KIND OF LINE TO SKETCH WITH 126[ ]

is the one which shall best enable you to insist on it and say, "I always said so" it turns up trumps, and yet to say, "I never meant anything of the kind" if it prove[s] to be wrong.

"KATTY[1] MY DEAR, 126[ ]

said Mrs. Jones after Jones had been playing, "now do go and play us something[ ] (as though what Jones had done was not playing).

THE PANTHEIST'S PRAYER 126[ ]

"If you want to eat or drink anything nice, do it through me, oh Lord!"

GOGIN[1] AND SMOKING 126[ ]

He said he had felt much better for giving it up. He felt the mere pleasure c[ ] existing more than he had done for some time. I feel this when I am smoking.

FOR LIKE AS A FATHER PITIETH HIS OWN CHILDREN &c.[1] 126[ ]

Yes, very like this.

UNITY AND GRAFTS 126[ ]

After saying that the unity of a tree lies not in the visible material connectio[n] between its boughs, but in the oneness of mind that exists among its buds, poin[t] this by sporting branches, grafts, and mistletoe, where the material connection r[e]mains but there is not true unity. The sap is the same sap, but when it comes to t[h]e alien bough it changes its mind.

October, 1883   Revised February 11, 189[ ]

MIND AND VIBRATIONS 126[ ]

I suspect strongly that all change of mind is dependent upon changes of vibra[ ]tions and that indeed the vibrations of matter are the mind of matter. I am not clea[r] about my own meaning, but if we consider vibrations and life (or mind) as one, an[d] life as nearly a series of inconceivably complex and recurring vibrations, we sha[ll] I think, connect the organic and inorganic more comfortably than in any other wa[y]

"Promise me solemnly," I said to her as she lay on what I believed to be her death bed, "if you find in the world beyond the grave that you can communicate with me--that there is some way in which you can make me aware of your continued existence--promise me solemnly that you will never never avail yourself of it." She recovered, and never never forgave me.[1]

THE BRAIN LAGS BEHIND THE BODY   1269

It takes a whale some seconds to know that its tail is stuck, and so Cambridge having Mr. Darwin's portrait painted (1879).

BELIEVING MOSES AND THE PROPHETS   1270

If they believe Moses and the prophets they are quite capable of believing one who said he had risen from the dead.[1]

SCIENTISTS AND LITERARY MEN   1271

The scientists say of me, contemptuously but quite truly, that I am not a scientist, but a literary man. What, I wonder, is a literary man if he is not able to weigh and reason upon the arguments with which scientists provide him? It seems to me that my opponents may indeed be scientists but they are not literary men. The mere scientist is a brickmaker. The literary man sets up as an architect, or at any rate, as a mason. Used in *Luck or Cunning*.[1]

MARRIED MEN   1272

are almost as bad as old maids.

SUBJECTS   1273

Academic distinction. The true wealth of a kingdom.

THE THREE SLADE PROFESSORS   1274

As a specimen of art-bullying, see *Pall Mall Gazette*, May 29, 1879.[1]

JESUS WITH ALL THY FAULTS I LOVE THEE STILL   1275

Jones said this one day. I said, "But we don't love him." "No more," said Jones, "did Byron love England very much."[1]

MY REVIEWERS AND SENSE OF NEED   1276

My reviewers felt no sense of need to understand me--if they had they would have developed the mental organism which would have enabled them to do so. When the time comes that they want to do so, they will throw out a little mental pseudopodium without much difficulty. They threw it out when they wanted to misunderstand me--with a good deal of the pseudo in it too.

See letter in the *Times*, June 12, 1879, from Sidney P. Holland.[1]

October, 1883   Revised February 15, 189

LIFE AND HABIT: THE CELLS NOT ALWAYS THE SAME   127

I said in *Life and Habit* that a colossal being looking at the earth through a micro scope would probably think the ants and flies of one year the same as those of th next.[1] I should have added—so we think we are composed of the same cells from year to year, whereas in truth the cells are a succession of generations.

H.L.B.G. AND THE GREAT RED YAWN   127

Taking up an American story book in an inn at Hurstpierpoint,[1] Jones and found these initials repeated several times. At length we discovered they stood fo Heaven's Last Best Gift. The same book spoke of the sun as giving a great red yaw before going to bed.

THE TEMPLES OF THE LORD   128

are made with other organs than hands.

GOD IS LOVE[1]   128

I dare say—but what a mischievous devil, love is.

MRS. WARREN[1] AND MISS SAVAGE   128

Mrs. Warren said she criticised everything. "I criticised D'Israeli's novels," sh said, "to his face, but I didn't know it was 'im.'" She also said her husband, walkin one evening at dusk in the Rosherville Gardens, overheard two people talking, on of whom he recognised by his voice as the Archbishop of York.

"What was there," he asked, "before creation?" Miss Savage said she was hardl surprised at the Archbishop's asking this question, "for," she said, "I don't know that myself." "Lor! don't you?" exclaimed Mrs. Warren. "Why my husband shoute out from the other side the walk 'Providence, to be sure,' and the Archbishop cam over and shook hands with him, and said he should preach upon it next Sunday a Westminster Abbey, and he did too."

I HATE THEM WHICH HATE GOD   128

but I don't find God sufficiently hating them which hate me.[1]

ɪinks of himself as a whole and not of his individual cells, unless he finds himself in
ɒuble with them. I wish I knew how to give him trouble enough to make him
ɔok after me a little more, without driving him into amputating me.

GOD   1285

ɑid Jones, is a licensed bogie. Servants must not frighten children with bogies, but
apas and mammas may. I remember my elder sister and myself asking our nurse
᾽ the world might come to an end that afternoon. We were told it might, so we be-
ɑn to scream, and screamed till we were told it mightn't.

THE ITALIANS SAY   1286

ɪangiare a modo suo, vestirsi a modo altrui.[1]

PORTRAITS OF ONESELF   1287

A man's work whether in music, painting or literature, is always a portrait of
ɪimself.

TWEEDLEDUM AND TWEEDLEDEE   1288

I saw a beetle attacking a cockchafer. It was God unable to make up his mind
ᴠhether he would be tweedledum or tweedledee.

HIDING AGAMEMNON'S FACE   1289

Whether this was wise or not I cannot say, but it was certainly cheap.[1] It is
ɒnly another way of painting the Red Sea to pass for the Egyptians who are sup-
ɔosed to be underneath it.

THE SUPREME WILL   1290

The Italians call it "L'ultima volontà."

GROWING NEW REPUTATIONS   1291

We can grow a certain number of new ones, as salamanders can grow fresh tails,
ɒut not too many, and we must not be too old.

TED JONES[1] ON ME   1292

Ted told his brother that I was a remarkable man, for I knew as much as other
,cientists but had never taken any trouble about it. He should have said I knew as
ittle as the other scientists but took less pains to appear to know what I did not
ᴋnow.

285

should be like a dog's barking. The dog should never bark at nothing, but he nee not always know exactly what he is barking at.

ART NOTE 129

If you have only a little time, do only a little thing.

MISQUOTATION 129

"Having your loins girded about with the breast plate of faith."[1]

THE SEVEN DEADLY SINS 129
Want of money, bad health, bad temper, chastity, family ties, knowing tha you know things, and belief in the Christian religion.

WINE AND MILK 129

are water which has had a long talk either with a vine, or with a cow, and has bee thoroughly satisfied.

ART NOTE: THE OLD MASTERS AND THEIR PUPILS 129

The old masters taught, not because they liked teaching, nor yet from any ide of serving the cause of art, nor yet because they were paid to teach by the parent of their pupils. The parents probably paid no money at first. They took pupil and taught them because they had more work to do than they could get through and they wanted some one to help them. They sold the pupil's work as their own just as people do now who take apprentices. When people can sell a pupil's work they will teach the pupil all they know, and they will see he does it. This is th secret of the whole matter.

ART NOTE: TRUTHS FROM NATURE 129

We must take as many as we can, but the difficulty is that it is often so har to know what the truths of Nature are.

TITIAN 130

The only thing of which I feel pretty sure about Titian[1] is that what he did cam pretty easy to him, and would not come very hard to any of us if we knew a few tricks of glazing. He was caught young, had a good eye, and the usual amount o *savoir faire*, was put under the best man that ever painted, was surrounded by the mo: promising young painters whom Bellini's fame could attract, knew how to do som good work, and how to hide bad work by glazing it. His colours had nothing t do with it, there is not an oil and colour shop in Seven Dials[2] where you could no get colours as good as or better than Titian ever painted with.

We do not fall foul of Christians for their religion, but for what we hold to be their want of religion--for the low views they take of God and of his glory, and for the unworthiness with which they try to serve him.

THE TRUE LAWS OF GOD   1302

are the laws of our own well-being.

REASON AND FAITH   1303

Reason is founded on faith and faith on reason; there is no "I know," but there is an "I think," which is found to answer all practical purposes.

THE HAND AND THE STOMACH   1304

The hand is a kind of mental stomach, wrapping itself round about things that we may digest them better with our minds, but it is so far a true stomach also that I imagine if a starving man were to hold a bit of raw beef well in his closed hand for four or five hours it would help to keep him alive; nevertheless he had better eat it if he can.

ELASTICITY IN THE MATTER OF FOOD AND ASSOCIATION   1305

The elasticity with which though our normal amount of food is so and so we can yet do the same work with a little less on a pinch, is part of the same story as association not sticking to the letter of its bond.

EATING AND PROSELYTISING   1306

All eating is a kind of proselytising--a kind of dogmatism which maintains that the eater's way of looking at things is better than the eatee's. We convert it, or try to do so, to our own way of thinking and when the food sticks to its own opinion and refuses to be converted, we say it disagrees with us.

MOTTO FOR MYSELF   1307

Nihil bene quod non jucunde.[1]

CHARLES JEFFRIES[1]   1308

said Mr. Withall could make his clients do so absolutely what he liked that they really ought to have independent professional advice.

HERBERT SPENCER   1309

When I try to read him--which I never, however, do--but when sometimes I have tried, I feel as a bee must feel when it goes buzzing up and down a pane of glass always hoping to be able to get out into the open air beyond and never succeeding. He[1]

has been clear enough sometimes and very good about Weismann[2] especially, sinc
the above was written.

INVALIDS 131

are people who do not know what to do with themselves when they have made
themselves.

BIOGRAPHY, OPENING FOR MY 131

Jones laughingly talked of writing my life. I said I would give him an openin
sentence, thus:
"The subject of this memoir was born of wealthy but dishonest parents Decen
ber 4, 1835. He inherited the dishonesty, but not the wealth of his family."

UNDERSTANDING 131

To understand is to follow side by side with the mind; to stand under, as
were, and alongside of, each step in a process, so as to have it all clearly before on

VELA'S DRAWING 131

I said of the drawing which old Vela[1] gave me (see *Alps and Sanctuaries*)
done by a Locarno schoolboy, that it was the hieroglyph of a lost[2] soul.

CHRIST FRESCO OF ARTO 131

The funniest fresco of Christ that ever I saw was at Arto above Pella on the
Lago d'Orta.[1] Christ is being led to crucifixion and turns round to Pilate with
a leer as though saying, "Crucifixion? I can do that little lot on my head."

FRESCO OF THE DEATH OF SOCRATES 131

I saw one at Civiasco between Orta and Varallo, on a wall: evidently done b
some freethinker to emulate the frescoes of religious subjects and preach fre
thought. It was more odious by far than any of its neighborus. "*Verba non animu*
mutant qui trans religionem currunt,"[1] or at least it often is so.

BOWING DOWN IN THE HOUSE OF CHRIST 131

I do not often do this, but I have to sometimes, and then I think of Naaman
bowing himself down in the house of Rimmon, and how he was told to go in peace.[1]

THE CLOVEN TONGUES OF FIRE 131

which sat upon the Apostles heads perhaps caught fire through friction against o
atmosphere on their descent from heaven.

s indeed about our bed and about our path, and spies out all our ways. We cannot ave even two or three gathered together, but what he will most likely be in the nidst of us.[1]

ENDNOTES

In the annotations that follow the first number is the number of Butler's note; the second, after the period, is the footnote number within the text of the note itself. The following persons, because they appear frequently in Volume I, have been identified only once in the endnotes here indicated:

1. Mrs. Boss - 247.1
2. Harriet Bridges (née Butler) - 348.1
3. Henry Festing Jones - 122.1
4. Charles Paine Pauli - 51.1
5. Eliza M.A. Savage - 22.1
6. Philip Worsley (uncle Philip) - 222.1
7. Reginald Worsley ("my cousin") - 216.1

Abbreviations used:

Letters	*Letters between Samuel Butler and Miss E.M.A. Savage: 1871-1885*, ed. Geoffrey Keynes and Brian Hill (London: Jonathan Cape, 1935)
Memoir	Henry Festing Jones, *Samuel Butler, Author of Erewhon (1835-1902): A Memoir* (London: Macmillan & Co., 1919).
Works	*The Shrewsbury Edition of the Works of Samuel Butler*, ed. H.F. Jones and A.T. Bartholomew. (London: Jonathan Cape; New York: E.P. Dutton, 1923-26), 20 vols.
Correspondence	*The Correspondence of Samuel Butler with His Sister May*, ed. Daniel F. Howard (Berkeley: University of California Press, 1962).
Family Letters	*The Family Letters of Samuel Butler, 1841-1886*, ed. Arnold Silver (Stanford: Stanford University Press, 1962).

Other quotations from Butler's letters are taken from the 16 volumes of correspondence housed in the British Library (Adds. MSS. 44,027). Considerable use has also been made of the unpublished materials in the Butler Collection at St. John's College, Cambridge, England. Identification of Handel's works are made in reference to the out-dated Chrysander edition, still the only complete edition of Handel.

1.1   Very likely the Congregational minister John Brown Paton (1830-1911), temperance crusader, an opponent of pubs, first Principal of the Congregational Institute at Nottingham (1863-1898). In later years Butler knew his son John Lewis Paton (1863-1946), who attended both Shrewsbury School and St John's College, Cambridge, and from 1898 to 1903 was Headmaster of University School, London.

3.1   T.H. Huxley, "On the Hypothesis that Animals are Automata and its History," *Fortnightly Review*, n.s., XVI, 555-580. Huxley, to demonstrate man is an automaton, describes the case of a French soldier who because of wounds received in battle suffered periodic loss of sensation except for touch. While in this state he behaved normally but became "an inveterate thief, stealing and hiding away whatever he could lay his hands on." See 1185.

5.1   Perhaps the model for Mrs. Cross, the Roughborough shopkeeper in *The Way of All Flesh* (ch. 42).

9.1   The first of several entries intended for a sequel to *Erewhon*. They are found frequently in vols. IV and V, covering the years 1890 to 1900, when Butler was editing these notes.

10.1   Gen. 2:25.

18.1   See note 1 to Butler's Preface.

19.1   An allusion apparently to the famous Nottingham pugilist (1811-1880), nicknamed Bendigo, who, because small in stature, relied on cunning to defeat larger opponents.

19.2   Gen. Sir Duncan Alexander Cameron (1808-1888), commander of the regulars in New Zealand from 1861 to 1865 during the Maori Wars in the North. He led the battles on Katikara in June 1863, and opened the Waikato campaign in July. He admired the valor of the Maoris who were usually outnumbered by the British.

20.1   Thomas Cass (1817-1895), an eccentric New Zealand surveyor and Butler's friend (while visiting England in 1867, Butler painted his portrait now hanging in Canterbury Museum). He was in the advance party sent out in 1848 (under Capt. Joseph Thomas) by the Canterbury Association to select a site for Canterbury Province, the Church of England settlement. Later as Chief Surveyor of Canterbury (1851-1867) he was active on commissions connected with the Province's development. Russell is a small town north of Auckland, named after Lord John Russell (1792-1878), twice Prime Minister of England.

21.1   Samuel Hewlings (1820-1896), a government surveyor like Cass (with whom he sailed, in 1841, on the *Prince Rupert* which shipwrecked off Capetown), Chief Surveyor of Canterbury Province from 1871-76, the first mayor of Timaru. In 1861 he married a Maori widow named Nga Hei in Geraldine; she bore him five half-caste daughters and a son.

22.1   The Berners Women's Club, at this time at No. 9 Berners Street; re-moved in 1877 to No. 64 (and renamed the New Berners Club for Ladies). From 1879 or 1880 to 1883 Miss Savage was its honorary secretary. Many of its members were "emancipated" women who (like Miss Savage) enjoyed satirizing marriage (the Club was in the same building as the offices of the National Society for Women's Suffrage). Miss Andrews, who claimed to be a descendant of Cromwell, is mentioned in Miss Savage's letters to Butler as a pillar of conventionality. He had met her once for fifteen minutes (so Butler recalled in 1901) during a visit to the Club. Miss Eliza M. A. Savage (1836-1885), the only daughter of the architect Humphrey B. Savage, met Butler at Heatherley's art school, sometime before 1871, and became his friend and literary advisor. Her encouragement kept Butler at his novel, *The Way of All Flesh*, which he put away after her death not to return to again. He had planned, as a memorial to her, to edit their correspondence with each other, a task he finally fulfilled in 1901. For further details, the reader may consult *Letters Between Samuel Butler and Miss E.M.A. Savage (1871-1885)*, ed. Geoffrey Keynes and Brian Hill (London: Jonathan Cape, 1935).

28.1   Butler was fond of "quoting from memory," that is, taking liberties with quotations (see note 953).

28.2   "You know, Maecenas, people ought to tell me the most important matters first." See Horace, *Epistle* I, 1, 1-3: *Prime dicte mihi, summa dicende Camena,/spectatum satis et donatum iam rude quaeris,/Maecenas....*

28.3   "But to retrace these steps and to return to the skies above, Beware, you Roman, of this labor, this dark matter." See Vergil, *Aeneid, VI*, 128-9: *sed revocare gradum superasque evadere ad auras,/hoc opus, hic labor est.*

28.4   See Oliver Goldsmith, "The Deserted Village," 1.174: "And fools, who came to scoff, remained to pray."

28.5   "The one good thing is not to be astonished at virtually anything: this bit of advice, if read three times, helps refresh you." See Horace, *Epistle* I, 6, 1-2: *Nil admirari propre res est una Numici,/Solaque quae possit facere et servare beatum.*

28.6   See Alfred Lord Tennyson, *In Memoriam*, XCVI, 10-12: "There lives more faith in honest doubt,/Believe me, than in half the creeds."

31.1   The spirit of the note is echoed by Overton's father in *The Way of All Flesh* (Chapter 1): "It is not . . . by the acts which [a man] has set down, so to speak upon the canvas of life that I will judge him, but by what he makes me feel that he felt and aimed at. If he has made me feel that he felt that to be loveable which I hold loveable myself I ask no more . . . ." Butler started the novel in 1873.

34.1   Samuel Butler (1600-1680), *Hudibras*, Part II, Canto III, 11.1-2. This and the previous note are the first referring to the neo-Lamarckian evolutionary theory Butler developed in *Life and Habit* (1877).

36.1   *Ernest Pontifex* was Butler's title for *The Way of All Flesh*, the alternate title chosen by R.A. Streatfeild (Butler's literary executor). See 1229.1 below. The idea appears in the chapter, "The Views of an Erewhonian Prophet concerning the Rights of Animals," added to the revised edition of *Erewhon* (1901).

293

38.1   On September 15, 1863, the Christchurch (New Zealand) *Press* carried a lengthy letter, "From our Mad Correspondent," signed Lunaticus, in which this notion is developed (reprinted in Joseph Jones, *The Cradle of Erewhon* [Austin Texas, 1959]. Butler's "Darwin among the Machines," signed Cellarius, had appeared in the *Press* for June 13, 1863.

40.1   This note, somewhat altered, was added to the judge's speech in Chapter XI ("Some Erewhonian Trials") of the revised edition of *Erewhon* (1901)

43.1   "Oh yes, she is still producing."

44.1   Of the Canada Tanning Extract Company, 131 St. James Street

45.1   Jason Smith (1835-1910), a class-mate of Butler's at St. John's College, remained a life-long friend. He was called to the bar in 1863 and became an equity draughtsman and conveyancer; occasionally he helped Butler with loans when he began buying rental property before he had access to his inheritance. Butler bequeathed his painting "Mr. Heatherley's Holiday" (now in the Tate Gallery) to him. Smith's rooms were at E 13, New Court, above Butler's at D 13.

46.1   Erewhonians consider illness a criminal transgression (see Chapters 10 and 11 of *Erewhon*, revised edition). This view of morality was perhaps influenced by George Drysdale's *The Elements of Social Science; or Physical, Sexual, and Natural Religion* (London: E. Truelove, 1854), published anonymously. Butler possessed a copy of the third edition (1860).

50.1   Toussaint Antoine Rodolphe Laflamme (1827-1893), well-known Montreal barrister, politician (a member of Mackenzie's Cabinet in 1876), and editor of *L'Avenir*, leader of the *Parti rouge*. Laflamme, then Queen's Counsel, represented Butler and the London directorship of the Canada Tanning Extract Company in legal battles with resident manager James Foley (note 144). In his correspondence (Vol. II) Butler calls Laflamme the best and leading member of the Canadian bar.

51.1   Charles Pauli (1838-1897), educated at Winchester and Oxford, youngest son of a Lübeck merchant who had settled in England. Butler met him at the Christchurch (N.Z.) Club and the *Press* offices (where he was then engaged) and upon his pleading, took Pauli with him to London and began paying for his legal training and maintenance. The friendship cooled, but upon their occasional meetings Pauli feigned hardship, and Butler unquestioningly continued to provide an annual allowance. Butler had persuaded him to invest in the ill-fated Canada Tanning Extract Company, and when it failed, paid him back his investments. He kept a photo of Pauli on his mantelpiece until the latter's death when Butler learned that Pauli had been a successful barrister all along, and in later years had lived in Grosvenor Gardens, yet had made no mention of him in his will. Butler had helped pay for Pauli's legal training; in 1867 Pauli was called to the bar. Butler's account of the friendship is found in Volume III of Note-Books.

57.1   During his final stay in Montreal (August to December 1875) Butler gave evidence in the Court of Appeals against the Canada Tanning Extract Company which the Court attempted to set aside on grounds of Butler's unorthodoxy. During cross-examination Butler replied that he believed in a first cause but not in a deity with "a turban and a flowing beard, and great drapery, as represented in picture books"; that he accepted the part in the Bible in which "it is said God is a Spirit," but not the part "in which we are told that God put his hand over Moses' face, and owed him his back" (Montreal *Gazette*, November 24, 1875, p. 2).

59.1   A series of engravings by William Hogarth (1697-1764), "Industry
d Idleness" (1747), depicting the contrasting lives of Francis Goodchild and Thomas
le, both silk weaver apprentices. Thomas ends his days on the gallows. Francis
comes Lord Mayor. The substance of this note was added to Chapter X ("Current
)inions") of the revised edition of *Erewhon* (1901).

59.2   The sentence that follows is overscored: Bad as the idle prentice is,
: virtuous apprentice is not much more attractive.

61.1   Job 19:25: "For I know that my redeemer liveth. . ."

62.1   i.e., the Grand Trunk Railroad of Canada, "that dreadful railway"
Butler called it in one of his letters. He invested in it and the Erie Railway, and
st some £600 in the venture.

69.1   The then Privincial Geologist to the Canterbury Government, John
ancis Julius von Haast (later Sir John) (1824-87). Born near Bonn, Germany, and
ucated at its university, he came to New Zealand in 1858. He was appointed Pro-
ıcial Geologist (1860), was a member of the Christchurch Club to which Butler
longed, and helped establish the Canterbury Museum whose first director he be-
me (1868). Butler maintained a correspondence with him after his return to Lon-
n. He was on one of his annual explorations of the Province's mineral resources
d the Rangitata River valley in company of his botanising friend Dr. Andrew Sin-
ıir (1796-1861), making Butler's hut (on Mesopotamia station) his base of opera-
ıns. It had been built in the previous October to serve as temporary home while
more spacious cottage next to it was still under construction. Butler's station
ıs located along the southern bank of the Rangitata, between Forest Creek and
ısh Stream.

69.2   Also Butler's overseer.

69.3   Henry Phillips, Jr., of Hakatere Station, several miles away on the
rth bank of the Rangitata, which he managed for his brother-in-law, T.H. Potts.
1857 Phillips had taken up a run close to Mesopotamia which Butler later bought.

69.4   Dr. Andrew Sinclair (1796-1861), both in Paisley, Scotland studied
:dicine at Glasgow and Edinburgh, became assistant surgeon in the Royal Navy,
d after leaving the service emigrated to New Zealand (1844), where as Colonial
cretary he helped build up New Zealand's civil service. He retired in 1856 to devote
nself to scientific pursuits, chiefly botany. He corresponded with Darwin, Huxley,
d Owen. He had joined von Haast's expedition (see 69.1 above) when he was
)wned trying to cross the Rangitata River to Butler's hut; he was buried on March
, 1861, in a spot between the river flat and Butler's hut.

69.5   Jonathan Swift, "On Poetry: a Rapsody," ll. 338-340.

72.1   James (Jimmy) Rawle, described as a "large yellowman," was t]
shepherd in charge of Mt. Possession, a station owned jointly by J.B. Acland (182
1904) and Charles George Tripp (1826-1897). When they dissolved their partnersh
in 1862, he became Acland's shepherd at Mt. Peel, the run bordering Butler's
Forest Creek. Acland and Tripp were the first white men to explore the Rangita
valley in the vicinity of what was to become Mesopotamia (1855 and 1856). But]
bought the small freehold from them at Forest Creek in June, 1860, where he s
up a V-hut as his first provisional lodging. Acland and Tripp both married daughte
of Henry John Harper (1804-1893), first bishop of Christchurch. Butler, it seem
upset Mrs. Tripp with his ideas and his attempt to "convert" her maid to them.

73.1   The daughter of Thomas Heatherley, proprietor of Heatherley
Art School in Newman Street where Butler studied (see 258.1 below).

74.1   Butler probably refers to Elizabeth Vassall Fox, Lady Holland (177
1845), who presided over the gatherings of intellectuals at Holland House and w
known for her acid tongue and haughtiness.

75.1   Thomas William Gale Butler had gotten in trouble in New Zeala
for shooting a policeman (who was saved by his belt) near the Rakaia River. I
returned to England "partially restored," and studied art at Heatherley's where But]
probably met him in 1870. He eventually died in a workhouse asylum in the 1890
Butler quotes him in Chapter V of *Life and Habit* (Works IV, 68): "Words produ
the appearance of hard and fast lines where there are none. Words divide . . . I
could *think* to you without words you would understand me better." Butler enjoy
airing his own unorthodox views at the studio.

76.1   Butler quotes from an advertisement for old Tokay, which Dr. Dru
recommends over malmsey for a patient ill "of diphtheria, hopeless phithisis, wi
ophthous tongue and throat, &c." (p. 10). Dr. Robert Druitt (1814-1883) was
well-known medical practitioner who wrote *Cheap Wines, their Use in Medici*
(1865).

77.1   Phillipians 4:8: ". . . whatsoever things are true, whatsoever thin
are honest, whatsoever things are just, whatsoever things are pure, whatsoever thin
are lovely, whatsoever things are of good report; if there be any virtue, and if the
be any praise, think on these things."

78.1   Allusion to John Dryden's "Alexander's Feast," set to music t
Handel in 1736.

81.1   That is, the garden of his father's rectory at Langar. See 313
below.

82.1   A Swiss summer and winter resort.

87.1   They are found in *Twelve Voluntaries and Fugues for the Org*
or Harpsichord with Rules for Tuning by the celebrated Mr. Handel, Book IV (Lo
don: Longman and Broderip, [1780]). The British Library copy of this edition w

ice in Butler's possession; his name is written on the title page; at the end of the les for tuning the eight chords of the scale he pencilled in this note: "These rules ere shown by my friend H.F. Jones to the late W.S. Rockstro [see note 190] who id they were those of one of the mean tone temperaments. S.B. December 16,)01." See note 790, and 790.1 below.

90.1   From the article "Maid-Servants."

91.1   Allusion to Matthew 18:20.

92.1   Allusion to the Committal Prayer of the Burial Rite (Book of Com- on Prayer).

93.1   That is, the teacher (the law) who leads us to Christ. The quota- on comes from Ga. 3:24.

97.1   "Congratulations to you on your strength." An allusion to Vergil's *eneid*, IX, 64.

98.1   John Hiram Haycock (1834-1890), Butler's school-fellow both at rewsbury School and St. John's College. He worked for the Home Office, occa- nally contributed to *Punch*, and in 1867 became rector of Seaton Uppingham. e played the chess game with Dr. Kennedy, the Shrewsbury Headmaster, that is tirized in Chapter 27 of *The Way of All Flesh* (see note 207).

98.2   Obadiah has but one chapter. See note 195.

98.3   Noah's son (Genesis 6:10).

103.1   Butler twice visited Charles Darwin (1809-1882) at Down in 1872 ee note 384). Though the visits were not a success, it was not until he worked on *ife and Habit* (between 1875 and 1877) that he found reasons for his long-lasting islike of Darwinism's founder. He told Francis Darwin that re-reading the *Origin f Species* made him aware of the antagonism between it and Lamarck's theory of *olution; he consequently eliminated from *Life and Habit* all support for "natural lection" to make it square with the Lamarckian view (*Memoir*, I, 257-60: letter [November 25, 1877.) In *Unconscious Memory* (1880) Butler claimed he had hoped) make *Life and Habit* an "adjunct" to Darwin's *Origin* since he was supporting e theory of evolution and at the time thought "natural selection" and evolution ere synonymous. Once he realized he could question "natural selection" without uestioning the theory of evolution, he was in a position to criticize Darwin's argu- ent in the *Origin* (see *Works*, VI, Ch. II).

106.1   I John 4:16.

110.1   The Peculiar People were an evangelical sect, founded in London 1838, that maintained vigorously the fundamentalist teachings of their faith and belief in the divine inspiration of the whole Bible.

113.1   This anecdote is found in Butler's account of his friendship wit Pauli in Volume III of the Note-Books. It had been relayed to Butler by one Captai Buckley, V.C., who had been with Pauli in San Francisco in 1860 or 1861.

114.1   See Romans 8:22.

115.1   See Luke 18:10-14.

121.1   Jones and Bonham (Bonham and Frederick after 1875), at 40 and 410 Oxford Street, were auctioneers, picture dealers, and importers.

122.1   The first mention of Henry Festing Jones (1851-1928), Butler constant companion and Boswell from 1877 on (in 1919 he published *Samuel Butle Author of Erewhon (1835-1902): A Memoir*; rpt. New York, 1968). He was th son of Thomas Jones, Q.C. (who died in 1869) and his wife Ellen; he received h B.A. at Trinity Hall, Cambridge in 1873. At the time of their meeting in 1876 (se 177.1 below) Jones was articled to a firm of solicitors (Paine, Layton and Cooper but he was unsuccessful in the legal profession and was supported by an allowanc from his mother. This was stopped when in 1886 Butler asked him to give up la to become his secretary at £200 *per annum*. He studied music, wrote a number songs as well as a children's opera (*King Bulbous*), for a time in 1878 he also studie at Heatherley's (see 258.1 below). In his account of their friendship (in Vol. I of the Note-Books) Butler states that he took to him immediately once, under h guidance, Jones -- a somewhat "square" fellow -- turned rebel.

123.1   "Madame Vigneau has had so many lodgers since we started tha she has become quite rich; and out of gratitude has had a four-dollar mass said fc the Company. This is the best mass money can buy in these parts. . ." (*Letters*, 92: letter to Miss E.M.A. Savage, July 10, 1874). The Company's works were a St. Leonard.

126.1   Published anonymously in March, 1873; the second edition bearin his name, was issued in September, 1873. The bulk of the book was written durin his holiday in Switzerland in August 1872. The argument, based on his unsigne pamphlet, *The Evidence for the Resurrection of Jesus Christ as Contained in th Four Evangelists Examined* (1865), suggests the theory that there was no death o the cross, and hence no Resurrection while the writer at the same time casts doub upon the theory's relevance.

131.1   From an anonymous review of *An Inquiry into the Process of Huma Experience* by William Cyples (1880); the reviewer quotes from Matthew Arnold' essay on Joseph Joubert (1754-1824), the French conservative moralist, in *Essay in Criticism, First Series* (1865).

140.1   See Matthew 25:36.

143.1   Overscored alternative conclusion to the sentence: that in anothe sense every man must rise again from the dead with his body. See note 42.

144.1   James Foley (1829-1900), of Lindsay, Ontario, resident manager f the Canada Tanning Extract Company in Montreal. He had patented a method r concentrating the tanning properties of 5 tons of bark into one ton of extract hich was twice as efficient in tanning than existing fluids. With four others he rmed a company out of which the Tanning Extract Company was established in ay, 1873. Butler, with the approval of Cmdr. C.N. Hoare (one of the Company's rectors and a major shareholder), had Foley removed in March, 1875, for falsify- g records of maintenance costs. In August Foley initiated legal proceedings against utler, had even warrants for his arrest prepared and an injunction issued to prevent utler from publishing damaging letters written by himself. On the advice of La- amme (see 50.1 above) they were published (*Extracts from Letters sent by Mr. oley to the Foreman of the Works of the Canada Tanning Extract Company [Limit- d]*). . .); Butler had Foley arrested for perjury and formally charged in November, 375, but the case was dismissed. It was during these proceedings that the attempt as made to set Butler's testimony aside (see note 57). For a full account of But- r's troubles see A.W. Currie, "Samuel Butler's Canadian Investments," *Dalhousie eview*, XXII (Jan., 1963), 109-25.

150.1   French-born trapeze-artists. Monsieur Leotard (1838-1870) intro- ced trapeze performances to England. Blondin (Jean Francois Cravelet, 1824- 397) performed all over the world, and once walked blindfolded on a high-wire ross Niagara Falls.

157.1   See for example Romans 2:11; Gal. 3:26; and Acts 10:34-5.

158.1   The figure of St. George by the Tuscan sculptor Donatello (Donato Betto Bardo, c. 1386-1466) is in the cathedral of Florence. Giovanni Tabachetti r Tabaguet) (c. 1568-1615) is the virtually unknown sculptor Jean de Wespin, ne of three sculptor brothers from the Belgian town of Dinant. Butler admired his ork in the chapels of the Sacre Monte at Varallo in Lombardy, Italy, and his schol- ly interest in it resulted in his study *Ex Voto* (1888), and his discovery of Taba- etti's Flemish background. His statues, like the Sleeping St. Joseph, are life-sized rra cotta figures, painted and often furnished with clothing and wigs, depicting cidents from Biblical history. Butler came to believe that a statue called "Il Vec- ietto" (the little old man), a great favorite of his, was Tabachetti's self-portrait e frontis-piece to *Works*, IX), but later changed his mind.

160.1   *Wild Oats*, an "illustrated weekly journal of fun, satire and burles- e," published in New York from 1870 to 1881.

162.1   Matthew 7:20.

164.1   Arthur Orton, a butcher living under an assumed name in Australia, aimed to be one Roger Tichborne who had been reported lost in a wreck off the ast of South America in 1854, and who was heir to the Tichborne House estate, ,000 a year, and a baronetcy. When in 1866 Tichborne's mother advertised for r lost son, Orton arrived in England to make his claim. She swore out an affidavit firming that he was her son, but died before she could be cross-examined. The st trial for settling the claim ended in March 1872 with Orton's conviction

on the charge of corrupt perjury, even though 85 witnesses, including the family
solicitor, under oath supported the claimant's contention. After a second trial (end
ing in February 1874), he was sentenced to 14 years imprisonment at hard labo
In 1884 he was released for good conduct, but not until 1895 did he confess to th
imposture. He died three years later.

165.1   Laura Thistlethwayte, a notorious courtesan (born either in 182
or 1832 in Ireland).   During the 1860's, as a result of a religious experience, sh
became an evangelical preacher.   She married, in 1852, Captain Augustus Thistl
thwayte, a wealthy gentleman who committed suicide in 1887.

168.1   [Editing date] : Notes 16-173 are on a page 35, originally numbere
34.   The verso side of p. 33 (that is p. 34, for Butler numbered both sides) bea
the editing date of November 27, 1891.   Apparently, then, Butler began his ne
session on November 25 with a new page, and on November 27 noticed the blar
verso of p. 33, filled it up with notes, renumbered the next page, and continue
with his notes on p. 36 (notes 174-180), the verso side of the renumbered pag

168.2   See Luke 7:37-50.

170.1   George McCulloch (born in 1821), Butler's fellow student at He
therley's Art School, was, in H.F. Jones's words, "an admirable draughtsman."
sculptor and painter of classical and historical subjects, he exhibited regularly
the Royal Academy between 1859 and 1901.   In 1873 Butler was still sending M
Culloch MS. portions of *The Way of All Flesh*, although his marriage in Novemb
1872 signalled the end of their friendship. See 1105.1 below.

174.1   Job 28:12-28: "But where shall wisdom be found? and where
the place of understanding? . . . And unto man he said, Behold, the fear of the Lor
that is wisdom; and to depart from evil is understanding."

175.1   See 75.1 above.   In a letter (February 14, 1900) to Robert Bridg
(1844-1930) defending his reading of Shakespeare's sonnets, Butler claimed that I
was not "a poetically minded man" and hence never read Keats or Shelley or Col
ridge "except such extracts as I occasionally see in Royal Academy Catalogue
(*Memoir*, II, 321).

176.1   Edmund Gurney (1847-1888) was a student at Heatherley's in 187
and a friend of Edward Hall (177.1 below).   He had received his degrees from Trini
College, Cambridge (B.A., 1871; M.A., 1874) and was a Fellow from 1871 to 187
from 1872 to 1881 he studied music and medicine; in 1881 he was admitted
Lincoln's Inn.   He is the author of the well-known musical treatise, *The Power c
Sound* (1880), and was a founder of the Society for Psychical Research (1882
He died of an overdose of narcotics in a Brighton hotel-room.

176.2   Ellen (Nelly) Farren (1848-1904), famous burlesque actress (pri
cipally at the Olympia and Gaiety Theatres), well-known for her excessive buffooner
and boy roles.

177.1   Edward Algernon Hall (1853-1933), a London merchant, school-
fellow of Festing Jones at Winchester and Trinity Hall, Cambridge (B.A., 1875; M.A.
1928), and a painting student at Heatherley's. His parents lived at Whatton Manor
near Langar and were good friends with the Butlers. When Hall lived in London,
Jones used to come to his rooms in Piccadilly after the Monday Popular Concerts
at St. James's Hall (Edmund Gurney [176.1 above] came often as well), and there
in January 10, 1876 he met Butler. Handel was Butler's musical idol (see notes 189
and 225). Jean le Cocq (Joannes Gallus) was a 17th century French composer. Butler
said he dropped Hall and Gurney when they declared their preference for Le Cocq.

181.1   The novelist Henry Kingsley (1830-1876), younger brother of Charles
Kingsley (1819-1875).

182.1   Butler's laundress for more than twenty years. She eventually became too drunken and decrepit for work, so in 1887, a year after the death of her
half-witted husband Robert--who did odd jobs for Butler--he dismissed her with a
pension and replaced her with the aunt of Alfred Cathie, the man servant he hired
in January, 1887. (See 246.1 below). Mrs. Doncaster died in 1888.

186.1   Charles Paine Pauli's mother (who died December 31, 1886), of
Huguenot extraction, wife of Emilius Pauli, a London merchant originally from
Lübeck, Germany. His business failed in the late 1860's and he was dependent upon
his wife's income from property settled on herself by her father, Dr. Berjew. Four
of her children survived into adulthood: Butler's friend; Charles, a son who served
in the consular service (Butler had known him in New Zealand where he was Resident Magistrate at Kaiapoi); another son who was an officer in the Army, and a
daughter who entered a convent; she drowned in 1874 or 1875 at Mt. St. Michel.

189.1   Domenico Scarlatti was born in Naples in 1685, the same year Handel
was born in Halle, Saxony; Handel died in 1759, Scarlatti in 1757.   The two met
then Handel visited the Italian music capitals in 1710, but at this time Scarlatti
had not yet developed the mature style for which he became known.

189.2   John Dunstable, musician and mathematician from Dunstable in
Bedfordshire; he died in 1453. He is considered one of the earliest musicians who
initiated the "schools" of the 16th century, and once was believed to have "invented"
counterpoint.

190.1   William Smyth Rockstro (1823-1895), once a student of Mendel-
sohn, was a well-known music teacher (Mme. Clara Schumann studied with him)
who contributed significantly to the revival of pre-Handelian English music. Early
in 1890 both Butler and Jones took lessons in strict counterpoint from him to aid
them in composing their "oratorio" *Ulysses*. Thus they learned the rules of counterpoint which had been the basis of Handel's art and of musical education in the 18th
century in general, and this helped Butler formulate his objection to post-Handelian
music expressed in the previous note. Giovanni Palestrina (c. 1525-1594) initiated
the era of vocal music from which these rules had been derived. The advent of tem-
pered instruments permitted Bach, for example, to modulate more freely than here-
tofore, and therefore take   considerable freedom with the codified rules. Hence

the significance of note 87.

193.1   Hebrews 13:2 "Be not forgetful to entertain strangers: for thereb
some have entertained angels unawares."

194.1   Nephew of Priam, King of Troy.

195.1   See note 98.

196.1   *The Christian Globe* (cost: one penny) was published from 187
to 1918 as an "Unsectarian and Independent Weekly Journal."

201.1   P. 106: "For, as it has been often observed, Judges are but mer
and there is no intoxication so rare, so ennervating, and so seductive as that whic
follows full draughts of contemporary goodwill." On March 9th, the Lord Chie
Justice, Sir Alexander Cockburn (1802-1880), was awarded in a Guildhall ceremon
the freedom of the City of London, the first member of the Judicial Bench ever s
honored. In the article to which Butler refers, the writer comments on the even
warning that Judges ought to remember that they should never regard "popula
approval as any element, however shadowy, to be looked for in the pursuit of the
duties."   Incidentally, Cockburn presided over the Tichborne case (see note 16
and 164.1 above).

203.1   Roman 8:28. The quotation is the epigraph of *The Way of A
Flesh*.

204.1   The parable of the sower, Matthew 13:3-9; of the shephered, Matthe
18:12; of the "husbandman" (the parable of the tares), Matthew 13:24-30.

205.1   Psalm 100:3.

205.2   II Samuel 11:3-17 and 12:1-9. The ewe-lamb is, however, meant a
a symbol of Uriah's wife whom David took as mistress.

207.1   Dr. Benjamin Hall Kennedy (1804-1889), successor to Butler's grand
father, Dr. Samuel Butler, as headmaster of Shrewsbury School (1836-1866), a wel
known classics scholar and teacher, educated at Shrewsbury and St. John's, Can
bridge (B.A., 1827; M.A., 1830: D.D., 1836). He was Regius professor of Greek a
Cambridge and Canon of Ely from 1867 to his death, and the author of a Lati
Grammar which served as the basis for the Public School Grammar (1871). In a not
(Volume II; June, 1888) Butler blames Kennedy's grammars for his not learnin
properly the rules of classical grammar. Kennedy was a "vehement" but "inspiring
man, and Butler expressed his strong dislike of him through the character of D
Skinner in *The Way of All Flesh*. In a letter to W.E. Heitland (June 20, 1889), Butle
said that he was "physically puny and timid, and Kennedy's March temperamen
was so distressing to me that I was virtually on strike during the whole time I wa
under him. . ." (*The Eagle*, XXXIV, 348-352).

213.1   Gin made in Holland.

214.1   See Matthew 10:16: ". . . be ye therefore wise as serpents, and harm-
·ss as doves."

215.1   Henry Hoare (1838-1898), Butler's school-fellow at St. John's Col-
·ge, Cambridge (B.A., 1861; M.A. 1869) later a partner and some-time acting head
f Hoare's Bank in Fleet Street. After his return from New Zealand, Butler and he
·ecame friends; Hoare in fact paid the production and printing costs for *Erewhon*.
ı 1873, he started some companies and persuaded Butler to call in his New Zealand
·arnings left behind under William Moorhouse's supervision (note 327)--some £8,000
·and to invest most of it in one of the companies, the Canada Tanning Extract Com-
·any. All of the investment schemes failed within two years, and Hoare, once earn-
ıg as much as £50,000 a year, was forced to file for bankruptcy, and was dismissed
·om the Bank. Butler lost most of his earnings. See also 144.1 above.

216.1   The first of many references to his favorite cousin, Reginald Edward
·'orsley (he died in Johannesburg in 1927), the youngest son of Philip Worsley (see
·22.1 below), Butler's mother's brother. "Reggie" in fact was the only Worsley
·ith whom Butler remained on cordial terms; he often took him on his walking
·ɔurs of the southern counties, and he appointed him one of the executors of his
·ill. After working for a time as accountant in Whitbread's brewery, Reginald Worsley
·ecame an architect and builder. He was also a violinist and participated in many
·atherings of amateur musicians. His children, occasionally referred to here, were
·dward ("Ted") and Amy, issue of a brief marriage which ended in divorce. But-
·r requested him to communicate the sayings of his laundress, Mrs. Boss (see 247.1
·elow).

218.1   Lucretius, *De rerum natura*, II, 1:

Suave, mari magno turbuntibus aequora ventis,
E terra magnum alterius spectare laborem
("It is sweet, when winds buffet the waters of
the great sea, to look out from the land at someone
else's great struggle. . .")

219.1   See II Kings 2:23-24.

222.1   Philip Worsley (1802-1893), eldest brother of Butler's mother, father
·f his cousin, Reginald Worsley (216.1 above). His wife, Butler's Aunt Philip (note
·30 and 530.1) was the former Ann Taylor, a descendant of the Taylors of Norwich.
·hough Butler occasionally visited the family home in Gordon Square (later in Re-
·ɛnt's Park), he had a strong dislike for his uncle who enjoyed telling Butler that
·'ewhon had sold well only because critics could not know it might have been by
·meone famous.

223.1   Matt. 22:30; Mark 12:25; Luke 20:35.

225.1   Handel visited Germany several times, the last time in 1750. But-
·r refers to his visits of 1719 and 1729. During the first visit he stopped at his home-
·wn of Halle to visit his old mother on his way to Italy. When Bach (then residing in
·ɛarby Cöthen) heard of his arrival, he supposedly set out to meet his former com-

patriot (whose music he held in high esteem), but missed him by a day. Ten yea
later, early in June 1729, Handel came to Halle especially to visit his mother wh
now lay dying. On this occasion, Bach, then at Leipzig and unwell, sent his so
Wilhelm Friedemann as emissary to request that Handel come visit him. He app
rently did not; by July 1 he was back in London.

227.1   John Worsley (1812-1886), a Bristol barrister-at-law, the "eccentric
younger brother of Butler's mother. According to Mrs. R.S. Garnett, the Worsle
family, staunch Unitarians, the descendants of Philip John Worsley (1769-1811
a sugar refiner of Arno Vale, Bristol, were "among the leading intellectual societ
of Bristol" (*Samuel Butler and His Family Relations* [London, 1926], 150). Butle
referring to this anecdote, wrote: "Whether he ate the cockchafer or no I kno
not. He never would wear a night shirt. He said it was an unnecessary expence, an
slept naked" (note on a letter of May 2, 1886). See note 518.

227.2   Brothers of John Worlsey: for Uncle Philip, see 222.1 above. Samu
Worsley (1803-88), gentleman of Clifton, Bristol, Philip's brother, was a geologi
whose fossil collection is in the Bristol City Museum. He was the founder, and
member of, the Bristol Naturalists' Society in 1862.

229.1   April 26, p. 7c: It was rumored that King Theebaw had died o
the small-pox then raging in Mandalay. Native astrologers declared that the "ev
spirits" were infuriated and had to be propitiated by human sacrifices.

237.1   Giotto di Bondone (1276? - 1337), the Florentine painter who
with his bold and vivid style, is considered the founder of the great line of Italia
Renaissance painters.

238.1   Vittore Carpaccio (c.1456-c.1526), Venetian painter. Some o
his best work is found in the Scuola di San Giorgio degli Schiavoni in Venice--a
altar-piece representing the Virgin and Child, and a series of pictures depicting scene
from the lives of Christ, St. Jerome, St. George and St. Trifon, the patron sain
of Dalmatia and Albania.

239.1   Jan van Eyck (c.1390-1441), Dutch painter, considered one of th
inventors of oil-painting. His work is a synthesis between medieval iconography an
highly detailed pictorial realism.

239.2   See note 198.

239.3   i.e., guide.

239.4   Gerrit (Gerard) Dou (or Douw) (1613-1675), Dutch genre painte
a pupil of Rembrandt. Frans van Mieris (1635-1681) was a pupil of Dou, as wa
Gabriel Metsu (1629-1667), a Dutch genre painter. All three are represented i
the National Gallery.

239.5   Rembrandt Harmensz van Rijn (1606-1669), the Dutch painte
(one of Butler's favorites), and the Spanish painter Diego de Silva y Velasquez (159S
1660).

241.1   One of Butler's cats.

241.2   The medical practitioner and astrologer, Michel de Notre Dame (1503-1566), famous for his obscure prophecies.

241.3   The legend of the seven Christian youths who hid in a cave in Mt. Celion during the Diocletian persecution (250 A.D.). They were walled in, and fell asleep to await the resurrection.

241.4   *Minga scuola*: "Not school."

241.5   Angera, Fobello, and Varallo are villages in the Piedmont of Italy frequently visited by Butler. A photograph of the latter scene at Varallo is in the Butler Collection at St. John's College, Cambridge.

242.1   Of the "first" edition (1879); see *Works*, V, 1740.

244.1   P. 9f. The writer is reminded by earlier series of letters dealing with sheep-flukes of William Cobbett's *Rural Rides*, from which he quotes Cobbett's expressed dislike for "prigs" who believe in the incarnation and yet confidently consider it irreconcilable to reason. To challenge them, Cobbett asks a series of questions of which the following is quoted in the letter: "What causes flounders, real little flat fish, brown on one side, white on the other, mouth sideways, with tail, fins and all leaping alive, in the inside of a rotten sheep, and of every sheep's liver? . . . Answer this Question . . . or hold your conceited gabber about the 'impossibility' of that which I need not here name."

246.1   His father's death on December 29, 1886 signalled the end of Butler's financial difficulties which had worried him since his investment losses in 1876. With his inheritance he was able to engage a man servant, Alfred Cathie, and live free of money worries for the remainder of his life.

247.1   Mrs. Boss was the laundress of his cousin Reginald Worsley (216.1 above), for Butler the incarnation of Mistress Quickly, whose coarse witticisms he delighted in and recorded throughout the Notebooks, particularly in a collection entitled "Mrs. Boss" and "Black-guardisms" bound up with Volume VI (included in large part in *Butleriana*, ed. A.T. Bartholomew [London, 1932]). She had an illegitimate son, Tom, who apparently was bigamously married to two wives, Topsy and Phoebe. Mrs. Boss is the original of Mrs. Jupp in *The Way of All Flesh*.

247.2   Alice Sarah Worsley (1832/3 - 1914), the spinster sister of Reginald Worsley (216.1 above), an amateur botanist, perhaps inspired by her aunt, Mrs. Anna Russell (née Worsley, a sister of Butler's mother) (1807-1876) who was "the most accomplished woman field botanist of the day. . ." (D.E. Allen, "The Botanical Family of Samuel Butler," *Journal of the Society for the Bibliography of Natural History*, IX, No. 2 (1979), 134).

249.1   The village some 20 miles south-east of London.

250.1   See 157.1 above.

257.1   See I Corinthians 15:32.

258.1   Thomas Heatherley (1825-1914), head of the art school in 79 New man Street, founded by James Mathews Leigh (1808-1860), where Butler studied from about 1867 on. It was attended also by such notables as D.G. Rossetti, Burne Jones, Millais, and Poynter. In the 1860's and 1870's Newman Street was an art ists' quarter. The quotation was not used in the novel, whose correct title was in fact *Ernest Pontifex, or The Way of All Flesh*. See 36.1 above.

258.2   Ecclesisastes 3:20-21: "All go unto one place; all are of the dust, and all turn to dust again. Who knoweth the spirit of man that goeth upward, and the spirit of the beast that goeth downward to the earth?" See note 773.

264.1   Office of the newspaper *The Land & Water Journal*, at that time at 176 Fleet Street.

265.1   See *The Way of All Flesh*, Chapter 83 (or 89 in D.F. Howard's edi tion [1964]), where this is said of Theobald Pontifex.

267.1   From *Acis and Galatea* (c. 1718).

267.2   *L'Allegro, il Penseroso ed il Moderato* (1740).

267.3   "Envy eldest born of Hell" from Act II of *Saul* (1738); "He was despised" from the *Messiah* (1741).

268.1   "Animal Intelligence," April 1, 1880, p. 448-479, an anonymous commentary on three works dealing with this subject. The writer does not consider the possibility of *a priori* knowledge, but believes that "rational behavior" origi nates in instinct, though he cannot decide, in the cases of insects and ants, how much is instinctive and how much is deliberate mental process.

268.2   See note 721.

276.1   From *Samson* (1743).

277.1   Butler misquotes; the original is in C.

279.1   [Editing date]: The almost two years that elapse between this and the last editing indicate Butler's absorption in his theories concerning the *Odys sey*. He had begun translating the epic in 1891; his first suspicion that the poem's setting was the area around Trapani, Sicily, was formed between January and May 1892. He announced his first conclusions in two letters to the *Athenaeum*, Janu ary, 30; and February 20. He made his first research journey to Sicily in July (re turning in September), another during the same months of 1893 (see 308.1 below). The results of his labors were published that year in Sicily as *L'Origine Siciliana dell'Odissea*, extracts from articles in *Rasegna della Letteratora Siciliana*) and in Eng land as *On the Trapanese Origin of the Odyssey* (a translation of the first with addi tions reprinted from *The Eagle*, the St. John's College magazine, October Term 1892, Part II, No. 45).

283.1   See note 278.

285.1   Butler began "Mr. Heatherley's Holiday" in the fall of 1873, and exhibited it, together with his portrait "A Child's Head," in the Royal Academy xhibition of 1874. Butler considered the former his most successful exhibition icture (he had exhibited several before), but after this he was unable to get his aintings accepted, and his attempts at becoming a painter "fizzled out" during e writing of *Life and Habit* in the fall of 1877. From then he painted only during acations. Instead of going to Heatherley's in the morning, or painting in his rooms, e began working in the British Museum Reading Room. This painting (now in e Tate Gallery) was apparently painted from a photograph (in the Butler Collection f St. John's College).

286.1   Butler apparently refers to views of Clifton, done when J.M.W. urner (1775-1851) was only twelve or thirteen, displayed in 1880 when the Royal allery exhibited much of its permanent collection of Turner.

288.1   Dickens was to be buried in Rochester Cathedral, but Arthur Stan-ey (1815-1881), Dean of Westminster from 1866 to his death, sent a letter to the amily requesting that he be interred in the Abbey.

292.1   "Habits of an Ant," p. 7c: because all means of extermination have iled to stop a species of Columbian ants from invading South American planta-ons, British authorities now litter the fields and roads with foliage refuse belonging) ants of the same species, but not connected with the invaders. The invaders "take anic, and hurry off to their own nests, and leave the field in question alone for ays."

293.1   Arthur Wellesley, First Duke of Wellington (1769-1852), the famous nglish field marshall. His funeral procession on November 18, 1852, from the lorse Guard's Barracks to St. Paul's (where he was interred) was witnessed by one nd a half million people.

295.1   William Ewart Gladstone (1809-1898), Prime Minister, from 1868) 1874; from 1880 to 1885; again in 1886, and from 1892 to 1894. He was also hancellor of the Exchequer from 1859 to 1866. Butler disliked him, particularly nce he was the opponent of Benjamin Disraeli (1804-1881), the Tory Prime Minister ı 1867 and from 1874 to 1880, whose politics and novels Butler admired.

295.2   The well-known auctioneering firm in King Street, St. James's.

297.1   In a letter to the *Times* (May 24, 1880), Dr. Joseph M. Granville, uthor of the *Report of the Lancet Commission on Lunatic Asylums* (1875-77), 1aintains that lunacy should be regarded like any other nervous disorder to which o stigma is attached. Hospitals, not asylums, should treat the malady, for the mind a functional aspect of life, a fact which suggests that insanity can originate any-here in the body. A respondent to Dr. Granville, in the letter to which Butler efers (p. 5b), objects to linking insanity with "stigma" and "disgrace"; he had 1ought, he writes, that modern physicians would not have applied such terms to e disorder, any more than to harelip, clubfoot, or "any other bodily deformity r disease." Associating immorality with illness is an Erewhonian custom.

298.1 Count Guido Borromeo (1818-1890) was a descendant of the asc tic St. Carlo Borromeo (1538-1584), archbishop of Milan, the first great Counte Reformation prelate who was canonized in 1610. The saint's father, Count Gilbe Borromeo, had also been a man of great sanctity; his cousin, Cardinal Frederic Borromeo (1564-1631) was known for his great charity during the famine of 162' 28. St. Carlo's uncle (his mother's brother) in 1559 became Pius IV. Count Guid owned the Castle of Angera (on Lago Maggiore) which Butler had visited sever times, and in the summer of 1878 he and H.F. Jones visited there (see *Works*, VI 237-239) on their first holiday together.

300.1 Genesis, Chapter 22. Ishmael was Abraham's son by Hagar, h wife's maid.

301.1 Honoré-Gabriel-Victore Riqueti, Comte de Mirabeau (1749-1791 orator and Constitutional monarchist who shortly before his death became Pres dent of the National Assembly. As a young man he had led a dissolute life, an his father had him arrested and incarcerated several times for indiscretions and debt in the Château d'If and on the island of Ré. Thomas Carlyle (1795-1881) write in Volume II of *The French Revolution: A History* (1837): "Hate him [Mirabeau not. . . Wild burstings of affection were in his great heart . . . So sunk bemired i wretchedest defacements, it may be said of him, like the Magdalena of old, that h loved much: his Father, the harshest of old crabbed men, he loved with warmtl with veneration" (Book III, Ch. 4).

302.1 Genesis 22:2-14.

304.1 See I Cor. 9:5.

304.2 H.F. Jones believes this incident took place in the Albergo del Angelo at Faido (Canto Ticino) when Butler stayed there in the late summer (1880.

305.1 Butler refers to "The Marriage of Geraint" (1859) in Tennyson *Idylls of the Kings*. It is based on a Welsh tale, "Gereint, Son of Erbin," one (eleven tales comprising the *Mabinogion*, translated between 1838 and 1849, an published by Lady Charlotte Guest (1812-1895). Earl Yniol is the father of Eni(Gereint's future bride.

307.1 *Endymion*, by the Author of Lothair [Benjamin D'Israeli] (Lo don: Longmans, Green & Co., 1880), 2 vols. Butler quotes the conclusion of th first volume. The character continues: "When you have succeeded in life accord ing to your views . . . you will, some day, sigh for real power, and denounce th time when you became a public man, and belonged to any one but yourself."

308.1 The following note covers almost 3 MS. pages in Butler's hand, th first of which is headed by the first editing date, the others by the second. Durinj the interval here indicated, Butler was preoccupied with his theory concerning th Sicilian origin and feminine authorship of the *Odyssey* and made his second journe to Sicily (July 14th to September 21st) to verify it (see 279.1 above). Jones b(

308

ves Butler intended to work the note up to article length for inclusions in a pro-
cted volume containing his *Universal Review* articles to be edited by Harry Quil-
r, editor of the short-lived journal (1888-1890). Nothing came of the project, but
n May 21, 1892, Butler wrote Quilter: "I have also an article in great part written
lled 'Croesus's Kitchen-Maid' which has nothing to do with Croesus or classics but
as, I fancy, a good deal of quiet devilment . . ." (*Works* XVIII, 259-60). Because
f his riches and power, Croesus, the last king of Lydia (560-546 B.C.), has become
e symbol for supreme wealth.

308.2   Roman adage: "he who acts through another acts himself."

313.1   Dr. Samuel Butler (1774-1839) was educated at Rugby (he was
school-fellow of W.S. Landor) and St. John's College, Cambridge. In 1798 he
ecame Headmaster of Shrewsbury School which he transformed into one of the
est public schools during the 38 years he held the post. He resigned it in 1836
) become Bishop of Lichfield, and moved to Eccleshall Castle (near Stafford), the
at of the bishops of Lichfield from the 13th Century to 1867. In 1798 he married
arriet Apthorp; their only son Thomas was Butler's father. One of their two daugh-
rs, Harriet, married John Thomas Lloyd of Shrewsbury, and their son was Butler's
ousin, Thomas Bucknall Lloyd (1824-1896), also educated at Shrewsbury and St.
hn's, who in 1880 was Vicar of St. Mary's, Shrewsbury, and from 1886 to his
eath Archdeacon of Salop. Butler's father was presented with the living of Langar-
m-Barnston, Nottinghamshire in 1834, and lived at the Rectory at Langar until
is retirement in 1876, when he returned to Shrewsbury. Archdeacon Lloyd was
anon Butler's executor. Mrs. Watchorn was a Langar woman who came in occa-
onally to do sewing. December 4 was, of course, Butler's fourth birthday: his
ther that morning had received the news that Dr. Butler had died about 1 a.m.
Works XI, 426-427).

316.1   From "For Unto Us" in Handel's *Messiah* (1741).

317.1   Tommaso di Giovanni, called Masaccio (1401-c.1428); Fra Filippo
ippi (1406-1469); Filippino Lippi (1457-1504); Domenico di Tommaso Bigordi,
alled Ghirlandaio (c.1448-1494); Antonio and Piero Pollaiuolo (1432-1498; c.1441-
1496); Alessandro di Mariano Filipepi, called Sandro Botticelli (1445-1510). All
f them belong to the 15th century Florentine school. Masaccio, who shows the
fluence of Giotto, one of Butler's favorites, developed an austere style which in-
uenced the early work of the Carmelite monk, Filippo Lippi. His son, Filippino,
ho studied with him and Botticelli, completed Masaccio's frescoes in the Branacei
hapel. Ghirlandaio painted in the style of both Masaccio and Filippo Lippi, whose
fluence is also visible in Antonio Pollaiuolo's paintings. Botticelli was probably
ained by Filippo Lippi, though his later work represents a reaction against Masac-
o, and reflects Filippo Lippi's later return to the luminous Gothic style admired
nd imitated by the Pre-Raphaelite painters with whose work Butler was acquainted.

318.1   In 1822, when William Blake was 65, he was commissioned to illu-
rate Dante's *Divine Comedy*, and consequently taught himself Italian. Virgil is
ante's guide in the epic; Tennyson's admiration of Virgil is expressed, for example,
"To Virgil" (1882).

321.1   Butler refers to *On Genesis of Species* (London, 1871), a synthes
of science and theology, by the English zoologist St. George Mivart (1827-1900
a copy of the second edition (1871) is in the Butler Collection at St. John's Colleg
Cambridge. It was this work which first opened Butler's eyes to the flaws in Darwin
argument (*Works*, VI, 24-27). Like Butler, Mivart rejected "natural selection"
sole agent in the development of species which, he insisted, proceeded teleologicall
Man, in view of his special attributes, developed as a being apart: "Man's anim
body must have had a different source from that of the spiritual soul which inform
it, owing to the distinctness of the two orders to which those two existences seve
rally belong" (p. 325). In the 6th edition of the *Origin of Species* (1872), Darw
responded to Mivart's criticism.

322.1   Mark 16:9 and Luke 8:2.

323.1   The *Messiah Quadrilles* (for piano) by Augustus Lashmare Tampl
(1837-1889), in his time one of the most renowned organ players in England, ar
composer for the piano. He attended Trinity College, Cambridge during Butler
time, and became the organist of St. James's Church, Marylebone where H.R. Hawe
was rector (see 404.4 below). In a note (dated August 26, 1901) to a letter fro
Miss Savage (December 15, 1875) he wrote: ". . . I did not like Tamplin, whom
knew well at Cambridge. Among other freaks he wrote *The Messiah Quadrille*
which I have vainly tried to see. They are sure to be clever--at least I should thin
they would be" (*Letters*, p. 112).

324.1   *A Treatise on Man, His Intellectual Facultie and his Education*, b
the French materialist philosopher Claude-Adrien Helvétius (1715-1771), translate
by W. Hooper, M.D. (London, 1777), 2 volumes. The third quotation reads: "B
he who is falsely learned [as the scholastic], has by degrees lost his reason when h
thought to improve it, and has purchased his stupidity at too dear a rate ever t
renounce it."

326.1   The Autotype Company (formerly the Autotype Fine Art Com
pany) at 36 Rathbone Place, photographic publishers and dealers in photographi
materials.

327.1   William Sefton Moorhouse (1825-1881), the second Superintenden
of Canterbury Province (1857-68), later Mayor of Wellington, whom Butler met i
New Zealand and held in high esteem ever after. James Edward Fitzgerald (1818
1896), the first Superintendant, also Butler's friend, founded the Christchurch *Pre*
(in May, 1861) to oppose Moorhouse and his policies. Moorhouse was considere
careless in financial matters, but he encouraged the building of railways, and sav
to it that the railway tunnel between Lyttelton and Christchurch was opened in 186
(see also *Memoir* I, 105-6). He was Butler's mortgagee, and for the rest of his li
Butler could not help feeling that when he called in his New Zealand investment
(in 1872), he had hurt Moorhouse. In the account of his friendship with Pauli (1898
he wrote that Moorhouse was "one of the very first and best men whom it was eve
my lot to cross--a man who had shown me infinite kindness and whom I never ca
think of without remorse. . ."

328.1   The first article, "The Effect of Lightning on Trees" (p. 7e) reports
he findings of a Swiss physicist who maintained lightning descends in "showers,
ince a single stroke affects many vines in a large circumference in a vineyard." The
econd, "A Shower of Lightning" (p. 6f), in corroboration of the above, recounts
ιow a little girl and several other people were enveloped, but not harmed, by a lumi-
ιous cloud immediately after lightning struck a nearby cherry-tree.

332.1   See Jude 9.

334.1   See note 170, and 170.1 above.

336.1   "He who has begun his task well has half done it." Horace, *Epis-
les* I, ii, 40.

338.1   *Times*, October 28, 1880, p. 5f. In the letter a French correspondent
ιsks: "Je prends la liberté de vous prier de vouloir bien me faire connaître s'il c'est
rai (comme je l'ai appris), que vous vous occupez le négociations de marriages."

344.1   Rev. (later Sir Rev.) Philip Perring (1828-1920), who studied under
)r. Butler at Shrewsbury (see 313.1) above; before leaving in 1848 he became head
ιf the school. After taking his B.A. and M.A. degrees at Trinity College, Cambridge,
ιe became the curate of St. James's, Piccadilly from 1855 to 1860, afterwards of St.
ohn's, Hackney. Upon his father's death in 1866 he became the 4th Baronet. But-
er, in preparation for ordination after taking his degree at St. John's in 1858, worked
everal months (until March, 1859) as amateur lay assistant to Perring, living with
ιim in dismal quarters in Heddon Street, in the slum district that was part of the
ιarish.

346.1   Mrs. Elizabeth Hudson, a native of Yorkshire, known as the "Rail-
ιay Queen," wife of the "Railway King" George Hudson (1800-1871) who amassed
ιn enormous fortune, eventually lost in litigations, through speculation schemes
ιnvolving the building of the railroad network in the North of England. She was
ιnown for her malapropisms and otherwise infelicitous use of the language as well
ιs her extravagant wit. See *Works*, VII, 124.

348.1   Harriet Bridges (née Butler) (1834-1918); in 1859 she married George
_ovibond Bridges, the brother of the later poet laureate Robert Bridges. Her hus-
ιand died after only seven months of marriage, but she continued to live with the
Bridges family on the Isle of Wight for some twenty years before returning to Wilder-
ιope House near Shrewsbury in 1879 where Butler's father after his retirement lived
ιith the younger sister May.

349.1   An allusion to Matt. 17:22 and I Cor. 13:2.

349.2   An allusion to James 2:17.

352.1   In Act III, Scene 5 of *Saul* (1738).

353.1   See Chapter XIII in the revised edition of *Erewhon*.

356.1   See I Peter 5:8 where this is said of the devil.

357.1   "The Church Congress," p. 4 a-c. Speaking on the previous day a Leicester (where the Congress was held), the Bishop pointed out that labourers i East London are indifferent to religion, though not because of hostility or "specula tive unbelief." If it is thought of at all, "it is thought of as a habit belonging to wholly different class from themselves, and to a class [i.e. the well-to-do] looke upon with no kindly regard."

358.1   The article (p. 5f) summarizes an essay by Sir John Lubbock i the *Journal of the Linnean Society*, XV, No. 83 (September 3, 1880), 137-187 detailing some of his experiments for demonstrating that ants communicate by som means "approaching to language."

359.1   Psalm 34:10: "The young lions do lack and suffer hunger; but the that seek the Lord shall not want any good thing." Verse 17: "The righteous cry and the Lord heareth, and delivereth them out of all their troubles."

360.1   James Artis Cooper, solicitor and partner with Paine, Layton an Cooper, Gresham House, City of London, died September 29, 1880, aged 43. Jone had been articled to the firm's head, Sir Thomas Paine (see 794.1 below); he wa admitted as solicitor in 1876, and subsequently became a "managing clerk," a pos tion he held until 1887 when Butler asked him to become his personal secretar (see 122.1 above). In 1878 he was shifted to the firm of Whithall and Compto (see 1308.1 below), but apparently was forced to return to his original position a Paine's in the Spring of 1881. Jones attended Cooper's funeral on October 1s

363.1   Miss Arabella Buckley (1840-1929), author (*The Fairyland of Sc ence* [1878]), in 1880 a lecturer in natural science, formerly secretary of the geol gist Charles Lyell (1797-1875). Butler made her acquaintance in 1878 at a dinne given by Mrs. Fanny Salter, the sister of his friend Haycock (see 98.1 above). Mi Buckley had attended a séance in December, 1865, at which both Butler and A.R Wallace had been present (*Memoir*, I, 316-7). In a note to one of Miss Savage's le ters Butler wrote that Miss Buckley "is a silly tattling log-rolling mischief-makin woman and I dislike her very much" (*Letters*, p. 196): Butler had known her hu band, Dr. Thomas Fischer, a medical practitioner, in New Zealand where he owne a sheep station ("The Grampain Hills") some twenty miles below Butler's "Mesopo tamia." He sold out in 1882 to return to England; he married Miss Buckley in 1883

363.2   Butler refers to a quarrel caused by the publication, in Novembe 1879, of *Life of Erasmus Darwin*, which Darwin, in the Preface, declared to be a translation of the article, "Erasmus Darwin und seine Stellung in der Geschicht der Descendenz-Theorie," by the scientific popularizer, Dr. Ernst Ludwig Kraus (1839-1903), which had appeared in the German periodical *Kosmos* in Februar of that year. When Butler checked the translation against the original, he discovere several new passages in the former, some condemning apparently his own reappraisa of Erasmus Darwin in *Evolution Old and New* (May, 1879). Because he had vouche

his Preface for the accuracy of the translation, Darwin was guilty, Butler erro-
ously concluded, of duplicity for passing off a covert condemnation of his own
forts as an unbiased opinion written prior, and hence without reference to *Evolu-
on Old and New*. Butler complained to Darwin, who explained he knew the article
d been altered, but since this was common practice, he saw no reason to mention
. Butler would not let the matter drop and aired his views in a letter to the *Athena-
m* of January 31, 1880 (p. 155). Darwin, on T.H. Huxley's advice, did not reply,
d Butler continued to nurse his grudge. The matter was cleared up posthumously
. *Charles Darwin and Samuel Butler: A Step towards Reconciliation* by H.F. Jones
ondon: A.C. Fifield, 1911).

363.3   Charles Crawley (1846-1899), a barrister specializing in insurance
w, was a life-long friend whom Butler met either through their common acquaint-
ce with Edmund Gurney and Henry Gurney (see 176.1 above) or at Heatherley's
t School which Crawley attended in the late seventies. He was active in the
orking Men's College, Great Ormond Street (he was its vice-principal from 1883
1887), and encouraged Butler to speak there. He and his wife drowned in the
ye near Tintern Abbey. Butler saw Darwin's son Francis (note 384, and 384.8
low), with whom he was still on friendly terms, for the last time at Crawley's
oms in February 1878, shortly after the appearance of *Life and Habit*. In a 1901
te to a letter of Miss Savage, referring to this meeting he wrote: "[Francis Dar-
in] was evidently a good deal upset with me--but quite civil. Speaking of attacks
established reputations he said that George Eliot had said to him a few days
fore 'If this sort of thing is to be allowed *who* is safe?' but whether or not this
as aimed at my attack on his father I could not determine" (*Letters*, p. 172).

363.4   Richard Garnett (1835-1906), author (*The Twilight of the Gods
888]; Life of Thomas Carlyle* [1887]) and at this time Superintendent of the
eading Room of the British Museum, and later (1890-99) keeper of Books, heavily
gaged in editing the library catalogue.

365.1   See note 172.

368.2   *Works*, VII, 64: he describes a dream in which he sees Handel at
organ: "I heard the great pedal notes in the bass stalk up and down, like the
ys of the Aurora that go about the face of the heavens off the coast of Labrador."
ora is a village in the Canton Ticino.

367.1   Overscored in MS.: to come to a decision as to what one likes best
d most permanently in connection with it,

367.2   See note 34, and 34.1 above.

369.1   Rev. George Barber Paley (1799-1880) became a fellow of Peter-
use, Cambridge (where he received his degrees) in 1825; he was Rector of Frecken-
m, Suffolk from 1835-1879. His eldest son was Butler's friend George Alfred
ley (1838-1866) who took his degree two years after Butler at St. John's (he was
prominent oarsman while there) and was called to the Bar in 1863. He died of ty-
us fever in February, 1866; Butler attended his funeral. The Miss Paley mentioned
his sister Beatrice Ann who eventually married Henry Hoare (see 215.1 above).

369.2   Between the winter of 1888 and the autumn of 1895 Butler was working on the biography of his grandfather (see 313.1), *The Life of Dr. Samuel Butler* (2 volumes), published in 1896, which required a review of Dr. Butler's voluminous correspondence which Butler's sisters had turned over to him. Rev. Samuel Tillbrook (1784-1835), who took his degree from Peterhouse, became both tutor and bursar in the College; the living of Freckenham was presented to him in May, 1829. He shared Dr. Butler's love for fishing and in Butler's view was the "most Shakespearean man" his grandfather had ever met.

369.3   The anecdote is worked into *The Way of All Flesh*, Chapter 11.

370.1   See 258.1 above.

371.1   Overscored in MS.: to those that adopt it

376.1   Quoted from a review of *Horae Helenicae* by John Stuart Blackie (London: Macmillan & Co., 1874) in the *Pall Mall Gazette* for August 22, 1874, p. 11b. The first quotation is part of the reviewer's summary of Homer's "theological" views: "A god is a supernaturally strong, amorous, beautiful, brave, and cunning man, who may on any given occasion be benevolently disposed to mortals or the reverse." The second quotation expresses the reviewer's dislike of the writer's attempt to systematize this "rude and slender theology" since Homer's morality, which is of a "sound" and "elevated type," renders this attempt unnecessary.

378.1   For the controversy about *Erasmus Darwin*, see 363.2 above, and note 363.

378.2   January 31, 1880, p. 155 (see 363.2 above). Butler again aired his grievance against Darwin in the *St. James's Gazette*, December 8, 1880 (p. 5), in response to a review of *Unconscious Memory* (December 2nd) in which Butler's quarrel was alluded to. Butler had placed "the whole story" on record in the first four chapters of his book where he traces the genesis of his ideas on evolution up to his public attack on Darwin.

378.3   Published in May, 1879; in it Butler distills the evolution theories of Erasmus Darwin, Buffon, and Lamarck, and compares them to Charles Darwin's theory.

378.4   Overscored in MS.: and had better be hung for a sheep than a lamb.

378.5   Butler refers to T.H. Huxley's article "Past and Present" in *Nature*, November 1, 1894, pp. 1-3. Huxley points out that no one now questions the theory that species have descended from common ancestors, and that this *volte face* in general opinion is due to Mr. Darwin's work, even though should specifically Darwinian ideas be swept away, the theory of evolution would remain since in its general form it is as "old as scientific speculation." In his note in Vol. V (dated November 3, 1894) Butler adds that this conclusion "seems to show that Professor

Huxley has at last begun to find Mr. Darwin out--or rather not to think it worth while to pretend longer that he has not done so."

380.1 In the Preface to *Evolution Old and New* (1879) Butler explains why he has adopted the musical practice of numbering his works with "opus" numbers. Had Handel numbered his oratorios, the "significance of the numbers on *Susanna* and *Theodora* would have been at once apparent, connected as they would have been with the number of *Jephtha*, Handel's next and last work, in which he emphatically repudiates the influence which, perhaps in a time of self-distrust he had allowed contemporary German music to exert over him" (*Works*, V, xv). *Susanna* (1749), and *Theodora* (1750) are not written in the customary Handelian oratorio manner; the first is almost an opera, the second an intimate work and the most overtly religious next to the *Messiah*. *Jephthah* reflects Handel's more usual public manner. In the strict sense, *Jephthah* was not Handel's last work, though the last finished before his blindness in 1752; he wrote the oratorio *The Triumph of Time and Truth* in 1756, which is, however, a third reworking of his *Il Trionfo del Tempo e della Verità* (c. 1708).

380.2 An occasional oratorio written in 1746 to celebrate the English victory at the Battle of Culloden in April, 1746.

380.3 The chorus, "He saw the lovely youth," telling the story of a youth raised to life by Christ, closes Act II of *Theodora*. Handel valued it more than any of his oratorios and regarded this chorus his best. The work was performed to almost empty houses during the first three performances in March, 1750.

380.4 A brief air following "Lord to thee each night and day" in Act III of *Theodora*. In G.A. Macfarren's edition, published by Novello in 1874, it is missing; Macfarren not only based his edition on Chrysander's (1858-1902), known for its unreliability, but felt free to bowdlerize the texts. John Clarke (Clarke-Whitfeld) (1770-1836), English composer and organist, edited *The Vocal Works of . . . Handel*, arranged for organ or piano-forte (6 vols.) (London 1805-8). Butler's Aunt Bather (see 729.1 below) gave him four volumes of the edition; and his cousin Reginald Worsley (216.1) later gave him the entire set.

380.5 *Theodora*, Act II.

382.1 The first quotation: "This is of such imposing majesty that I cannot praise it sufficiently." The Latin of Dr. Butler (who thought Nemea VII to be "the most unpleasant ode of any in Pindar"): "This is a work of such obfuscation that I should like never to have written it or at least have seen it destroyed." The note is found in Dr. Butler's heavily annotated copy of *Pindari Carmina* edited by Christian Gottlob Heyne (London: G. and W.B. Whittaker, 1823), now in the Butler Collection at St. John's College, Cambridge. Dr. Butler apparently refers to the *Pindari Carmina* edited by Heyne's pupil, Ludolf Georg Dissen (1784-1837), published in Gotha and Erford in 1830. Butler added his own comment to his grandfather's note (dated May 2, 1889): "This note is my favourite."

384.1 Down House, Darwin's home in Beckenham, Kent.

384.2   Butler first visited Darwin during the week-end of May 21, 1872. Erewhon had come out in April.

384.3   Butler's dialogue, "Darwin on the Origin of Species," a brief exposition of Darwin's theory, was published anonymously in the Christchurch, New Zealand, *Press* for December 20, 1862 (see *Works*, I, 188-195). A copy was sent to Darwin, possibly by Butler's friend, Julius von Haast (see 69.1 above). In any case, Darwin recommended it to an English journal because it was "remarkable from its spirit and from giving so clear and accurate a view" of his theory. Darwin's letter to Butler is not extant. On his return to London he sent Darwin a copy of his anonymous pamphlet, "The Evidence for the Resurrection of Jesus Christ as Given by the Four Evangelists Critically Examined."

384.4   In the Preface to the second edition of *Erewhon* (dated June 9, 1872) he wrote that "nothing could be further from my intention" to reduce Darwin's theory "to an absurdity" in the Machine Chapters, that "few things would be more distasteful to me than any attempt to laugh at Mr. Darwin; but I must own that I have myself to thank for the misconception, for I felt sure that my intention would be missed, but preferred not to weaken the chapters by explanation, and knew very well that Mr. Darwin's theory would take no harm. The only question in my mind was how far I could afford to be misrepresented as laughing at that for which I have the most profound admiration. I am surprised, however, that the book at which such an example of the specious misuse of analogy would seem most naturally levelled should have occurred to no reviewer; neither shall I mention the name of the book here, though I should fancy that the hint given will suffice." Butler had written Darwin earlier about the critics' misunderstanding of the Machine Chapters (May 11, 1872), and had then told him his target, which he would identify should a second edition be called for, had been Bishop Joseph Butler's *The Analogy of Religion* (1736) (see *Memoir*, I, 156-57).

384.5   Erasmus Alvey Darwin (1804-1881) was Charles Darwin's elder brother. Both had attended Shrewsbury School. In his *Autobiographical Recollections* (1876) Charles Darwin wrote: "Nothing could have been worse for the development of my mind than Dr. Butler's school, as it was strictly classical, nothing else being taught, except a little ancient geography and history. The school as a means of education to me was simply a blank." He attended Shrewsbury School from 1818 to 1825--his father, Dr. Robert Waring Darwin was at the time the town's leading medical practitioner--and was a schoolfellow of Thomas Butler, Butler's father. The two spent the summer of 1828 together on a reading party at Barmouth when both were students at Cambridge, Charles Darwin at Christ's and Thomas Butler at St. John's.

384.6   St. George Mivart, *On Genesis of Species* (1871). Darwin was to respond to Mivart's criticism in the 6th edition of the *Origin* (see 321.1 above). Butler did use Mivart's book to bolster his own theory in *Life and Habit* (1877) and to criticize Darwin's.

384.7   Charles Darwin's son (1845-1912), later Sir George, the astronomer and mathematician. Butler visited him at Cambridge during a November week-end in 1873 (see also note 385). George Darwin had read mathematics at Trinity College, Cambridge (he graduated in 1868), but then studied law; he was called to the bar in 1874 (though he never practiced), and it was not until he read a paper on the influence of geological changes on the earth's axis before the Royal Society in 1876 that he established himself as scientist. In 1879 he was made a fellow of the Society; in 1883 he became Plumian Professor of Astronomy at Cambridge. See Butler's note 791.

384.8   Charles Darwin's son, Francis Darwin (1848-1925), later Sir Francis, botanist, reader in botany at Cambridge from 1888 to 1904, at this time his father's secretary and research assistant, was on good terms with Butler until *Life and Habit* appeared. Before this, they dined or went to concerts together. It was he who pointed out, as Butler remembers, the Hering article that had anticipated Butler's theory (see *Works*, VI, 23-24). See also 416.1 below. This second visit took place during the first week-end of November, 1872. See also 363.3 above.

384.9   *The Fair Haven* was published in March 1873. Butler composed it during the summer and autumn of 1872.

384.10   See note 363.

384.11   Thomas Woolner, R.A. (1825-1892), one of the original members of the Pre-Raphaelite Brotherhood, who had made a bust of Charles Darwin at Down in 1868.

384.12   *The Expressions of Emotions in Man and Animals* (1872).

384.13   Letter of April 1, 1873 (*Memoir* I, 186-7): "What has struck me much in your book is your dramatic power--that is to [say] the way in which you earnestly and thoroughly assume the character and think the thoughts of the man you pretend to be. Hence I conclude that you could write a really good novel."

385.1   See 384.7 above.

394.1   *Svelare*, to unveil; *svegliare*, to awaken.

395.1   See 75.1 above.

397.1   Luke 15:11-32. In Christ's parable the father, upon the return of his son, rejoices by celebrating the event with a fatted calf.

400.1   Butler had sent Dr. Harvey Goodwin (1818-1891), Bishop of Carlisle, a copy of *Unconscious Memory* in which he had cited Goodwin's condemnation of the obscurantism of scientific jargon, in "The Philosophy of Crayfishes" (from the October 1880 issue of *Nineteenth Century*). See *Works* VI, 199. In his letter (November 18, 1880) Butler wrote that if those who begin "with an all-pervading supreme intelligence" find nothing inharmonious with their assumption in the theory of evolution, and if those, like himself, who begin with "tabulae rasae" and find themselves driven to purposive evolution and to "the action of a supreme, all-pervading mind or purpose in both organic and inorganic matter; then,

317

surely, we may be upon the eve of the removal of other misunderstandings, and it is well that those who most heartily desire such a consummation should put anything they think may tend, however little, towards it in the way of those whom they hope it may concern" (*Memoir* I, 345). He let Miss Savage see the Bishop's acknowledgement of the book, and this was her reply on November 24 (*Letters*, p. 240). See also *Correspondence*, pp. 90-91.

404.1   Henry John Furber (fl. 1830-1865; died after 1885), the 4th generation of London violin-makers; he carried on his business as dealer and maker in Grafton Street, Fitzroy Square. His father and teacher, John Furber (fl. 1810-1845), made violins on the Nicolò Amati pattern.

404.2   Reginald Worsley (216.1), Butler's cousin, was a violinist. Charles Gogin (1844-1931), a painter and illustrator who exhibited regularly at the Royal Academy from 1874 to 1885, had met Butler at Heatherley's; they remained on good terms, and Butler trusted him as an authority on art, though he regarded him as one who kept studying and putting off painting. In later life he kept a studio at Shoreham. The friendship was briefly interrupted when Gogin married Alma Broadbridge in the spring of 1894, a painter of domestic subjects (she occasionally exhibited in the Royal Academy and Suffolk Street Gallery) who also had been a student at Heatherley's in the 1870's. Gogin drew the human figures for Butler's drawings in *Alps and Sanctuaries* (1881), and painted two portraits of Butler in 1896 (one now in London's National Portrait Gallery, one in Chapin Library). In a letter dated December 7, 1880 (in Chapin Library) Butler wrote: "I am now writing my magnum opus but that is not to see light till years after I and most now living are dead--so that I am telling the truth the whole truth and nothing but the truth, but please don't tell about it." Clearly, a reference to *The Way of All Flesh* (1903).

404.3   The reference is unclear; possibly David Hyam, of David Hyam & Co., dealer and importers of Hounsditch who dealt in musical instruments.

404.4   The Broad Churchman Rev. Hugh Reginald Haweis (1838-1901) received his B.A. in 1859 from Trinity College, Cambridge. He was rector of St. James's, Marylebone, where he encouraged musical performances; an able violinist (he studied with one of Paganini's students) with an interest in violin-making, he wrote articles for newspapers and books on musical and theological subjects (*Music and Morals* [1871]; *Old Violins* [1898]), and was much in demand as speaker. He preached in colonial cathedrals, and toured the U.S., giving the Lowell lectures in music at Boston in 1895. Tamplin, the organist (see 323.1 above), played in his church. Since Haweis was active as undergraduate in the Cambridge Musical Society, Butler may have met him while at St. John's. In a 1901 note to one of Miss Savage's letters he declared his dislike for both him and Tamplin (*Letters*, pp. 111-12).

405.1   Mlle. Clémence Dubois was an acquaintance of Jones and of the Paine family (see 360.1 and 794.1 below).

406.1   Alfred Cathie (1862-1937?), the man-servant Butler employed from January, 1887 on. With the exception of notes 561 to 563, the remainder of Volume I is type-written, though often corrected in Butler's hand. All preceding notes, except for the typed notes 333 to 381, are also in Butler's hand.

407.1   When Sir Charles Mordaunt (1836-1897), MP for Warwickshire from 1859 to 1868 and in 1879 its sherriff, brought a suit of divorce on charges of adultery against his wife, Harriet Sarah, née Moncrieffe, the Prince of Wales was subpoenaed to appear as witness at the trial because two correspondents were his friends and because Lady Mordaunt had accused the Prince of misconduct toward herself. He took the stand (the trial lasted from February 16 to 25, 1870), denied any misconduct and was cleared. Lady Mordaunt had been declared legally insane, but the House of Lords decided her husband could bring divorce proceedings against her. The Prince's connection with the trial, however, was resented in some quarters, and he was hissed (as Butler points out here) at his next theatre appearance after the trial and at the Epsom race course.

409.1   See note 384.

409.2   The review, generally favorable in spite of an unkind conclusion, appeared in the *Spectator* for April 20, 1872 (pp. 452-4). It identified the Ydgrunites as the moral norm of the tale, an interpretation Butler approved in a letter to the *Spectator* for February 15, 1902 in response to its unfavorable review of both the revised edition of *Erewhon* and *Erewhon Revisited* (*Spectator,* February 8, 1902, p. 253.) Butler did not add his name to *Erewhon* until the so-called "5th edition" which appeared sometime after April of 1873.

414.1   A species of lynx native to southwestern Asia.

415.1   This case is quoted from Robert B. Carter's *On the Pathology and Treatment of Hysteria* (London: John Churchill, 1853) in Chapter XIX of William B. Carpenter's *Principles of Mental Physiology* (London: H.S. Knight & Co., 1874). Three of the child's fingers were cut off, and the mother's fright immobilized her; the attending surgeon had to treat the corresponding fingers of the mother's hand, which had become swollen and inflamed though healthy before the accident. Dr. Brian Tuke wrote *Illustration of the Influence of the Mind Upon the Body* (London: J. & A. Churchill, 1872) from which Carpenter quotes as well. Butler had met Carpenter (1813-1885) at a séance on December 8, 1865 at the home of John Marshman, whom Butler had apparently met in connection with his New Zealand venture for at one time Marshman was the Immigration Officer and Agent-General for the colony in London. Apparently a shower of beautiful roses descended from the ceiling to the table. Butler wrote in his diary: "Transparent humbug. A.R. Wallace [the biologist and friend of Darwin's] and Dr. Carpenter both there: the former swallowing everything, the latter contemptuous as well he might be" (*Memoir*, I, 127). Miss Arabella Buckley (see 363.1 above) also attended.

416.1   *The Principles of Psychology*, Volume I, 2nd edition (London: Williams & Norgate, 1870): Spencer states that "experiments show that the so-called nerve-current is intermittent--consists of waves which follow one another from the place where the disturbance arises to the place where its effect is felt. The external stimulus in no case acts continuously on the sentient centre, but sends to it a series of pulses of molecular actions" (152). These waves constitute subjective feelings, both simple and compound, since each wave "has for its correlative a shock or pulse of feelings. . ." (154). In *Unconscious Memory* (1880) Butler in cluded his translation of a lecture by Karl Ewald Hering (1834-1918), Professor of Physiology at the University of Prague, entitled *On Memory as a Universal Function of Organized Matter* ("Über das Gedächtnis als eine allgemeine Funktion der organisierten Materie"), delivered first at the Imperial Academy of Sciences at Vienna, May 30, 1870, and published in England in Volume LXXII of the Proceedings of the Royal Academy of Sciences, Division III, December, 1875. Hering proposed that sensations and feelings were caused by the motion or vibration within the molecular structures of nerve-fibers, and that the phenomenon of memory as well as of identity consequently could be resolved into the uninterrupted patterns of vibrations set up by various external and internal stimuli. Like Butler, he considered heredity a type of memory, a passing on, so to speak, of vibration patterns. Butler's attention was directed by Francis Darwin to a reference to the lecture in an article by Ray Lankester in *Nature* for July 13, 1876, "Perigenesis v. Pangenesis--Haeckel's New Theory of Heredity" (pp. 235-238) while he was writing *Life and Habit* (1877). He deliberately ignored it until he had completed his book.

416.2   On page 190 of *Psychology* Spencer points out that the relation between feelings is of short duration when compared to the feelings themselves because transmission through a nerve-fiber is rapid in comparison with the transformation it sets up in a nerve-center. But on page 191 he declares that "such unrelational feeling as smells" can call up remembrances because the olfactory centers are "outgrowths from the cerebral hemispheres." Spencer's book is discussed in *Luck or Cunning*? (1886/7) (*Works*, VIII).

417.1   See quotations under 416.1 above.

420.1   Right Hon. Sidney Lord Herbert of Lea (1810-1861), well-known liberal-conservative Peelite, Secretary for War under Gladstone and Palmerston; George Herbert (1593-1633), the well-known devotional poet; Lord Edward Herbert of Cherbury (1583-1648), his brother, the deist philosopher; Auberon Herbert (1838-1902), political philosopher of radical persuasion; Lady Elizabeth Herbert of Lea (died in 1911), wife of Lord Herbert; Herbert Spencer (1820-1903), the philosopher.

420.2   Herbert Campbell (1844-1904), immensely popular music-hall performer who appeared regularly in the Drury Lane pantomines from 1882 to his death, and for many years a member of the stock company of the Grecian Theatre. He was a man of Falstaffian girth and cheerfulness, with a booming voice, known for his irreverent, blunt, broad satire on topics of the day. Max Beerbohm considered him the epitome of the British character.

421.1   See 247.2 above.

421.2   Leopold Silberberg, active in London during the 1880's. The Argyll Rooms was at this time (its name changed again in 1882) an upper middle class nightclub and dancing casino located in Great Windmill Street, Piccadilly. In 1894 it became known as the Royal Trocadero Music Hall.

422.1   See Chapter 66 (67 in D.F. Howard's edition) of *The Way of All Flesh*.

423.1   See Butler's sonnet "There doth great Handel live," written sometime after 1898 (*Works*, XX, 428).

425.1   Edward R. Worsley, son of Reginald Worsley who by this time was divorced from his wife. Many of the Worsleys lived in Clifton, Bristol, the home of the family for several generations.

428.1   John Baldwin Buckstone (1802-1879), author of numerous comedies, considered in his time one of the finest "low" comedians, renowned for his portrayals of comic characters in Shakespeare's plays, a favorite of Queen Victoria. He was manager of the Haymarket Theatre from 1853 to 1876. On June 2, 1849, at the Lyceum Theatre he played one of the witches in a production of *Macbeth*.

430.1   Reginald Worsley's daughter, Teddy's sister (see 425.1 above). For Alice S. Worsley, her aunt, see 247.2 above. The Worsleys were all staunch Unitarians.

435.1   The first examinations at Cambridge for the B.A. degree.

436.1   H.F. Jones's landlady when he was living in New Ormond Street.

436.2   In the gardens of the Grecian Theatre (which allowed smoking and drinking) there was singing and dancing: attached to them was a saloon, "The Eagle." Herbert Campbell (see 420.1 above) was a member of the stock company.

440.1   The painter and illustrator Henry Marriott Paget (1856-1936). He and his wife (see 441.1 below) studied at Heatherley's art school; Butler considered him at this time "one of our most promising young painters" (*Correspondence*, p. 81). He exhibited at the Royal Academy from 1879 to 1894; his younger brother Sidney was a well-known illustrator of the works of Scott and Conan Doyle. *The Quiver*, a popular illustrated journal "designed for the defence of Biblical truth and the advancement of religion in the houses of the people" was published in London and New York from 1861 to 1890.

441.1   Mrs. Paget, wife of H.M. Paget (440.1 above), daughter of Dr. William Farr. Butler had known her and her husband since they were children. She, as the others here mentioned, studied at Heatherley's. For Miss Broadbridge see 404.2 above. Miss Yate may refer to Miss Carrie Yates, later wife of the painter Thomas Cooper Gotch (1854-1931). Butler for a time was on friendly terms with him, but in a letter to H.M. Paget (May 20, 1880) he finds Gotch "has a screw loose somewhere" and can do nothing with him. In August he writes to the well-known painter H. Scott Tuke that he should come only with Paget or Jones, for he is "tired" of Gotch. He studied for a time in Paris under J.P. Laurens.

442.1   James Savage (1833-1855), a sizar at St. John's College (admitted in 1851), often sat with Butler at the scholar's table. A laborer found him dead in a ditch at Comberton; after an inquest at Madingley it was determined he had died of apoplexy. The bootmaker's shop of R. Flack stood just outside the main entrance of St. John's.

442.2   George William Fisher (1835-1898), a student at Christ's College, Cambridge (B.A., 1857); he was the mathematics master at Shrewsbury School from 1860 to 1872.

443.1   Butler joined the Century Club (founded in 1867) in 1872 or 1873: it was a society of Oxford and Cambridge worthies who met once a week. Butler was a member of a committee that drew up plans for what would, after 1882, become the National Liberal Club. Among the members of the Century were such notables as Thomas Hughes, J.S. Mill, John Bright, Frederic Harrison, Leslie and Fitzjames Stephen. Butler withdrew from the club when he felt it became increasingly political (he had joined it as an avowed conservative), and because it might simply merge with the new National Liberal Club. By 1882 the Club in fact ceased to exist.

444.1   Sancton Wood (1816-1886), railway architect and district surveyor of Putney and Roehampton. He built stations for Eastern Counties Railway; Cambridge railway station was largely his work.

445.1   See 222.1 above.

446.1   Handel's musical setting (1736) of John Dryden's second ode to St. Celia.

447.1   A painting by William Hogarth completed about 1758.

448.1   See 258.1 above.

449.1   "Movements of Plants," p. 409. Darwin explains how certain plants rotate their leaves to escape radiation. The leave of the Phyllantus sometimes "rise in the morning from their nocturnal vertically dependent position into a horizontal one, without rotating, and on the wrong side of the main petiole. . . . I have never before heard of a plant appearing to make a mistake in its movements; and the mistake in this instance is a great one, for the leaflets move 90^{c} in a direction opposite to the proper one."

450.1   The Essex village of Nazeing; Butler spells it "Nasing."

451.1   Charles Grant Blairfindie Allen (1848-1899), Canadian-born writer who settled in London after 1876, author of several "hill-top" novels, a contributor of popular scientific articles (drawing a moral from nature and evolution) to the *St. James's Gazette, Cornhill Magazine*, the *Pall Mall Gazette*, and other journals. Many of his articles appearing without by-line in the *St. James's Gazette* were collected into *The Evolutionist at Large* (1881) and *Colin Clout's Calendar* (1883), and bear such titles as "A Wayside Berry," "Amongst the Heather," "A Pretty Land-Shell," "A Sprig of Crowfoot." Butler met him at the home of Edward Clodd (Allen's biographer), a banker and science advocate, a member of the Century Club (443.1 above); and an admirer of Butler. Their friendship was strained after the publication of *Unconscious Memory* (1880), because of Butler's anti-Darwinian position. In June, 1881, Allen published "The Romance of a Wayside Weed" in *Cornhill Magazine*, XLV, 703-16.

452.1   Thomas Layton (1849-1929), solicitor, at this time partner in Paine, Layton, and Cooper (renamed Paine, Layton and Pollock) (see 360.1 above). In 1885 he formed his own firm.

454.1   See 430.1 above.

454.2   Ez. 33:19: "But if the wicked turn from his wickedness, and do that which is lawful and right, he shall live thereby."

456.1   See 22.1 above.

457.1   Edward Armitage (1817-1896), painter of historical and Biblical subjects, appointed in 1875 professor and lecturer on painting to the Royal Academy where he exhibited regularly from 1848 to his death.

457.2   See 404.3 above.

460.1   W. Stewart Duncan, *Conscious Matter, or the Physical and the Psychical Universally in Causal Connection* (London: David Bogue, 1881). Duncan cites *Life and Habit* in support of his theory. In his copy Butler underlined the following: "In other words, every body, large or small, has its own ego, and this, whether it be an organic or inorganic body." Butler copied large excerpts from the book, bound up in one of the volumes entitled "Notes and Extracts, Italian etc." now in the Chapin Library. See General Note on the Text.

461.1   P. 296: Butler is quoting from the author's conclusions cited in a review of *Les Maladies de la Memoire*, by Th. Ribot (Paris, 1881).

462.1   From "On Fruits and Seeds,' *Fortnightly Review*, XIX, n.s., 426-455.

464.1   P. 13f: John Tyndall (1820-1893), physicist and successor to Faraday as Superintendent of the Royal Institution, objects in this letter to the belief that Carlyle was incurious and even hostile to science.

464.2   April 30, p. 9f. During the weeks prior to this, several letters deal
with the moral implications of vivisection. Richard Hutton writes to object to the
support eminent scientists such as George Romanes give to vivisection. Hutton was
a member of the Royal Commission which in 1876 found that prominent scientists
did claim that one ought to be cruel to animals for the sake of science.

468.1   The wife of his uncle Philip Worsley (see 222.1 above), the former
Ann Taylor (1806-1877), daughter of the wealthy and well-known mining engi-
neer and mine owner John Taylor and mother of his favorite cousin Reginald.
See 530.1 below.

470.1   Albert Grant (1830-1899), known as Baron Grant, has been called
"the pioneer of modern mammoth company promoting" (DNB). By means of
various financial schemes he amassed enormous sums until court litigations left him
penniless. King Victor Emmanuel made him a baron. He was apparently a fraudu-
lent speculator who knew how to display his forceful and impressive character.

471.1   "Relations," p. 5d-e. The anonymous writer argues that filial
bonds and loyalty to one's relatives ought to have sensible limits; the reverence
for ancestry is an encumbrance in our social life since it imposes dubious claims
on our affections.

473.1   Dr. Benjamin Kennedy, the Headmaster. See 207.1 above.

474.1   From Handel's *Messiah* (Job 19:25).

475.1   P. 12c. Charles Bradlaugh (1838-1891), the notorious and popular advocate of free-thought. After standing twice for Northampton, he was returned in 1800, and in May presented himself in the House of Commons claiming
the right "to affirm" instead of swearing the oath prescribed by law. This set of
a controversy that was to last six years and involve Bradlaugh in eight actions in
the courts. In April, 1881 he consented to be inactive while the Government introduced a bill allowing for affirmation, but it was dropped. Only after the general
elections of 1886 did Bradlaugh take his seat unchallenged. He helped pass a bill
legalizing affirmation as a substitute for the oath in both the House of Commons
and the law courts. Roundell Palmer, first Earl of Selborne (1812-1895) was Lord
Chancellor from 1872 to 1874, and again from 1880 to 1885.

476.1   Jean-Baptiste-René Robinet (1783-1820), French philosopher,
naturalist, grammarian, and sometime Royal Censor. He developed his materialist
and evolutionary theories (which he was to reject before his death) in this work
as well as in *De la nature* (1761). See 541.1 below. The following is the context
of Butler's quotation: "Chacun [des productions de la nature] a son existence à
part, et aucun n'est isolé ou indépendent. Chacun a des rapports plus au moins
proches avec tous les autres, et les extrêmes se communiquent encore. Ils procé-
dent les uns des autres d'une manière si intime et si nécessaire que chacun a la raison
suffisante de son existence dans celui qui le précede, comme il est lui-même la
raison suffisant de l'existence de celui qui se suit" (p. 2). Butler published *Evolution
Old and New* in 1879 to document, in order to question Darwin's originality, the

theories of evolution developed by eighteenth and early nineteenth century think-ers.

480.1   Pierre Louis Goreau de Maupertuis (1698-1759), French physicist and mathematician (see 542.1 below); Denis Diderot, the philosopher, writer, and encyclopedist (1713-1784); he contributed to the materialist treatise by d'Holbach, *Système de la Nature* (see 543.1 below).

484.1   His sheep-run Mesopotamia; in the spring of 1861 Butler was build-ing his second home there (see note 69 and 72.1 above).

484.2   An employee on the run.

485.1   See note 327.1 above.

485.2   "Nothing comes from nothing."

490.1   The letter is referred to in note 464 (see 464.1 above).

492.1   Miss Frances Powers Cobbe (1822-1904), Unitarian crusader in the name of various causes, including women's rights. She was in 1875 one of the founders of the National Anti-Vivisection Society (and its honorable secre-tary until 1884), and in 1898 the founder of the British Union for the Abolition of Vivisection. In her letter of April 19 (p. 11b) she objects to Darwin's publish-ed opinion (April 18, p. 10b) that the Royal Commission investigating vivisection practices had found the charges of cruelty lodged against British physiologists to be false. Instead, she replies it found them to be true. Darwin answered her in turn (April 22, p. 11b), she then contradicted him once more (April 23, p. 8d), and this correspondence elicited the letter from commission member Hutton refer-red to in note 464 (see 464.2 above). The following paragraph appeared in *The Examiner* on December 25, 1880 (p. 1439a): "Some reports having been afloat to the effect that Mr. Darwin's health is not good, it may be well to state that he suffers from nothing worse than occasional stomachic derangement, caused by his five years' voyage in the *Beagle* long ago. Otherwise Mr. Darwin is hale and sociable, goes to bed before ten and rises to work at six, and enjoys having the best novels of the day read to him by Mrs. Darwin--not a bad sign for a man in his seventy-second year, who has read and thought much." *The Examiner*, a weekly review, ceased publication with the February 28, 1881 issue.

495.1   June 17, p. 11f. The letter explains how electricity is stored in the Fauré battery (or "secondary battery").

496.1   P. 5a-c. Sir William Wilson Hunter (1840-1900), who entered the Bengal Service in 1861, executed over a period of 12 years as Director-General of the Government of India, a statistical survey of India published as *The Imperial Gazetteer of India* (14 volumes). Butler refers to a review of the first 6 volumes that is unreserved in its praise of Hunter's research and literary excellence.

500.1   In the village of Bushey. Butler refers to the inscription again in Volume II of the Note-Books (March, 1885).

502.1   Dr. Erasmus Darwin (1731-1802), Charles Darwin's grandfather, physician, naturalist, published his theory of evolution in *Zoonomia* (1794), arguing that all creatures undergo continuous changes which are produced by their own exertions, which in turn are triggered by their perception of need. Butler summarizes Dr. Darwin's natural philosophy in Chapters 13 and 14 in *Evolution Old and New* (1879 and 1882).

504.1   See note 207.1 above.

505.1   "Intelligence of Ants," by George J. Romanes, pp. 992-1008. The article catalogues the characteristics of ants; much of it summarizes the work of Sir John Lubbock (see 1030.1 below): ants have a sense of color, smell, taste, and direction; have a memory, can communicate with each other, distinguish friend from foe among their kind; have emotions, nurse and "educate" their young, keep aphids as their "cows" and even keep pets; practice slavery, fight wars, and put their dead out of the way.

506.1   Job 28:20-22.

511.1   Butler refers to the German philosopher Eduard von Hartmann (1842-1906) who in *Die Philosophie des Unbewussten* (1869) developed a vitalist and anti-mechanistic theory of evolution, referring many of the phenomena o[f] living organisms to the activity of an unconscious force (*Urwillen*); but it is conceived as impersonal and independent of the personality and activity of the organism. Butler referred all unconscious activity to memory which was heritable and shaped by the efforts of countless individuals; he made clear the difference between his theory and von Hartmann's in *Unconscious Memory* (1880). Ted Jones is Edward James Jones (1854-1889), H.F. Jones's brother who joined the Geological Survey of India, where he died of dysentery.

512.1   A village south of Reigate, Surrey.

516.1   See note 1213.

518.1   See 227.1 above.

519.1   See *Works* VII, pp. 173-74. Butler was working on the book at this time; it was published at the end of 1881 by David Bogue (though dated 1882).

520.1   An allusion to Matthew 22:37-40.

523.1   Arthur Perrhyn Stanley (1815-1881), Dean of Westminster Abbey from 1863 to his death on July 18 of this year. He had studied under Dr. Thomas Arnold at Rugby, and wrote *The Life and Correspondence of Dr. Arnold* (1844). Known for his charity and religious liberalism, he championed free inquiry into the Bible, had defended the *Essays and Reviews* of 1860, and had permitted ministers and laymen of other denominations to preach in the Abbey's pulpit. For Teddy, see 425.1 above.

524.1   *Works*, VII, 26-27.

526.1   *Works*, VII, pp. 44-45.

530.1   Mrs. Anne Pring (1792-1866), wife of Captain Daniel Pring of
Ivedon Pen (near Honiton in Devon), a Commander in the Royal Navy. His sister,
Ann Rowe Pring, in 1805, married the mining engineer John Taylor (1779-1863),
founder of the firm John Taylor & Co. of London, and their daughter Ann married
Philip Worsley in 1832, and thus became Butler's "Aunt Philip" (see note 468).
Mrs. Pring, originally from Dundee, met her husband in Heligoland, and was one
of the few wives who travelled with her husband while he was in the navy. He
died in 1847 in Jamaica. She continued to live at Ivedon, in the parish of Awliscombe (some two miles from Honiton) which belonged almost entirely to the Pring
family; she is buried in Awliscombe churchyard.

531.1   See 363.1 above.

531.2   See 523.1 above.

531.3   Tom Taylor (1817-1880), barrister, journalist and critic, author
of numerous burlesques and comedies, at the time of his death the editor of *Punch*;
he died in July of 1880; George Eliot died in December of the same year, Thomas
Carlyle in May of 1881. Butler had a decided dislike for the latter two. Benjamin
D'Israeli (Earl of Beaconsfield), the Tory statesman had died on April 19th of this
year (see 295.1 above).

534.1   Gaudenzio Ferrari (c. 1481-1546), the Italian religious painter
and sculptor whose works Butler admired, is represented chiefly in Milan and the
churches of outlying Piedmont towns and villages. One of his principal works, here
referred to, decorates the dome of the Church of St. Gaudenzio at Novara, entitled
'Grand' ancona con l'Annunziazione, il Presepio, la Madonna e santi."

535.1   *Works*, VIII, 98. *Luck or Cunning* was published in November,
1886.

536.1   The *padrona* of the Hotel del Angelo at Faido (Canton Ticino)
where Butler stayed when passing through. Morra, Arto, Pella and Civiasco are
villages to the east of Lago Maggiore in the Italian Piemont.

536.2   That is, an old woman "with great absence of spirit."

536.3   See note 43.

537.1   See 534.1 above. Vercelli is a town east of Novara.

537.2   Bernardino Lanini (c. 1520-1578), born in Vercelli, painter of
religious subjects, pupil of Gaudenzio Ferrari. He worked mostly in Milan and
Novara.

538.1   See 425.1 above. Bingfield is a village in southern Northumberland. For Aunt Alice, see 247.2 above.

538.2   Mrs. Edward Enfield, née Honora Taylor, the youngest daughter
(born in 1814) of the mining engineer John Taylor and his wife Anne, the sister
of Commander Daniel Pring (see 530.1 above), and hence Teddy's great-aunt. Edward Enfield (1811-1880) had been an officer of the Royal Mint: from 1878 on
he was the managing chairman and treasurer of the University College Hospital
London.

539.1   Quoted (somewhat inaccurately) from an article on p. 5d-e.

540.1   P. 9e, quoted from an article reviewing a speech by Charles Bradlaugh (see 475.1 above).

541.1   *Vue Philosophique de la Gradation Naturelle des Formes de l'Etre
ou les essais de la Nature qui apprend à faire l'homme* (Amsterdam, 1768), by J.B.
Robinet. The quotation is Butler's translation of the French. See 476.1 above

542.1   That is, Maupertuis' *Venus physique, contenant deux dissertation,
l'une, sur l'origine des hommes et des animaux; et l'autre, sur l'origine des noirs,*
published anonymously at the Hague in 1746. The book contains a brief history
of ideas about sexual reproduction, a summary of Harvey's experiments on generation, and discussions of such subjects as heredity, foetus formation, white Negroes,
and the origin of the Black race. See note 480.1 above.

543.1   The quotation is translated from "La Philosophie de Diderot
Le Dernier Mot d'un Materialiste," pp. 695-708, by the French anti-materialist
philosopher Paul Janet (1823-1899).

544.1   Gottfried Wilhelm Leibniz (1646-1716), the German philosopher,
scientist, engineer, and encyclopedist who sought to harmonize the mechanistic
Cartesian methodology with scholastic and Aristotelean philosophy.

545.1   Rev. Mark Wilks (1831-1894), for more than 30 years the minister
of Holloway Congregational Church, one of the founders of the School Board
system in London, known for his iconoclastic and pro-Darwinian views. Butler
met him at one of Clodd's at-homes (see 451.1 above), one of several "Revolutionary Robespierrian" (Note-Books Vol. II, July 1885) he met there. In a letter
to him (May 17, 1882), Butler defends his view that T.H. Huxley, in the articles
on "Biology" and "Evolution" for the *Encyclopedia Britannica*, 9th edition, believed
in spontaneous generation but not in natural selection.

550.1   See note 524 where Butler refers to the same pages (*Works*, VII
26-27).

555.1   *The Echo*, well-known half-penny liberal evening paper published
from 1868 to 1905.

556.1   See 404.1 above.

561.1   A slightly different typed copy of this excerpt, subtitled "Genesis II," is in the Butler Collection at St. John's College; the allusion is to Gen. 1:1-4 and other Biblical passages. Henry Festing Jones, in a note (1917) appended to this copy explains that his friend, Herbert Phipson, gave or lent him a copy of the *Index* issue which Jones then showed to Butler. For Ted Jones see 511.1 above. The *Index* was a weekly paper dedicated to complete secularization, published from 1870 to 1886 in Boston and Toledo, Ohio. See issue for December 10, 1874 (vol. V, no. 259), p. 593. Butler quotes with slight alterations.

561.2   Allusion to Luke 8:10 and Mark 4:12.

561.3   In the type-written version in St. John's College Library, Lamarck is not mentioned in "verse 26"; preceding this "verse" is the following which Butler deleted: "Then arose Lamarck also a prophet of Evolution, neither would they hear him."

561.4   In the type-written version "the Unknowable" is "the Lord."

562.1   P. 10c. The article ("Frog-Development in Relation to Food") is about the effect of food, such as beef and algae, on tadpole growth.

563.1   P. 7f: an insert recording observations about a species of honey-making ants in Manitou, Colorado, similar to those found in Mexico.

564.1   By his grandfather's will Butler had a reversionary interest in the Whitehall estate at Shrewsbury, contingent upon the death of his father. Several times Butler tried to get his father to make the reversion absolute by cutting off the entail. On the last occasion, in 1879, Butler, having exhausted the finances salvaged from his disastrous Canadian investments, had argued that with absolute interest he would be able to maintain himself. Canon Butler refused but provided him with an annual allowance of £300. Then suddenly in February, 1881, his father asked him to sign a deed which in effect cut off the entail, allowing Butler to borrow the money for the purchase of leasehold property from which he was to realize a small income.

569.1   In *Alps and Sanctuaries* (1881), Butler, attacking professional schools for painters, advises students never to look at old masters, "and to consign Raffaelle, along with Plato, Marcus Aurelius Antoninus, Dante, Goethe, and two others, neither of them Englishmen, to limbo, as the Seven Humbugs of Christendom" (*Works*, VII, 135). When Butler later published the chapter in which this passage occurs ("Considerations on the Decline of Italian Art") in *Selections from Previous Works* (London: Longman, Green, and Co., 1890), he had "Beethoven" printed in small letters at the foot of the page, without a footnote number to link it to the main text (p. 301).

570.1   James 4:7: "Resist the devil, and he will flee from you."

571.1   See *The Way of All Flesh*, ch. 23.

575.1   *Henry IV*, Part I, I.ii.

575.2   *Henry IV*, Part II, V.v.

576.1   The barrister William Phipson Beale (later a baronet) (1839-1922) was a friend of both Butler and H.F. Jones. Butler met him aboard the *Prussia* in June, 1874, when he made his first voyage to Canada to investigate the Canad Tanning Extract Company (see n.1 to Butler's Preface). His wife Mary was als a close friend of both Jones and Butler. Phipson Beale introduced Butler to th botanising metal manufacturer Alfred Tyler (1824-1884) to whom *Luck or Cur ning?* (1886/7) is dedicated.

576.2   Butler describes the village of Fucine, northeast of Turin, in Chap ter 13 of *Alps and Sanctuaries* (*Works*, VII, 142-146).

576.3   "Total Eclipse" and "How Willing my Paternal Love" are from Handel's oratorio *Samson* (1741-2).

577.1   Henry and Charles Kingsley, the novelists.

580.1   The wife of Dr. Robert Ellis Dudgeon (1820-1904), homeopathist for 40 years editor of *The British Journal of Homeopathy*, inventor of "subaqueou spectacles" and a pocket sphygmograph, and Butler's personal physician. He wrot the utopian romance, *Colymbia* (obviously modeled on Butler's *Erewhon*), publishe anonymously by Trübner at the end of 1872; and *The Prolongation of Life* (1900)

584.1   A custom, practiced by barbarians of antiquity, which dictate that the father take the mother's place during her normal confinement, and becom the recipient of congratulations and solicitations usually due to the mother.

585.1   See note 503.

588.1   The keeper of the inn, St. Lawrence Hall, at St. Leonards, outsid Montreal, where Butler apparently stayed for a time. See also 123.1 above. Th Mr. Rae here referred to may be John Rae (1796-1872), author and economist for a time headmaster of a grammar school in Hamilton, Ontario.

589.1   Butler's reference here is unclear: Bulstrode is a river northeast o Montreal.

590.1   See Matt. 12:31: "All manner of sin shall be forgiven unto men but the blasphemy against the Holy Ghost shall not be forgiven unto men."

591.1   See *Works*, VII, 226-7.

592.1   *Othello*, III.iii, 155.

596.1   *Works*, IV, 39-40: a man digests his dinner "as a matter of course, unless it has been in some way unfamiliar to him, or he to it, owing to some derangement or occurrence with which he is unfamiliar, and under which therefore he is at a loss how to comport himself. . . ."

597.1   Psalm 19:1.

600.1   In the revised edition of *Erewhon* (1901), Butler added this idea to the judge's speech to the convicted consumptive (Chapter 11).

601.1   See 384.8 above.

607.1   See *The Way of All Flesh*, Chapter 5.

612.1   Matt. 10:34, and Luke 12:52.

614.1   Miss Savage encouraged him to begin *The Way of All Flesh* (1903) in the spring of 1873, shortly after the publication of *The Fair Haven* in March, 1873. See also *The Way of All Flesh*, ch. 32, where Alethea is made owner of Miss Savage's irrevence.

617.1   "My friend Jones continues very ill, & we are anxious about him, but he is certainly better today. The scarlet fever part of the story was very mild, but it has been followed by rheumatism, & other complications. . ." (*Correspondence*, 97-98: letter to May Butler, December 17, 1881). Jones caught the fever in November at Midhurst; Butler helped nurse him back to health.

620.1   See 420.1 above.

621.1   Euclid begins his *Elements* with five "common notions" and five postulates for which no proof is possible. By Butler's time such mathematicians as Wolfgang Bolyai (1775-1856) and Nikolaus Lobachewsky (1793-1856) had substituted other postulates from which sets of non-Euclidian geometries were constructed. The quoted phrase is used by Euclid to indicate conclusions that do not logically follow.

621.2   A reference to Matt. 11:29-30.

622.1   The satiric epic poem by his namesake, Samuel Butler (1613-1680).

624.1   "Everything true is beautiful." Faido, in the Canton Ticino, was usually Butler's headquarters on his holiday excursions to northern Italy.

625.1   Butler refers to Darwin's *The Formation of Vegetable Mould through the Actions of Worms with Observations on their Habits* (London: John Murray, 1881). The passages cited express Darwin's uncertainty as to whether the actions of worms (when closing their burrows with leaves, for example) are signs of a "simple reflex action," or of strong inherited instincts, or "some degree of intelligence."

625.2   Darwin claims that in plugging their holes worms are not guided by "special instincts," though they possess a "general instinct" for doing it, for they experiment until they "at last succeed in some way," thus showing a "capacity" many higher animals do not have.

625.3   *Origin of Species*, Ed. VI, 233. [Butler's note.]

625.4   *Origin*, Chapter VIII: "It can be clearly shown that the most wonderful instincts with which we are acquainted, namely, those of the hive-bees and of many ants, could not possibly have been acquired by habit."

625.5   P. 242 [Butler's note]. See *Works*, IV, 197ff.

625.6   "Professor" in original.

625.7   Butler quotes from a review of Darwin's *The Formation of Vegetable Mould. . .*, p. 2a-b.

625.8   "Lowly" in original.

625.9   "Dr." in original.

625.10   *Works*, VIII, 215-217. *Luck or Cunning?* was published at the end of 1886.

627.1   See also *The Way of All Flesh*, ch. 21 and 58.

627.2   Overscored: was visible to the eye of faith rather than that of reason.

628.1   See 404.2 above.

629.1   The allusion is to 1 John 4:19.

633.1   This is Butler's argument in *The Fair Haven* (1873).

633.2   Allusion to Psalm 90:4.

635.1   See 363.1 and 363.4 above.

637.1   Mrs. Ellen Jones (1828-1900), Jones's mother, was the only daughter of Rev. William Carmalt, headmaster of a school in Putney. She married Jones' father Thomas (1812-1869), a barrister, in 1845. Cathy (Katty) is Jones's sister. Butler disliked both, but the mother he regarded as one of the most malicious and contemptible women he had ever known. Her remark was incorporated into *The Way of All Flesh*: see ch. 11.

639.1   Angela Georgina, Baroness Burdett-Coutts (1814-1906), the well known philanthropist, principal partner of the banking firm Coutts and Company n the Strand, and grand-daughter of its co-founder Thomas Coutts. In February, 1881, she married Mr. William Ashmead-Bartlett.

641.1   This occurred during the excursion on which Jones caught scarlet fever (see note 617, and 617.1 above).

644.1   Sir Francis Bacon (1561-1626), the scientific philosopher and moralist. See chapter 9 of *The Way of All Flesh* where he refers to him as Pecksniff Bacon. "Dr." here means "debtor."

645.1   *Works*, VII, 251.

647.1   ". . . few of us can see the lightest trifle scratched off casually and idly long ago, without liking it better than almost any great thing of the same, or ever so much earlier date, done with purpose and intention that it should remain" (*Works*, VII, 211).

647.2   Bryce Wright, mineralogist and expert in precious stones, had his shop at this time in Great Russell Street; Furber is the violin-maker in Grafton Street (see 404.1 above).

649.1   An allusion to Matthew 26:11 (Mark 14:7; John 12:8).

650.1   An allusion to Matthew 18:7 (Luke 17:1).

654.1   See 443.1 above.

655.1   March, 1877, p. 1 ("Prefatory Sonnet"):
            Those that of late had fleeted far and fast
            To touch all shores, now leaving to the skill
            Of others their old craft seaworthy still,
            Have charter'd this; where, mindful of the past,
            Our true co-mates regather round the mast,
            Of diverse tongue, but with a common will
            Here, in this roaring moon of daffodil
            And crocus, to put forth and brave the blast. . . .

656.1   Herbert Edwin Clarke (1852-1912), a clerk in the firm of A.L. Elder & Co. (the firm had dealings with New Zealand imports), poet and short story writer. Butler had met him through Jones whose college friend John Elder was the son of the firm's head.

656.2   The book was thus issued by David Bogue in November 1881, though both sets bear the date 1882.

666.1   See 363.1 above. Compare this note to conclusion of note 384 and note 679.

668.1   "Some do indeed preach Christ even of envy and strife; and some
also of good will. . . . What then? notwithstanding, every way, whether in pretence
or in truth. Christ is preached; and I therein do rejoice, yea, and will rejoice."

670.1   See 327.1 above.

670.2   Robert Burton's *The Anatomy of Melancholy* (1621); Bishop
Joseph Butler's *The Analogy of Religion Natural and Revealed, to the Constitution
and Course of Nature* (1736), a well-known defense of Christianity against Deists.

673.1   In Yorkshire.

674.1   Butler refers to the time when his family still lived at Langar Rec
tory. Job Heathcote was a miller from nearby Bingham who died in February
1882, aged 65.

679.1   See note 666.

681.1   Act I, "I am the Captain of the *Pinafore*."

684.1   It is unclear who Patty Roscoe was, but is certain to have been
related to Richard Roscoe (1833-92), a London solicitor whose first wife was Honora
Worsley (1837-79), the daughter of Butler's uncle Philip Worsley (see 222.1), and
thus his cousin Reginald's sister (Amy is Reginald's daughter: see 430.1). Mr. Ros
coe's second wife was Charlotte Wicksteed (born in 1855), daughter of the Rev
Charles Wicksteed, a Unitarian minister. Honora was Mrs. R.S. Garnett's mother.

687.1   From "Canonical Books of the Buddhists," p. 3d, where this saying
is cited.

689.1   Butler embarked for New Zealand on the *Roman Emperor*, clear
ing Gravesend on October 1. He developed his doubts when, as lay assistant at St
James's, Piccadilly (see 344.1 above), he could not distinguish between the behavior
of his baptized and unbaptized pupils. On the voyage out he read Edward Gibbon's
Decline and Fall of the Roman Empire (1774-81).

691.1   Jonah 2:1-10; Daniel 4:14-30.

695.1   Radley School, Abingdon, which Jones attended from 1865 to
1869.

697.1   Henry Latham (1821-1902), from 1848 to 1888 fellow of Trinity
Hall, Cambridge (Jones's College), and Master from 1888 to his death.

700.1   See Matthew 4:1-11.

701.1   A slum dwelling, not far from Clifford's Inn, of the kind described
in Dickens' *Bleak House*, Chapter 1.

705.1   "I remember in one monastery [in northern Italy] . . . the novice taught me how to make sacramental wafers, and I played him Handel on the organ as well as I could. I told him that Handel was a Catholic; he said he could tell that by his music at once. There is no chance of getting among our scientists this way" (*Works*, VII, 51).

707.1   See notes 416 and 417. On p. 147 Spenser points out that the substance of mind can not be known, since this substance itself changes when acted upon; cognition is consequently an unseparable interrelationship between a "something acted upon" and "something acting upon it." Section 13 of *The Principles of Biology* (London: Williams and Norgate, 1880) deals with the effects of undulations or waves of various kinds (heat or light) on chemical compounds.

713.1   Henry Brett and Co., Old Furnivall's distillery, 26 and 27 High Holborn.

717.1   This quotation and those in note 718 are found in "Baboo-English," *Times*, April 11, 1882, p. 8c-e. The source of the quotation in note 717 is an Anglo-Indian newspaper article about Sir George Campbell, former Lieutenant-Governor of Bengal.

718.1   Extract from a Calcutta newspaper.

718.2   This is a biography (1876) of a member of the High Court of India, written by Chindronauth Mookerjee.

719.1   Jean-Baptiste Lamarck (1744-1829), the French naturalist who in his chief work, *Philosophie Zoologique* (1809) outlined the theory of evolution. Butler summarizes Lamarck's theory, based as his own, on the principle of inherited habit, in *Evolution Old and New* (1879).

719.2   P. 9c-e.

719.3   The anonymous treatise, *The Vestiges of the Natural History of Creation* (1844), written by Robert Chambers, presents a bold if derivative theory of evolution. By 1846 it had gone through five editions, eleven by 1860.

719.4   Edward Gibbon (1737-1794), whose *The History of the Decline and Fall of the Roman Empire* (1774-81) Butler read on his voyage out to New Zealand.

719.5   Darwin wrote two monographs on the sub-class Cirripedia, published in London by the Ray Society in 1851 and 1854.

719.6   P. 9e-f.

719.7   April 21, 1882, p. 4f-g: The *Origin* "closes with a beautiful and devout expression of belief in divine wisdom that orders the life of the world. But in spite of Darwin's simple faith, his views were twisted by unwise men."

719.8   The enlarged second edition was published in 1882. In the Preface (dated April 21, 1882) Butler wrote: "It being still possible for me to refer to this event in a preface, I hasten to say how much it grates upon me to appear to renew my attack upon Mr. Darwin under the present circumstances" (*Works*, V, xiii). In the Appendix Butler included excerpts from reviews of the first edition which all record Butler as a fool for wishing to give some credit for the theory of evolution to Darwin's forerunners.

719.9   Leader, p. 11f.

719.10   Vol. XXV, p. 597: "Charles Darwin."

719.11   "In *Life and Habit* I said: 'To the end of time, if the question be asked, Who taught people to believe in Evolution?' the answer must be that it was Mr. Darwin. This is true; and it is hard to see what palm of higher praise can be awarded to any philosopher" (*Works*, V, xiii).

719.12   "Mr. Darwin's Work," p. 5b-6a.

719.13   P. 5a-b. Butler wrote to object to the *Gazette's* hostile review of *Unconscious Memory* (1880) in which the identification of instinct and heredity with memory is dismissed on grounds that it had been developed in Spencer's work on psychology (see 416.1 above). In the letter Butler challenged the writer to refer to passages in *Principles of Psychology* where Spencer develops this identification.

719.14   Frederick Greenwood (1830-1918), journalist and editor of the *St. James's Gazette* from 1880 to 1891, formerly editor of the *Pall Mall Gazette* until its owners (in 1880) decided to turn it into a radical paper.

719.15   The naturalist Alfred Russell Wallace (1823-1913) sent Darwin his MS. of a fully developed theory of evolution exactly like the one Darwin was at the time (June, 1858) still setting down. Wallace consented to Darwin's proposal that his MS., and a sketch Darwin had made of his theory in 1844, be published together by the Linnean Society in order to establish the priority of both their claims. The two papers were read and published in 1858 without causing the slightest stir. It was the geologist Sir Charles Lyell (1797-1875) who urged Darwin to write the *Origin*.

719.16   In the Introduction to the *Origin*.

720.1   The Bishop of Carlisle, Dr. Harvey Goodwin (see 400.1 above) preached Darwin's funeral sermon on May 1, 1882 in Westminster Abbey, on the text of Colossians 2:10. It began: "It is always difficult and delicate to speak concerning the departed; besides the well-known maxim which tells us that we should say concerning the dead nothing but what is good, there is the duty also of saying nothing but what is true, what is necessary, what is wise, and what is profitable." Butler wrote his father that to begin this way "was rather hot" (*Family Letters*; p. 210: letter of May 22, 1882). The Latin proverb here alluded to (from Diogenes

Laertius) translates "Speak no evil of the dead but only what is good."

721.1   Sir William Thackeray Marriott (1834-1903) received his B.A., like Butler, in 1858. He was ordained deacon, but in 1862, after refusing orders, began to study law instead, and was called to the bar in 1864. He stood as a Liberal for Brighton in 1880, was elected but quarreled with Liberal policy; he successfully ran as a Conservative in 1884 and remained an M.P. until 1893. Under Lord Salisbury's two terms as Prime Minister he was judge advocate general; he was knighted in 1888. In a letter to his father (May 7, 1882) Butler wrote: "I saw Marriott. . . a few days ago. He said to me 'I shan't join the Conservatives'--and then added 'not *yet*.' Which I think means that he would be very glad to do so on the first chance. I do not like him, but he is an able man. [I don't believe he is. S.B. 1901]" *Family Letters*, p. 208.

721.2   See 215.1 above.

722.1   Henry Crabb Robinson (1775-1867), barrister of the Middle Temple, one of London's leading intellectual lights, a founder of the *Athenaeum Club* (1824) and of University College, London (1826), a close friend of Wordsworth, Coleridge, Lamb, Southey, and Goethe (he had studied and travelled in Germany from 1800 to 1807). During the later years of his life he regularly invited friends, most of them quite distinguished, to Sunday morning breakfasts and occasional dinner parties at his residence in Russell Square. Robinson distributed his entire library among these friends.

722.2   Richard Worsley, brother of Butler's favorite cousin Reggie; Sir George Scharf (1820-1895), first secretary of the National Portrait Gallery (opened in 1859); its director from 1882 to 1895; John Pattison of the Middle Temple, a judge of the Queen's Bench; George Edmond Street (1824-1881), well-known architect, designer of the new law courts in the Strand.

722.3   See 222.1 above. Butler's uncle Philip lived in Gordon Square at this time (in the 1860's).

722.4   *Italy, a Poem*, in two parts, by Samuel Rogers (1763-1855), published anonymously at first in 1822 and 1828 respectively. The 1830 edition of the complete poem is illustrated with engravings by Turner. See 722.1 above.

723.1   In reviewing natural philosophers in his *Temporis Partus Masculus* (1653), Francis Bacon dismissed the work of the English Franciscan Roger Bacon (1214-1294) (which stood under the influence of hermetic philosophy), along with that of Paracelsus and Severinus, even though all three "in their chance ramblings hit upon some useful things. . . and manage by a mechanical skill to arrive at continuing inventions" (quoted in F.H. Anderson, *The Philosophy of Francis Bacon* [Chicago: University of Chicago Press, 1948], 108).

724.1   Mrs. Elizabeth Geldart (1809-1883), wife of Thomas Charles Geldart (1797-1877), barrister and Master of Trinity Hall from 1852 to his death. Edward Anthony Beck (1848-1916), also a barrister whom Jones knew while at Trinity Hall, was a fellow of the College from 1871 to 1902, its Master (1902-1916), as

337

well as its Vice-Chancellor (1902-06).

725.1   See 724.1 above. Dickens' son was of course Henry Fielding Dickens (1849-1933), who had matriculated at Trinity College in 1868, and would eventually become a barrister.

726.1   Cf. Heb. 11:5 and 2 Kings 2:11.

727.1   Caroline Fox (1819-1871) the daughter of a prominent, wealthy Quaker family (they ran a shipping company, G.C. Fox & Company) who from age 16 kept a journal in which many Victorian worthies are sketched, published posthumously as *Memories of Old Friends, Being Extracts from the Journals and Letters of Caroline Fox of Penjerrick, Cornwall, from 1835-1871* (ed. Horace N. Pym) in 1882. Butler quotes an entry for February 18, 1847. Barclay was her brother Robert Barclay Fox (1817-1855) who also kept a journal and was a friend of J.S. Mill and Thomas Carlyle.

727.2   In original: and heard of it at

728.1   "Mr. Darwin on Earth-Worms," *Fraser's Magazine,,* n.s., XXVI (January, 1882), 46-51: the article is a discussion of the habits of worms in which Paley describes his own studies of worms to corroborate (with occasional demurrers and without the customary tone of deference), some of Darwin's findings. Frederick Apthorp Paley (1815-1888), a Johnian (B.A., 1838), sometime tutor at Cambridge, was a classical scholar with an interest in botany and archeology. He became a Roman Catholic in 1846, and later taught classics at the Catholic University College, Kensington. He was a grandson of the 18th century divine William Paley and had attended Shrewsbury School under Dr. Butler to whom he was related (his mother, an Apthorp, was the sister of Dr. Butler's wife).

728.2   "Charles Darwin: A Farewell Offering," pp. 322-331.

729.1   Mrs. Mary Bather, eldest sister of Butler's father, second wife of Rev. Edward Bather (1779-1847), Vicar of Meole Brace near Shrewsbury. Canon Butler was his curate until 1834, when he removed to Langar. Aunt Bather was Butler's favorite aunt; he visited her regularly while at Shrewsbury School. She played the piano and introduced him to Handel's music, and left him four volumes of Clarke's edition of Handel (see 390.4 above).

729.2   The first quotation concludes Chapter XXI (XXIII of the revised edition); the second is found in Chapter XX (XXI, revised edition).

730.1   Richard Worsley (see 722.2 above).

730.2   Butler's father wrote (in the Preface to *A First Year in Canterbury Settlement* [1863]) that after having paid for his berth "important alterations were made in the arrangements of the vessel, in order to make room for some stock which was being sent out to the Canterbury Settlement. The space left for the accommodations of the passengers being curtailed, and the comforts of the voyage seeming likely to be much diminished, the writer was most providentially induced to change his ship, and, a few weeks later, secured a berth in another vessel" (*Works*, I, 63).

731.1   In *Histoire naturelle des Oiseaux* by Georges-Louis Leclerc Buffon (1707-1788), the French naturalist (and Linnaeus's opponent): "Dans l'homme où tout doit être jugement et raison, le sens du toucher est plus parfait que dans l' animal où il y a moins de jugement que le sentiment. . . ." (Paris: Imprimerie Royale, 1771), 2. Butler quoted from *Histoire Naturelle* in his *Evolution Old and New* (1879) to show that Buffon had developed a consistent theory of evolution.

735.1   Frederic Galland Sykes (c. 1832-1912), who received his B.A. from St. John's College, Cambridge in 1857, eventually became the Vicar of Dunsforth, Yorkshire (1865-1911). Butler used to go to his rooms, where on one occasion he met the composer Sir William Sterndale Bennett (1816-1875) (*Memoir*, I, 49-50).

735.2   Incidentally, Mendelssohn, inspired by the Taylor sisters, Susan, Honora, and Anne (Butler's aunt Philip: see 530.1 above), dedicated three piano fantasies to each of them; he considered them among his best piano compositions. The sisters met Mendelssohn when he stayed at the Taylor home Coed Du, near Honeywell in Flintshire, in September, 1829.

735.3   This might be Mrs. Miriam Longden, wife of Rev. William George Longden (1836-1898), fellow of Queen's College, Cambridge, from 1860 to 1872.

735.4   Rev. Cornwall Smalley (1814-1888), a fellow Johnian (B.A., 1837), the curate of St. Matthew's Chapel in Bayswater from 1859 to 1867.

739.1   Antonio Rosmini-Serbati (1797-1855), Italian philosopher, and Roman Catholic priest, founder (1839) of the Institute of the Brethren of Charity, known as the Rosminian fathers, who had a novitiate in England (Wadhurst, Sussex). After the publication of *Alps and Sanctuaries* (1881), Butler came to know the Rosminians at Ely Place, Holburn (see notes 765 and 773); their Italian brethren maintained the sanctuaries at St. Michele which Butler had described in his book. To Miss Savage he wrote (letter of February 24, 1882) that he was "flirting hard" with the Rosminians (*Letters*, p. 273).

739.2   Thomas Davidson, *The Philosophical System of Antoine Rosmini-Serbati* (London: Kegan, Paul, Tench Co., 1882). Rosmini, as a philosophical opponent of Kant and Hegel, attempted to base his system not on logic so much as on the "facts of consciousness": "Rosmini cordially agrees with Kant and his school. . . in holding that 'all our knowledge begins with experience'; but he finds grave faults with them for not clearly showing what they mean by experience" (p. 10). Butler apparently wrote a review once of a work by Rosmini, but it has not been found.

743.1   That is, a simple unknown by a complicated greater unknown.

753.1   "Inequality among Individuals," p. 10e: the article reports on the findings of a study of differences among individuals of the same sex, in primitive and civilised societies. "But the rule is that the equality and similarity of individuals which characterize inferior races diminish with the progress of civilisation. . . . [there are greater differences] among the older than among the younger of animals and men. . . among the strong than among the weak."

754.1   "Charles Darwin," by John Fiske, *Atlantic Monthly*, pp. 835-845: a fulsome appraisal of Darwin (placing him next to Aristotle, Newton, and Descartes) and the *Origin* (before its publication no opinion deserving the name "scientific hypothesis" had been advanced on the subject"). The article in the *Monthly Journal of Science* is referred to in note 728. "Newton and Darwin," by R.A. Proctor, in the *Contemporary Review*, pp. 994-1002: Darwin's theory has the same relation to biology as Newton's laws of gravity have to astronomy; both Newton and Darwin have extended man's conception of natural law.

758.1   Inaccurately quoted from Diderot's *Histoire Naturelle des Oiseaux*. See 731.1 above.

760.1   The issue for June 3, p. 7f.

765.1   Father William Lockhart (1819-1892), who received his B.A. from Exeter College, Oxford (1842), was the first of the Tractarians to "go over" to the Catholic Church in 1843. John Henry Newman, whom Lockhart had joined at Littlemore in 1842, condemned his decision at the time. From 1843 to 1845, Lockhart (a kinsman incidentally of Sir Walter Scott's son-in-law) studied under the Rosminians in Rome (see 739.1 above), joined the order in 1845, and worked in the Order's mission field in England. When the church of St. Etheldreda's in Ely Place, Holborn was put up for sale, he bought and refurbished it. It was reopened for worship in 1879, and Lockhart remained as Rector of the Church until his death. Butler met him sometime in June, 1882 when, in response to his description in *Alps and Sanctuaries* (1881) of St. Michele (a sanctuary kept by the Rosminians), he was invited to dine at St. Etheldreda's refectory (*Memoir*, I, 374).

765.2   Lord Frederick Cavendish (1836-1882), a prominent official in the Liberal government, was appointed chief secretary to Earl Spencer, the Lord Lieutenant of Ireland, in May of 1882. Thomas Burke (1829-1882) was the Under-Secretary for Ireland since 1869. Both men were stabbed to death in Phoenix Park, Dublin, by a clandestine group called "The Invincibles," on May 6, the day Cavendish was sworn in.

771.1   "The Marriage of Giovanni Arnolfini and Giovanna Genanni" by the Dutch painter Jan van Eyck (c. 1390-1441). The National Gallery acquired the painting in 1842. The husband, wearing a large black hat, is holding the hand of his bethrothed. Aunt Worsley is probably his "Aunt Philip" Worsley who died in 1877 (see 468.1 above).

773.1   Fr. Lockhart was a close friend of John Henry Newman (see 765.1 above) who in 1870 published the *Essay in Aid of a Grammar of Assent*, detailing the philosophical method underlying belief in the Catholic Christian faith. For Ely

Place, see 765.1 above.

781.2   From the Vulgate: *"Quis novit si spiritus filiorum Adam ascendat sursum, et si spiritus jumentorum descendat deorsum."* See 258.2 above.

775.1   See 739.2 above. Thomas Davidson (1840-1900), philosopher and teacher of classics, a Scott by birth, emigrated to the United State and founded the "Breadwinner's College," a New York City settlement for Russian Jews, and the Fellowship of the New Life, a society for promoting the development of the "inner" man. Though no Catholic, he was influenced by Rosmini's philosophy. Fr. Lockhart had edited the translation of a life of Rosmini in 1856 and was to edit yet another in 1886.

781.1   A popular novel by the novelist and journalist Walter Besant (1836-1901).

782.1   The famous Italian actress Adelaide Ristori (1822-1906) played the title-role in a translation of Paolo Giacometti's *Elizabeth, Queen of England* (1853) at the Drury Lane Theatre during July, 1882. Harry Nicholls (1852-1926), burlesque actor, principal comedian for fourteen years at Drury Lane, author of numerous pantomimes, farces, and comic songs, played Davison, Keeper of the Seal. Ristori alternated this play with *Macbeth*, playing Lady Macbeth, Nicholls playing the third witch. (Butler, according to his own biographical chronology in Volume III, saw both plays in July.) In the previous month, Nicholls had appeared as Mrs. Sinbad in *Sinbad, the Sailor: or The Tar that was "Pitched" Into*, a burlesque by Frank W. Green produced at the Royalty Theatre. In *Sinbad the Sailor* by E.L. Blanchard, one of the popular Drury Lane Christmas pantomimes (performed both in 1882 and 1883), Nicholls played Professor Hanki-Panki.

783.1   Sophie Amelia Prosser (1808-1882), Charles Dibdin's daughter, contributed regularly in *Leisure Hours* and *Sunday at Home* during the last years of her life; she was author of several children's books, such as *Original Fables and Sketches* (1864) and *Cicely Brown's Trails* (1871), most of them published by the Religious Tract Society. Her husband was the Rev. William Prosser, Vicar of Asby Folville, Leicester.

784.1   Butler was in Shrewsbury from the 25th to the 29th of July to attend the formal opening on July 28th of the new buildings of Shrewsbury School (the subject of the next five notes). In the 1860's the old school had been judged by a Royal Commission to be in need of improvements. Some 27 acres of land at Kingland, Shrewsbury, were purchased (some of it belonging to Butler by virtue of his entail) and plans for an entirely new set of buildings drawn up. The opening, attended by "old Salopians," many of them distinguished, began with Holy Communion at St. Mary's Church at 8 a.m. (since the new chapel had not been completed), followed by the morning service at 11:30 during which the sermon was delivered by the Bishop of Manchester. After a luncheon the assemblage moved to the Corn Exchange where speeches were held and school prizes distributed. The celebration came to a close in the evening with the annual school concert in the Music Hall. Butler's father read the first lesson during the morning service; the celebrant at Holy Communion was Butler's cousin, Thomas B. Lloyd (see 313.1 above), Vicar of St. Mary's.

784.2   "If you're anxious for to shine," Act I of Gilbert and Sullivan's *Patience* (1881).

784.3   Henry Whitehead Moss (1841-1917), headmaster of Shrewsbury from 1866 to 1908, a position he inherited from Dr. Kennedy (see 207.1 above) whose pupil he had been. Moss attended St. John's College, Cambridge, graduated as Senior classics and was elected a fellow.

785.1   From the Morning Prayer Service, after the Lord's Prayer.

786.1   George Augustus Chichester May (1815-1892), barrister, and the Lord Chief Justice of Ireland from 1877 to 1887.

786.2   Canon Edward James Geoffrey Hornby (1818-1888?), Rector of Bury, Lancashire, from 1850 on. After leaving Shrewsbury, he attended Merton College, Oxford, and received his B.A. in 1839, his M.A. in 1843.

787.1   James Fraser (1818-1885), who studied under Dr. Butler and Dr. Kennedy, an authority in educational affairs, was Bishop of Manchester from 1870 to his death. In his sermon he criticized the purely utilitarian view of education: "The cry is, 'Give us what will pay, and pay immediately. Give us that education for our children which will turn them out at the earliest age with the largest amount of practical knowledge, convertible with the least possible delay in coin.' Horace tells us that boys trained on this system will never become poets. They will never become what Pericles boldly says every Athenian citizen became--'able to play the greatest number of parts in the state with the happiest appropriateness.'"

788.1   Henry Cardogan Rothery (1817-1888), one of the top boys Dr. Butler left at Shrewsbury when he retired from the Headmastership in 1836. He practised law in both ecclesiastical and admiralty court and was the Commissioner of Wrecks from 1876 to 1888. For the Butler-Darwin quarrel, see note 363, and 363.2 above.

790.1   Found in *Twelve Voluntaries and Fugues for the Organ or Harpsichord with Rules for Tuning by the celebrated Mr. Handel*, Book IV (London: Longman & Brodsnip, Music Sellers to the Royal Family, n.d.). It contains rules for tuning in mean temperament, the eight chords going up in fifths from C to E major, and down from F to E flat major. The copy of this volume in the British Library has Butler's signature on the title-page, and the following note below the rules: "These rules were shown by my friend H.F. Jones to the late W.S. Rockstro [see 190.1 above], who said they were those of the mean tone temperaments. S.B. December 17, 1901." For Butler the fact that Handel played and composed in mean temperament was crucial, for it prevented him from mixing his diatonic style with the chromatic style which well-tempered tuning made possible.

791.1   That is, George Darwin. See 384.7 above.

791.2   Issues for November 24 and December 1, pp. 79-82 and pp. 103-107 respectively. "A Glimpse through the Corridors of Time," by Prof. Robert S. Ball (Royal Astronomer of Ireland, professor of astronomy in the University of Dublin), is a lecture delivered in 1881 in Birmingham. He considers George Darwin the discoverer of "tidal evolution," the concept that the length of day is influenced by the moon's motion. Darwin took exception to some of Prof. Ball's deductions in the January 5 issue (pp. 213-14).

791.3   The first letter (January 5, 1882, p. 217), signed by A. Dupré, explains that Kant dealt with the influence of tidal actions in a lecture of 1754, a century before "any of the authorities mentioned by Prof. Ball." Huxley replied (January 12, p. 241): in his 1869 address as President of the Geological Society he had given credit to Kant's work, and the book-buying public has no excuse for overlooking it. A critique of Darwin's reply to Ball (791.2) appeared in another issue to which Darwin, however, did respond without mentioning the subject of covert attribution.

792.1   The Lombard painter Bernardino Luini (c. 1480-1532) was one of Butler's favorites, though an imitator of da Vinci's style. He and another Butler favorite, Gaudenzio Ferrari (534.1 above), were for a time students under Stefano Scotto who ran a school in Milan "more or less a rival to that of Leonardo da Vinci" (*Works*, IX, 76). Butler refers to "Noé deriso da Cain."

793.1   This episode occurred the night of Jones's arrival at the Albergo Riposo at Varese, in August 1878 (see *Memoir*, I, 281-283). Butler's reply broke the ice between the two.

793.2   Marcus Aurelius Antoinus (121-180), Roman Emperor (161-180) and stoic philosopher. The reference is to the *Meditations*, I. 17.

794.1   The New Law Courts were opened on December 7, 1882; both men were knighted in ceremonies at Windsor Castle: Thomas Paine (1822-1908), senior member of Paine & Layton, Solicitors, at Gresham House (see 360.1 above), the firm to which Jones had been articled; Sir Thomas, in Butler's words, "shunted" him off to another firm in 1878 (Withall & Co.). Sir Francis Roxburgh (1820-1891), barrister, was another member of the firm and became Queen's Counsel in 1866, a Bencher in 1867.

797.1   Butler had left for northern Italy in August (1882) of this year, and was trapped in Verona during the heavy flooding in September which washed out all but one bridge and immobilized the railroad.

799.1   P. 2a: This letter to a Jena University student had been quoted in a lecture by Prof. Ernst Haeckel (a friend of Darwin's and his champion in Germany) at the Natural Science Congress in Eisenach, Germany; a correspondent sent a translation of it to the *Gazette*. It is dated June 5, 1879: in it Darwin explains that "Science and Christ have nothing to do with each other" except to make one cautious; that he believes no revelation has been given man, and that everyone must decide about the future life from "vague and contradictory probabilities."

801.1   See 425.1 above.

802.1   "It is art to hide art" (Ovid, *Ars Amatoriae*, II. 213).

803.1   See 430.1 above.

814.1   Philip Worsley of Bristol (1834-1917) was the eldest son of the elder Philip Worsley (see 222.1); in the summer of 1861 he married Anna Taylor, who died at Torquay in February, 1906. Her mother cannot be identified, though apparently she was related to the Taylor family branch to which Philip's mother (née Taylor; see 468.1 above) belonged. The younger Philip helped H.F. Jones draw up the Worsley--Butler pedigree for the *Memoir* (I, 17), in which neither his wife Anna nor Reginald's (his brother's) wife is listed. For Amy, see 430.1 above. The younger Philip was a member of the Bristol Naturalist's Society, and head of a firm manufacturing alkali. The couple had two sons. Butler's relation with this cousin ended with the marriage.

815.1   The reference is to Sir Walter Scott's narrative poem, *The Lady of the Lake* (1810).

818.1   See 170.1 above.

820.1   John Nicholas Trübner (1817-1884), author, editor, and translator, was the head of the publishing firm on Ludgate Hill that had brought out *Erewhon* and *Life and Habit* (1876).

820.2   David Bogue (he died in 1897), the publisher at 3 St. Martin's Place (originally in partnership with Robert Hardwicke) was declared bankrupt in June, 1885. After Trübner had insulted Butler about the failure of *Life and Habit*, he went over to Bogue, who then published (at Butler's expense) *Evolution Old and New* (1879; 1882); *Unconscious Memory* (1880), and *Alps and Sanctuaries* (1881). Bogue had offered Butler £100 for the latter, but backed down when it had been completed. When Bogue's firm failed, Trübner "begged me, almost with tears in his eyes, to come back to him, which I did, remaining with that firm till it became a limited liability company" (*Memoir*, I, 294). Longman published Butler's three Homeric books and his edition of Shakespeare's sonnets.

820.3   i.e., "a man of one book."

823.1   Mrs. Boss's bigamous son.

823.2   i.e., Butler's cousin Reginald.

824.1   Butler purchased his camera lucida in Paris in September on his way home from Verona (see 797.2 above) as an aid for making sketches. ("What a lot of time I wasted over that camera lucida to be sure!" he wrote on a letter to Miss Savage [*Memoir*, I, 377].) The Cock "ale-house," frequented by such worthies as Samuel Johnson and W.M. Thackeray, stood then at 201 Fleet Street, but was torn down in 1887 to make room for a branch office of the Bank of England. It appears to have stood exposed because of the construction of the New Law

Courts practically next door, and its demolition seemed imminent. Soon after its destruction a new Cock tavern was erected across the street, at No. 22.

824.2   Tennyson, while living in London in the 1830's, used to frequent the Cock to consume his "pint of port." His poem, "Will Waterproof's Lyrical Monologue" (supposedly "made at the Cock"), published in 1842, made the tavern notable. It begins:

> O plump head-waiter at The Cock,
> To which I must resort
> How goes the Time?

The waiter was apparently displeased by the poem.

825.1   See *In Memoriam* (1850), xxvii, 15-16.

826.1   The prayer is from the Communion Ceremony.

830.1   The highest peak (3,279 ft.) in the Glyder Range, North Wales.

830.2   The Butler family's man-servant, called "William Williams, the Butler's butler."

830.3   He brought them on his return from his holidays (referred to in note 793) in September, 1878.

831.1   "Speech of Animals," *Journal of Science*, January, 1883, p. 1-7: the point made is that birds, the parrot for example, do connect sounds to specific outer events; in the case of apes, comprehension of speech will be merely a matter of intelligent training.

833.1   Butler usually ordered his meat on his way to the British Museum, and though buying most of it elsewhere, he occasionally bought cooked meat and some round in Mrs. Lucy Ann French's shop in 61 Fetter Lane.

834.1   See 258.1 above.

837.1   Allusion to Lord Byron's "Destruction of Sennachireb": "The Assyrians came down like a wolf on the fold. . . ."

839.1   See 45.1 above.

839.2   The comment following the date is in Butler's hand and appears to be a later addition to the note.

841.1   The Winter Exhibition of 1883 at the Royal Academy featured the work of both Dante Gabriel Rossetti (born 1828) and John Linnell (born 1792); they had died in April and January, 1882, respectively.

841.2   Henry Wallis (1830-1916) was influenced by the Pre-Raphaelites early in his career and painted the well-known "The Death of Chatterton" (1856).

He was a regular exhibitor at the Royal Academy from 1854 to 1877. In 1872, Butler met Rossetti at his London home, shortly after the publication of *Erewhon* (during Butler's brief lionhood). He wrote Miss Savage that he disliked Rossetti's "face and his manner and his work, and I hate his poetry and friends. He is wrapped up in self-conceit and lives upon adulation" (*Memoir*, I, 164: letter of September 23, 1872). In a letter of March 15th, 1883, he wrote her that Rossetti's pictures "have made me so angry that I cannot see any good in them at all" (*Memoir*, I, 383). He had met Wallis in January, 1867, liked him then, but changed his mind at this 1872 meeting. The third person was the Pre-Raphaelite painter William Bell Scott (1811-1890) whom Butler did not object to.

844.1   Thomas Butler, born in 1837, attended Warwick School, and St. John's College, but left under mysterious circumstances. He was a heavy drinker. He married a poor Welsh girl, Henrietta ("Etta") Rigby, but often disappeared for a month at a time, eventually abandoning her and their four children whom Canon Butler then supported. In 1880 Thomas was discovered living in Brussels with a prostitute. He died on Corsica in November, 1884, though the death was not heard of until early 1885. Butler was at least on friendly terms with him until after 1871. In a letter to his father (November 26, 1881), Butler wrote that none of the family should communicate with Tom, and that his sister May particularly should recognize him only as "a disgrace to us all who is to be put aside once and for all, and with whom no words are to be bandied " (*Family Letters*, 194).

846.   Butler refers to Turner's "Tintagel Castle, Cornwall" (1822).

849.   The Cheviot Hills form a mountainous range along the border of Scotland and England.   Chiltern   Hundreds is a section of Buckinghamshire over which an appointed stewart held sway to seize robbers who hid away in the Chiltern Hills. Since 1750 this stewartship has been a sinecure, retained by the Chancellor of the Exchequer, to be applied for when an M.P. desires to resign his post. Members of Parliament are forbidden by law to resign directly.

852.1   The medical physiologist Andrew Wilson (1852-1912), lecturer on Physiology and Health to the George Combe Trust, brought out two books on evolution in 1882: *Leaves from a Naturalist's Note-Book*, and *Chapters on Evolution*. The Christmas, 1882 issue of *The Graphic* (p. 2) reprints one of his lectures entitled "A Few Words Concerning the Care of the Skin and Complexion." In it he warns against fancy scented soaps and recommends Pear's "as a satisfactory and scientifically prepared article," declared by several scientific authorities to be "a pure soap, well calculated to cleanse and purify the skin."

855.1   Miss Helen M. Johnson, since girlhood a friend of Miss Savage's, had been a student at Heatherley's art school, and at one time directed a drawing class. She lived alone at this time in Gower Street, her parents, brother and sister being dead; after 1882 she moved to Leigh, near Tonbridge. Butler described her as "a dear good silly little chirrupy lady artist with a spinal complaint that gave her at times excruciating pain, and in the end killed her, a year or two, or it might be rather more, after Miss Savage's death [February 22, 1885] " (*Letters*, p. 285, see also p. 395). She exhibited her paintings, chiefly landscapes, at various London societies between 1865 and 1881.

346

856.1   See 363.4 above.

856.2   See note 578.

859.1   Samuel Butler (1612-1680). When the first portion of the poem was published in 1663, he emerged for a brief period from the obscurity of his profession as clerk and secretary; his subsequent literary efforts did not secure him the preferments he had hoped for, and he died in relative obscurity and poverty. See note 1226.

860.1   2 Cor. 19: "For ye suffer fools gladly, seeing ye yourselves are wise."

862.1   Butler refers to his brother Tom (see 844.1 above). The little-go was a preliminary examination at Cambridge.

864.1   Butler refers to the Amsterdam Ship Canal, built between 1865 and 1876; it restored Amsterdam's importance as a commercial port.

865.1   Butler deleted this note following note 865; "unfair" is written next to it:

DR. JOHNSON

The worst thing I know about him is that he left all his money to a black servant.

869.1   Miss Cornelia Knight (c. 1757-1837), poetess, lady companion to Princess Charlotte from 1806 to 1814, when the Prince Regent dismissed her. She returned to the Continent, lived in France, Italy, and Germany, and died in Paris. As a Tory and Bourbonite, she was a favorite friend of France's Charles X who was deposed in 1830. Pius VI, who reigned from 1775 to his death in 1799, opposed the anti-ecclesiastical measures both of Emperor Joseph II and of the French Revolution. He lost much of the papal state and was incarcerated by the French and deported to Valence. The papers of Dr. Butler (see 313.1 above)--those, that is, Butler did not destroy while writing the biography of his grandfather (*The Life and Letters of Dr. Samuel Butler* [1896]) are now in the British Library.

870.1   See Chapter III and XII.

871.1   In the MS. Butler overscored this note that was to follow:

THESE NOTES

do in a way contain a sort of narrative--for some of them got set down soon after the event with which they deal, and so there is a certain chronological relation between them. At the same time I am posting up the accumulated notes of years and a note many years old will come next one of the last week, or half a dozen pages of eight or nine years old notes will come together, and then be followed by recent ones. When I have come to the end of the old notes--which will not be for some time--then those that follow will be chronological. Suppose Shakespeare to have done something of the kind with his sonnets--writing new ones as he wanted them, and tinkering up old ones in between whiles. I don't think this was the way in which they got so mixed, but it is one out of the many ways in which they might have done so.

Butler wrote "See Vol. V, p. 115" at the head of this note, to refer to his note on the Shakespeare Sonnets, found in the volume on p. 116 (dated December 21, 1896). Butler rearranged the sonnets sequence in 1898, and published the arrangement in his *Shakespeare's Sonnets Reconsidered* (1899).

873.1   Butler refers to Chapter 17, "Shadows of the Coming Race" of George Eliot's *Theophrastus Such* (1879), which does bear some resemblance to Chapters 21-22 of *Erewhon* (1872) (23-24 of the revised edition). For Darwin's *Erasmus Darwin* (1879), see 363.2 above.

873.2   *The Coming Race*, published anonymously late in 1871 by Edward Bulwer-Lytton (1803-1873). Butler believed the enthusiasm which greeted *Erewhon* in March, 1872--it remained anonymous until 1873--was due to a suspicion that it formed the sequel to Lord Lytton's popular utopian romance.

875.1   Probably Robert Doncaster, second husband of Mrs. Doncaster, Butler's laundress (see 182.1 above). He was half-witted and did odd jobs for Butler.

876.1   The reference is to the apostles' regard for Christ's healing power (Mark 7:37).

877.1   The bill for the 1882 Christmas pantomime advertise the "Grand Procession of the Kings and Queens of England, from William the Conqueror to the Present Day, and Historical Incidents in their respective reigns." The list is divided into the two royal houses; under Elizabeth's name we find the "significant historical incidents" listed in the order here reproduced.

880.1   Tradition has it that Molière read his comedies to his fellow actors and their children, as well as to his maid-servant La Forêt, for purposes of discovering what they thought of them. He was to have tested her once by reading a play not his own, but she was not deceived.

884.1   The Erinyes (or Furies) of Greek mythology avenged the murder of relatives or the violation of the rules of hospitality and asylum.

885.1   *Champagne, A Question of Phiz*, a burlesque by Henry Brougham Farnie and Richard Reece, first produced at the Strand in 1877. William Sydney Penley (1853-1912) was a comic actor who began his career as a singer in the Chapel Royal (in 1862) and subsequently sang in several choirs. He turned to the theatre in the late 1870's, and succeeded Beerbohm-Tree in his role in Charles Hawtrey's *The Private Secretary* (1884).

885.2   Claude Marius (Claude Marius Duplany) (1850-1896), French-born actor, first appeared in London at the Lyceum in 1870. He performed in plays at the Strand, and was stage manager of several theatres in London, Australasia, India, and South Africa.

885.3   See note 1016. Butler concludes in *Life and Habit* (1878) that the reason some races of animals and men change and improve while others do not is the absence of a desire to go farther. The presence or absence of this desire depends upon the surroundings of the individuals, "which is simply a way of saying that one can get no further, but that as the song (with a slight alteration) says:

> 'Some breeds do, and some breeds don't,
> Some breeds will, but this breed won't,
> I tried very often to see if it would,
> But it said it really couldn't, and I don't think it could.'" (*Works*, IV, 163)

888.1   The Flemish painter Peter Paul Rubens (1577-1640) ran a large studio in Antwerp.

889.1   The allusion is to "The Psalter, Day 4" in *The Book of Common Prayer*: "Cleanse thou me from my secret faults." The prayer derives from Psalm 19.12.

890.1   In Chapter V of his *Autobiography* (1873), John Stuart Mill singles out music as the art which had always brought him pleasure. In a state of nervous depression, however, "I was seriously tormented by the thought of the exhaustibility of musical combinations. The octave consists only of five tones and two semitones, which can be put together in only a limited number of ways, of which but a small proportion are beautiful: most of these, it seemed to me, must have already been discovered...."

891.1   See 170.1 above.

892.1   Horace, *Odes*, IV. xii. 27: "*Dulce est desipere in loco*" (It is sweet to forget one's wisdom on occasion). Butler is alluding also to "*Dulce et decorum est pro patria mori*" (It is sweet and proper to die for one's country): *Odes*, III, ii. 13. The second quotation alludes to *Hamlet*, III. iv. 66-67: "Could you on this fair mountain leave to feed/And batten on this moor?"

894.1   See 844.1 above.

895.1   *Works*, vii, 86.7.

899.1   *Works*, vii, 87.

900.1   Butler refers to note 325.

903.1   See *Memoir* I, 367 where Butler addresses this witticism to Miss Savage (letter of January 31, 1882). The priest-King Melchisedec is not furnished with a genealogy in Genesis 14.

904.1   That is, "every egg" comes "from an egg."

905.1   The parenthesis is added in Butler's hand to the typescript. See note 415, and 415.1 above.

906.1   Exodus 20:5.

911.1   A London slum.

913.1   Arnold developed this concept in *Culture and Anarchy* (1869). The third edition of the essay had appeared in October, 1882.

913.2   Odes III, 3, 49: Butler refers to the passage which translates, "Let Rome be bold as to disdain the gold that earth conceals and therefore is better hidden rather than to gather it up greedily with hands that profane all sacred things to practical ends."

913.3   London publishers. Cassell's published books and periodicals on religious subjects.

913.4   The largest lending library in London, founded in 1842 by Charles Edward Mudie (1818-1890); he often bought large numbers of popular books, but avoided stocking books he considered immoral.

913.5   1 Cor. 13:8.

914.1   See 170.1 above.

915.1   Psalm 130:3: "If, then, Lord, shouldest mark iniquities, O Lord, who shall stand?"

915.2   *Measure for Measure*, V. i. 439.

916.1   This overscored note was to follow 916:

ANALOGY BETWEEN MIND AND AND MATTER

Calms and storms in the air are like the calms and storms that affect stocks upon the stock exchange. They are money currents-- "the usual flow of gold &c."

916.2   Epicurus, *Epistle to Menoeceus*; in the second paragraph he writes that the gods exist, that it is impious to accept the common beliefs about them, and that they have no concerns with men. Epicurus may be elaborating *Iliad* 24. 825-26.

919.1   *Hamlet*, II. ii.

921.1   A hamlet in northern Surrey.

921.2   *Works*, IV, 54.

923.1   "My heart leaps up" (1807): "The Child is father of the Man. . . ."

923.2   *Works*, IX, 210. The parenthesis was added later.

926.1   This note following note 926 is overscored:

AUSTRALIAN AND NEW ZEALAND WEEDS

I am told (with what truth I know not) these will not hold their own in England: they have been sown over and over again, but are invariably chocked out in a very short time; whereas European weeds, like European men, overrun and oust the native growths abundantly. The plants seem to have borrowed some of the civilisation of the men.

928.1   Mrs. Anna Russell (née Worsley) (1807-1876), sister of Butler's mother and his godmother. In 1844 she married Frederick Russell of Burlington near Bristol; she was "the most accomplished woman field botanist of the day..." (D.E. Allen, "The Botanical Family of Samuel Butler," *Journal of the Society for the Bibliography of Natural History*, IX, 2 (1979), 134).

929.1   P. 11c, "Mr. Proctor's Astronomical Lectures": among "the greatest lessons which science had learned and taught were these, that occupied space was practically infinite, occupied time practically eternal, the reign of law without beginning and without end knowable to us." Proctor stated these views again in the *Contemporary Review* for June, 1882, 994-1002: "Newton and Darwin" (see note 754). Butler copied these remarks into his "Life and Habit, Vol. II" notebook (see note on the text). R.A. Proctor (1837-1888) was a Johnian (B.A., 1860), honorary secretary of the Royal Astronomical Society 1872 to 1873, and thereafter a science lecturer.

931.1   Parenthetical comment is added in Butler's hand. Mrs. Jane Smart Monk was the wife of James Henry Monk (1784-1856), the high church bishop of Gloucester from 1830 to his death. She was the only daughter of Rev. Hugh Hughes (1745-1830) of Nuneaton and his wife; he was Headmaster of the Free Grammar School of Nuneaton, and rector of Hardwick, Northamptonshire. Their son, Thomas Smart Hughes (1786-1847), canon of Peterborough from 1827 to his death continued both Hume's and Smollett's Histories. He had been a pupil of Dr. Butler at Shrewsbury, and winner of the Browne medal at Cambridge in 1806. His eldest son was Thomas Hughes.

933.1   "Parasites in the Human Body," p. 9f.

936.1   Butler refers to the poem "Heredity" by Thomas Bailey Aldrich (1836-1907), the American poet and novelist, editor of the *Atlantic Monthly* from 1881 to 1890.

937.1   P. 6d: insert about an accacia plant in Virginia, Nevada, that "went very mad" when transplanted.

939.1   Very likely this note was occasioned by a bout with "brain-fag," and the recurrence of noises in his head in the spring of 1883; he had first suffered the latter as well as a growth on the back of his neck in 1866. Both symptoms, he said, did not subside greatly until sometime after his father's death.

939.2   Added in Butler's hand. Butler's father died December 29, 1886; his will left Butler in easier financial circumstances.

940.1   See 729.1 above.

941.1   He wrote about this to Miss Savage (see *Memoir*, I, 383: letter of March 15, 1883).

944.1   The fugue in e minor, from Suite IV in *Suites de Pièces pour le Claveçin* first published in 1720; and Fugue VI in G from *Six Fugues or Voluntaries for the Organ or Harpsichord*, published in 1735. In *The Way of All Flesh* Overton asks little Ernest Pontifex what he thinks might be inscribed on his aunt Alethea Pontifex's tombstone. He replies by suggesting the first three bars of the "old man fugue" (Chapter 36).

949.1   That is, on Jones's and Butler's return from Italy.

950.1   During the construction of the New Law Courts (see 794.1 above), the famous Temple Bar that separated the Strand from Fleet Street to form the entrance to the City of London, was demolished. In its place was erected the Griffin (then much disliked), a pedestal in the middle of the street surmounted by the mythical bird.

951.1   Charles Stuart Parnell (1846-1891), who headed the Irish Land League which fought for Irish farmers' right to land, was arrested in 1881 and interned in Kilmainham Prison, Dublin; his imprisonment sparked widespread agrarian crime. In the spring of 1882 he (with other Land-leaguers) was released on the understanding (referred to as the "Kilmainham Treaty") that he would procure an end to this crime if the Government in return would provide relief to farmers for arrears in their rent. When shortly afterwards the Phoenix Park murders (see 765.2 above) occurred, the Government resorted again to coercive tactics.

952.1   Philip Dormer Stanhope, the 5th Earl of Chesterfield (1694-1773), politician remembered for his witticisms and letters to his natural son (published in 1774).

953.1   The large London lending library.

953.2   See *Works*, VII, 48: "Mr. Tennyson has said well, 'There lives more doubt'--I quote from memory--'in honest faith, believe me, than in half the systems of philosophy,' or words to that effect." Butler misquotes *In Memoriam*, XCVI, 10-12.

956.1   *A First Year in Canterbury Settlement* (1865), composed of Butler's letters home to his family which his father edited. Butler's edited correspondence, now in the British Library, comprises sixteen volumes.

957.1   A well-known fishmonger in Bond Street.

957.2   Jones identifies him as old Mr. Brooke, rector of Gamston, that
is the Rev. Joshua Brooke (1761-1851) who was rector of Gamston from 1812
to 1851, and vicar of Colston Bassett from 1800 to 1834, both in Nottinghamshire. But Butler may refer to his son, with the same name (born in 1810), who
became vicar of Colston Bassett in 1834 and of Owthorpe (Notts.) in 1879. Old
Mr. Brooke is remembered by Butler in Volume III of the Note-Books (note for
May, 1887) as a man who had been present at the Handel Commemoration of
1784.

957.3   i.e., "the very words."

958.1   The Neopolitan composer (1685-1757), later court harpsichordist
in Madrid. He was a frequent companion of Handel during the latter's stay in Venice
during the season 1709-1710.

961.1   "Memory and Personal Identity," by Roden Noel, pp. 380-387.
The article, a critique of materialist theories of mind, deals with the questions of
the sense of identity and consciousness. The Pantheistic conception of unconscious
identity is rejected, and the author concludes that if a person's influence abides
after death, it is because his identity abides: "our present isolated [life]. . . is not
our true personality. We have yet to attain that. . . . Our true being is in others,
and theirs in us."

962.1   Three essays from *Nature* by George John Romanes (1848-1894)
were reprinted in *Charles Darwin: Memorial Notices* (London: Macmillan & Co.,
1882). In one Romanes explains that Darwin had a "fixed habit of mind to seek
opinions as well as facts from every available quarter," and in another that he took
delight in "helping every one in their work . . . in throwing out numberless suggestions for others to profit by, and in kindling the enthusiasm of the humblest tyro
in science."

965.1   The Bishop, the Rt. Rev. Charles W. Sandford (1828-1901), a
voluminous author of pastoral letters, in a letter to the *Times* (April 3, p. 12b)
had objected to the practice of sending English patients to Monte Carlo for their
health, a place where "the very scum of Europe" gathers. He objected to plans for
a new English church there since it would only serve to attract English visitors to
a place of "temptation and iniquity." Several replies followed; on April 25 (p.
6f) the Bishop defended his objection to the proposed church. A letter follows
from William Wright, then the English chaplain at Monaco who held services there
though he had not been licensed by the Bishop. He considers the town safer than
English sea-side resorts, the church as a deterrent to the evil of gambling.

966.1   "Charles Darwin: His Biographer and His Traducer," pp. 203-
210. A reprint from *Nature*, which also appeared in *Charles Darwin: Memorial*

Notices (see 962.1 above): the article rejects as unfounded the one criticism voiced amid the general praise of Darwin by Henry G. Atkinson who had quoted Carlyle as having declared Darwin an atheist and possessed of "'very little intellect.'"

968.1   See 186.1 above.

969.1   The article (p. 6 d-e) is a review of *Souvenirs d'Enfance et de Jeunesse* by Ernest Renan (1823-1892), the biblical critic and author of *Vie de Jesu* (1863). He records his happy childhood in Tréguier (Brittany), and regrets his loss of faith that attended his study of ancient languages.

969.2   Added in Butler's hand.

927.1   In the original edition (London: Trübner & Co., 1878); see *Works*, IV, 43.

973.1   Samuel Charles Whitbread (1796-1879) was head of Whitbread's brewery in Chiswell Street, Finsburg, London, and one of the founders of the British Meteorological Society in 1850. Philip Worsley (see 222.1 above) was a partner in the brewery; his son Reginald, Butler's cousin, worked there for a time as a clerk (see note 117.9).

975.1   *The Vestiges of the Natural History of Creation* (1844). See 719.3 above.

976.1   Butler must refer to the son of Philip Taylor (born in 1786), the brother of John Taylor (1779-1863), the grandfather of his aunt Worsley (see 530.1 above). Edgar Taylor (dates unknown) was probably an engineer like his father who had his own engineering firm in London.

976.2   Richard Porson (1759-1808) was a well-known Greek scholar in his time, and Regius Professor of Greek at Trinity College, Cambridge, a post he attained despite losing his Fellowship for declining orders.

977.1   Aunt Bessie, that is, Elizabeth Worsley, died in August, 1894, aged 85. During the last years of her life she lived at Clifton, Bristol, with another woman friend.

977.2   i.e., Mrs. Philip Worsley (see 530.1 above).

977.3   Alice S. Worsley (see 247.2 above).

977.4   Daughter of Butler's counsin Reginald Worsley (Alice's brother).

979.1   For Heatherley's, see 258.1 above. Thomas Sadler was an obscure painter (in 1881 he exhibited one painting at the Royal Academy) who later lived in very straightened circumstances. For a time he worked as a stage painter. Butler found him a bore, but asked him to read the MS. of *The Authoress of the Odyssey*.

980.1　　　　For Clarke, see 656.1 above. Alexander Lang Elder (1815-1885) was head of the firm of Elder & Co. in whose employ Clarke was. The poem, "A Reminiscence of Corot" is found in his *Songs in Exile and other Poems* [1879]):

> Above, the tender leaves, grown wan and gray,
> 　　Half mingle with the quiet gray-grown sky;
> Below, the wondrous misty moonbeams lie, --
> Dim shafts of light across the flower-strewn way, --
> And 'twixt the solemn stems two lovers stray,
> 　　'Neath the great arch of boughs that meet on high;
> 　　While over all sweet Evening, lovingly,
> Like Salmacis melts in sweet Night away
>
> The spell of it grows on us as we stand,
> 　　The stillness, the deep calm and the repose, --
> 　　　　The sadness making all more sweet, -- and we
> Down the dim avenue go hand in hand,
> 　　Watch the mists gather and the evening close
> 　　And speak no word for very ecstasy.

Jean Baptiste Corot (1796-1875) was a French landscape painter.

982.1　　　　The children of the solicitor Arthur Russell Malden (1851-1913) and his wife Rebecca. He was a friend of H.F. Jones's, his fellow student at Trinity Hall, Cambridge (B.A., 1873). From 1879 to his death he practiced in Salisbury, was secretary to the Bishop of Salisbury, and Mayor of the city in 1895.

983.1　　　　See note 721 and 721.1 above.

984.1　　　　The Venetian master Giovanni Bellini (c. 1430-1516) was one of Butler's favorites. Both Titian (Tiziano Vecellio [1477-1576]) and Giorgione (Giorgio Barbarelli [1478-1510]) studied under him in the 1490's and for a time apparently worked together.

985.1　　　　Sarah Worsley, the sister of Butler's mother, of Clifton, Bristol. John Laird Muir, 1st Baron Lawrence (1811-1879), well-known for his distinguished service in India, raised in 1864 to Viceroy and Governor-general of India. During the second Afghan war (1878-1880), he attacked the government's policy in the Afghan which was designed to consolidate the territory under British rule.

985.2　　　　For Miss Buckley and Mr. Garnett, see 363.1 and 363.4 above.

985.3　　　　Reginald Bosworth, *Life of Lord Lawrence* (London: Smith, Elder & Co., 1883).

987.1　　　　Left out by Butler: "belief; he yearns to believe in God; he seems to think that his soul needs belief, but"

987.2   *Walk in the Regions of Science and Faith* (London: John Murray, 1883), by Harvey Goodwin, D.D. (see 400.1 above) contains a criticism of *A Candid Examination of Theism* (1877) by Physicus (George John Romanes) constituting a warning against facile rationalism.

989.1   A town in Tuscany.

989.2   "I can work the earth pretty well, but I have no head for geography."

991.1   Painting by Henry Stacy Marks, R.A. (1829-1898), illustrator, genre painter, and regular exhibitor at the Royal Academy from 1853 to 1897. The painting was sold at Christie's in 1877.

991.2   "The Death of Raffaelle," by Henry N. O'Neil, A.R.A. (1817-1880), genre and historical painter, like Stacy, regular exhibitor at the Royal Academy.

992.1   Luke 18:24.

995.1   P. 6d.   George Grove (1820-1900) was a civil engineer, the secretary to the Society of Arts and the Crystal Palace, as well as the first Director of the Royal College of Music.   He published *Grove's Dictionary of Music and Musicians* between 1879 and 1889, for which he received an honorary knighthood. Papé, as the letter explains, "clarionet" player in the Crystal Palace Band, died in September, 1874; Grove wrote the conductor, Mr. Manns, to inquire about the time of the funeral.   Later, on May 1, 1883, Grove and Manns were listening to a rehearsal of a Schubert symphony in the Palace, and Grove said how well Papé would have played the passages.   Mr. Manns then told him that on this very day he had discovered Grove's old letter stuck in his letter box.   Before this meeting the two had never mentioned Papé's name.

1001.1   In July, 1882 (see 784.1 above).

1002.1   Exodus 2:3: "And when she could no longer hide [the child Moses], she [his mother] took for him an ark of bulrushes, and daubed it with slime and with pitch, and put the child therein. . . ."

1004.1   P. 96: the notice announces the death in Berne of the physician Dr. Valentin (born in Breslau in 1810), former Professor of Physiology at the University of Berne, author of a handbook on evolution published in 1835.

1005.1   David Garrick (1716-1779), the most highly regarded actor of his time, dramatist, and director for many years of the Drury Lane Theatre. His Victorian counterpart was Henry Irving (1838-1905), like Garrick famous for his Shakespeare roles, a manager as well, of the Lyceum Theatre. He was knighted in 1895.

1007.1   Richard Entwistle, Pauli's intimate and wealthy friend who became an alcoholic and died in 1894 or 1895, leaving Pauli his sole executor. Butler writes about him in the account of his friendship with Pauli, bound into Volume III of the Note-Books.

1009.1   Maximilain Robespierre (1758-1794), the French Jacobin politician active during the Reign of Terror.

1009.2   Brother of the artist Henry Stacy Marks (see 991.1).

1010.1   Leslie Stephen (1832-1904), the English critic and philosopher (knighted in 1904). He seems to have become acquainted with Butler after *The Fair Haven* came to his notice in 1873. Butler wrote a positive review of Stephens' *Free-Thinking and Plain-speaking* (1873) in *The Examiner* for December 20, 1873 (pp. 1265-7). When Butler once again charged, in *Unconscious Memory* (1880), that Darwin had been dishonest in his dealings with him, it was Stephens and T.H. Huxley who persuaded Darwin not to respond.

1010.2   *The Science of Ethics* (London: Smith, Elder & Co., 1882).

1013.1   Mrs. Susanna Reeve (1788-1864) was the eldest daughter of John Taylor of Norwich (1750-1826), the grandfather of Reginald Worsley's mother Ann. See 530.1 above. Mrs. Reeve's husband, Henry Reeve (1780-1814), had been a well-known physician in Norwich. Their only child, Henry (1813-1895) was editor of the *Edinburgh Review* from 1855 to his death.

1016.1   Of the original edition (London: Trübner & Co., 1878); see *Works*, IV, 163.

1016.2   See note 885.

1017.1   Of the original edition (London: David Bogue, 1880); see *Works*, VI, 23-24: the friend said "that the theory which had pleased him more than anything he had heard of for some time was one referring all life to memory."

1019.1   See Chapter 37 and 86. Butler disliked Beethoven's and Mendelssohn's music.

1020.1   "As cheers the sun," Act II of *Joshua* (1747).

1021.1   See 637.1 above.

1024.1   Apparently Edward Herbert Draper (1841-1911), assistant master at Shrewsbury School in 1868; he was called to the Bar in 1870 and practiced on the Midland circuit. From 1878 on he was Clerk of Skinners' Company.

1025.1   See 637.1 above.

1026.1   It was a custom for members of the Salvation Army who were regarded as particularly valorous in their duties to choose for their names certain words to which music had given larger significance. Thus, "Hallelujah Butler" or "Praising Page."

1028.   See 982.1 above.

1030.1   P. 6c, the obituary notice announcing the death of William Spottiswoode (1825-1883), the President of the Royal Society for the previous four years: "Mr. Spottiswoode was the type of a student of science almost peculiar to this country, one who does not follow science as a vocation, but as an avocation, who cultivates it from pure love in the leisure left him by the busy life of a man of business or affairs. We have had several notable examples of this class of investigator, but among living men we need only mention the names of Sir John Lubbock and Mr. De La Rue." Sir John Lubbock (1834-1913), a banker by profession, was also a botanist and animal physiologist who wrote several books in these fields. Warren De La Rue (1815-1889), by profession a printer, was an inventor, chemist, astronomer, and author of numerous scientific papers.

1031.1   See 190.1 above.

1031.2   Handel suffered a paralytic stroke in May, 1737, possibly brought on by his unsuccessful efforts in the raging opera war between himself and rival cliques supported by the nobility. That year he was unable to attract sufficient audiences either to the Haymarket Theatre or to Covent Garden. He suffered another collapse of health in 1745 after he had been forced to cancel some of his projected concerts. The turning point in his career came about 1749 (when he was 64), by which time he was composing only oratorios that his audience generally preferred to the by now unfashionable Italian opera. Handel received a pension of £200 from George I, his former employer when still Elector of Hanover, and a confirmation of another £200 pension was bestowed by Queen Anne. Later, the Princess of Wales, Caroline, presented him with yet another pension of £200. However, despite many financial setbacks, Handel was never bankrupt as 19th century biographers were inclined to suggest.

1032.1   See 985.1 above.

1032.2   Mrs. Hutchings, who lived in Shrewsbury, was the sister of Sarah Worsley (née Savery), the wife of Philip Worsley (1769-1811), a sugar refiner of Arno's Vale, Bristol, father of Butler's mother, his uncle Philip, and aunt Sarah. The Worsley children, including aunt Sarah, used to visit the Hutchings at Shrewsbury, and there it was that Canon Butler met his future wife.

1033.1   See 363.4 above.

1033.2   An immensely popular historical and psychological romance by Joseph Henry Shorthouse (1834-1903), written from 1866 on and published privately in 1880. Butler noted that Mudie's had 1000 copies of it in circulation in 1882; but he wrote his sister Harriet that he was seldom "more displeased with any book. I think it deserves to be classed with *Wilhelm Meister, Andreas Sinistram, Sartor Resartus* and a few others that I cannot call to mind at this moment" (*Memoir*, I, 373: letter of June 8, 1882).

1033.3   See 939.1 above.

1034.4   The letter is found in *Memoir*, I, 388.

1038.1   Located on the Belvedere marshes. Sheerness is on the river Medway where it enters the Thames.

1042.1   See note 791, which refers to the same matter.

1042.2   P. 214.

1042.3   In the original edition (London: Hardwick & Bogue, 1879); see *Works*, V, 316, and IV (*Life and Habit*), 211. Butler is quoting a passage found in the 6th edition of the *Origin* (1872), Chapter VII.

1042.4   *Nature*, November 24, 1881, p. 81 (from the first of the two-part paper referred to at the beginning of the note).

1042.5   See 791.3 above.

1042.6   P. 241.

1042.7   Letter in *Nature*, February 16, 1882, pp. 360-1: the letter was written from aboard ship at Southampton.

1042.8   In *Nature*, p. 265. Dr. Samuel Haughton (1821-97), who published on various scientific topics including geology and physics, became president of the Royal Zoological Society of Ireland in 1883, and Registrar of Trinity Medical School, Dublin.

1043.1   "Inheritance," p. 257. Darwin describes two cases which suggest the tendency "in any new character or modification to reappear in the offspring at the same age at which it first appeared in the parents, or one of the parents...." In one instance, a man, whose hair turned grey at twenty had two daughters who became grey at twenty; in the other, a man whose thumb was deformed when a boy, had two daughters, and two grand-daughters, who inherited the deformity.

1045.1   Oliver Madox Brown (1855-1874), the son of the Pre-Raphaelite painter Ford Madox Brown (1821-1893), began to paint at age 8, and to write poetry and tales at 17. His tale, *The Black Swan*, was published in altered form as *Gabriel Denver* by Smith & Elder in 1872; two years after his death it was publish-ed in its original form with the original title. A second work, *The Dwale Bluth*, was turned down by the *Cornhill Magazine*. He died, not yet twenty, of blood-poisoning. Butler knew the Madox Brown family, but dropped them after his return from Canada in December of 1875.

1045.2   July 21, 1883, pp. 69-70: the reviewer of *Oliver Madox Brown: a Biographical Sketch* by John H. Ingram, speaks of the inappropriateness of the comparison with the poet Thomas Chatterton (1752-1770), yet "it would be diffi-cult to recall any other English man of letters who, dying at so early an age... left behind him such remarkable, if fragmentary work."

1046.1   P. 498: the matter is reported in a letter to the editor.

1047.1   A pamphlet published in 1880. Mrs. Margaret Watson was the wife of the Rt. Honorable William Watson (Lord Watson) (1828-1899), Lord Advocate of Scotland (1876-1880) and Lord of Appeal in Ordinary from 1880 on. The letter belongs to 1856, before her marriage in 1868, and continues: "That's a pleasant thing to think of, as one of the wise adjustments of this life of ours." The italics are Butler's.

1049.1   See note 719.

1049.2   P. 5. The sentence continues: ". . . must ever form a landmark in the annals of human inquiry, not inferior in importance to the 'Principia' of Newton in astronomy, or in metaphysics to the 'Critique of Pure Reason' by Kant."

1049.3   P. 5-6: "Charles Darwin."

1049.4   P. 5: "[The *Origin*] is no longer shunned as a banned treatise. Years ago it was removed from the 'Index Expurgatorium,' for, whatever may be our opinion. . . ." The sentence concludes: ". . . aims at a loftier plan than that of an anachronism to avoid mastering not only the facts of that book, but also its conclusions."

1051.1   The Chorus of Act IV (1744).

1056.1   *The Globe*, November 21, 1878, p. 3: in a letter to the editor (dated November 16), a correspondent complains of the levity with which the conclusion of the Metropolitan Water Board, that Thame Water is contaminated, was set aside by having someone drink a tumbler of unfiltered river water. The letter ends with this question.

1058.1   *Times*, November 26, p. 96; Shipley announces in his letter his reasons for going over to Rome ; an editorial attack on Shipley's position is on p. 7c-d. The Rev. Orby Shipley (1832-1916), a graduate of Jesus College, Cambridge, was a prolific writer on religious subjects, and served 23 years as an Anglican priest, last at St. Alban's Church, Holborn. He became a Roman Catholic in 1878 (he had been an ultra-ritualist Anglican). The letter to the *Times* from which Butler quotes is reprinted in Shipley's *Principles of Faith in Relation to Sin.*

1060.1   Butler may be referring to Edward Somerset, second Marquess of Worcester (1601-1667), prominent in the service of Charles I, and associated with experiments in the development of the steam engine; Roger Bacon was the English Franciscan philosopher (1214-1294). See note 723.

1063.1   *Lieder ohne Worte*, a series of piano pieces in eight books by Felix Mendelssohn-Bartholdy (1809-1847), published between 1830 and 1845. The pieces made the composer enormously popular in England (even though he had his misgivings and declared that they were meant chiefly for ladies), and inspired countless imitations. See also 735.2 above.

1065.1   There were three Giovanni Bellinis in Pesaro at the time: "The Coronation of the Virgin" ("L'Incoronazione della Virgine"), an altar-piece painted for the church of S. Francesco (Butler had this one in mind, since it is mentioned in the 1878 Italian edition of Vasari); a crucifixion and a painting entitled "Il Padreterno Benedicente" ("God the Father Blessing"), now in the Civic Museum of Pesaro, have been attributed to Bellini only since 1894.

1068.1   Horace, *Epistles*, V, 53-54: *"Quaerenda pecunia primum est; virtus post nummos."* ("The search for money comes first; morality after cash.")

1069.1   See 784.1 above; for Mr. Moss, see 784.3 above.

1070.1   See note 227, and 227.1 above.

1071.1   P. 6; Sir Edward Becket Denison (1816-1905), later (1874) Baron Grimthorpe, a well-known lawyer and controversalist, was active in both church affairs and architectural work (he designed the clock and drew the specifications of the Big Ben bell for the tower of the Houses of Parliament). In the mid-90's Butler corresponded with him on matters involving the Homeric question.

1072.1   Written in by Butler: "until Copernicus's time it was most convenient to us to think this--still"--possibly intended as an insert between "but" and "it."

1073.1   Added in Butler's hand.

1074.1   See note 1063.

1076.1   See 404.2 above.

1077.1   P. 7: "A few instances have occurred where timber, growing on peaty land, in a very dry season, the soil itself taking fire, has been burnt, but in most other cases it is only the dead or defective trees that burn, the green timber being scorched, not burnt, but since the scorching, if severe, kills the tree, it becomes necessary to cut the timber within a year or so, or the grubs will injure it, though, if removed within a year, there is little injury done, since the grubs do little more than penetrate the almost worthless sapwood the first season, so that the timber might all be removed before serious loss is suffered, and if the timber landowner would expend annually the same percentage he is willing to spend to insure other property of like value towards putting his timber property in a safe condition, he could so place it that it would be difficult to set it on fire so as to do any serious injury, so that, with proper legislation, and an enlightened public opinion to lead the American to look upon the tree as one of his best friends, there should be little danger from fire."

1080.1   Sophie Larkin, a comic actress who made her London debut in 1865 and was active for more than 30 years in London, frequently appeared in comedies at the Vaudeville Theatre. In August, 1883, she appeared in *Confusion*, a popular farce by Joseph Derrick (from which Butler's quotations are taken), playing the part of Miss Lucretia Tickleby.

361

1089.1   See *Bradshaw's Hand-Book to Normandy and the Channel Islands*, by Herbert Fry (London: W.J. Adams, [1865]), pp. 51-53; 60-64. According to legend, Matilda, wife of William the Conqueror (1028-1087) wove the Bayeux tapestry depicting events of the Norman conquest of 1066 to prove his right to the English Crown. Arlette was the mistress of Robert le Diable, Duc de Normandie, and the mother of William. The story here relates how the Duke saw Arlette, a simple peasant girl, and persuaded her to be his mistress despite her father's objections. When the Duke's escorts asked her to hide within a large cloak so that her sojourn might go unnoticed, she insisted that she would go like the daughter of a respectable man, intent on increasing "her honor and wealth"; when at the castle she was requested to enter by the rear gate, she refused and demanded the main gates be opened, as presently they were.

1091.1   The poem was first published in Volume XX of the Shrewsbury Edition of Butler's *Works* (1926).

1092.1   Matthew 8:14.

1093.1   See 536.1 above; *Come son scandalezzato*: "Oh dear, I am scandalized."

1096.1   Samuel Carter (1805-1878), solicitor to the London and North-Western as well as the Midland Railway Companies (the latter post he held from 1835 to 1868).

1105.1   Martha McCulloch (née Guttridge), born in 1846, the wife of the painter George McCulloch (see 170.1 above). They were married on November 6, 1872. Butler apparently did not get along with her.

1106.1   In Act III of Richard Wagner's opera *Lohengrin* (1848) Lohengrin, a knight of the Holy Grail, requires of Elsa, his bride, never to ask his name or origin. But she does ask the question ("Im fernen Land") and that means, as Lohengrin will explain in the next scene, that he must now return from whence he came.

1106.2   The note following 1106 is overscored:

PARTHENOGENESIS

Consider the bearing of this on the supposition that heredity is due to memory: and consider its bearing on heredity generally.

1109.1   Originally: true, indeed incontrovertible.

1110.1   In the oratorio *Messiah*.

1111.1   Matt. 3:7 and Luke 3:7: "Oh generations of vipers, who hath warned you to flee from the wrath to come?"

1120.1   See the end of Chapter V: the chords are found in the Prelude from the Second Collection of *Pièces pour le Clavecin*, first published in 1733; there are several gigues in this set.

1120.1   Romans 8:23.

1124.1   *The Contemplation of Nature*, 2 vols. (London: Printed for T. Longman, T. Becket, and P.A. de Hondt, 1766), by the French *philosophe* and naturalist Charles Bonnet (1720-1793). Originally published in Amsterdam in 1764 and 1765 as *Contemplation de la Nature*. Notes 1124 to 1130 refer to this work.

1125.1   Op. cit., I, 83.

1126.1   Bonnet continues: "and does not the soul herself occasion it, by an effect of her will? If she were not *attentive*, she would not experience any fatigue. She acts then on the fibres, which are the seat of this fatigue." Bonnet explains here his theory that for every object of the soul's will there is a specific fibre in the brain.

1127.1   In the text: "imagination."

1127.2   "Right and Wrong: the Scientific Ground of their Distinction," by W.K. Clifford, in Vol. XVIII (1875), pp. 770-800. The article explains that the moral law and the actions of conscience are as much a subject for science as is chemistry: any moral act can be referred to some sort of motor stimuli.

1128.1   Butler quotes Bonnet on this subject in *Unconscious Memory* (1880): see *Works*, VI, 59.

1129.1   On these pages Bonnet deals with gradations in rock formations, in animals and plants: "Such is the nature of the gradations between beings, that they oftentimes differ from each other by slender shadowings; and such is the narrowness of our capacities, that none but the stronger and more striking marks attract our notice." Bonnet, nonetheless, considers species immutable.

1130.1   Bonnet describes the behavior of sensitive plants, and of the polyp, which because it displays animal characteristics, constitutes "one of those connections whereby the *vegetable* and *animal kingdom* are united."

1137.1   P. 8: the letter is a memorial for one of his students, a Japanese Buddhist monk, who died this July in Japan after his return from Oxford, where he had studied English and other languages. Max Müller finds it hard to think that all the work of this good man will now bear no fruit, and explains how on his departure he looked again and again at Max Müller's house where he had spent the "happiest hours of his life." Once professor and student had watched a sunset on Malven Hills: " 'That is what we call the eastern gate of our Sukhavati, the land of Bliss,' " he said, "He looked forward to it, and trusted he should meet there all who had loved him, and whom he had loved, and he should gaze on the Buddha Amitabha--*i.e.*, 'Infinite Light.' " Rt. Hon. Friedrich Max Müller (1823-1900), well-known philologist, educated at the universities of Leipzig and Berlin, was appointed Taylorian Professor of Modern Languages at Oxford in 1854, and was Corpus Professor of Comparative Philology from 1868 on.

1138.1   P. 51, "Automatic Machinery": the article describes a weaving plant that at night produces cloth without human assistance save that of an engineer.

1138.2   "New Inventions--Remarkable Increase and Cheapening of Production," pp. 78-79. The article refers to the same plant as the *Times* article above, at Oak Mills, Low Moor, near Bradford. The mill runs 132 hours a week, producing 200,000 yards of fabric of different patterns and thickness. "At present" the machines work "on what we may term forty-eight hour 'shifts,' " and are "able to produce every known fancy yarn. . . ."

1144.1   P. 46. The article deals with the life history of the phylloxera. Each of seven successive generations of these lice differ from one another: from the third generation on they are winged; the seventh generation leaves eggs behind from which hatch lice resembling the first generation.

1152.1   See 404.1 above.

1155.1   In his *The Spirit of Laws*, Book XVI (under the heading "Of the Slavery of the Negroes").

1157.1   See 511.1 above.

1157.2   Radley School, which H.F. Jones also attended (695.1 above), known also as St. Peter's College, Radley, Abingdon.

1158.1   French for "worldly" or "vain."

1160.1   P. 1f. The advertisement refers to the Prague painter Gabriel Cornelius Ritter von Max (1840-1915), a painter of sentimental and religious subjects.

1170.1   1 John 3:15.

1177.1   A village in West Kent.

1178.1   See 222.1 above.

1179.1   See 973.1 above.

1180.1   Edgar Roscoe, born in 1871, was the son of Richard Roscoe (1833-1892), solicitor with Shaen & Roscoe of Bedford Row, London; his wife Honora (1837-1879), was Reginald Worsley's sister.

1181.1   Dr. Edmund Alexander Parkes (1819-1876), until his death Professor of Hygiene at the Army Medical School at Chatham,   wrote *On Personal Care of Health*, published posthumously in   1876 by the Society for Promoting Christian Knowledge. In it he claims that married men have fewer illnesses than single men, for (among other reasons) marriage protects a man from "the most serious temptations and dangers to health. . . ."

1183.1   Published anonymously in 1844 by Robert Chambers (1802-1871), prolific author and editor, partner in the Edinburgh publishing firm of W. & R. Chambers. See also note 719 and 719.3 above. Butler quotes, not quite accurately, from the tenth edition of 1853.

1185.1   The source of the following conclusions is the same article cited in 3.1 above (*Fortnightly Review*, n.s., XVI (1874), 555-580).

1190.1   "Si l'on veut donc que le siège des sensations soit dans la tête, il sera dans les meninges, & non dans la partie medullaire du cerveau, dont la substance est toute différent" (*Histoire Naturelle, Générale et Particuliere, avec la description du cabinet du Roi* [Paris, 1758], 14). See 731.1 above.

1192.1   See 363.1 above.

1192.2   Issue of May 31, 1879, pp. 682-4. Butler quoted from the review in the second edition of *Evolution Old and New* (1882) and in *Unconscious Memory* (1880): "When a writer who has not given as many weeks to the subject as Mr. Darwin has years is not content to air his own crude, though clever fallacies, but presumes to criticize Mr. Darwin with the superciliousness of a young schoolmaster looking over a boy's theme, it is difficult not to take him more seriously than he deserves or perhaps desires. One would think that Butler was the travelled and laborious observer of Nature, and Mr. Darwin the pert speculator, who takes all his facts secondhand." See *Works*, V, 34; VI, 39-40.

1195.1   See note 722. See also 722.1 and 722.3 above.

1197.1   Boadicea, the British queen of the first century, during a revolt of Britons against the occupying Romans, led a sack on the Roman town of Verulanium (which lay on the outskirts of the present St. Albans in Hertfordshire). Anne Boleyn (1507-1536), Henry VIII's second wife, was not connected with the town. Butler records having heard this anecdote recently in a letter to his sister May (according to Daniel F. Howard) in August, 1886 (*Correspondence*, 165-66).

1198.1   A Surrey village near Hampton Court.

1199.1   Isidore Geoffrey St. Hilaire (1805-1861), a French zoologist. Butler cites the commentary on Buffon found in St. Hilaire's *Histoire naturelle générale des regnes organiques* (3 vols., 1854-62) in *Evolution Old and New* (1879; second edition, 1882).

1205.1   Andromeda, daughter of Ethiopia's king Cepheus, claimed to be more beautiful than the Nereids. As punishment for her conceit, Poseidon flooded the land and permitted a sea-monster to terrorize it. Cepheus was counselled that the remedy for the affliction was to expose Andromeda to the monster, and she consequently was chained to a rock on the seashore. Perseus saw her, fell in love with her, and Cepheus granted his wish to marry her on condition he kill the monster. He did so, and thus freed Andromeda.

1205.2   Thomas Ballard, an obscure, indigent painter who lived in Newman Street, one of Butler's friends, a fellow student at Heatherley's Art School who later painted scenery for theatres. He exhibited very occasionally at the Royal Academy between 1865 and 1877. See also *Memoir* I, 138-139.

1205.3   ". . . when Andromeda and Perseus had travelled but a little way from the rock where Andromeda had so long been chained, she began upbraiding him with the loss of her dragon, who, on the whole, she said, had been very good to her" (*Works*, IV, 112).

1206.1   The name given to the teacher whose first duty it was to help students pass examinations.

1207.1   See 158.1 above; in note 158 Butler expresses a different sentiment.

1209.1   Allen (see 451.1 above) in this article (pp. 487-505) compares Darwin's theory of evolution with Spencer's (as propounded in the latter's *Principles of Psychology*) to conclude that Darwin's "spontaneous variation principle" (much as he respects it) cannot be applied to the genesis of the nervous system, or to the difference of mental development among individuals and races. Spencer shows how the individual depends mainly "upon the doings and gains of his ancestors, as modified and altered by himself," and Allen goes on to indicate how this may explain the rise of extraordinary individuals in complex societies.

1218.1   British bankruptcy laws were continually revised from 1858 onward; on August 25, 1883, the New Bankruptcy Act was passed, superseding, or finally consolidating, numerous bankruptcy amendment acts promulgated between 1867 and 1882.

1219.1   The Vokes were a family of dancers and actors, two men and three women, all children of a London costumier. They usually acted together as the "Vokes family" or the "Vokes children" in pantomines mostly of their own invention, both in England and the United States. The family made its debut in London in 1868. Victoria Rosalie Sarah Vokes (1853-1894) first appeared at the Surrey Theatre in 1854, and was a member of the family from 1861 to 1884. Theodosia Rosina Vokes (1858-1894) first appeared at the Alhambra Palace, and was a part of the family until 1870, when she married and retired from the stage.

1221.1   John O'Groat's House, popularly considered the northernmost point of the Scottish mainland is a place on the coast of Scaithness, Scotland, the legendary site of an octagonal house erected by a Dutchman, John Groot, to settle a squabble between eight families over seating arrangements at table during feasts.

1222.1   The St. Bartholomew's Day massacre began in Paris on August 24, 1572, and lasted well into October: it was a brutal attempt to murder prominent

French Protestants, the Huguenots, who consequently fled France in great numbers. In 1598, under Henry IV, the Edict of Nantes was promulgated, giving the Huguenots religious liberty; in 1685, however, Louis XIV revoked the Edict and thereby initiated further emigration of Protestants, many of them France's most gifted and prominent citizens.

1223.1   Butler refers to the advertisement slogan for Pears's soap: "Cleanliness is next to godliness."

1226.1   According to literary tradition, Samuel Butler (1612-1680), author of *Hudibras*, died in extreme poverty of consumption in Rose Street, Covent Garden. The first part of the long satiric poem appeared in 1663, but despite the admiration of Charles II and other prominent nobles, Butler received no preferments, and lived the next seventeen years in obscurity and narrow circumstances.

1226.2   Obviously this note does not belong to September; very likely Butler was filling out this "September page" with notes belonging to October.

1227.1   Job 1:21: '. . . the Lord gave, and the Lord hath taken away; blessed in the name of the Lord."

1229.1   The complete original title for the novel was *Ernest Pontifex or The Way of All Flesh, A Story of English Domestic Life*. See 36.1 above.

1229.2   See 258.1 above.

1235.1   Butler inverts 1 Timothy 1:15.

1237.1   This reference is incorrect. The article Butler refers to has not been found.

1239.1   In the passage of *De rerum natura* referred to Lucretius explains that only the fittest and most useful races of animals survive, that mixtures of widely differing breeds, that is, wide crosses, are not possible (for, as in the case of plants, "each . . . comes forth after its own manner, and all preserve their separate marks by a fixed law of nature" [11. 923-24: tr. by Cyril Bailey in *Titi Lucreti Cari* (Oxford University Press, 1947)]); and that though early man was uncivilized and had no knowledge of agricultural or mechanic arts, he was of a hardier constitution.

1242.1   An Italian spa on Lago Maggiore.

1243.1   Butler's uncle Philip Worsley, Uncle Sam's brother, lived in Chester Terrace. Samuel Worseley (1804-1888) of Clifton, Bristol, married Eleanor Parkes who died in 1879, aged 76. He was an amateur geologist, and founder-member of the Bristol Naturalists' Society (1862), though he never was (perhaps because of the disability Butler mentions) an active member, and took little or no part in its work. His fossil collection was sold at the time of his marriage in 1849 to the British Institute (now the Bristol Museum). He left a small legacy to Butler. See

D.E. Allen, "The Botanical Family of Samuel Butler," *Journal of the Society for the Bibliography of Natural History*, IX, 2 (1979).

1244.1   See p. 10 c-3. Sir Antonio Panizzi (1797-1879), when a young barrister at Modena, was implicated (in 1823) in a conspiracy against Francis IV, the reigning Duke of Modena (1814-1846), was arrested and sentenced to death. He fled to England, and after some years of teaching Italian and Italian literature, he was appointed Assistant Librarian to the British Museum where he rose to considerable eminence as Keeper of Printed Books. He retired in 1866, and received the K.C.B. in 1869. He expanded the Museum's library, initiated the modern catalogue, and had the Reading Room built. Butler refers to the following anecdote in the article: When Panizzi years later met the Duke of Modena again in Vienna, the latter expressed delight at his former subject's success and "congratulated himself on his having been the cause, however indirect, of Panizzi's good fortune." Panizzi reminded him that his "chances of success would have been small" had the Duke had his will. He, however, insisted on the justice of having condemned him and was vexed Panizzi would not agree. Later, in recalling the incident, Panizzi contended that "after all, the Duke was right, and all had happened for the best. Next to that of being hanged, there could hardly, he thought, have been a less enviable lot than that of being pardoned by the Duke's clemency."

1247.1   See 511.1 and 637.1 above.

1253.1   A village in eastern Sussex.

1254.1   Cf. Luke 24:25.

1255.1   II Samuel 12:3: "But the poor man had nothing, save one little ewe lamb, which he had bought and nourished up. . . ." Radley is Radley School, Abingdon. See 695.1 above.

1256.1   II Samuel 12:20: ". . . then [David] came to his own house; and when he required, they set bread before him, and he did eat."

1262.1   H.F. Jones's sister Cathy. See 637.1 above.

1264.1   See 404.2 above.

1265.1   Psalm 103:13: "Like as a father pitieth his children, so the Lord pitieth them that fear him."

1268.1   Butler inserted this invented anecdote in a letter of 1879 to Alfred Russell Wallace (see 719.15 above) in which he explained his rejection of spiritualism. Butler was introduced to Wallace (who had written a review of *Life and Habit* for the March 1879 issue of *Nature*) at Paddington Vicarage; he had met him earlier, as well as Miss Arabella Buckley (see 363.1 above) in 1865, at a séance in the home of Mr. Marshman, the Agent-General for New Zealand. Wallace was apparently impressed by the seance, and corresponded with Butler on the subject after their second meeting (see *Memoir*, I, 316-18).

1270.1   Luke 16:31:   "If they hear not Moses and the prophets, neither will they be persuaded, though one rose from the dead."

1271.1   *Works*, VIII, 11-13.

1274.1   Butler refers to a letter signed by three Slade Professors of Fine Art, A. Legros (University College, London), W.B. Richmond (Oxford), and Sidney Colvin (Cambridge), objecting to the *Gazette*'s criticism of Burne-Jones's paintings, especially of his "Annunciation", which is depicted as a sorrowful event. The letter reads: "Having regard to what seem to us the entirely mistaken and misleading strictures lately published [May 16, pp. 11b-12a] in your columns concerning certain points in the pictures by Mr. Burne Jones exhibited this year at the Grosvenor Gallery, we wish to be allowed to express an opinion that the works in question, and most especially the Annunciation, are of the very highest order both of imaginative and technical power, and such as not only do honour to the English school of painting, but would have done honour to any school at any period of history."

1275.1   Allusion to Byron's *Beppo*, stanza 47: "England, with all thy faults I love thee still!"

1277.1   P. 146.   Holland defends his picture "On Honour" against the charge (levied by the anonymous critic of the Royal Academy Exhibition on June 6, p. 4e-f) that it showed a figure smoking a cigar, dressed in apparel worn some sixty years before "the introduction of that weed in England." Holland cites Hall's Encyclopedia of 1790 (the period of the figure's dress) to show the inaccuracy of the criticism, and hopes the Editor "will insert these few lines as some proof that I have not been guilty of an anachronism. . . ." Philip Sidney Holland (1855-1891), a genre painter, was active in London between 1877 and 1884.

1278.1   See *Works*, IV, 104-105.

1279.1   Near Brighton.

1281.1   1 John 4.

1282.1   Mrs. Warren seems to have been a charwoman or caretaker at the New Berners Club for Ladies (see 22.1 above) of which Miss Savage was honorary secretary in 1883. The Archbishop of York at this time was William Connar Magee (1821-1890), formerly Bishop of Peterborough.

1283.1   Psalm 139:21: "Do I not hate them, O Lord, that hate thee?"

1286.1   "Eat to please yourself, dress to please others."

1289.1   When Agamemnon returned to Argolis after the capture of Troy, his wife Clytemnestra murdered him in revenge for sacrificing their daughter Iphigenia: she surprised him alone in the bath, and before slaying him, threw a cloth over his face.

1292.1   See 511.1 above.

1295.1   Ephesians 6:14-16: "Stand therefore, having your loins girt about with truth, and having on the breastplate of righteousness. . . ."

1300.1   See 984.1 above.

1300.2   A London district.

1307.1   "Nothing good that is not pleasing." See Cicero, *Tusculans* V, 84: "*nihil bonum nisi voluptatem, ut Epicurus. . .*" (nothing is good except pleasure according to Epicurus).

1308.1   A solicitor friend of Jones, connected with the firm of W.H. Whithall & Compton of Bedford Row; its head, William Whithall (1831-1907) engaged Jones from 1878 to 1881, when he returned to the firm of Sir Thomas Paine (360. 1 above).

1309.1   Added in Butler's hand.

1309.2   August Weismann (1834-1914), professor of zoology at the University of Freiburg, in 1885 developed the "Keimplasmatheorie" (germ plasma theory), postulating that the plasma of reproductive cells alone is the carrier of hereditary components. Since these cells differ in structure from soma cells, the changes in the latter cannot affect changes in the former, rendering impossible the transmission of acquired characteristics. This anti-Lamarckian theory Spencer attacked in four articles published in the *Contemporary Review*, 1893-4 (included in the second edition of Volume I, *Principles of Biology* [1898]; he rejected Weismann's belief that natural selection was the all-sufficient agent of evolutionary change, and supported the principle of the inheritance of acquired characteristics, which, so he claimed (not quite correctly) had been fully accepted by Darwin.

1313.1   Vincenzo Vela (1820-1891), an Italian sculptor living in Ligornetto, father of the painter Spartaco Vela (1854-1895) mentioned in *Alps and Sanctuaries*. See *Works*, VII, 126-27.

1313.2   Crossed out: dammed.

1314.1   In the Piemont district.

1315.1   "The spirit is unchanged when it enters into another religion."

1316.1   See 2 Kings 5:17-19.

1318.1   Matt. 18:20.

NAME INDEX